Historic Meetinghouses and Churches of New Hampshire

Historic Meetinghouses and Churches of New Hampshire

Glenn A. Knoblock

America Through Time®
Adding Color to American History

America Through Time is an imprint of Fonthill Media LLC
www.through-time.com
office@through-time.com

Published by Arcadia Publishing by arrangement with Fonthill Media LLC
For all general information, please contact Arcadia Publishing:
Telephone: 843-853-2070
Fax: 843-853-0044
E-mail: sales@arcadiapublishing.com
For customer service and orders:
Toll-Free 1-888-313-2665

www.arcadiapublishing.com

First published 2019

ISBN 978-1-64399-139-1

Typeset in 10pt on 13pt Sabon
Printed and bound in England

Acknowledgements

The seeds for this book were sown about twenty-five years ago when my wife, Terry Knoblock, was attending the University of New Hampshire, where she gained her Bachelor of Science. One of her gen-ed. classes was an "Introduction to Architecture" course, her final paper a study of the famed church built at Templeton, Massachusetts, by Elias Carter. While I cannot recall all of the details, being a historian, I offered to take the several hours' trip from New Hampshire to Templeton to take some pictures for her paper. While there, I somehow managed to get the name of the keeper of the church to arrange an impromptu tour, one of the highlights being a climb to the top of the steeple from within. The paper Terry wrote, and my pictures from that trip, sadly, are long gone, and while my memory of that visit has always remained strong, the idea of writing about historic meetinghouses and churches would not evolve until many years, and many published books, later. When this book project came to the forefront several years ago, Terry and I visited nearly every one of structures discussed in this book together because of our shared love for New England architecture, both for research and photographic purposes. These journeys were a wonderful experience, and while she takes no credit for this book, I cannot thank Terry enough for being there with me almost every mile of the way (and there were many of them, well over 3,000 as we crisscrossed the state on our many day-trips) and to say that I could not have written this book without her support and encouragement is an understatement.

During the course of researching and writing this book, I have come into contact with many individuals in various towns who have offered their help and expertise, oft-times helping to uncover some obscure fact, providing data, or pointing me to previously unknown sources of information. To these individuals, listed below in no particular order, I offer my thanks and appreciation; Dianne Burrington (Grafton); Dan and Lisa Rothman (New Boston); Mary Atai (New Boston); Linda Smith (Madison); Joy McCorkhill, Library Director, Jefferson Public Library;

Walter and Carol Baird, for their extensive tour of the Danville meetinghouse and for providing documentary material; Beatrice Jillette (Goshen); Arlene Bassett and Ben Winter, for their informative tour of the Sandown Meetinghouse; Eric Small (Seabrook); Matthew Thomas (Fremont); Arnold Goodrum (Colebrook); Patricia Sapienza (Stratham); John Mullen, Middleton Heritage Commission, for his tour of the old Middleton Town Hall; Victor McLean, for his tour of the Newington church; Andrea Fitzgerald, Historian, Lisbon Area Historical Society, for sharing her research on churches in Bath and Lisbon; Christine Hadsel, for allowing the use of her photograph of the Washington Town Hall theatre curtain; Rev. Margaret Bickford of the Wentworth Congregational Church, for her help with Wentworth and Pittsburg churches; Sandra Doolan of All Saints Parish, Lancaster, for providing information on St. Agnes Church in Jefferson; Rev. Stephen Silver, First Congregational Church, Lebanon, for his tour of the church interior; Don Davis, for his tour of the North Sutton meetinghouse; Heidi Thoma, Library Director, Sutton Free Library; Rev. David Richardson, for his tour of the Webster Congregational Church; Rev. Peter Howe, for his tour of the Washington Congregational Church; Michael Ransmeir, for providing information on The Church of the Epiphany, Lisbon; Thomas Merkl, Library Assistant, Gordon-Nash Library, New Hampton; Eileen Widner, for her photograph of the Amherst Meetinghouse weathercock. My apologies go out to anyone that I may have inadvertently missed, but please know that I value your help to the same high degree even if your name does not appear here.

Finally, I cannot help but thank several individuals, architectural historians James Garvin, David Ruell, and Lisa Mausolf, as well as historian Peter Benes, whose expertise has informed me during the course of writing this book and, in some cases, during the longer course of my career as a historian, author, and lecturer for the New Hampshire Humanities. While they were not directly consulted for this work, and thus bear no responsibility for any mistakes I may have made, their published works and documentary reports, mostly in the form of National Register of Historic Places Inventory Nomination Forms, have been vital sources of information.

The reader should note that while this work covers all regions of the state, of those cities and towns that are documented (just over half in the entire state), not every church in a given town is represented. This was done mainly in order to keep this work at a manageable size and, in some cases, to avoid repetition, though it is much more extensive than originally planned (and for that I heartily thank my publisher and editor), and not because a particular town or structure was deemed unimportant. My methodology involved studying every city or town in the state and then visiting nearly three-quarters of them for further evaluation. The easiest decisions involved those truly historic structures that have already been well-documented in book form, many of them located in the Seacoast, Monadnock, Merrimack Valley, and Dartmouth–Lake Sunapee regions. However, it was my priority to also include historic structures with interesting histories in the Lakes and White Mountain regions, as well as the North Country (a.k.a. the Great North Woods), that are virtually unknown to those who live outside the communities in which they are found. Though several twentieth-century churches are represented here, my primary focus were those structures built in the eighteenth and nineteenth centuries. In the end, I hope the reader will find the book well-balanced and one that gives an informative and interesting view of the entire state.

All photographs and images in this book are by the author or from the author's collection unless noted otherwise.

CONTENTS

Introduction

Meetinghouse and church buildings have long been a part of every New Hampshire town history in one way or another. Not only were they often the first public buildings to be built in a given town, but they are often the most impressive such structures when it comes to their size, architectural details, extensive history, and, of course, the community values and ideals they represent. After all, when one thinks of the classic New Hampshire town, who cannot help but think of a white church on the village green? Over the years, a number of publications, including individual town histories and books, local newspapers, and magazines, have helped to document the most historic of these buildings. However, with very few exceptions, it is the southern or Seacoast areas of the state that receive the most attention. The work you are now starting to read covers every region in the state and documents examples of historic meetinghouses and churches from Sandown and Rindge in the south, Dover and Milton to the east, Claremont and Lyme to the west, Pittsburg and Berlin to the north, and numerous other towns in-between. It is also important to note that my focus here is not just on Congregational and other Protestant denomination structures, but those of other faiths as well, as they too add to New Hampshire's rich religious, architectural, and cultural history. Despite its attention to architectural details, this work is far from being just a study in architecture. Instead, it provides an equal focus on key aspects of the history associated with these structures in a variety of areas, including specific construction and builder details, notable ministers and town-folk associated with them, and interesting events with which they are associated. The details given, often found buried in old town or church records and published town history books that are often 125 years old or more, are interesting and informative of a way of life that has long-ago vanished, including a religious revival that filled church pews sparked by a deadly lightning strike (Alton), a meetinghouse whose timbers were cut in the season of the "old moon" (Washington), a church that was the spiritual home of a Civil Rights martyr (Keene), a black sheep who occupied the minister's pulpit (Cornish), and a church that was twice broken into by a rival religious group (Colebrook). Indeed, while many today may view these picture postcard and calendar worthy structures as quiet and dignified symbols of a simpler past, sometimes they were anything but that, being, instead, a place where civic and religious matters often came to a head and disputes, confrontation, and conflict were commonplace. Anyone who has attended an annual town meeting in New Hampshire has probably gotten a taste of what the old days must have been like. While the oldest meetinghouses and churches in the state are here given their due, so too are many other later-day buildings from the mid- to late nineteenth century included due to their local importance, as well as several churches of note that date from the twentieth century. Overall, a sampling of structures from 125 towns and cities across the state are presented herein, making this work the most comprehensive of its kind, and whether you are an armchair historian or hope to use this book on the road as a travel guide, some interesting facts and details await your discovery and, I hope, lead to an even greater understanding and appreciation of New Hampshire's meetinghouses and churches and the history that they encompass.

PART I

The Meetinghouse Era in New Hampshire

1

In the Beginning-The Meetinghouse Concept

New Hampshire was first settled on a permanent basis by white Europeans in 1623, though it had been home to Native Americans for thousands of years and its shores had been touched by European explorers and fisherman many years before this. However, unlike the Plymouth settlement to the south in what would later be the colony and future state of Massachusetts, New Hampshire's earliest settlements were not always motivated by religious ideals, but ones of commerce. Indeed, the land that comprises New Hampshire today was part of a large grant of land made in 1622 to Sir Ferdinando Gorges and Captain John Mason and stretched from the Sagadahoc (now Kennebec) River in Maine southward to the Merrimack River in northern Massachusetts. In 1629, the men split these holdings, with Mason taking the portion that lie between the Piscataqua River and the Merrimack and extending 60 miles inland. The first settlements in the state were made at Dover and Portsmouth (now in the town of Rye) and were primarily fishing and trading stations, but salt-works and the planting of crops were also major activities. The first meetinghouse in New Hampshire, then, was not erected until 1634—that being in Dover. As can be seen, carving out a new settlement from this ocean-side frontier and making a living was the first priority of the inhabitants, or so it would seem. It is important to remember that though New Hampshire's first colonists were not all of the same religious bent as the Pilgrims in Plymouth and the Puritans in the Massachusetts Bay colonies, religion was still important to them; services in the early years were conducted, albeit on a scattered basis, in privately-owned buildings such as homes and even barns and not officially designated houses of worship for the main reason that, at this time, a church was defined by colonists not as a tangible building, but by the group of people who worshipped in communion together. Thus, their "church" could be found wherever they gathered together to pray on the Sabbath. This was one of the ideals first brought over by the Pilgrims and Puritans in Massachusetts, the concept that grand church structures or cathedrals, and the fancy trappings surrounding them and, most importantly, the large and corrupt (to them) organizations that operated them (especially the Catholic Church, but also the Church of England), were not only unnecessary, but also needlessly hindered the worship of God in its purest form. The Congregationalist form of worship founded in Massachusetts and brought to New Hampshire, becoming the dominant Protestant sect through the entire Colonial period, was an outgrowth of these ideals, whereby they rejected a central church authority and instead believed in local church rule and the extensive participation of laymen in the church. It is not surprising, given this background, that the meetinghouses built during the colonial period were not considered sacred buildings and, at least early on, were quite plain in appearance. Moreover, as their name implies, these meetinghouses had a dual purpose, serving as a place where civic affairs were conducted, like the traditional town meetings to elect public officials, and to discuss and vote on town affairs, while on the Sabbath serving as a house of worship, with services conducted by a minister whose annual salary was paid by mandatory contributions (in taxes or goods such as firewood or livestock) from every town member, whether they agreed with his preaching or not. Not until after 1819, as we shall discuss shortly, did the concept of the meetinghouse come to a legal end. In coming to America, these separatists hoped to purify (thus the term "Puritans") the church, so to speak, by returning to the basics of worship without being persecuted for their beliefs. It is one of the great myths of American history that our country was founded on the ideals of religious freedom for all, for while the colonies in Massachusetts welcomed those of like religious beliefs, dissenters were persecuted, banished from the colony altogether, and sometimes even put to death. The New Hampshire religious experience early on was unique and from its earliest days the colony become a magnet for many groups, both dissenters and conformists to Puritan views, because of its proximity to Massachusetts, but also because, after the death of Mason in 1635, it fell under the rule of Massachusetts, from 1641–1680, 1689–91, and, finally, from 1702–1741, when the two colonies, at least in terms of governance, separated for good. Interestingly, after the settlement of New Hampshire's first towns in 1623, the next two towns to be established, Exeter and Hampton (both in 1638), were polar opposites in terms of Massachusetts influence. Exeter was founded by Reverend John Wheelwright, who came to America in 1636, and, within six months, his preaching and association with Anne Hutchinson had offended the local magistrates so much that he was jailed and subsequently banished. He came to New Hampshire in 1638 and purchased a tract of land with a small group of followers, that same year erecting the second known meetinghouse in the colony. The town of Hampton was also founded in 1638, but this by a group of Puritans in good standing from Lynn, Massachusetts, led by Reverend Stephen Bachiler. When a division in the Lynn church arose, Bachiler and his supporters "thought it best to remove to some other place" and initially looked on Cape Cod, but eventually came northward to Hampton, building a log meetinghouse.[1] Separation events such as this one that resulted in the founding of Hampton were common among the Congregational churches—whether a portion of the church had a disagreement over doctrine, or simply wanted to establish a congregation that was closer to home (sometimes for both reasons), local church rule made it possible.

2

Which Came First, Meetinghouse or Town?

The building of a meetinghouse was an important milestone in any New Hampshire or New England town, for the simple reason that not only was it the only town-owned building in the early colonial days but it was the figurative capstone to a town—homes and barns, grist and sawmills alone signified a settlement, but it was the meetinghouse that served as the seat of government and made a town a town. How and under what circumstances these meetinghouses were built from New Hampshire's first settlement through the first decades of the nineteenth century is fascinating and occurred in a variety of ways. In the oldest towns in the state, these meetinghouses were built near the center of compact settlements as part of the development of the town. However, as these and other towns grew in size, additional parishes were established, and meetinghouses were often built by a town to serve outlying areas as it was difficult and often dangerous to travel to the originally established meetinghouse. In those days of horse and foot travel, a miles-long trek on the Sabbath to attend meeting was a tiring experience on the best of days in the summer, but downright brutal in the winter. In cases like this, which was quite common, the meetinghouse itself predated the formal establishment of the town. For example, the town of Greenland was formally part of Portsmouth's southern holdings, but residents were granted their request to establish a separate parish in 1706, and later, in 1721, it was set-off as a separate town altogether. Likewise, in Hampton, the swath of land south of the Taylor River and north of the New Hampshire border was established as the town's Third Parish in 1709, with a new meetinghouse built in 1711. Eventually, in 1726, Hampton Falls received a grant as an independent town. Throughout the colonial period, in similar fashion, portions of a town far distant from the meetinghouse would petition to be set off as a separate town, and in the aftermath of doing so built their own meetinghouses. The town of Canterbury was incorporated in 1741, its remote northern portion, some lands located between the Merrimack and Winnipesaukee rivers, were referred to as the "north fields." When that area's inhabitants became more substantial in number and became weary of travelling the long distance to Canterbury's meetinghouse, they petitioned the legislature to be set off as a separate town, the town of Northfield being granted in 1780, though their meetinghouse would not be built until 1793.

While the above models would hold true throughout the colonial period, another set of circumstances arose that resulted in meetinghouses being built. New Hampshire's expansion westward from the seacoast and to the north and the establishment of new towns was achieved by the granting of townships by several different authorities. Many towns, such as Newport and Lancaster, were formed based on grants made by Royal Governor Benning Wentworth, who was quite active in such endeavors and amassed a large fortune from the proceeds of these grants. Other towns, such as Newbury, Stoddard, Sanbornton, and Wolfeboro, were granted by a private association known as the Masonian Proprietors, who were a group of high-powered men who came to own the rights to the former land of Captain John Mason. In these towns, while the land itself was granted (also for a profit) to groups of individuals, the right to form a town was not included and these new settlements had to petition the provincial authorities to be formally recognized as a political unit. Finally, other townships, such as Rindge and Winchester, on the New Hampshire–Massachusetts border were granted by Massachusetts authorities, mainly Governor Jonathan Belcher, when New Hampshire was under that colony's political rule. No matter how these towns were granted, it was usually included within the provisions of such grants that a meetinghouse be built within a specified number of years under varying conditions. New Durham, for instance, was granted in 1749, with the requirement that a meetinghouse be built within six years after there was peace between the English, French, and the Indians. Wolfeboro, granted in 1759, was given eight years to have "a convenient house built for the public worship of God" after peace in the same running conflicts, known as the French and Indian Wars (1688–1763) was achieved.[1] On the other hand, the town of Sutton, granted in 1749, was given no time limit even though it was stated that a meetinghouse "shall be built," while Sanbornton, granted in 1748, had to build their meetinghouse within ten years, but Stoddard, granted in 1742, was given only four years' leeway. While it is not always fully understood how these negotiations regarding such building took place or why there was such a disparity in the time allotted to build a meetinghouse, one thing is clear; the formation of these towns was first and foremost an economic venture, and while religion was still important to many settlers, life on the frontier did not always prove conducive to building a meetinghouse in a timely fashion and early worship and town meetings alike were held either in private homes, barns, or a local tavern. Many towns, in fact, missed the deadlines imposed in their grants for building a meetinghouse, but none suffered any consequences for doing so.

3

Siting the Meetinghouse

Once a town held a public vote and decided to build a meetinghouse, perhaps the most important detail to be decided was its location. Most charters had simple language stating that the meetinghouse should be built on a plot of land that was conveniently situated. As to details, these were usually left to the inhabitants of the newly granted town, though the 1748 charter for New Ipswich is unusually detailed, stating "That a Convenient Meeting House be built … as near the Center of said town and at such place as the Major part of the Interest of the Grantors and Grantees shall Determine by a Major Vote in publick Proprietors Meetings."[1] The siting of the meetinghouse was of vital importance for both economic and practical purposes—the land closest to it was usually the most valuable in town because of its close proximity not just to the meetinghouse, but such local businesses as taverns, merchants, and tradesmen shops that clustered around what would eventually become a village center, while the convenience of having but a short distance, or no distance at all, to travel to attend Sabbath services and public meetings was highly desirable. As any realtor will tell you today, "location, location, location" is what determines property value, and this same ideal held true regarding the meetinghouse in early days. Because it was such a big decision, the vote as to where to build the meetinghouse was always a well-attended event, and often contentious! Many towns formed committees to make this decision, these usually consisting of the prominent men who were active in settling the town. The first meetinghouse site in Francestown (then called New Boston Addition) took two years to arrange in the early 1760s, even though the site was chosen "right off."[2] Surveys were often conducted in order to find the geographical center of a given town, this method, in an ideal situation, being the easiest and least biased way of making such a decision. However, problems with this geo-centric method often arose—perhaps the center of the town was located on some un-moveable feature, like rock outcroppings, that made it impossible to build. The Sandown meetinghouse, for example, was supposed to have been built in the center of the town, but when town officials found that this was in a swamp, they had to choose another location. Perhaps the most contentious event in siting a meetinghouse occurred in Hopkinton beginning in 1765. The first site was chosen at a location on Putney's Hill, but this vote was soon rescinded and a site on the plains was chosen, though tradition states that other sites were also discussed. When the final decision was made, many in town were unhappy about it and made their displeasure known and held a grudge for many years. Finally, in 1787, things came to a boil when it was suggested the meetinghouse be moved. It was first voted that the meetinghouse would stay in its current location, but in early 1788, a committee of twelve men was chosen to find a place for the meetinghouse. In December of that year, they recommended against moving the meetinghouse, and three days after their recommendation was accepted in February 1789, the meetinghouse was burned to the ground by a young man, Abel Rowell. With the town at an impasse, it was recommended that men from three other towns, Lyndeborough, Gilmanton, and Washington, be called in to look at the situation objectively and render a report on the site where a new meetinghouse would be built. These men accepted the challenge and published their decision within weeks in a letter to the officials of Hopkinton. The site on the hill was voted against because it could serve only the northwest part of the town, while a site near the schoolhouse was so close to the old meetinghouse as to be not worth consideration and, in the end, they recommended, and the town accepted, that the new meetinghouse be located on the site of the original one recently burned. The town accepted this report in March 1789 and later that same year built the meetinghouse that sits on the site today. As for Rowell, he was imprisoned in nearby Amherst from 1790 until his eventual release in December 1793. It is interesting to note that the historic Rowell's Covered Bridge in West Hopkinton was named after the Rowell family of local landowners who lived on Putney's Hill and surely preferred that location for a meetinghouse site.

Another interesting example in the siting of a meetinghouse, one that shows the influence of prominent individuals, may be found in Effingham. When that town was considering where to build their meetinghouse in 1798, like Hopkinton, they also had a difficult time deciding, in this case between Lord's Hill and the Drake's Corner areas, and after being deadlocked during the course of a dozen town meetings, subsequently chose a committee of "disinterested persons" from neighboring towns to make the decision. While their decision was likely supposed to be unbiased, these men held their meetings at the tavern of Isaac Lord (he being reimbursed by the town for their "rum and victualling" expenses), Effingham's most prominent merchant and tavern keeper, whose establishment and home was located just across the street from the site where the committee recommended, and the town accepted, that the meetinghouse be built.[3] Lord won out in almost every aspect of this decision, as not only did he build the meetinghouse, located in what is now called the Lord's Hill Historic District, but his tavern directly benefitted from the increased traffic.

Finally, as can readily be seen, many towns had difficulties in keeping everyone happy with their siting decisions. Because those farthest away from the meetinghouse often faced great hardships to attend meeting, such outlying areas were the ones that were most susceptible in later years to forming their own local parish and building their own meetinghouse closer to home. In many cases, as previously discussed, the establishment of a second parish or the desire for their own meetinghouse sometimes led to that part of town breaking away and petitioning the authorities to be recognized as a new town altogether. This subsequent loss of people and land to the original town meant, in reality, a loss in revenue for the original town (and fewer individuals to pay the expense of supporting the town minister), as well as a reduction in the physical size of the town altogether. However, one town had the foresight when building their first meetinghouse to anticipate this problem. Sutton was first granted in 1749, but because of the French and Indian Wars, its settlement was delayed, the town was subsequently regranted in 1784. Religious services were first held, according to tradition, in a log structure in the mill village area, but finally, in 1794, the possibility of building a substantial meetinghouse was discussed. However, the tradition of locating a meetinghouse in the center of town was unworkable, as town officials commented to state authorities:

> ... our town being seven miles ... in length, and but five miles in width, being mountainous and extremely broken ... the centre of said town being so inconvenient, the land poor and broken for two miles each way, not fit for settlements, nor no leading road by said centre.... There are two main roads already laid out, leading through each end of the town, which serve the country and the inhabitants of the town better to build two meeting houses one on each main road which we think will better accommodate the inhabitants. And upon this consideration we have gone forward to build two small meeting houses.[4]

This was, indeed, a commonsense and agreeable solution for all to a challenge that many other towns had difficulties overcoming.

Sandown Meetinghouse, built 1774–75.

4

Raising the Meetinghouse

Once a given town had chosen a site for their meetinghouse, whether it be the first in town or an eventual replacement in later years, the details of its building were attended to. The first step came at a town meeting, where a committee of men were usually chosen to study the issue and make recommendations as to the size of the meetinghouse and some of the building details, as well as who would be hired to either be its master builder or who would frame the structure out, and when the work might start. Amherst in 1738 designated that their first meetinghouse be 45 × 22 in size, while Dover's second meetinghouse built in 1652 was specified to be 40 feet long by 26 wide, with six windows, two doors, and to have a "tite" cover.[1] In Bedford, the current historic First Presbyterian Church was specified to be 71 × 51 in 1831. As to the style of the meetinghouse, it was a tradition early on that towns were influenced by the meetinghouses built in surrounding towns, and thus when specifications were drawn, specific directions were made in some cases as to copying these details. In Boscawen, their first meetinghouse, built in 1738 of logs, was designated to be 40 feet long, the same as nearby Rumford (modern day Concord), but 2 feet higher. In 1772, the first Francestown meetinghouse was directed to be as good as the meetinghouse in Lyndeborough, though when the meetinghouse was finally finished in 1788, it was directed to be finished "after the form of the meeting house in Dedham that this meeting house was Pland by."[2] This may seem an unusually distant influence but it makes perfect sense as some of the town's earliest settlers were from that Massachusetts town and must have admired its meetinghouse. This copying of meetinghouse and church forms seems to have been especially pronounced in the Monadnock region, all because of one man. Master builder Elias Carter built a fine church in Templeton, Massachusetts, in 1811, whose design was extensively copied in New Hampshire, resulting in a chain of related meetinghouses that historian Peter Benes refers to as the "Templeton run." However, the influence was not in all cases a direct one: the 1815-built Troy meetinghouse was directly influenced by Templeton, their building committee directed to examine the Templeton meetinghouse in person. The next building in this run, the 1817 Fitzwilliam townhouse (built in 1816, destroyed by fire, and rebuilt in 1818 in the same form), was probably directly influenced by Templeton, but the 1818 Dublin meetinghouse (no longer extant) was copied from Fitzwilliam, while the 1819 Hancock Meetinghouse was copied in size, construction, and form from Dublin. The other churches in this Templeton run include Acworth (1821, possibly built by Elias Carter himself), Newport (1822), Jaffrey (1823), and Keene (1829).

Surviving town meeting records also show in some cases that details were worked out as to who would supply such key materials as wood for the frame and the stone for the foundation (often called the "underpinning"), and, in rarer cases, specifics as to paint color and other finish work, to be discussed in more detail shortly. In Bedford, Hugh Riddle built the stone underpinning for the 1755 meetinghouse, while in 1832, the same work was done by his nephew, Benjamin Riddle, for the First Presbyterian Church at a cost of $418. In Northfield, the committee accepted bids from fourteen individuals, each to provide about 500 boards at a price varying from 9 to 13 shillings (the equivalent of about $65–$95 in today's currency) and delivered to one man designated to be in charge of receiving the lumber. The timber for the framing and supports typically consisted of local woods, pine, oak, birch, cedar, and beech, these "sticks" measuring anywhere from 6 to 60 or more feet long, with hackmatack (Eastern larch) roots sometimes used for supports and bracing. Of course, along with these details, funds for paying for nails, window glass, and the services of a builder were also detailed. If the meetinghouse was a replacement

Woodcut, artist's conception of first Dover Meetinghouse, from Wadleigh's *Notable Events in the History of Dover* (1913). Once located on what is now Dover Point Road, this meetinghouse was notable for the defensive stockade thatsurrounded it. Though long gone, the site of this meetinghouse is today a historic site.

Acworth Meetinghouse, built 1821.

structure, it was often the case—in the tradition of true Yankee frugality—that materials from the old meetinghouse were recycled for use in its replacement. Among the many towns that saved in this manner were Gilsum (1789, boards reused, old nails straightened), Acworth (1821), Sanbornton (1834, the foundation, frame, and window glass from the old meetinghouse reused), and the Smith Meetinghouse in Gilmanton (*c.* 1839).

Once the day was chosen for the meetinghouse to be raised, further plans had to be made for this important community event. First and foremost was the availability of the needed manpower—most towns designated that every able-bodied man in town would be required to provide one full day of labor, starting early in the morning, often 6 or 7 a.m., and continuing until dark, unless other circumstances, such as bad weather, arose. The early meetinghouses were small in size and likely required fifty men or less and a town could usually draw from its own population to fill this need, the work usually requiring about two full days. However, in later years, when meetinghouses were larger in size or more complicated in design (such as having a bell-tower), this time could easily be doubled, or even longer. In these instances, a given town would appeal to neighboring towns for help; when Temple raised its meetinghouse in 1781, they appealed to the neighboring towns of Peterborough, Wilton, and New Ipswich for an additional forty-five men, while in 1795, Greenfield asked for fifty-four men in all from the towns of Temple, Wilton, Lyndeborough, Francestown, and Hancock.[3] Thus, these meetinghouse raisings were often not just town events, but significant regional events as well. As befits such an important occasion, there was much fanfare and celebration at the raising of a meetinghouse—an oration and prayer by the town minister was traditional to get things going, while the ladies of the town would provide food and refreshments, and spectators came from near and far to witness this momentous and interesting event. Also present were vendors selling their wares and entertainment in the form of jugglers, singers, and other itinerant artists. One New England tradition at these raisings, which would surely raise eyebrows on a town construction site today, was the serving of prodigious amounts of rum to the master-builder and his crew of workmen. The funds for these spirits were paid for by the town and the procuring of the rum in advance was a major part of preparing for the raising. In Amherst in 1771, the town voted to procure the rum for the raising of its meetinghouse, "not exceeding 8 barrels," the modern equivalent of 256 gallons.[4]

Finally, when the frame of the meetinghouse was ready to be raised into place, the men having had their first drink of rum, the master-builder, with a bottle of rum in one hand, stood on the upper most beam—or "plate" as it was called—and to great cheering was hauled upward along with the frame, in this raised position visible to all the workmen under his command and the raising commenced at a steady pace. The process of framing a meetinghouse has been discussed in many other works, but because the details were not written down in contemporary sources, there is much we do not know. We do know that block and tackle and men standing on ladders were used in the raising process, as were simple derricks, windlasses, yokes of oxen, and such simple tools as pike and gin poles to provide hoisting and holding power. Once the frame was raised, temporary bracing timbers were employed to keep things in place. As anyone who has witnessed a modern-day barn raising can attest to, the whole must have been quite the combination of a noisy spectacle and a nice feat of engineering. Cuts, sprains, bruises, and splinters among the builders were certainly part of the experience, as any carpenter knows, and falls from the frame during construction were not uncommon, but most of the time, meetinghouse raisings went off without a major hitch. In Andover, during the raising of the two-story Union Meetinghouse at the center in June 1822, only one person, Daniel Smith, was injured, this happening when a large joist fell from the beams, striking him in the head and splitting his jawbone to the chin, but he was "fast recovering."[5] However, the town of Wilton was not so fortunate; during the raising of that town's meetinghouse on September 7, 1773, a tree trunk that was being used as a temporary support for the tie beam of the frame and the two sets of rafters being constructed above cracked in half and collapsed, sending the fifty-three men standing on the beam or working on the rafters plummeting to the ground 27 feet below. Moments before, master-builder Ephraim Barker had been warned that the support was unsafe, but disregarded it with scorn, at least according to tradition. Three men died almost instantly, another succumbed to his injuries the next day, while another man suffered greatly until dying four days later. Every other man suffered injuries of one type or another, such as broken ribs, crushed ankles, and cuts and gashes from falling axes and other tools, the whole scene said to be quite bloody. After a day of fasting and prayer to reflect on this horrible event, building would eventually resume, the tie-beam whose support gave way being found useable, though, incredibly, it hit the ground again while being lifted due to a failure in the equipment. This time nobody was hurt, and by the end of September, the frame was fully raised.[6] The meetinghouse would serve the town for many years before being destroyed by fire in December 1859.

With the frame of the meetinghouse now in place, the next step, taking place over several weeks or more, was to sheath the frame, leaving openings for the doors and windows, shingling the roof with the wood shakes commonly used during that time, installing the clapboards on the outside of the building, and framing out the doors and windows, and, if enough glass had been obtained, actually installing the windows—though many meetinghouses went without window glass installed, often for several years or more, due to the high expense. Now, with the basic form of the meetinghouse in place, the building was open for use and finish details could be considered.

5

Finishing the Meetinghouse

Like many people who have a great affection for the buildings of old, you may now, at this point, have pictured in your mind's eye the finished product of the builders of olden days, a "typical" white-washed New England meetinghouse, sitting all nice and pretty on the town green. However, in reality, this was not the scene that our New England ancestors saw with their own eyes for months or sometimes even years after their new meetinghouse was erected. In fact, it was far from it. With all the time, energy, and money spent on deciding to build a meetinghouse, finding a site, and raising the frame, many towns in the immediate aftermath of the raising seemed to have what might be called "meetinghouse fatigue," and the final finishing details, including painting the building and finishing the interior, which included building pews, the minister's pulpit, finishing the gallery (the upper level of seats in a two-story meetinghouse), and even installing window glass, took a considerable amount of time to complete and, in rare cases, were never completed. The first meetinghouse in Raymond was erected in September 1766, but right away, the town wanted to move it—it sat uncompleted for thirteen years, until early 1779, when it was torn down, the timbers sold and later used to build a bridge.

In most cases, money was the issue when it came to getting a meetinghouse finished in full; many, like the town of Wilton in 1773, could not get voters to approve the funds needed for finishing, so other means of funding had to be found. The common method of doing this, especially later in the colonial period, was to sell the box pews inside the meetinghouse, and space in the gallery, to the highest bidders. In an earlier time, the 1600s through the early 1700s, the seating of the meetinghouse, as it was termed, was usually by assignment based on social rank: the wealthiest and most prominent individuals or families in town getting the best seats in the house, so to speak, with family pews located on the ground floor and the minister's family pew usually closest to the pulpit. During this time period, once the seating was arranged, each man or head of household was responsible for their own space. In Stratham, when their first meetinghouse was built in 1718, "Each man was obliged to build his own pew; keep it in repair; to maintain all the glass against it; and he must build too on the spot assigned him.... There was, however, one exception to this, for the town of Stratham solemnly voted 'that Mr. Andrew Wiggin shall have Leberty to set in what seat he pleaseth in the meeting house.'"[1] In the gallery, throughout the colonial period, single men and women were separated, each sitting on their own side, while some towns even had separate box pews in the gallery for slaves or indentured servants. In later years, when the seating of the meetinghouse was more democratic, pews were put up for bid and anyone (provided, in most cases, that they were town residents) with enough money could buy the pew of their choice. Likewise, reserved spaces on the benches in the gallery above could also be purchased, and it was by the raising of these private funds that a town raised enough money to finish their meetinghouse inside and out. However, while in some towns disputes arose and it could take months or years to iron things out regarding pew sales, this does not mean the meetinghouse went unused—Sabbath day services or town affairs usually took place even in unfinished meetinghouses, though seating might consist of simple log benches that offered little in the way of comfort. The settling of pew sales and the subsequent building of the pews was, perhaps, the second most important event, aside from the raising, in the life of a meetinghouse, for the simple reason that while the structure of the meetinghouse was owned collectively by the town, the pews in the meetinghouse, which were conveyed by a legal deed, were a space, just like any traditional plot of land, owned by individual town members who could sell or will their pews to other individuals at their own desire. Of this practice of owning pews, a New Castle historian commented in 1884 that "To get a square pew and find themselves seated in it, gave those early Christians the same sense of superiority and self-satisfaction that an opera box gives their descendants."[2] While this old-fashioned practice of selling pews would eventually die out, especially after the second decade of the nineteenth century, it has never entirely disappeared in New Hampshire; the Stark Union Church in Stark Village is wholly owned and administered by the Pew Owner's Association and has been since the church was built in 1853. Today, only in a few historic New Hampshire meetinghouses, including Newington, Sandown, Danville, Fremont, and New Hampton, do these box pews survive to give us a glimpse of what the interior of a colonial-era meetinghouse looked like, they being distinguished by their numbered paneled entrance doors, hinged seats within which folded up when their owners stood to sing, and the finely turned balusters between the railings mounted on the top of the box pews.

As to the interior finish details, of central importance was the minister's elevated pulpit, in the earliest times usually located on the wall opposite the front entryway and reached by a small stairway consisting of eight or ten steep steps. One common form of this feature has been called the "wainscot" pulpit because the front of it was paneled, including the central three-paneled projection where the minister stood to give his sermon, and the paneled walls that flanked it.[3] The front was decorated to

Danville Meetinghouse. Interior view of pulpit wall.

Sandown Meetinghouse. View of slave pew in gallery.

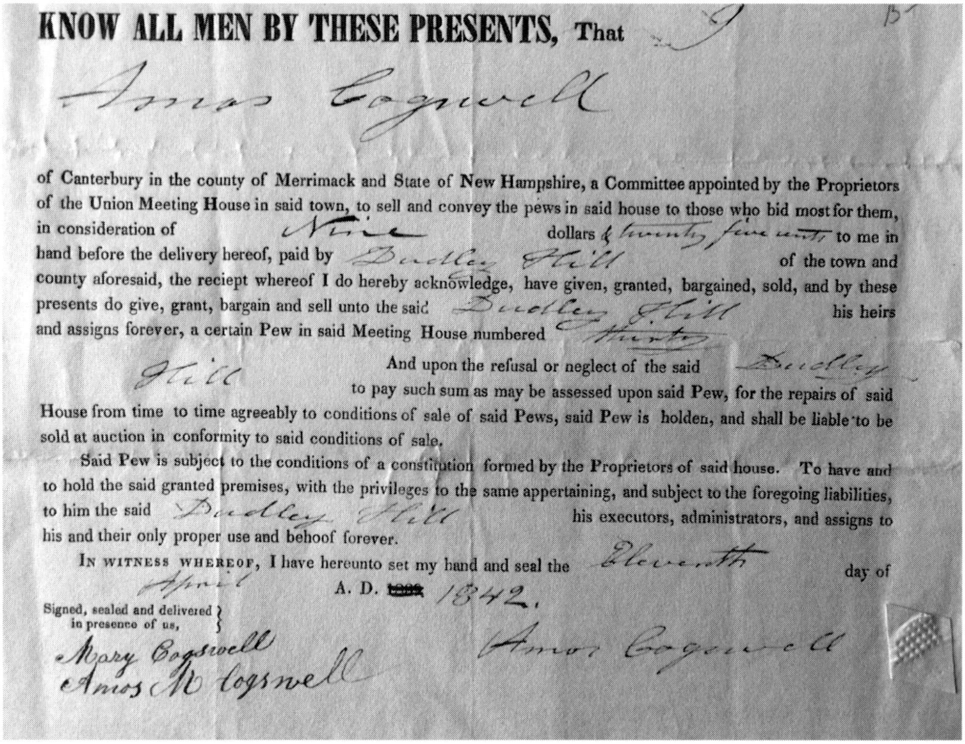
KNOW ALL MEN BY THESE PRESENTS, That

Amos Cogswell

of Canterbury in the county of Merrimack and State of New Hampshire, a Committee appointed by the Proprietors of the Union Meeting House in said town, to sell and convey the pews in said house to those who bid most for them, in consideration of Nine dollars & twenty five cents to me in hand before the delivery hereof, paid by Dudley Hill of the town and county aforesaid, the reciept whereof I do hereby acknowledge, have given, granted, bargained, sold, and by these presents do give, grant, bargain and sell unto the said Dudley Hill his heirs and assigns forever, a certain Pew in said Meeting House numbered thirty

And upon the refusal or neglect of the said Dudley Hill to pay such sum as may be assessed upon said Pew, for the repairs of said House from time to time agreeably to conditions of sale of said Pews, said Pew is holden, and shall be liable to be sold at auction in conformity to said conditions of sale.

Said Pew is subject to the conditions of a constitution formed by the Proprietors of said house. To have and to hold the said granted premises, with the privileges to the same appertaining, and subject to the foregoing liabilities, to him the said Dudley Hill his executors, administrators, and assigns to his and their only proper use and behoof forever.

IN WITNESS WHEREOF, I have hereunto set my hand and seal the Eleventh day of April A. D. 1842.

Signed, sealed and delivered in presence of us,

Mary Cogswell
Amos M Cogswell

Amos Cogswell

Original pew deed, Union (Worsted) Church, Canterbury, 1842. This document shows the sale of pew No. 30 by original pew-holder Amos Cogswell to a fellow townsman. Such deeds were kept by families for years and were every bit as important as land deeds. (*Author's collection*)

varying degrees, usually including such architectural details as pilasters or columns and decorative molding. Directly behind the pulpit was a large window, giving the minister enough light to read from in the daytime, while flanking it were columns and pilasters. In Dunbarton, the town directed that there be one circular-headed window in back of the pulpit for their 1789-built meetinghouse. Above the pulpit was the sounding board or canopy, which helped to deflect sound and project the minister's voice, especially important for those hellfire and brimstone sermons. These sounding boards were usually octagonal shaped when suspended from the ceiling, and when attached to the wall were usually five-eighths of an octagon in shape. Like the pulpit front, they usually had some form of decorative carving and molding, and many were topped off with a finial—that in Jaffrey in the shape of a pineapple, while those in New Ipswich and Henniker were in the form of an acorn. One additional pulpit detail, which shows not only outstanding craftsmanship, but also the lengths a town might go to in order to show off their meetinghouse in fine fashion despite the additional expense, was their decorative paint schemes. In the historic Sandown meetinghouse, the corner pilasters on the pulpit front and those flanking the pulpit window were (and still are) painted white with light blue veining in order to imitate fine marble, as is the folding deacon's table at the base of the pulpit, while the pilasters on the front of the pulpit of the historic Danville meetinghouse, as well as that which once stood in New Ipswich, were painted a reddish-brown to imitate mahogany wood. In most cases, we do not know who crafted these pulpits and other interior woodwork details—in some cases, perhaps most, local skilled builders and/or woodcarvers whose names were not recorded did the work. However, one prominent man known to have been a pulpit and pew-maker was Major John Dunlap (1746–1792), a professional furniture-maker and joiner, born in Chester and practicing his trade in Goffstown and Bedford. He also trained his younger brothers, Samuel and William, in these trades. In 1783, John Dunlap, according to his account book, drew up plans for the pulpits in Temple and Londonderry, while about 1785, he built the pews for the Bedford meetinghouse.[4] Of the interior features and paint schemes in New Hampshire meetinghouses, town records give us a few clues; the historic meetinghouse at Barnstead Parade had a pulpit that was "clay" in color with an octagonal sounding board; in Hanover, the 1795-built meetinghouse that once stood on the north side of the college green had an interior that was painted white with a light tinge of blue; the 1808-built meetinghouse in Sullivan had its pulpit front, as well as stairs, balusters, support columns, and gallery front all painted light blue; Hampton's third meetinghouse, built in 1675, had clay walls "smoothed over and washed with white lime and made hansom";[5] the meetinghouse in Gilsum, built 1790, had a stone gray interior with a pulpit and canopy and pews painted a Prussian blue, the pulpit and canopy copied from the town of Surry; the 1796-built meetinghouse in Swanzey had angels painted on the wall behind the pulpit; and the 1795-built meetinghouse in North Sutton had its gallery front and pillars, as well as the pulpit and sounding board painted a "brilliant" green, with white walls throughout. All of these interior details combined—the pulpit and woodwork details and paint colors used—were well-thought out and, in many cases, greatly debated at town meeting, and together show the great pride taken in these communal structures. As with the exterior paint colors chosen for many earlier meetinghouses (see below), these details also give us a startling glimpse of the colorful preferences of our New England ancestors before the advent of latter-day Greek Revival and Victorian-era stylistic influences that are more familiar to our day and age.

In these later days, perhaps the most controversial change to a meetinghouse or church interior was the addition of a stove. Remembering that Sabbath-day sermons were long, drawn-out affairs lasting for hours, the winter season caused many hardships to these colonials, not the least of which was enduring the bitter cold in unheated meetinghouses. Attendees, for sure, bundled up as best they could, but the extremities were always a problem. Attendees were sometimes allowed to bring personal foot-stoves, but these soon came to be banned as they were a real fire danger and caused the loss of many a wooden New England meetinghouse. However, by the early 1800s, new stove technology had been invented and churches began to

Sandown Meetinghouse. Interior view of pulpit wall with slave pew at upper right.

Wall mural detail, attributed to John Avery, Middleton Town Hall.

Interior view of box pews from the gallery, First Congregational Church of Webster.

explore the possibility of adding full-size heating stoves to their building, as well as the requisite chimney for venting smoke. The Presbyterian Church in Windham would not install a stove for heating until 1828, a seeming latecomer, but folks in Fremont had to wait even longer. Though a stove was proposed in 1829, "old-timers objected to such modern contraptions, and regarded these proposed changes as an indication that the younger generation was becoming too soft."[6] Eventually, in 1840, the Fremont meetinghouse gained two stoves, paid for by private subscription. Elsewhere, Jaffrey had one installed sometime between 1818 and 1820, while Hampton installed their own in March 1821, the town historian later commenting "behold-an innovation!"[7] The decision to add a stove always engendered much debate and controversy, as is demonstrated by events in Amherst and Francestown. In the former, the town in 1818 refused, upon petition, to purchase a stove for the meetinghouse, the response being that "Even the Indians have stoves in their meetinghouses. Is it not astonishing that civilized and enlightened people have none ... a word to the frozen will-we hope, be sufficient to make them weatherwise?"[8] Apparently, this appeal fell on deaf ears and a stove for Amherst was not purchased until 1824, and only then by private subscription. In Francestown, a stove for the meetinghouse was proposed about 1822, but was "vigorously dismissed." Later that fall, "A few of the more progressive spirits bought one in Claremont, did deliberately set it up in the meetinghouse, and did kindle a fire in it.... Some could not sleep for fear of being burned up."[9] This last comment is interesting, and we presume that they did not mean their sleep in the meetinghouse during the minister's sermon was disturbed. In any case, the town eventually voted to let the stove remain and the matter seemed to have been settled. In modern times, with the advent of central heating systems, these early stoves have been removed, their only remnant the markings on the wooden floor where they once stood and holes where stovepipes used to be. In the towns of Danville, Fremont, and Sandown, the stoves were removed from these early meetinghouses and the interiors restored to their original configurations.

Once the pews were sold to the highest bidders and the necessary funds were raised, the finishing of the meetinghouse might be commenced, though the expenditure of these funds was still controlled by town vote and it was not uncommon for a meetinghouse to go unfinished for five, ten, or even twenty years, though some meetinghouses were completed in good time. In Warren, their historic 1818-built meetinghouse was finished by 1819, except for being painted. Others were not so diligent. The first meetinghouse raised in Fitzwilliam in 1770 was not finished for over twenty years, with the pulpit window and two upper-end windows not installed until 1791. In Francestown, the meetinghouse raised by John Quigly in 1775, at the outset of the American Revolution, was not finished until 1788 "due to poverty and the hardships of war."[10] In Windham, their 1798-built meetinghouse did not fit out its gallery until 1805 (building slab seats with no back) and did not entirely finish the building until 1814. The town of Hampton had a varied track record; its third meetinghouse, built in 1675, was not occupied until 1680 and its finishing was delayed by the Indian wars, though their fourth meetinghouse, built in 1719, was finished within a year. The town of Amherst, too, had troubles with their first meetinghouse; raised in 1739, the floors were not laid, nor the doors hung or pulpit built, until 1743, window frames were voted to be made in 1744, as well as to have walls and ceilings plastered, and while it was voted to finish the meetinghouse in 1747, it was still not finished by 1753. Some final examples of finishing delays include Antrim (built 1785, finished 1791), the historic meetinghouse in Barnstead Parade (built 1788, finished 1799), Bedford (built 1755, finished 1775), and the historic Canaan meetinghouse (built 1792, finished 1797).

One interesting detail are the color choices made for the exterior of New Hampshire's meetinghouses. It is here that the myth of the white-washed meetinghouse, at least in Colonial times, has been demolished by research in town records and the old town history books, in this later source, the evidence existing in plain view. In fact, white-washed meetinghouses and churches did not become common in New Hampshire, and all of New England, until the early nineteenth century for two reasons. The first being that white-lead paint was expensive in the seventeenth and eighteenth centuries, while, second, the Greek Revival style of architecture that was popular in America from the 1820s into the 1850s made white a fashionable color for meetinghouses and many were painted this color during the time period. When it comes to the actual paint colors used, what little we do know, from the research of Peter Benes and others, is fascinating and paints an entirely different picture of what early meetinghouses must have looked like. The 1789-built meetinghouse in Gilsum was perhaps the most striking, being "Coloured A Bright Orring" (orange), the doors a stone gray, and the cornices and window trim white.[11] Also striking were the meetinghouses in Alstead and Washington, both once painted with red ochre. Yellow in several shades was popular throughout New Hampshire; the historic meetinghouse at Barnstead Parade was once painted yellow with a red roof, while the 1802-built North Parish meetinghouse in Charlestown was "a tawdry yellow, which did not render it externally, very attractive."[12] In Mont Vernon, the historic 1781-built meetinghouse, now the town hall, was painted in 1821 "with two coats of good paint and oil, the trimmings with white lead, the body of the house a bright yellow, composed of 2/5 of white and 3/5 a French yellow, the doors of a Mahogany color."[13] In Keene, their 1786 historic meetinghouse was painted white or a light yellow, with green doors, while Kensington's meetinghouse in 1823 was shown in drawings as being yellow with bright orange doors and a brown roof.[14] Also painted yellow or a related shade at some point in their existence were the following meetinghouses: Union Episcopal Church in Claremont, Hancock (a straw color in 1807); Mason (1795, a straw color); Rindge (built 1796, yellow with a red roof before 1839); Sullivan (1822—yellow tint with white trim, copying Keene); Wilton (based on a nineteenth-century model, which is now lost); Temple (1781—a copy of Wilton); Surry (1789—painted like Keene); Walpole (1789—straw color); and Monroe (1800), whose meetinghouse was nicknamed "Old Yellow." Despite the high cost of white lead paint, some towns did paint the meetinghouses this color—the historic meetinghouse in Hancock was voted to be painted white in 1806, but the following year changed their mind, but the meetinghouses in Candia (1795), Hollis (1804), and Littleton (1815) were painted white, while that in New Ipswich was originally a cream color. As for the historic Chester meetinghouse built in 1773, in 1785, the town "voted that the money which the pews shall fetch shall be laid out toards colloring [*sic.*] the meetinghouse," but does not specify the color, though white is suspected, and, not surprising given their close proximity, the Sandown meetinghouse followed their example.[15] Finally, though painting was commonly done, many towns did not go to the expense to do such and instead left their meetinghouses to be naturally weathered. The first meetinghouse in Fitzwilliam, erected in 1770, was never fully painted, while that erected in Orford had unpainted clapboards that grew so dingy and blackened from the weather over the years that it was said to resemble an old coffin.

6

From Meetinghouse to Church

Once raised and open for business, the meetinghouse was the most important building in any town, symbolic of the town's permanent establishment and the *de facto* center of local power and decision-making. Early meetinghouses in many towns were short-lived structures, often being replaced with larger and more substantial versions as the town grew in size and prospered within a relatively short time span. This was especially true for the early towns in the Seacoast: Hampton's first meetinghouse, built in 1637, was replaced in 1640 by a larger one that lasted for thirty-five years. In Dover, Exeter, and Portsmouth, the interval of time between their first and second meetinghouses was similar; Dover's first meetinghouse, the first in New Hampshire, was built in 1634 and lasted until 1653, while Exeter's first meetinghouse, completed in 1638, was replaced in 1652. Portsmouth completed its first meetinghouse in 1640 and replaced it in 1657. Though early meetinghouses in New Hampshire have not survived into modern times, many later-day Colonial-era meetinghouses have had a long and useful life; the oldest remaining meetinghouse in the state, though much altered, at Newington has stood since 1711, while that in Hampstead dates from 1745. The other meetinghouse survivors that pre-date the American Revolution are those in Nashua (1747—Bird's Meetinghouse), Danville (1755), Greenland (1756), Westmoreland (1764), Seabrook (1765), Dover (1768—Quaker Meetinghouse), Londonderry (1769), Amherst (1771), Surry (1771), Claremont (1773—Union Episcopal), Sandown (1773), Chester (1774), and Jaffrey (1775).

During the course of their "lives," events great and small took place inside these meetinghouses; the decision as to who would be hired as the town minister and preach in the meetinghouse every Sabbath day was an important one, and it included much wrangling over the minister's salary and whether his brand of theology was suitable for the town, often involving the prospective candidate giving a guest sermon on a chosen Sabbath day in order to gauge his oratory skills. Other important events

Claremont, Union Episcopal Church, built 1773.

include Election Day proceedings where eligible townsmen cast their votes in the town's voting box, the reading of important proclamations and bills from the state level and higher, and discussions of issues of the day, including such events as the American Revolution and proceedings regarding the formation and ratification of our state and national constitutions that took place afterwards. It was also in the meetinghouse where important decisions were made on local military matters, including the choosing of town militia officers and deciding upon local expenditures for training and outfitting and, in times of war, such as the French and Indian Wars and the American Revolution, the enlistment of soldiers. Not to be forgotten is the fact that these meetinghouses also served as local courthouses where trials and other legal proceedings were sometimes held—when justice was meted out at the local level, it often took place just outside the front door of the meetinghouse, where the stocks were usually located. In short, it was in these meetinghouses that every important issue of the day, both religious and secular, was debated and decided. However, change was in the wind by the 1760s as religion in New Hampshire (and New England as a whole) was undergoing slow but inexorable changes. Though they may not have known it, the seeds of separation of church and state were being sown by New Hampshire's citizens in the years before the Revolution as the old religious order was being challenged. One eventual result was the end of the meetinghouse-era.

7

Changes in the Standing Order

It is at this point that a brief history of the predominant religious denominations and how they came to be established in Colonial-era New Hampshire must be discussed. It is through this complicated but interesting lens that we can better understand the evolution of the state's meetinghouse traditions and how these structures' usage has evolved, as well as how new church buildings were subsequently built solely for religious purposes.

As previously discussed, religion in New Hampshire from the beginning was based on the Puritan or Congregational model from Massachusetts, and this order would remain the dominant form throughout the Colonial period. New Hampshire towns were, in effect, parish towns, founded early on Congregationalist principles, which became known as "the Standing Order." The Puritans rejected an ecclesiastical hierarchy (like the Catholic and Anglican churches) that included bishops, archbishops, and a pope, and instead believed in the power of the local congregation, in combination with the fellowship of their neighboring churches. Thus, ministers could share pulpits with one another when the occasion called for such, and neighboring ministers could even be brought in or consulted to solve a town's dispute with their own minister or if extra guidance on a matter was required. Note that this fellowship extended only to their fellow Congregationalists and they did not hold fellowship with other religious orders, with the exception of the Presbyterians, who first practiced in the colony at Londonderry about 1719 and, later on, the Calvinistic Baptists. The Presbyterians, whose beliefs were much the same as the Congregationalists, had their origins with the Church of Scotland. They had a strong following among the Scotch-Irish settlers in the Merrimack Valley in such towns as Londonderry, Windham, Bedford, and Antrim, as well as in Peterborough and on the Seacoast in Seabrook, while a few towns, such as Goffstown, had both Presbyterian and Congregational influences.

Also established in New Hampshire early on, first at Portsmouth by 1640, was the Anglican Church (later known as Episcopalians in America). This was the Colonial

American version of the Church of England and the church in New Hampshire followed their practices, though the head of the church in England, the Archbishop of Canterbury, exercised no authority outside that country. This denomination is a reformed Catholic church whose history as an independent group began when King Henry VIII renounced papal authority after a political dispute in 1534. Members of this church early on in New Hampshire tended to be wealthy merchants or those serving in the royal government bureaucracy, including royal governors themselves. Though not a separatist group like the early Puritans/Congregationalists, the Anglicans co-existed with them on a largely friendly basis because their members were among society's elite. Even after the break with England spurred on by the American Revolution, many churches of this sect were established in the post-Revolutionary War period and beyond.

Catholicism, on the other hand, was downright despised and banned in New Hampshire in Colonial times, and its members would continue to be discriminated against in New Hampshire well into the twentieth century (more on that later). The peaceful Quakers, too, were despised in New England, their members being very ill treated in Massachusetts, being banished and even executed for their beliefs, while early on in New Hampshire, they were treated much the same way, with three young women of that sect in Dover—Ann Coleman, Mary Tompkins, and Alice Ambrose—being seized by local authorities in 1662, stripped to the waist and whipped, the whole event witnessed by Reverend John Reyner, who stood there laughing. Banished from the colony, they were transported by cart and subsequently whipped at Hampton and Salisbury before the proceedings were eventually halted. As can be seen, the Standing Order was a powerful one intimately intertwined with the local government, they effectively being one and same. Changes in the Standing Order began to appear with religious revivals that began to occur in the 1730s and intensified with the period of religious revivals known as "the Great Awakening" in the 1740s. By this time, the hellfire and brimstone Puritan theology was fading in popularity—it taught that only a few elect individuals would ever achieve salvation, and that the destination of one's soul was pre-ordained and could not be changed by one's "good works" during the course of a lifetime. It was not a joyous religion by any means, and enthusiasm faded by the early 1700s, but a revival was eventually started, first in England and later in America's middle colonies, and eventually, by 1740, to New Hampshire and the rest of New England. Led by such itinerant ministers as John Wesley (the founder of Methodism), Rev. George Whitefield, and Gilbert Tennant (a Presbyterian), their preaching was joyous and emotional, imparting the message that salvation might be had (there were still no guarantees) by an individual achieving a state of grace through a recognition of their sins, prayer, Bible study, and, of course, church attendance, as well as leading a good life by having high moral standards. These ideas, enthusiastically accepted by many, despised by others due to the emotional outpourings of religious fervor, brought about changes in the meetinghouse and a challenge to the Standing Order.

George Whitefield first came to New Hampshire in 1740, preaching outside to large crowds in Hampton (where it was windy and his voice could not be clearly heard) and Portsmouth; in some cases, he was invited to speak in local meetinghouse pulpits, but at other places he was not welcome. Indeed, one problem of the Great Awakening for the Standard Order was that there were many itinerant preachers at work who refused to respect the traditional boundaries of local town parishes and preached in other minister's jurisdictions without permission. This revival led to a conflict even among Congregationalists, pitting "Old Light" ministers, who clung to the old ways, and the "New Lights," who heartily embraced the new form of worship. These battles led to disputes in many towns and effectively opened the door to other religious sects, including the Baptists, Free Will Baptists, Methodists, and, even later, Unitarians and Universalists.

The first group to benefit from the Great Awakening in New Hampshire were the Baptists. Though the first Baptist Church in America was established by Roger Williams in Rhode Island in 1638 after he was banished from Massachusetts, its adherents were few in New Hampshire. The first Baptist church to be organized in the colony was in Newton in 1755, led by Rev. Walter Powers, with subsequent Baptist churches founded by the end of the American Revolution in Stratham, Deerfield, and Richmond (all in 1770), Brentwood, Lebanon, and Westmoreland (1771), Marlow (1777), and Meredith, Sanbornton, and Rumney (all in 1780). While this group was at first a dissenting one, it split into several distinct movements, including the Calvinistic Baptists, whose hellfire and brimstone brand of theology was not greatly different from that of traditional Congregationalists, and the more liberal Free Will Baptists.

The Free Will Baptist Christian movement has its roots in the General Baptist movement in England, but in America, it consists of two branches that evolved separately from one another: the Palmer line was founded in North Carolina in 1727, while the Randall line was founded independently in New Hampshire in 1780 by New Castle native Benjamin Randall while living in New Durham. He was originally a Baptist but rejected their Puritan views on predestination and believed that the Bible was the very will of God and that individuals, of their own free will, could accept or reject faith. This group was very popular in the Lakes Region and early local churches were established in 1780 in New Durham, Loudon, and Strafford, with subsequent churches established in Tamworth (1781), Middleton and Pittsfield (1791), Wolfeboro (1792), Gilmanton Iron Works (1794), Canterbury (1798), and Unity and Gilford (1799). From 1800–1809, an additional twenty-six towns formed Free Will congregations all over the state, including Ossipee (1807), Thornton (1800), Piermont (1806), and Lebanon (1801). Many of these groups were inspired by itinerant Free Will Baptist preachers, including noted preacher John Buzzell, a native of Barrington and friend of Benjamin Randall who was ordained in 1792 and traveled widely to spread the faith. Eventually, by 1835, the Randall line split into two groups based on differences in theology, one led by Buzzell and another led by Jeremy Bullock, who was active in Maine and in towns along the Maine–New Hampshire border. In some towns, such as Ossipee, the dispute between the Buzellites and Bullockites, as they were called, within a Free Will Baptist congregation over matters of theology led to breakaway groups forming their own church.

The Methodists, too, were active in New Hampshire, but followed a slightly different model at first, employing circuit riders who travelled periodically all across New England and New Hampshire, preaching to small groups of followers, giving their sermons in private homes and often in local schoolhouses, and sometimes, as in Fremont, the local meetinghouse. They were especially active in northern New Hampshire, where Northern Circuit riders preached in many towns, including Stratford and Whitefield. In this later town, it is said that the foundation for the Methodist circuit riders was built by a woman known as "Mother Hutchins," who came to town in 1813 and preached in her log home, "where she shed the new light among her neighbors," as well as preaching a series of meetings in nearby Lancaster in the winter of 1816–1817.[1] Eventually, Methodist ministers would come to settle in many New Hampshire towns and formed local congregations.

Finally, there were those individuals who believed in the Universalist and Unitarian doctrines, liberal brands of theology that have a long history (the two formally united in 1961 as the Unitarian Universalist Association), their basic tenets wholly rejecting the Puritan hellfire and brimstone teachings, instead believing in a loving God and that everyone would achieve salvation. One of the key figures in this group was Universalist minister and writer Hosea Ballou, a native of Richmond, New Hampshire, who preached in Portsmouth (1807–1815) and at many other places in Massachusetts and Vermont and was the founder of several Universalist publications and magazines. One great event in the history of this church took place in Winchester, New Hampshire, in 1803, where a General Convention of Universalist ministers from all over America, including Hosea Ballou, met and formulated a statement of the Universalist faith known as the Winchester Profession.

As can be seen from the above accounts of these later religious groups, New Hampshire men and women played a significant role in their founding, formulation of doctrine, and subsequent spreading of their faith. While many traditional Congregational ministers did not take kindly to these new groups of worshippers being gathered in their town, these sects soon became resentful about being forced to pay taxes to support a religious denomination whose beliefs they did not subscribe to—conflict in the meetinghouse was inevitable.

8

Time of Transition and Change

Disagreements in many towns about which type of minister to support were not uncommon in the decades between the time of the Great Awakening and the American Revolution, but these disputes became heightened in the 1780s as our state and federal governments were being organized. There was much debate, of course, regarding how much power should be retained by the states *versus* the central government, and issues of taxation and religion were details that were always in the forefront. With New Hampshire's ratification of the United States Constitution in 1788, the ninth state to do so, the Constitution went into effect. Among the recommendations by the "Convention of the Delegates of the people of the state of New Hampshire" was that "Congress shall make no laws touching religion, or to infringe the rights of conscience." Despite this recommendation, there were no immediate changes in the state regarding the town support of a minister and the forced payment of taxes. However, the year 1791 was an important one: it was at this time that the Bill of Rights to the Constitution was established at the national level, stating in the First Amendment and the Establishment Clause that "Congress shall make no laws respecting an establishment of religion, or prohibiting the free exercise thereof." Thus, the Constitution prevented the government from preferring any one religion over another. New Hampshire followed suit in part that same year when the Act for Regulating Towns was passed, which, while not as grand in statement or scope, made some changes. This law stated that local taxpayers were still obligated to pay taxes for the support of the town minister, now hired by selectmen, and for the construction and maintenance of a building for religious and town services (a meetinghouse) but did provide an exemption for those who belonged to a different sect, as long as they were paying to support another minister on a private basis and could provide a certificate to prove their exemption. The law made no provision for those who did not wish to support a religion of any kind and they were still required to pay the ministerial tax. With the burden of proof on the objector, disputes arose in many towns as many of these sects, such as the Free Will Baptists and Methodists, were served by itinerant preachers who spread their faith free of charge and were not settled pastorates as was common in the old Congregational order. Because of this, many that applied for exemption were denied by town selectmen, not surprising as an approval would mean less revenue being paid in a town to support the hired minister and a heavier financial burden for those who did support the standing order. In Hampton Falls in 1803, Elias Smith led a new religious group in town, and by 1809, twenty-one of his followers were exempted from paying the ministerial tax. Smith was also active in nearby Greenland, where his preaching gathered new followers in 1808, reducing the numbers and "pecuniary ability for a season" of the established church. In Rindge, the town granted just three exemptions in 1796, but that number rose to seventeen in 1800 and twenty-five by 1819. Likewise, in Hampstead, the established Congregational order was challenged in the late 1770s, when the church was "greatly weakened by divisions, occasioned by the intrusion of flaming sectarian exhorters among them."[1]

Despite all these types of disputes, the New Hampshire law of 1791 would remain in force until 1819, when the state passed the Toleration Act. In this law, the state ended the practice of town ministry support, except for those already settled with a contract, and that citizens were not required to belong to or pay for the support of any religious group. This act also stated that taxes could be voted on and assessed to support the maintenance of the meetinghouse that was owned by and used for town purposes. The bill was first proposed in 1816 by newly-elected representative Rev. Dan Young, a Methodist minister from Lisbon, and it took three years to achieve passage. Finally, three decades after New Hampshire made the U.S. Constitution the law of the land, religious freedom was finally achieved, at least for Protestant sects. Catholics and those of any other faith were still restricted by the state constitution from holding elective office, a ban that remained in place until 1879 after a constitutional amendment would finally pass.

In the aftermath of the Toleration Act, however, the use of the town meetinghouse for strictly secular affairs would change only gradually. Buildings intended for worship built after 1819 were generally called a "church," while meetinghouses that were formerly used as houses of worship but were now used strictly for secular affairs might continue to be referred to as meetinghouses, though many eventually came to be called the "town-house" or "town hall." In some cases, religious groups—whether they be Congregationalist, Baptist, Methodist, or another denomination—soon moved to new church buildings built for that specific purpose and with privately raised funds (usually from among the church members) within a short time period. This occurred in Acworth, where previously the town had debated repairing the old meetinghouse and allowing its use by other denominations. The Congregationalists, however, fought this tooth and nail and the meetinghouse fell into disrepair. After the Toleration Act was passed, Congregationalists built a new house of worship (today often referred to, incorrectly, as the Acworth Meetinghouse) in 1821, while the old meetinghouse was torn down and a new town hall was built next door to the church on the town common. However, not all towns acted right away; in Northwood, the meetinghouse continued to be used as a house of worship until 1840, while that in Raymond was used by Free Will Baptists, then Methodists, before it finally became a town hall sometime in the late 1830s. In Fitzwilliam, their meetinghouse built in 1817 continued as a house of worship and town meeting place until 1832, when the Congregationalists built their own edifice, while the 1814-built meetinghouse in Troy remained under the ownership of the original proprietors until it was sold to the town in 1853. In Rindge, their historic 1796-built meetinghouse became town owned in 1839, with the church society being its tenant; to this day, the building is shared, with the town offices located in the lower level while the rest of the building is occupied by the United Church of Christ. Thus, it can be seen that the ties that bound New Hampshire town government and organized religion were not fully severed in 1819 and, in many cases, a relationship between these two entities exists today. Most town meetinghouse interiors, as a result of these legal and resulting social changes, would eventually be reconfigured from the 1820s through the first decades of the twentieth century. Most commonly, galleries were replaced with a full second floor, which were reconfigured for their new intended use as a religious or civic space, the same being true for ground level spaces as well. It is at this time that original pulpits, sounding boards, and box pews, now deemed out of fashion, were removed and largely discarded. In their place, town office spaces were created, library space and kitchen facilities sometimes added, and, in many cases, community stages were added to accommodate such public entertainments as plays and music concerts. However, annual town meetings were still held here and it is interesting to note that many election polling places today in New Hampshire towns are located in local churches (as well as town halls and schools); while this may seem odd to those from different parts of the country, such a relationship hearkens back directly to the meetinghouses of old where voting and religious services were held under the same roof.

One common situation after 1819 was to allow shared use of the meetinghouse for different religious groups in a given town. This was done in South Hampton, where "The town threw open the Meeting-house to other denominations, according to the desire and in proportion to the amount of taxes paid by the friends of the several systems of doctrine."[2] In Jaffrey, their historic meetinghouse continued to be used for church services, and their citizens charged a ministerial tax, until 1831, though the meetinghouse was shared by Congregationalists, Baptists, Unitarians, and Universalists in its final years, each allowed a set number of Sabbath days. In fact, this sharing of the meetinghouse on an equalized basis among the different religious groups in a town was a common solution to an otherwise thorny problem.

In regards to private church buildings, now that these religious groups were operated on a private basis, many built structures of their own, of which some today are considered historic churches. Whether they were Congregationalist, Baptist, or

Theater curtain, Washington Town Hall. This curtain, made by the O. L. Story Company of Boston, was installed *c.* 1900–10 in the upper floor of the meetinghouse, which used to be the gallery. (*Photo courtesy Christine Hadsel*)

some other denomination, each had to privately finance their own building costs and, in most cases, their own land acquisition costs where the church might stand. While a number of private churches were built in New Hampshire prior to the Toleration Act, many more would follow suit after 1819. The use of donated land was a relatively common way for a church to find a home, this usually contributed by one of the church members, or land was bought outright from money raised by a given congregation. In Keene, their historic 1786-built meetinghouse was originally located on the town common, but in 1828, it was moved to an adjacent site on donated land once the Congregational Society became its owner. Later on, in such towns as Manchester, Berlin, and Colebrook, land was donated by local companies, usually textile mills, whose workers would attend the church eventually built. However, in many towns, local religious groups were small in number and did not have the funds to raise their own church building. One common solution was for these groups to band together and pool their resources to build a church, each group using the building on an alternating basis. These structures, often referred to as "union meetinghouses," were built all over the state, but were very common in the Lakes Region and northern New Hampshire, where Free Will Baptists, Methodists, Congregationalists, and other groups united for a common goal. The historic 1853-built Union Meetinghouse in Stark is a perfect example of this kind of church building, while the town of Wolfeboro had four such churches located within its boundaries at one time.

Finally, while there were many Congregational, Presbyterian, Baptist, Free Will Baptist, Anglican, Methodist, Unitarian, and Universalist church buildings that would come to be built in New Hampshire after 1819 when age of the meetinghouse was ended, one other factor also contributed to the increase in churches in the state and representation of other religious groups. This was the influx of immigrants in New Hampshire that began in the 1830s with the coming of the Industrial Revolution and the advent of the textile industry in such places as Manchester and Dover, and later on, after 1850, in such northern towns as Berlin and Lancaster with the advent of the logging industry. Early immigrants came from Ireland and French Canada, but they also came in smaller numbers from many other countries, including Greece, Sweden, Germany, and even Russia. Immigrants from Quebec, just over the international border with Canada, were large in number, and many French-Canadian enclaves were established in New Hampshire towns and cities. The same was true of the Irish. The city of Manchester, with its large-scale mill operations, was perhaps the most diverse in terms of immigrants and remains so to this day—here can be found the 1869-built St. Joseph's Cathedral and the 1880-built St. Marie's Church, both serving French-Canadian populations; the 1887-built Gethsemane Lutheran Church; the unusual Saint George Greek Orthodox Cathedral; as well as churches for a number of other denominations. It is also in Manchester that the first mosque for the Islamic faith is being built in the state. Though its construction began in 2000, it has long been delayed due to a lack of funds and difficult national political issues stemming from the devastating terrorist attacks on September 11, 2001, whose consequences have trickled down to the local level. Those who opposed the building of the mosque should not be too smug that such a long delay will mean the mosque will never be built, nor should those who hope to see it to come to full completion lose all hope. While the ultimate fate of this project is yet to be decided, a twenty-year delay or more in finishing a church was, as we have seen, a commonplace occurrence in New Hampshire early on, albeit in a society that was more homogenous. Among these immigrants from other countries, French-Canadians predominated in the state and the city, where over half of all mill workers by 1900 belonged to that ethnic group. Similar to Manchester in its diversity is the gateway city of Nashua; an industrial center as well, it also has had a large immigrant population over the years, including many French-Canadians. Like Manchester, immigrants still form an important part of Nashua's population and new religious groups, too, have established a presence. When the historic St. Francis Xavier church was closed by the Catholic Diocese, the church was subsequently sold to a group of Coptic Christians who now call the church their home and are striving to repair and renovate the church. A final example is Berlin in the North Country, which was also home to a large French-Canadian population, causing the building of the first St. Anne Church in 1882, and later, with the influx of Russian immigrants, the building of the onion-domed historic Holy Resurrection Orthodox Church in 1915, the first Russian Orthodox church in the state.

Above: Islamic Society of Greater Manchester Mosque. Construction began in 2005 and remains unfinished to date.

Right: Nashua, St. Mary & Archangel Michael Coptic Orthodox Church (former St. Francois Xavier Roman Catholic Church), built 1896–98.

In regards to other religious groups whose churches are represented in this work—those of the Jewish, Catholic, Lutheran, and Greek Orthodox faiths—these groups too were all established in the state to serve immigrant communities. In regards to the Jewish faith, two historic temples may be found: one in Portsmouth and one in Bethlehem. The state's first known practicing Jews were Abraham and Rachel Isaacs, who arrived in Portsmouth from Prussia sometime in the mid-1780s. Abraham was an auctioneer and shopkeeper and was known for closing his store on Saturdays, the Jewish Sabbath (Shabbat). However, the Isaacs were apparently the only Jewish family in town and no temple would be established in Portsmouth until over a century later, in 1910, when Temple Israel, the first in the state, was finally organized to serve a small but growing population of Jewish families. In the White Mountains, the town of Bethlehem was (and still is) known for its clean and pollen-free mountain air; by the 1870s, the town became a tourist destination for Jewish families from all over New England and New York seeking relief from hay fever allergies. In fact, the Hebrew Hay Fever Relief Association was established here in 1919 and was in operation for many years. Eventually, a temple was organized in that town in the 1920s.

Adherents of Catholicism were at first not welcome in New Hampshire, and while they were discriminated against from Colonial times down into the twentieth century, the first Catholic church to be built in the state was the historic 1824-built St. Mary's Church in Claremont, constructed under the guidance of Rev. Virgil Barber, his home once being directly attached to the structure. However, the first Catholic parish to be organized in the state was in Dover in 1830, its primary members being Irish immigrants who worked in the local mills. Catholicism in New Hampshire grew at a slow pace early on and was controlled by bishops in Boston and Portland, Maine, but finally, in 1884, the Diocese of Manchester was established by the church, it covering all of the state. The state's first bishop was Denis Mary Bradley, an Irish immigrant from County Kerry who came to Manchester at the age of eight.

Finally, the Lutheran and Greek Orthodox churches became established in the state with later waves of immigrants—those from Sweden and Germany organized Lutheran churches in Berlin and Manchester in the 1870s and 1880s. The Gethsemane Lutheran Church, founded in 1882 by Swedes who came to work in the city's textile mills, was built on land donated by Amoskeag Mills in 1887. Likewise, Greek immigrants arrived in large numbers in the state from the 1890s to 1924, with Manchester and Nashua being destination cities due to the vast opportunities for employment in their mill operations. It is no wonder that today the city is home to St. George Cathedral, which was established in 1905, as well as The Assumption Greek Orthodox Church (founded in 1936 after a split with St. George) to serve a growing population that soon became, though not the largest, one of the most vibrant and influential immigrant communities in the city.

In the end, no matter what faith they represented, many beautiful meetinghouses and churches have been built in New Hampshire to serve its citizens, with survivors today representing over 300 years of growth and change in the state.

Claremont, Old St. Mary Roman Catholic Church, built 1823.

PART II

The Architecture of Meetinghouse and Church

Having discussed the circumstances in which these structures were built and the faiths they represent, it is now time to take a look at them from an architectural point of view. Indeed, it is these details—their lofty clock towers and spires, detailed doorways, impressive windows, and ornamental attributes—that catches even the most causal observer's eye. Just as the way in which New Hampshire citizens have practiced religion has changed and evolved over the years, so too have these building types and details also changed. Because there are already many available works on the architecture of meetinghouse and church forms in New Hampshire and New England readily available (some found in the source bibliography at the end of this book), this section focuses on the basic elements of what can be immediately discerned by the layman in this book's pictures, or while visiting in person, and how they have evolved over the years. Examples of meetinghouses and churches listed here are given by town, with their building date in parentheses. Further details about and pictures of these structures may be found in the individual town listings in Part III.

9

Early Meetinghouse Types

In most cases, the surviving meetinghouse and church structures of today, if viewed by New Hampshire's first settlers from the 1620s through the early 1700s, would be vastly different, even shocking, to what they were used to. Architectural historians like Edmund Sinnott have categorized these early meetinghouses and churches built between the seventeenth century and about 1825 into four different types. However, the classification for a given edifice in many towns changed over the years as an original structure was often changed or altered over the course of its lifetime to serve both changing needs (like a larger congregation) and changes in decorative norms. Indeed, just as clothing styles have changed over the years, so too did meetinghouse and churches change; what was once considered a proper meetinghouse or church when first built might later come to be considered old-fashioned or even "crude" in later years, resulting in alterations, editions, or outright replacement. In this aspect, larger towns seemed to lead the way, influenced perhaps by a larger, more diverse, and better travelled populace, while rural communities tended to be more conservative and stick with the "old-fashioned" way of doing things for a longer period of time. This is amply demonstrated by the historic meetinghouses built in Exeter and Fremont. That in the large town of Exeter (a center of commerce and once the state capital), the First Parish Meetinghouse, was built from 1798–1800, and though built by talented local builders, it "Was widely admired at its completion" and was studied by out-of-state builders, a very elaborate and beautiful structure.[1] The meetinghouse in Fremont, located just miles away from Exeter in a rural setting, was built in 1800. As historian Matthew Thomas comments: "Its builders looked backward for its design and were content to judge its appropriateness by comparing it with the many meeting houses that existed in surrounding towns, most of which had been built before 1775."[2] As Thomas further notes, Fremont was perhaps oblivious to the changes in architectural trends then taking place, but its small population, then shrinking, would not have had the resources to erect anything other than a more practical building in a form that was once quite popular. Despite the differences in style and wealth embodied in this comparison, the Fremont Meetinghouse, because of its very simplicity, is still an architectural gem in its own right.

The earliest meetinghouses built in many towns in New Hampshire were in the form of a log house and probably nearly identical to the homes then being built, though larger in size. Of these, there are no survivors, nor even contemporary sketches of what they may have looked like. The second meetinghouse built in the state—that in Hampton in 1637—was built of logs and had a bell, but nothing else is known. That built by John Hutchinson in Portsmouth in 1657 was 40 feet square and used logs with a 9-inch diameter, while that in the border town of Dunstable built in 1685 was also a log house. Towns settled later on in the Merrimack Valley Region in the 1730s, such as Penacook (modern day Concord) and Boscawen, also built log meetinghouses, as was probably also the case for towns in the North Country. The first log meetinghouse in Penacook was 40 feet long by 25 feet wide and was copied by Boscawen built in 1735. These meetinghouses and churches were in all likelihood crude indeed—the 1808-built Methodist meetinghouse on Meeting House Hill in Stratford "furnished a refuge from the heat for the sheep which ranged at will through the unfenced wilds. Their noise often interfered with the service.... Elder (Antipas) Marshall once called to them in the middle of his sermon 'Bleat away, we can make as much noise as you can,'"" while "Elder Lord vehemently declaimed against making or allowing the house of God to be made a sheep pen."[3] Of course, early structures like these were merely built for convenience and most proved to be rather temporary in nature until a proper meetinghouse could be built.

Artist's conception, first Concord meetinghouse in log cabin form, from Bouton's *History of Concord*, 1856.

The first formal meetinghouses to be built have been termed Type I meetinghouses by architectural historians and were built between the 1630s and about the first decade of the 1700s. Only one of this type survives in all of New England, the famed Old Ship Meetinghouse, built in Hingham in 1681. Meetinghouses of this type were largely square in plan and had a four-sided hipped roof, very steep, which might be topped off with a turret or cupola. Where this form originated is a subject of debate among architectural historians: some claim it is a uniquely American design, while others believe that meetinghouses similar in design were constructed by separatists in Holland and England. It seems likely both ideas are true and that Puritans built meetinghouses in similar form to those they built in Europe, but modified their designs so as to be useful in their New World environment. Once again, we know little about the New Hampshire meetinghouses of this form. Exeter's second meetinghouse, built in 1652, was likely in this form, measuring 20 feet square. That built in Dover in 1653 was larger, measuring 40 × 26 feet. It had a turret added in 1665, and two years later, it was fortified with walls that were 8 feet high and enclosed a 100-foot-square area where inhabitants could gather in times of danger. This was an important feature as towns like Dover, Durham, and Exeter were truly on the frontier and endured devastating Indian raids well into the 1730s. One very late example of this type was built in Wentworth some time after that town was granted in 1766. Described as being "nearly square … with its four-sided roof and no steeple," the "Old Meetinghouse" burned down in April 1828, replaced by the current Wentworth Congregational Church.[4]

The Type II style of meetinghouse became popular by 1710, with examples built as late as 1800. Attributes of this type of meetinghouse include its barn-like appearance,

Artist's conception, first Jaffrey meetinghouse, a Type I-style structure square in plan with four-sided hipped roof. From Cutter's *History of the Town of Jaffrey, New Hampshire*, 1881.

oblong in shape with a steeply pitched roof rising to a ridgepole. This form usually had entrance doors at each end, with a main entrance on the front, with the pulpit located on the side opposite the main entrance. This form was often termed by colonial builders as having a "flat" roof because its angle of pitch was much less than that of Type I meetinghouses with hipped roofs. It likely got its start in Boston with the building of the Brattle Church in 1699, then the largest church in all of New England. This new form raised eyebrows among the Puritans and soon was copied throughout New England.[5] Churches of this style are known for certain to have been built in New Hampshire in Portsmouth and Newington in 1712, the later still surviving in an altered form. The state has an outstanding collection of Type I meetinghouses remaining; that in Sandown, built in 1773–74, is regarded as the finest example of this type, but that in nearby Danville, built in 1755, is nearly its equal and can lay claim to being the oldest meetinghouse in the state existing in its original, unaltered form. In this same area may also be found the previously discussed 1800-built Fremont meetinghouse, possibly the last of its kind built in the state. It is notable for its two side porches (which look like additions) that cover the stairways that lead to the second story gallery inside, this feature being a space-saver for the interior and once very common. Finally, there is the old Webster Meetinghouse, built in 1791. Now restored, its exterior is a beautiful example of this simple yet quintessentially New England type of meetinghouse. In addition to these originals, there are some notable surviving meetinghouses of this type that have been altered with the addition of a bell tower and/or steeple, including those in Newington (1712), Hampstead (1745), East Derry (1769), Jaffrey (1775), Washington (1789), Canaan (1793), Lempster (1794), North Sutton (1795), East Alstead (1798), and Barnstead Parade (1799). However, while viewing these meetinghouses today, if you can picture them without their added bell-towers or steeples you can still see their distinctive Type II origins.

While the Type II meetinghouse style would have a long reign in New Hampshire, further changes began to occur by the 1790s, influenced in part by the beginning of a true separation between church and state. Not only were new churches being built by specific denominations who were not bound by Congregationalist traditions, but even among those of the Standing Order, whose meetinghouses were used for both secular and religious affairs, "a feeling began to grow that their meetinghouse, as well, should be a less secular building and more a House of the Lord."[6] It was in this atmosphere that the Type III meetinghouse style was born and reigned supreme from about 1800–1830. Structures of this type are characterized by an elaborate main entrance of two or three doors (the side entrances being eliminated) with the pulpit located at the opposite end. This entryway often had a projecting two-story porch decorated with flanking strips of ornamental woodwork called pilasters, a decorative element made to look like columns, or a portico supported by actual columns, often four in number. Above this entryway was usually a square bell-tower of two or more stages, partially supported by the roof, the whole thing sometimes topped off with a cupola or spire. The style of churches built during this time are also important because they signaled a change from

Danville Meetinghouse, built 1755. This is New Hampshire's oldest Type II-style meetinghouse.

the vernacular to academic form of architecture. In the vernacular tradition, buildings were designed and built by local builders who had no formal training. This all changed with the advent of architecture as a profession, where builders now received formal academic training and studied the art of architecture through the ages to become not just builders, but men capable of blending both pleasing aesthetics and utilitarian aspects in the structures they designed. To be sure, many local builders were able to achieve these goals without the benefit of formal training, but this was the time of influence from such architects as Englishmen Christopher Wren (St. Paul's Cathedral, London, 1697) and James Gibbs (St. Martin-in-the Fields, 1724), whose famed London churches were studied in America and admired for their form, and the rise of such influential American architects as Connecticut's Asher Benjamin (1773–1845) and Bostonian Charles Bullfinch (1763–1844). New Hampshire has many original Type III meetinghouses, notable examples being those in Lyme (1810), Troy (1814), Fitzwilliam (1818), Warner (1818), Hancock (1820), Acworth (1821), Newbury (1821), Webster (1823), Gilmanton (1825), Peterborough (1825), Haverhill (1827), Loudon (1827), Hampton Falls (1828), Lebanon (1828), Wentworth (1828), New Castle (1828), Dover (1829), Unity (1831), and Bedford (1832). Other notable examples which were originally built in the Type II form but were later altered include those in Keene (built 1786, altered 1826), Mont Vernon (built 1781, altered 1837), Rindge (built 1796, altered 1839), and Francestown (built 1801, remodeled 1834).

Left: Unity Town Hall, built 1831. A Type III-style meetinghouse, built originally for the town's Free Will Baptists.

Below: Façade view, Francestown Meetinghouse. Shown here are the pilaster and modillion details that were added during renovations in 1834.

10

Other Notable Church Styles and Types

In addition to the specific meetinghouse and early church types previously discussed, there are a number of other noteworthy architectural styles found among New Hampshire's historic churches that help to give its city and townscapes a pleasing diversity. As will be seen below, many of these architectural styles were blended with one another.

The Federal Style, which came into vogue about 1790 and was widely popular for the next fifty years, was, ironically, influenced by the designs of professional English architects. Its proponents, men like Benjamin and Bullfinch, each of whom added their own unique element, are considered America's first trained architects. Features found on Federal-style churches include elaborate moldings of a geometric design, including windows and doorways with a keystone-shaped lintel, doorways with sidelights and fanlights above, and delicate pilasters and columns. Many Type III meetinghouses have Federal-style elements in their designs. Excellent examples of churches featuring Federal details are those in Exeter, Newbury, and Acworth.

Beginning about 1825 and lasting throughout the nineteenth century there came the Greek Revival style, termed by historian Edmund Sinnott Type IV. Churches of this type are notable for their great ornamentation and a portico of varying depth supported by four columns (usually of the Doric order), or with ornamental pilasters, the whole front resembling a classic Greek temple. Excellent examples of this style include that in East Andover (built 1796, remodeled in 1840), Nashua (Unitarian-Universalist Church, built 1827 by Asher Benjamin), Portsmouth (Unitarian-Universalist Church built 1824–28), Hampton Falls (Unitarian Church, built 1838), Northwood (Congregational Church, built 1840), and New Hampton (1854). Relatively few examples of pure Greek Revival-style churches are found in the state, perhaps because "New Hampshire was slow to adopt the Greek Revival mode," and this style was likely deemed to be too ostentatious for most New Hampshire small towns.[1] However, many churches were built in rural areas that used Greek

Above left: Exeter, First Congregational Church, built 1798–1800. This Church is considered one of the finest Federal-style churches in New Hampshire.

Above right: New Hampton Community Church, built 1854. Detail view of the portico and its supporting columns with pediment above, giving the building its classical Greek Revival appearance.

Below: Orford, West Congregational Church, built 1855. This view of its façade shows the distinctive pinnacles and pointed window that are hallmarks of the Gothic Revival style.

Revival elements in a more subdued manner. It is also interesting to note that New Hampshire and New England church builders also modified the proportions of their Greek Revival buildings in regards to roof and pediment, constructing them with a more steeply-pitched roof in order that they could better handle the heavy snow-loads of New England winters.

The Gothic Revival-style churches, prominent from the 1830s up to the Civil War era, are known for their steeply pitched roofs, pinnacled steeples, crenelated towers reminiscent of a medieval castle, quatrefoil trim, and arched windows, sometimes in a variety of sizes. However, not all churches employed all these features, and in many instances, a church builder employed two or even three different styles, with, say, Gothic, Greek Revival, and other elements combined to create a distinctive design. Gothic Revival edifices are easy to identify and offer a pleasing alternative to the more traditional church styles of earlier times. Excellent examples, in no particular order, can be found in Newport (1821), Orford (1855), Bath (1873), Claremont (1836), Dunbarton (1836), Charlestown (1843), Lancaster, Laconia (1930), Bethlehem (1930), Keene (1864), and Manchester (1860).

The Italianate style reigned from about 1840–1880 and is noted for its tall windows and, most notably in New Hampshire churches, wide eaves that are supported by large and often ornate paired brackets. Rusticated blocks of stone, or wood cut to look like stone, termed "quoins," were also used on the corners of some church buildings. While Italianate homes are distinguished by their flat or low-pitched hip roofs, this was not an Italianate feature generally employed by church builders. Because of these differences, Italianate inspired churches can be difficult for the layman to identify. Excellent examples with these features may be found in Alton (1854), Portsmouth (1855), Penacook (1858), Epsom (1861), and Laconia (1877).

The Romanesque Revival style was popular from 1840–1900. Buildings in this style are usually noted for their brick or stone construction and large size with multiple towers and varying roof lines, as well as semi-circular arched doors and windows. In regards to this style and church construction, their size and associated building costs largely limited them to the state's largest cities, with notable examples found in Nashua (1894), Penacook (1897, a wooden structure), and Concord (1904).

The Stick-style design, prevalent from 1860–1890, is highlighted by highly decorative stick-work that is applied over the horizontal siding of a structure, giving it the appearance of offering functional support, and steeply pitched gabled roofs. Notable examples can be found in Claremont (1853), Charlestown (1880), and Berlin (1883).

The Shingle style, popular from 1880–1900, is, as its name implies, distinguished by the uniform covering of structures with unpainted wooden shingles, with steeply pitched roofs with multiple levels and small sash or old-fashioned casement windows with many lights. Several examples are found in the state, including the Emmanuel Church in Dublin (1888) and The Church of the Epiphany in Lisbon (1911).

Left: Portsmouth, North Church, built 1854–55. This side view offers a view of the building's Italianate details, including the paired brackets supporting the eaves and the tall and narrow rounded-arch windows.

Below: Nashua, The First Church Congregational, built 1893–94. Its massive stone construction, tower, and varied roof line are all predominant features of the Romanesque Revival style of architecture.

Right: Claremont, Trinity Episcopal Church, built 1852. The façade of this building offers an excellent view of its Stick-style construction, with its steeply pitched roof and applied decorative timbers that appear to offer support.

Below: Dublin, Emmanuel Episcopal Church, built 1888. The finest Shingle-style church in the state, highlighted by its distinctive shingled roof and old-fashioned windows.

One highly distinctive category are those churches that were built using an Eclectic style beginning in the late nineteenth century and lasting well into the twentieth century. Churches of this design combined recognized styles like Gothic Revival with other styles, often more than one, to create a building that was completely unique. Indeed, Eclecticism was all about an architect's ability to design an original creation rather than copying a tried and true form. These are buildings that, once seen, are hard to forget because of their exquisite details. The three outstanding examples found in the state are the First Congregational Church in Keene (built 1788, remodeled 1859), the United Baptist Church of Lakeport in Laconia (1892), and the Holy Resurrection Orthodox Church in Berlin (1915).

While we have discussed the various meetinghouse and church styles, it is worth noting that all of these structures also fall into several different categories of houses of worship. The vast majority under discussion in this work are public houses of worship, with the meetinghouse being the first and foremost example, as nearly everyone in the community attended this structure for one reason or another, whether religious or civil. The churches that succeeded them, or the meetinghouse that became a church, was also a public structure, but of a slightly more limited basis: in order to attend the church, which was open to most nearly everyone in the community, all that was required was an interest in or a profession of faith for which the church building represented. This model stills holds true today; if you have an

Laconia, United Baptist Church of Lakeport, built 1892. This Victorian-era Eclectic-style church combines elements of several different architectural styles to create a distinctive and unique building that commands attention.

interest in a particular church, members of the public are generally free to enter and attend church ceremonies. However, not all houses of worship were or are open to the public, a small number being classified as private chapels. Such structures as these, built in many architectural styles, are privately owned and were not open to the general public, and include those built by individual, wealthy families as their own private place of worship, as well as those built to serve a select population, such as a private school, hotel, or even a summer camp community. Examples of the former include Trinity Church (1797) in Holderness, built by prominent settler and politician Samuel Livermore and privately owned by his descendants until 1854; The Church of St. John the Evangelist (1867), built by the famed Stark family; and the Ivie Memorial Church of the Messiah (1930) in Bethlehem. It is interesting that all of these structures were built by those who were Episcopalians, but not surprising, many adhering to the Episcopal faith, since early Colonial times, were higher up on the social and economic ladder, while Episcopal dioceses in general were more loosely organized and allowed for these structures to be built. Examples of those private chapels owned by a small or select group include the Emmanuel Episcopal Church (1888) in Dublin, originally built by wealthy Boston Episcopalians who summered there and now serving the privately-owned Dublin School since 1935; the St. Matthews Episcopal Chapel (1894) in Sugar Hill, first built by a local hotel to serve its wealthy summer guests but now open to the public; and the Wonalancet Union Chapel (1880), a summer chapel privately-owned by the Wonalancet Corporation since 1892 but one that is open to all denominations, as its name implies. The effect these structures have had on their communities is simple: "The chapels have a deep hold on generations of summering families. Many people, along with some newcomers, mark the major passages of their lives in the chapels: baptisms, weddings, even memorial funerals," they being "a place where people can actively cultivate the spiritual when, maybe in the rest of their lives, life has gotten too busy to do that."[2] As a group, all of these structures are rather distinctive and quite charming in their architectural detailing—though that in Bethlehem has a more somber appearance in keeping with its medieval styling—and offer a unique and intimate setting for worship or meditation, which was, really, the original cause for their construction from the very beginning.

It may also be helpful here to clarify some of the terminology for churches in the Catholic and Episcopal faiths. In these faiths, there are structures described as "churches," "mission" churches, and "cathedrals"; while all of them are churches in their truest sense, those given the title of mission churches were those located in areas that were initially where these faiths were attempting to gather followers—their activities were not locally self-supporting like an established church, but rather from the diocese that established the mission. Often, when missions are thought of in the historical sense, one may hearken back to the efforts of Puritan ministers and competing Catholic priests of colonial times going into the wilds of northern New England to Christianize Native Americans, all in the ultimate goal to save

Bethlehem, Ivie Memorial Church, built 1930. This Gothic Revival church was built to commemorate the loss of a loved one and never fulfilled the role of a traditional Episcopal parish church.

souls, gain new adherents to spread their faiths, and, pragmatically speaking, to gain important allies. The efforts to spread the faith continued on in rural New Hampshire even into the 1800s, and though such missions were no longer fraught with danger, there were still many places, such as the towns of Claremont and Wakefield (Sanbornville), where opportunities existed and missionary churches were built to further the goal of spreading the faith. Finally, there is that house of worship called a "cathedral"; they are additionally important as the principle church of the diocese of which they are a part of and the church associated with the bishop of the diocese. The Roman Catholic Diocese of Manchester, for example, is responsible for all of New Hampshire, with St. Joseph's Cathedral (built 1869) in Manchester being the home of current Bishop Peter Anthony Libasci, as it has been for all bishops since New Hampshire gained its own diocese in 1884, chosen by the first to hold the office, Bishop Denis Bradley. The term "cathedral" conjures up images of large and elaborate churches, like those famed in Europe, but that need not be so; the Gothic Revival-styled Ste. Marie Church in West Manchester, built in 1880, is a much more elaborate building in an architectural sense than St. Joseph's, but it is a parish church.

11

Meetinghouse and Church Details

In this section, we will take a look at some of the exterior details of these historic structures that catch the eye, such as windows, doors, steeples, and decorative woodwork, and how these elements have changed over the years.

Windows and Shutters

It has often been said that, for people, the eyes are the window to the soul. One could make the case that the windows of a meetinghouse or church have the same visual, and perhaps spiritual, effect. Not only are we drawn to them visually, they being the key feature of any building, but they also offer immediate clues as to that building's style and, often, its intended purpose. The windows in New Hampshire's earliest meetinghouse were casement windows, which were hinged on one or more sides and opened inwards. The glass panes in these windows were of diamond-shaped crown glass, small in size, the individual panes separated and held in place by lead strips. In Portsmouth's first North Parish meetinghouse built in 1657, the individual panes were 4 inches long and 3 inches wide. As we have seen, glass windows in early meetinghouses were rare and many were not installed until years after a structure was built. This is because window glass was very expensive in the American colonies, and while some was produced in locations as close as Boston, it was still costly to obtain and in many cases was imported from England until after the American Revolution, when glass-making in America became more common.

The casement window style was popular until the early 1700s, when sash windows, first invented in either Holland or England, became the norm. Sash windows (also called hung sash windows) are distinguished by their moveable panels that slide up and down, with the style still a popular one to this day in the building trade and a classic throughout New England. The moveable panels of this style of window consist of individual panes of glass, often referred to early on as "lights," separated by wood strips known as "muntins." A typical arrangement for sash windows in New Hampshire and New England meetinghouses and churches has both panels with three rows of four windows each, resulting in twelve panes of glass in each sash, the whole window arrangement known as twelve over twelve windows (12 × 12). However, there was no hard and fast rule and the size of a meetinghouse's windows and the number of panes of glass in each was often determined by a variety of factors, including the time period when the structure was built, cost, the setting and size of the structure and the amount of interior light desired, and prevailing stylistic concerns. Though the 12 × 12 configuration, by an informal survey, was the most common over the years in New Hampshire, there were many deviations: the Monadnock Church in Colebrook has a 6 × 6 configuration (typical in many period colonial homes); the East Alton Meetinghouse employs an 8 × 8 configuration; the Canaan Congregational Church has 20 × 20 windows; the Province Road Meetinghouse in Belmont 15 × 15; the Hampstead Townhouse 16 × 12; the North Wilmot meetinghouse 16 × 16; and that in Dunbarton a combination of 12 × 8 (upper) and 20 × 20 (lower).

As to the type of glass used in these windows, crown glass—which was hand-blown and formed into a flat circular sheet on a table while still fluid—was the first, the resulting diamond-shaped panes being used as they resulted in the least amount of waste. This method was very expensive, but produced clear glass that had little distortion. Crown glass was eventually replaced by broad (sometimes called "cylinder") glass, which was hand-blown into a long tube shape and then cut and flattened out on a sheet of iron. This type of glass was less clear and produced many imperfections and bubbles, but was less expensive. Some of New Hampshire's surviving meetinghouses, including those in Danville and Sandown, still have some of their original glass in which these imperfections are visible. It is, perhaps, understandable why town fathers may have resorted to this less expensive glass: the windows in the meetinghouse in Sandown, for example, contain, all told, 1,080 individual panes of glass. Of these, it is estimated that about a third are still original, the remainder being lost over the years, including many during the infamous 1938 hurricane that devastated New England and wrought much damage among New Hampshire meetinghouses and churches. As I have previously alluded to, glass was difficult to come by and it often took quite some time before a meetinghouse's windows were fully complete. In many cases, individual panes were donated by townsfolk, while early on, those whose box pews were located next to a window were required to furnish their own glass. The town of Bedford offers some interesting glass details in the building of their first meetinghouse in 1755. It was not until 1757, two years after the structure was raised, that a committee was formed to obtain sash windows and the glass for them, but the glass was not procured until 1766. However, it was decided to not use it at that time, the panes subsequently "lent out to various inhabitants of the town."[1] Among the holders were Rev. John

Right: Sandown Meetinghouse, 16 × 12 sash window detail.

Below left: Lisbon, Lisbon-Llandaff Shared Ministry Church, sash window detail.

Below right: Belmont, Province Road Meetinghouse, 15 × 15 sash window detail.

Houston and Deacon Gilmore (twenty-four squares each, equivalent to one full window's worth), who held onto them, though it is unclear if they actually used it in their own homes, until at least 1768.

In addition to the traditional sash windows, many New Hampshire churches also have other windows that are decorative in nature, their distinctive shapes adding to the overall architectural styling of a given structure in dramatic fashion. One of the earliest to be used was the "compass-headed" or rounded arch window. This style of window was first used in Anglican churches in Boston and beyond in the late 1600s to illuminate the pulpit, but by the mid-1700s, it was used in Congregational meetinghouses all over New England.[2] Excellent examples in New Hampshire include the historic meetinghouses in Sandown and Jaffrey. In the Monadnock region, the famed meetinghouses in Hancock, Acworth, and Westmoreland, as well as that of a similar style in Newport (most part of the Templeton run), are distinguished by an oval pediment window surrounded by decorative elements, while in other churches, elliptical (Bedford and Campton), circular (Ossipee and Gorham), and diamond-shaped (Troy) windows would later come to be used. Another specialty type used was the Palladian window, its origin coming from sixteenth-century Italy. This style of window, found in dramatic form on meetinghouses in Acworth, Westmoreland, Lyme, Hancock, North Wilmot, and Webster, consists of three windows, the central one being a large arched window, flanked by two smaller rectangular windows with decorative columns in-between. Finally, by the early 1800s, Gothic-style arched or pointed windows also became popular. Early on, the Gothic effect was commonly achieved by topping off regular sash windows with arched or pointed fan louvers or trim work, as was done in Sanbornton, Chichester, and Dunbarton. In many cases, the glass sash panes capped with fan louvers were replaced many years later by fixed stained-glass windows. True Gothic-style windows, both in arched and rosette form, resembling those fashioned in medieval Europe, can be found on the stone churches in Bethlehem, Manchester, Peterborough, and Keene, to name just a few. As glass-making progressed in America, by the late 1800s, non-traditional window styles were also employed.

Along with these various types of windows, many meetinghouses and churches were also fitted with exterior shutters. One of the earliest references comes from Portsmouth, where the 1657-built meetinghouse was outfitted with shutters "to draw backwards and forwards" in 1670, these supplied by John Pickering at a cost of 30 shillings.[3] While these today tend to be merely a decorative element (fixed in place) on modern buildings, early on, these shutters were moveable, mounted on hinges, and served two purposes. The first of these was for protective purposes; window glass was expensive, so shutters were important in protecting the glass from breakage during times of bad weather. They also likely served, in the case of the earliest meetinghouses in towns like Dover, Exeter, and Oyster River (Durham), as protection for the inhabitants within the meetinghouse during times of Indian attacks. These earliest shutters were probably not louvered like the shutters we

Right: Jaffrey Meetinghouse, compass-headed pulpit window detail.

Below: Lyme Meetinghouse, Palladian window detail.

think of today, but were rather of stout board and batten construction, similar to those found on the 1798-built New Hampton Town House. Later-day fixed-louver shutters were also important for these structures in terms of regulating the temperature inside. In times of hot weather, shutters kept the sun from shining directly through the windows and heating up the interior, at the same time offering ventilation and air circulation, while in times of inclement weather, the louvers helped direct rain away from the window opening. There has been little study of this aspect of meetinghouse architecture to date, and it is likely that few original shutters from the colonial era have survived due to their exposed nature. In many other cases, shutters that are merely decorative in nature have been added to remodeled or restored churches and meetinghouses. Functioning shutters on meetinghouses and churches can be found in a number of locations, with those in Westmoreland, Acworth, Francestown, and Lebanon offering up fine examples.

Doorways

This aspect of meetinghouse and church architecture is also quite interesting, but is often taken for granted. The earliest meetinghouses made of logs and built in no specific architectural form likely only had one doorway, but by the mid-1600s, the three-doorway configuration became the standard for New Hampshire and all of New England. Doors were located on the east, west, and south sides of the meetinghouse, the main entry being on the south side, with the pulpit inside located on the north wall. Throughout the colonial era, these doorways had specific uses, with the main entrance typically reserved for the minister and his family, as well as important visitors, while the side doorways were segregated—one designated for women and the other for men. Type II meetinghouses, those with a second-story gallery, often had the stairways to the upper floor opposite these side entrances fully enclosed and sided, this feature being termed a "porch." Twin porch meetinghouses were once common throughout New England, but in later-day remodeling efforts, these porches were often removed. Today, only two remain in all of New England, that in Fremont, New Hampshire, as well as one in Rockingham, Vermont. Those meetinghouses built with three porches, two on the sides and one for the main entrance, were, on the other hand, rare, but the old townhouse in Milton, before its mid-nineteenth-century remodel, was one of them. The porch feature of these old meetinghouses was not intended to be decorative, but was a space-saving feature; by having the gallery stairs built outside the main floor-plan and enclosed from the elements, more floor space was available for pews inside. In addition to these three doors, some meetinghouses even had private entryways for prestigious pew owners, one notable example being that in Newington for Col. John Downing (1684–1766), who was even buried in a spot right near his entryway. When the church was remodeled in 1890, Downing's personal entryway became the main entrance for the building.

New Hampton Town House, 20 × 15 sash window and board and batten shutter detail.

Rindge Meetinghouse, entryway detail.

Fremont Meetinghouse, built 1800. Shown at each end are the distinctive porches, once a common feature, but now a rarity.

By the late 1700s and early 1800s with the building of Type III and Federal-style meetinghouses and churches, the side doorways were eliminated and the doorway(s) was moved to one end, the pulpit inside located on the opposite wall. With this change, two or three evenly spaced doorways were often utilized, the old tradition of segregated entryways for men and women still followed (this was especially true for Shaker meetinghouses), though a single door was often used. Highlights of meetinghouses and churches built during this time period were doorways framed on each side with glass panels (known as sidelights), sometimes accompanied by a transom, as is found in Sandown, or fan-shaped window ("fanlight") above, the later featuring tracery in the form of a rayed or spider-web design. Excellent examples of doorways featuring sidelights may be found in Haverhill, Hampton Falls, Ossipee, Tuftonboro, Kensington, Peterborough, and Rindge, while that in Acworth features both sidelights and a beautiful fanlight.

As to the actual doors of these structures, those built before 1700 utilized simple batten doors, consisting of unframed vertical wood planks, usually two layers on exterior doors, that were held together ("battened") by boards mounted horizontally or diagonally (often in a "Z" or "X" pattern). The door was attached to the doorframe by iron strap hinges, some quite ordinary, others more ornate, with ends that might be shaped like a heart or a leaf. Since batten doors were unframed, the seasonal contractions of the wood used in their construction caused sticking problems at certain times of the year. However, after 1700, the raised panel door came into use and the seasonal contraction problem was largely solved because

Acworth Meetinghouse, door detail showing sidelights with fanlight above.

the frame and the recessed panels interlocked with each other without the use of nails. In the colonial era, the number of recessed panels in these doors varied from between four and eight panels, with six probably the most common. This style of door became very common in home and meetinghouse construction, and remains popular to this day. Because the configuration of these paneled doors resembles a raised cross, this type of door is today sometimes called a "cruciform" door. However, while the image of the cross found in these panels cannot have escaped the eyes of our Puritan ancestors, I have found no early contemporary records that show that such a term was used to describe these doors in New Hampshire. Finally, regarding historic meetinghouse and church doors, it must be commented that probably only a small percentage today are originals that date back to when the structure was first built, and for two reasons: first, being a heavily used component of a given building, a moveable part exposed to the weather, doors wore out over the years and were no doubt changed; second, when many meetinghouses were moved, altered, or otherwise renovated, it is reasonable to assume that doors were also changed or replaced. In the end, while many doors today appear to be ancient, it takes a trained expert and a thorough examination of a door's components, the type of wood used, how it was put together, the type of paint used, and even the type of hardware used, such as hinges and locks, to determine with any degree of accuracy whether it might be an original, a later era replacement, or a more modern reproduction. To this last point, some historic meetinghouses, most notably those in North Sutton and Sandown, retain their original locks, while others have what

Left: Lempster Meetinghouse, six-panel cruciform door detail with iron strap hinges at top and bottom.

Below: Wilmot, North Wilmot Union meetinghouse, door handle detail.

appear to be period hinges or latches, but in this area, we must be careful as well because these moveable fixtures, made of wrought iron, also usually broke down and had to be replaced over the years. While most of this hardware was likely simply crafted by the local blacksmith, a description of the original door-latch for the 1797-built Bradford Center Meetinghouse, made by local gunsmith Richard Cressy, offers intriguing details: "The handle was plated with brass. Two angels are carved on the thumb-piece, and an angel's head and wings are engraved on the handle. Just above ... is engraved this sentiment: 'While Truth and Benevolence reign within, the Angels keep the door.'"[4]

Bell Towers and Steeples

These features are easily the most identifiable architectural feature of many historic meetinghouses and churches, but also ones whose evolution and acceptance are generally misunderstood. Though it seems natural that every religious edifice must have these skyward-reaching features, it was not always so. To distinguish between them, bell towers and steeples are primarily differentiated by how they are attached to the meetinghouse or church; bell towers were typically later additions to an existing structure, usually replacing a side porch, and are not roof-mounted. A steeple, whose principal parts include a tower, and possibly a belfry to house a bell, a lantern, and a spire (not all steeples have these last three components), whether an original part of the structure or a later addition, is erected over or on top of the original roof line. Early on, these bell enclosures were usually fully exposed, though later on, they might be partially open or fully enclosed with louvers utilized to allow the emission of sound.

As has been discussed regarding early meetinghouse styles, Puritans in New Hampshire did not generally employ such features until the late 1600s, and even then, they did not gain full popularity until after the 1720s. We do not know for certain when the first bell tower or steeple was erected on a New Hampshire meetinghouse—it may have been in Hampton in 1637. Tradition states this log meetinghouse had a bell, but we do not know how it was mounted, whether on the meetinghouse itself in a turret or cupola above or on a post next to it. The 1657-built meetinghouse in Portsmouth was fitted with a "substantial turret" and a bell was added to it in 1664.[5] On the Isle of Shoals, their 1685-built meetinghouse had a belfry and a bell. In some New Hampshire towns, it is possible that bell towers that were built were separate structures from the meetinghouse itself. Though no specific mention of them is found, examples were built not far away in Massachusetts, including one in Lexington in 1714. The first substantial addition of any kind in New Hampshire was probably that for Portsmouth's 1712-built meetinghouse; a belfry and bell were added in 1720, and a 150-foot-tall spire in 1730. The oldest remaining meetinghouse in the state—that in Newington, built in 1712—gained its belfry and bell sometime before 1744. As has previously been mentioned, many Type II meetinghouses would later have bell towers added at one end of the structure, often replacing an entrance porch. It is interesting to note that in many cases, town rate-payers were not willing to pay for bell towers, bells, or steeples at public expense, and in a number of towns, contributions were made by private citizens to pay for these added architectural features. On the seacoast, the town of Exeter's fourth meetinghouse, built in 1730 by John Folsom, had a bell tower added in 1731 and a "high steeple" erected in 1738, all paid for by private funds, though when the steeple blew down in 1775, it was rebuilt at town expense. In Hampton, their fifth meetinghouse, built in 1797, had a steeple finally added in 1811, built by Jeremiah Hobbs at a cost of $811.[6] In western New Hampshire, the 1802-built North Meetinghouse in Charlestown also had a steeple built by private subscription. In some cases, the bell tower was both a public and private venture affair—in Jaffrey, their 1775-built meetinghouse has a bell tower that was added in 1823. The tower was built by privately raised funds, though the bell was furnished by the town. Finally, in many cases, especially after 1800, bells were donated by local individuals and organizations, it being a great honor to provide the town with such a notable feature. In Rindge, their 1796-built meetinghouse, with a steeple built by John and David Barker for $330, had a bell donated by Reverend Seth Payson, whose offer to provide a bell in 1794 spurred the building of the new meetinghouse. In Sullivan, their third meetinghouse, built in 1848, has a bell purchased in 1860 with funds donated by James Comstock ($50) and "considerable money" raised by the Ladies Circle of Industry.[7]

As to steeples, these come in many different forms in New Hampshire, having anywhere from one stage up to as many as six stages of varying sizes, with three stages being the average. Single-stage steeples were probably first utilized in the 1600s, perhaps in the form of a simple turret or cupola. One interesting example is that in Marlborough for the 1834-built Federated Church. Two-stage steeples with such Gothic features as crenelated towers and pointed finials are easily found throughout New Hampshire, many of them in rural areas, and are easy to recognize and pleasing to the eye. These include examples in Stark, Sanbornton, Chichester, Stoddard, and Litchfield. Simple two-stage steeples, with short towers and open cupolas, are also found, with nice examples in Belmont, Pittsburg, and Jefferson, while those in Loudon center, Meredith, Portsmouth, and Gilmanton are more elaborate, the last two examples having upper stages decorated with eye-catching Federal-style details. With three-stage steeples, greater heights are gained with varying effect. Some, like that in Loudon, are simple in form, reflective of their rural location, while others are more elaborate, with outstanding examples in diverse forms found in Westmoreland, Exeter, Lancaster, Northwood, Penacook, Wentworth, and Warner, the last notable for the Palladian window in its first stage. With four-stage steeples, the architect is in his element and even more elaborate details begin to be added, often including a lantern (called a "lanthorn" in Colonial times) stage that is usually octagonal in form and is decorated with oval windows, or painted with oval shapes that resemble windows (most likely a cost saving measure due to the high cost of window glass). The Congregational church in Acworth is probably the finest four-stage steeple in the state, though those in Newport, Dover, Amherst, and Lebanon are almost its equal, while more subdued examples can be found in Rindge, Sandwich, and Goshen. With five-stage steeples, we are entering more rarified air and, not surprisingly, of the six of this kind in the state, four of them are found in the Monadnock Region in Hancock, Peterborough, Fitzwilliam, and Jaffrey, while the other two are located in the large cities of Portsmouth and Concord. These are truly impressive edifices and while those in Hancock and Fitzwilliam are probably the best known among historians, all offer stunning architectural details that highlight the abilities of their builders. Finally, there is one six-stage steeple in New Hampshire, that for the 1786-built United Church of Christ in Keene. The amount of detail incorporated into this unusually styled church is truly a sight to behold.

Finally, it should be noted that most meetinghouses and churches in New Hampshire, and much of New England, prior to the nineteenth century that had a steeple or bell tower usually only had a single spire projecting skyward. However, at least one meetinghouse in New Hampshire—that in Salisbury Heights—was built in 1791 with twin spires, having a bell tower at each end of the structure as it was originally constructed, a feature that was later removed. However, with the advent of the Gothic Revival style of architecture, twin spires became more common by the late nineteenth century, their appearance indicative of a prosperous church organization. While Catholic Church buildings most commonly featured twin spires, as may be found in Berlin (St. Anne) and Nashua (St. Aloysius of Gonzaga, one tower lost due to fire), other denominations also built churches with twin spires, notable examples being the First Baptist Church in Newport and the First Congregational Church in Littleton.

In relation to steeples, now is a good time to mention three related steeple components that are often found on New Hampshire meetinghouses and churches: bells, weathervanes, and clocks. While discussing these highlights in full would require a book-length treatment for each, the brief details that follow should offer some clarity as to their use.

As previously discussed, bells were mentioned early on in New Hampshire by the mid-1600s, but we know little about them, except that the earliest steeple-mounted bells came from England. That for Portsmouth's 1713-built North meetinghouse was hung in 1720 but cracked about 1764. It was subsequently sent "home" to be recast, but was lost when the ship carrying it to England sank in a storm off the Massachusetts coast. A brand-new, 800-lb bell was subsequently purchased with privately-raised funds, cast by Lester & Pack of London at the Whitechapel Bell Foundry.[8] Such bells were important in every town, as they were not just rung to call the faithful to worship, but they also tolled in times of danger or crisis, and to note the passing of both local citizens and state and national figures as well. The bell

Above left: Fitzwilliam Town House, tower and steeple detail. Note the Gothic pinnacle on the open belfry stage, while the stage above features balustrades with Federal-style urn finials at each corner.

Above right: Keene, United Church of Christ, tower and steeple detail. This Eclectic-style church's tower features a variety of details, including Federal, Greek Revival, and Italianate elements, making it one of the finest to be found in the state.

made by Paul Revere for Milford's meetinghouse in 1802 is still in operation today and has been rung to mark the death of every United States president except George Washington. One paid town position of old was the bell ringer, a man employed to ring the bell (and probably see to it that the rope was in good condition) whenever it was required, as well as at regular times on the Sabbath. In two towns, African-American Revolutionary War veterans were paid as bell ringers, Pompey Peters for Exeter (1776—the bell rung at 1 and 9 p.m.) and Drover Minor in Londonderry (1781). Today, the sound of such bells being tolled in New Hampshire towns and cities offers not just an old-fashioned sound to our modern ears, but also a unique connection to the past. By the early 1700s, there were bell foundries operating in the American colonies, but the most recognized and famous name among American bell makers is that of the famed Revolutionary War patriot, Paul Revere. Already skilled as a metalsmith with his own foundry, he made the first bell to be cast in Boston in 1792 and worked on his own until he brought his sons into the business. Revere continued as a bell founder until his retirement in 1811, after which his son, Joseph, and two grandsons carried on the business up to 1828. From 1828 to 1843, the company operated as the Revere Copper Company. For the 1792–1828 timeframe, there are complete account books detailing the 398 bells cast by Paul Revere & Son. After this time period, records are less complete and bells made by the later company are still being discovered from time to time. To complicate things, Paul Revere, Jr., left his father's employ about 1801 and may have also made bells independently until his death in 1813 in partnership with George Holbrook (full documentation is lacking), these bells being simply marked "Revere Boston," in contrast to the elder Revere's bells, which carried their year of casting and often some kind of inscription. Because of the fame of the Revere name, a meetinghouse or church possessing a Revere bell is a lucky one indeed; the oldest and most prestigious of these bells are those cast by Revere himself between 1792 and 1811. New Hampshire has three of them: that in Milford (802 pounds), now in the Town Hall belfry, was cast in 1802 and was originally mounted in Eagle Hall, the town's meetinghouse; that in the Congregational Church in Newington was cast in 1804 and weighs in at 505 pounds; and that in Hopkinton's First Congregational Church was cast in 1811, the year the old midnight-rider retired, weighing in at a whopping 1,158 pounds. Those bells cast at the Revere foundry from 1811–1828 are second in importance, and there are nine remaining in New Hampshire, all but one in their original location, in the following towns: North Hampton (1816—once located in the second meetinghouse, moved to the 1844-built town hall), Hancock (1820), Effingham (1821), Newport (1822—one each in the Congregational Church and the First Baptist Church), Deerfield (1826), New Boston (1826), New London (1826), and Keene (1828—Baptist Church). Nine towns have churches with bells from the Revere Copper Company, they being Chatham, Claremont (Universalist Church), East Alstead (Second Congregational Church, now in the town museum), Greenland (Methodist Church), Haverhill, Henniker, Jaffrey (United Church), Keene (Unitarian Church), and North Conway (First Baptist Church). Finally, Hampstead has a bell made in 1811 by Paul Revere, Jr., probably in partnership with George Holbrook. In addition to the Revere bell foundry, there were several other bell foundries in operation that supplied bells to New Hampshire houses of worship, the most important being the Holbrook Bell Foundry, started by George Holbrook in 1816 in East Medway, Massachusetts, he having learned the trade under the Reveres, and operated by successive generations until 1880. Among the Holbrook bells found in the state's churches (not a complete list) and the dates when they were cast are those at Durham (1823), Amherst (1839), Boscawen (1847), Windham (1847), Antrim (1865), and Keene (1873). Yet other important bell foundries were those operated in Boston by Henry Hooper and William Blake, both former apprentices to Paul Revere. Hooper bells date from 1838–1868, while bells from William Blake's foundry date from 1820–1890, which he operated separately from his partnership with Hooper. Hooper bells can be found in Nashua (First Baptist Church, 1854) and Wolfeboro (First Congregational Church, 1856), while Blake bells are quite common, the firm being perhaps the largest bell foundry in America in its heyday. Finally, it must be noted that bells often became damaged or lost by fire, or cracked while being rung in many churches over the years and were often recast, what was left of the metal that was useable being melted down to make a new bell. In fact, many original Revere bells were recast by Hooper and Blake in later years, so are no longer truly Revere bells, including examples in Fitzwilliam (recast 1881), East Jaffrey (1850s), Lempster, Westmoreland (*c.* 1848), Greenfield (1827 and 1847), Franklin (1902), and Exeter (Baptist Church—1882). For more information on this interesting subject, the reader is advised to consult Eva Speare's *Historic Bells in New Hampshire* (1944).

Many a meetinghouse or church steeple was finished off by adding a substantial weathervane. This decorative weather device probably made its first appearance on New Hampshire meetinghouses in the late 1600s and became popular in the early 1700s, remaining a staple on religious and civic buildings ever since. Crafted at first by local blacksmiths or metal workers, and later, after the 1850s, by weathervane manufacturers in Massachusetts and New York, these vanes took many different forms, with the banner-style form predominating. This style was deliberately chosen for their resemblance to the heraldic flags of medieval England that flew above local castles and battlements, as the meetinghouses they flew above in the new country were also centers of power and authority. One of these banner types, that called a swallow-tail banner with a forked-tail design, was often humorously termed a "long-john" weathervane because of its resemblance to that traditional article of cold weather clothing flying on a clothesline. This style of weathervane was very popular, especially in the Monadnock region. Other banner styles employed astronomical symbols like the sun and moon, and delicate scroll-work in the shape of a heart and floral designs, each having both secular and religious meanings. Such weathervanes were crafted from wood, copper, and brass, and in order to be visible from the ground, they were often up to 7 feet long and mounted on wooden or iron spindles that might be twice their length. The men who crafted these often made them as part of their contribution to a new structure being built, they themselves being church members in good standing. That for the 1823-built Webster Congregational Church was made of wrought iron by Joseph Morse, along with a lightning rod, at a cost of $5.50.[9] That for the Presbyterian Church in Bedford, built in 1832, was crafted by blacksmith Nathan Kendall; representative of the phases of the moon, this distinctive vane was said to be hung on one of Kendall's crowbars. Other notable weathervanes of local make are found on meetinghouses and churches in Jaffrey and Stratham. For a wider discussion of meetinghouse and church weathervanes, the reader is advised to consult the author's book titled *New England Weathervanes* (2018).

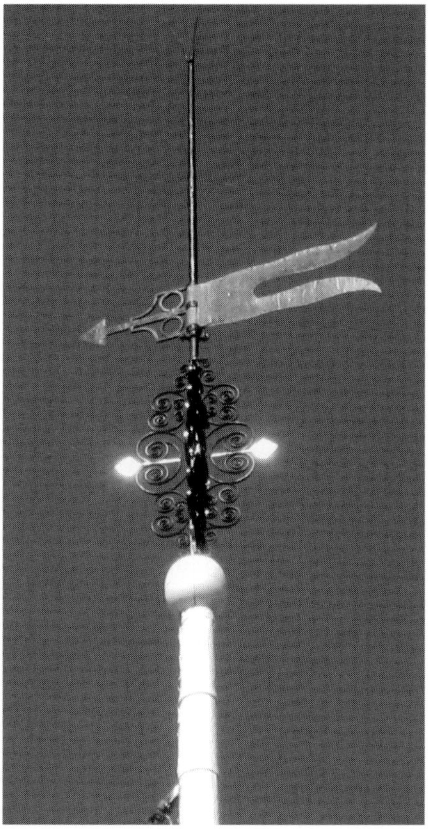

Above left: Webster Congregational Church, weathervane detail. This vane is of the swallow-tail banner type, distinguished by its forked tail.

Above right: Weathercock crafted by Thomas Drowne of Boston, Amherst Meetinghouse. (*Photo courtesy of Eileen A. Widner*)

Finally, we come to the tower clocks. Clocks were a steeple addition that came on the scene much later, even though their use in old England dates back to the 1200s, with that in Salisbury Cathedral said to date back to 1386. The first meetinghouse clocks made their appearance in New England in the mid-1700s, but New Hampshire churches did not apparently feature them until the early 1800s. Early examples include that in Chester (1804), whose dial cost $22.14, but never worked very well and was subsequently replaced in the 1850s, again in the 1870s, with the current clock installed in 1882. That for the meetinghouse in Amherst was installed in 1815. It was made by local clockmaker Luther Elliot from a design by Claremont clockmaker and inventor Thomas Woolson. Their appearance on New Hampshire churches is important as it coincides with the period when the state was an important clockmaking center, with notable makers in Boscawen (Benjamin Morrill), Claremont (Thomas Woolson), and Charlestown (Stephen Hasham).[10]

Later on, many churches in the state would use clocks from large out-of-state makers, the most prominent being the E. Howard & Co. clockmakers, which got its start in Boston in 1858 and lasted well into the twentieth century. As with bells and steeples, clocks were often gifted to the town; that in Dover was installed in 1835 by Benjamin Morrill at a cost of $300, which was paid for by public subscription, while that in Meredith's First Congregational Church was donated in 1903 by Miss Virginia Ladd. In Peterborough, their church clock was installed in 1856 after a clock festival was organized by a local women's group. Perhaps the most identifiable church clock to be gifted in the state is that found on the steeple of the Hampton Falls Baptist Church—it does not have standard clock numbers, but rather letters that spell out "Memorial Gift" when read in clockwise fashion. This clock, nicknamed "Ellen" by the town, was gifted in 1894 by merchant John Brown in memory of his wife, Ellen, after her death in 1893. It is interesting to note that because many of these clocks were gifted, they remain town-owned to this day, even when they are in what are now privately-owned church buildings. While church clocks were at first wound by hand, many were later electrified so as to save the trouble of having to have someone wind a massive clock mechanism daily or every few days. However, some towns, such as Hancock, still hold to the old traditions. Their meetinghouse clock is still wound by hand. Bob Fogg, Sr., began winding the meetinghouse clock there in 1965 and did so continuously on his own for fifty years. In 2016, his son, Bob Fogg, Jr., began to take over the job, though his father still helps out on occasion. In the past, other towns also entrusted this job to the same individual for decades on end: in Chester, when their Howard clock was installed in 1882, Robert Hazleton climbed the 108 stairs to the clock tower every day for the first sixty years of its existence, while today in Webster, Reverend Dave Richardson, who grew up right next door to the church he would eventually come to pastor, attends to the First Congregational Church clock regularly. Of the many church clocks in New Hampshire, some of the most notable include those in Orford and Dover. The former has an original Morrill clock that was installed in 1850 and has only recently had its maker identified. That in Dover exists in a few remnants only, the original Morrill clock, installed in 1835 and replaced after 1870 by a Howard clock. In Salisbury, the First Baptist Church clock was made about 1839 by Josiah Green, a local builder, and has rare diamond-tipped hands. The work of Charlestown clockmaker Stephen Hasham may be found in Cornish Flat; he was a native of Boston who moved to New Hampshire by the 1780s and became a clockmaker, as well as a builder, and operated the Eagle Hotel. In Northwood, the old Baptist Church (now in poor condition) has a clock made by Thomas Woolson, but its age is uncertain. Many other meetinghouses and churches throughout the state, too numerous to list here, have clocks dating from the mid-nineteenth century down to the last half of the twentieth century. No matter how old they are, these meetinghouse and church clocks are town icons of varying repute; when they are in good repair and keep good time, they are a useful and unique historic part of

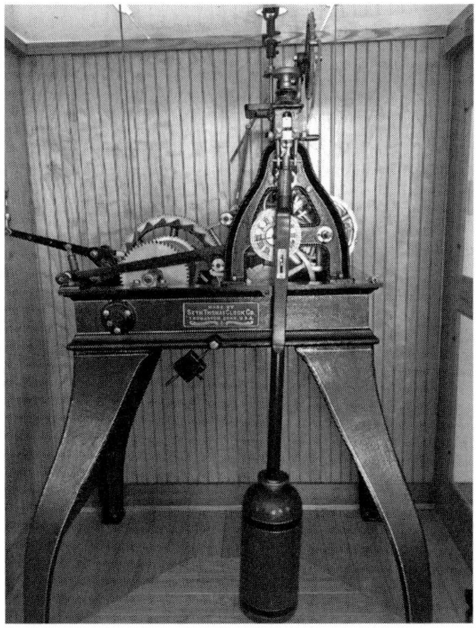

Right: Sutton, First Free Will Baptist Church tower clock mechanism detail. While most operating clock machinery like this is located high in the tower, this one, a later addition to the church, was placed on a lower level where it is visible to the public.

Below: Hampton Falls, First Baptist Church, Ellen Brown Memorial Clock detail.

the local skyline and a source of town pride. However, when they have become inaccurate or quit working altogether and fallen into decay, they are at best a town joke (even a broken clock is correct twice a day) and at worst a highly visible and sad reminder of a town landmark that has seen better days.

Finish Details

One aspect of historic meetinghouse and church architecture that stands out is the detailing that can be found on them. Features on some structures are highly decorative and intricate, while on others they are more subdued or subtle in their detailing. Though I have previously discussed the various styles of meetinghouse and church architecture and the hallmarks of each that incorporate such details, here we will take a closer look at some of the most easily observed of them and offer examples of each. Learning to identify these details is easy and offers an even greater appreciation for the builders of old. After studying them, it is easily understood why the saying "They don't make them like they used to" really does apply when we compare our historic structures to those built today, even allowing for changing tastes and styles.

What follows is a simple, top-to-bottom guide to some of the most common of the architectural features found on period meetinghouses and churches.

Bay

This term, from which the bay window is derived, refers to the number of window openings on the wall of a structure, specifically in regard to the long wall or main façade of a meetinghouse or church. For example, a meetinghouse with three windows on its façade and five on the long side would be described as being three bays wide and five bays in length.

Pinnacles

These are small spires, often pyramid in shape, that are mounted on steeples and are a highlight of structures built in the Gothic style. It is a very common feature throughout the state, with one of the most interesting uses being found on the steeple of the First Congregational Church of Dunbarton.

The Pediment

This triangular-shaped decorative feature is one of the most readily identifiable and a classic element found in Greek Revival architecture. Located on the main façade just below the roof line, it is formed by two raking cornices above with a horizontal cornice below. The recessed triangular area within these cornices is referred to as the "tympanum" and may be plain, decorated, or contain a small window, fan, or louvre. In some cases, a pediment might be found above a portico, supported by

Gilmanton Community Church. This side view shows the four-bay configuration of the building's long side.

Dunbarton Congregational Church, tower detail. This distinctive view shows the Gothic pinnacles that surround the golden dome of the church.

Hancock Meetinghouse, pediment detail. Note the oval window with olive branches beneath, both elements common amongst the Templeton run of meetinghouses in the Monadnock Region.

columns. Outstanding decorative pediment examples are found on Monadnock region meetinghouses in Fitzwilliam, Hancock, Acworth, Peterborough, and Westmoreland, as well as on the brick churches in Newport, Haverhill, and Concord. There are many other pleasing pediments, executed in a more subdued fashion, most by local builders, found throughout the state, those in Lisbon, New Hampton, Kensington, Francestown, and Newbury being among the best.

Entablature

This horizontal decorative woodwork, located at the top of a wall, often just below the pediment if one exists, and supported by pilasters or columns, is another element of classical architecture. It consists of three elements; the upper portion is called the "cornice," or simply "molding"; in the middle is the "frieze," consisting of an ornamental band of woodwork in some cases, while in other cases just a plain, flat board; and below this is the "architrave," a plain or ornamented beam or board supported by pilasters or columns. In some cases, each of these three elements of the entablature are easy to identify, while in many others, especially in rural areas, these features are very simply done and quite subtle and hard to distinguish. Excellent and highly decorated and visible examples of full entablatures may be found in Exeter, Hampton Falls, Fitzwilliam, and Hancock. More subdued but readily visible examples of this element are found in Amherst, Nashua, Gilmanton, and Hopkinton.

Hampton Falls, First Congregational Society Unitarian, entablature detail. This full entablature, supported by fluted columns, is very finely executed.

Modillions

This feature is a small decorative bracket or corbel that supports a cornice. These might come in scroll form or, later on, in block form, and often supported raking cornices. Excellent, albeit non-traditional examples in a triangular shape with a square base are found on Monadnock region churches in Hancock, Acworth, and Fitzwilliam, while more traditional modillions are found on churches in Francestown, Haverhill, Newbury, Penacook, and Keene.

Dentils

This distinctive, non-supporting element consists of a row of small tooth-like blocks that are part of the cornice. Excellent examples of this finish work are found in Keene and Lyme.

Fan Louvers

This type of decoration, found on many Federal- and Gothic-style churches, is ornamental woodwork executed with radiating slats of wood and, as their name suggests, are usually semi-circular or arched and pointed in shape, though there are other examples that are triangular and circular in form. These decorative devices, fashioned in the same manner as shutters, were usually placed in pediment areas

Fitzwilliam Town House, modillion and capital details. The triangular shaped modillions above, as well as the Ionic order columns, are exquisite details carved in wood for this and other meetinghouses in the region.

Keene, United Church of Christ, dentil, modillion, and column details. The dentils, a row of small blocks below the larger block modillions, and the finely carved Corinthian capitals are all exquisite details that distinguish the architecture of this church.

Newbury, Center Meeting House, window details. The fan louvers above the 20 × 20 sash windows are a fine Federal-style element of this meetinghouse's architecture.

or on the steeple, as well as embellishments above sash windows. In some cases, they are purely decorative, while others were used to cover otherwise open areas, allowing for ventilation and, when found on steeples, sound emission for bells. An extreme number of meetinghouses and churches in this study share this easily identifiable feature, though the Center Meetinghouse in Newbury, the Lower Warner meetinghouse, and the Unity Town Hall offers pleasing examples of their use.

Pilasters

This type of ornamentation consists of a flat, ornamental strip or board set vertically on the façade below the entablature and pediment. Though purely decorative, it is fashioned to represent a column, and it has all of its three elements—a base, a shaft, and a capital (see below). Such a feature, used on many Federal- and Greek Revival-style buildings, is found in many different forms, from the very simple to those that are quite elaborate. Those historic meetinghouses and churches found in Exeter, Lebanon, Hancock, Francestown, and Acworth offer up some of the finest examples of pilasters, while those in Amherst, New Durham, Sandwich, East Andover, Hopkinton, and Chester offer examples executed by rural builders with varying degrees of ornamentation.

Francestown Meetinghouse, pilaster detail. The towering pilasters that flank this meetinghouse' doorways are topped with nicely carved volutes that are matched by the smaller pilasters that flank the central entryway.

Columns and Capitals

This supportive element is perhaps one of the most easily recognized architectural features among the state's historic churches, and one that is a highlight of the Greek Revival style. Relatively few early churches feature this element, likely because a full-on Greek Revival-style church was considered too costly and perhaps too ostentatious. Columns are distinguished by one of the five orders to which they belong; Doric, Ionic, and Corinthian columns originated in Greece, while the Tuscan order was developed by the Romans. All of these are part of the classical orders. A fifth order, called Composite, was also developed by the Romans and combines elements of the Ionic and Corinthian orders. Columns, topped off with a capital, are used to support a projecting porch or portico, with the entablature and pediment above, the whole resembling an ancient Greek temple. Each of the orders is distinguished by their decorative form: the Tuscan order is the most solid of the orders, with a very simple capital and can be found on the South Church Universalist Unitarian in Portsmouth and the Unitarian Universalist Church of Nashua; the Corinthian order, distinguished by fluted (grooved) columns with capitals decorated with acanthus leaves and scrolls, is the most decorative of the Greek orders and is only represented by one structure in our study, the beautiful United Church of Christ in Keene; the Ionic order is second in terms of ornateness, and two buildings, the Fitzwilliam meetinghouse and the Bedford Presbyterian Church, have columns of this type, distinguished by their capitals with elaborately decorated scrolls (called "volutes"); the Roman-developed Composite order is next in terms of ornate qualities, employing volutes in their capitals—one church in our study, the Dublin Community Church, employs this type of column; and finally, the Doric order is distinguished by its plain, round capitals and fluted columns and is the simplest of the classical orders. Seven meetinghouses and churches in our study employ the Doric order, but in two distinct forms, and all but two have Doric capitals, but the column itself is not fluted, a slight change often found among rural American builders; these are found in Troy, Westmoreland, New Hampton, Lebanon, and Concord. However, two outstanding Greek Revival churches, those in Hampton Falls and Northwood, employ true Doric columns that are fluted. As to the number of columns employed in these structures, the average number is four. However, there are exceptions: the churches in Nashua and Bedford employ six, while the New Hampton Community Church and the Dublin Community Church each employ two. All but one employ columns crafted of wood, the South Universalist Unitarian Church in Portsmouth being an impressive stone structure. It is interesting to note that, in some cases, the wooden columns do not extend all the way to ground level, as is traditional, but instead rest on a base of granite blocks. It was once thought that these blocks were later additions because the original columns had rotted at their base and needed

Northwood Congregational Church, column details. These fluted columns of the Doric order make this church one of the finest of New Hampshire's Greek Revival-style houses of worship.

Dublin Community Church, capital detail. The columns of this church were carved in the Composite order and feature finely carved volutes on the corners of the impost block above.

shoring up. However, many architectural historians today now believe that such column bases were in fact originally constructed in this manner, with the intent of avoiding rotting problems. The use of granite blocks supporting columns can best be found in the Westmoreland and Fitzwilliam meetinghouses.

Antae

Antae are square pillars or supportive piers located opposite a door or entryway, terminating a wall. When they are used in conjunction with supportive columns in between, the structure is said to be "*in antis*." Antae are not found on all structures with columns and *in antis* church buildings are rare in New Hampshire, being found only in Hampton Falls.

Portico

This term indicates a porch on the façade of a building, supported by columns. In Greek Revival-style meetinghouses and churches, an entablature and pediment are above the columns of the portico. Excellent examples may be found on the churches in Concord, Greenland, Bedford, and Bradford.

Vestibule

This refers to a fully enclosed room or space between the outer door and the interior space of a meetinghouse or church. This feature is a significant part of many meetinghouse and church designs, no matter what their style, and one that is highly visible due to its location on the gable-end façade. It is also, in many cases, an important structural feature that serves to offer support to a tower and steeple above if such is present. In some cases, like the Quaker Meetinghouse in Dover and the Center Harbor Congregational Church, the vestibule is small, only one story high, and serves both a decorative and functional role (offering weather protection), but offers no structural support. However, many vestibules are towering in size, matching the height of the gable end, and offer partial support to a tower and steeple above, as is found in East Andover, North Wilmot, and Salisbury. Depending on the design of the church or meetinghouse, the vestibule may only project slightly from the main block of the building, leaving no room for side windows, as is the case with the South Congregational Church in Newport, and the Congregational Church in Hopkinton, or it may have a larger projection, like those found on the meetinghouses in Exeter and Lyme. Finally, because the vestibule is in many cases the largest part of the façade, it is also the area, like an artist's canvass, where the architectural style of the building is often fully realized, sometimes in beautiful and elaborate form as may be seen in Hancock and Acworth.

Window Caps

This feature, as its name implies, is one found above a window, consisting of an ornamented horizontal band of wood in the form of a frieze, cornice, or a single molding. It can be found on many meetinghouses and churches in the state, with those in Exeter, Stark, Lisbon, and Danville offering a wide range of examples from the ornate to the simple.

Board and Batten

This term refers to a type of exterior wall covering in which vertical boards run from the sill to the eaves, with the cracks between them covered with narrow raised strips of wood (termed "battens"). This type of siding, contrasting greatly with the traditional New England horizontal clapboard siding, came into vogue beginning about 1845 and was popular for its decorative aspects only, not because it was a better or more economical type of siding. Excellent examples of board and batten siding are found in period Episcopal churches in Sanbornville, Charlestown and Lancaster.

Quatrefoil and Trefoil ornamentation

This type of carved woodwork can be found on many Gothic- and Victorian-era churches, they being fashioned in a recessed or opened manner. The quatrefoil, distinguished by four intersecting curves, resembles a four-leaf clover without its stem, while the trefoil is formed in a three-leaf shape. Both are traditional Christian symbols; the quatrefoil is found in decorative form on many European cathedrals and is said to represent a stylized crucifix, or perhaps the Four Evangelists (Matthew, Mark, Luke, and John). Likewise, the trefoil is by ancient tradition a symbol of the Holy Trinity, its three lobes representing the Father, the Son, and the Holy Spirit. Excellent examples of the use of these elements can be found in Claremont, Hampton Falls, Charlestown, and Berlin.

Above: Charlestown, St. Luke's Episcopal Church, board and batten siding detail. The raised strips of wood, known as battens, cover the gaps between each individual board, giving this style of structure a distinctive look.

Left: Claremont, First Congregational Church, quatrefoil trim detail. The recessed quatrefoil trim is a highlight of the tower details of this Gothic Revival-style church.

Buttress

The buttress is an architectural structure built against or projecting from a wall, which serves to act as a support for that wall. These features come in several different forms and have been in use since ancient times, featured prominently in European cathedrals. Their use in New Hampshire churches is not common, but three excellent examples are found in the old St. Francois Xavier church in Nashua, St. Agnes Church in Jefferson and St. John the Baptist Episcopal Church in Sanbornville.

While the above are the most common and easily observed architectural features in early meetinghouses and churches, there are a number of others that are either less common, less observable, or those that more technical in nature and fall outside the scope of this work. For those wishing to learn about some of these additional features in detail, the reader is referred to two excellent sources, *New Hampshire Architecture* (1979) by Bryant F. Tolles, Jr., and *The Historic Churches of Belknap County* (1995) by David Ruell.

Sanbornville, St. John the Baptist Episcopal Church, buttress detail. This detail, most notably found on the Gothic cathedrals of medieval Europe, are a prominent part of the base of this church's corner tower, being shingled and topped off by mini-gables with trefoil cut-out trim.

12

The Builders

The builders of New Hampshire's historic meetinghouses and churches were a varied group of men. Many early builders are unknown, and of those men whose names are known, often details about their lives are lacking. However, town records and old town histories can often fill in some gaps. In any case, these builders can be divided into several different categories from the early colonial days down to the twentieth century: the local builder; the regional builder; and the professional architect.

The local builder was certainly the most common tradesman when it comes to New Hampshire, and he was the first from the earliest colonial days. This was a man who had building skills, often employed as a housewright, and was someone who worked very much on a local basis. It is possible he built only one meetinghouse or church during his lifetime in the town in which he lived, and that that structure may have been his most notable achievement. Depending on where he lived, it is possible that he was employed by a neighboring town to build their meetinghouse based on both his proximity, but also his reputation. However, his travels from home would not have been far, probably less than 10 miles. Because the names of many early builders are unknown, both due to lost records, but also because the builder was unnamed, it is almost certain that the builder employed was a local man known to all, very likely a member of the church congregation in good standing, and often, but not always, prominent in town affairs. It is also possible that such a man was a member of the town's building committee, a group formed in many communities when it was decided to build a meetinghouse. While in some cases this committee merely decided who to hire for the job, in other cases these were the men who did the building.

The first known builder of a New Hampshire meetinghouse was Richard Knight, who built Hampton's second meetinghouse in 1640. He arrived there from England about that same year and set up a sawmill, but seems to have gotten in some trouble with thieving activities and moved to Rhode Island by 1645 to escape punishment. Here, he worked as a house carpenter and seems to have become a model citizen.

In contrast, the builder of Dover's second meetinghouse in 1653, Richard Waldron, was one of the town's and the New Hampshire colony's most distinguished citizens. He built the meetinghouse (possibly at his own expense) in exchange for being granted the lucrative timbering rights in the town. Waldron came to Dover from England about 1635, building mills on the Cocheco River and becoming very wealthy and influential, later serving as deputy to the Massachusetts General Court in 1654 and acting President (governor) of New Hampshire in 1681–82. He was tortured and killed at his home during an Indian raid on Dover in 1689.

Another pre-1700 builder was Valentine Hill, who built the first meetinghouse in the Oyster River (Durham) Parish of Dover in 1656. He first came to Boston from England in 1636 and was a merchant, trader, and builder, constructing a wharf there in 1641. After being granted land in Oyster River in 1641, he built a sawmill and even received permission to build a canal connecting two local rivers. He also built a small house, on the banks of the Oyster River in 1649, which was expanded in size by later generations and today operates as the Three Chimneys Inn & ffrost Sawyer Tavern.

Later examples of local builders include John Folsom of Exeter, Josiah Clark of Nottingham, Col. William Gregg of Londonderry, William Parkhurst of Canaan, the Barker brothers in Rindge, Thomas Kennedy of Goffstown, the Spauldings in Sullivan, and Daniel Page in Sutton. Folsom built Exeter's second meetinghouse in 1730, and though we know little about him, he likely learned the carpentry trade from his father, Peter, who was paid to mend the town stocks in 1717. Josiah Clark, employed as "Master Workman in Building the whole of the Frame & Steple," built the new meetinghouse in Stratham in 1767, discussing the details with Samuel Lane of that town over "a nip of Punch" at Folsom's Tavern in nearby Greenland.[1] Col. Gregg, whose family emigrated to town from County Antrim in Ireland, was a farmer, distinguished Revolutionary War soldier, and town citizen, as well as "master workman" who built the first meetinghouse in neighboring Antrim in 1785. William Parkhurst of Canaan "was a handsome young man, cool headed and of firm nerves" and was injured during a bad fall while building his town's meetinghouse in 1792.[2] He remained unconscious for quite some time and his wife, Sally, who had been busy preparing dinner for the workmen, came to her husband's side and was "weeping bitterly." After a time, the injured builder "opened his eye and, upon learning what had happened, said to her; 'Sally, don't you see, if you spend your time crying and wringing your hands, that you won't have dinner ready, and all these men will be hungry.'"[3] Parkhurst did survive the fall but did not finish the meetinghouse nor build any other buildings, being severely crippled the rest of his life, though he was licensed to sell "spiritous liquors" in 1798 from his home on Broad Street. In Rindge, John and David Barker, possibly with the help of their brother, William (a carpenter and tanner), built the big meetinghouse there in 1796. The contract awarded to them at a cost of $3,316 did not initially include the steeple, which was awarded to John Priest for an additional cost of $330. Soon after, however, the steeple contract was also given to the Barkers. John Barker was a farmer (killed by a bull in 1819 and buried in the church cemetery), while David, a deacon in the church, was both a farmer and carpenter. In Goffstown today, one can visit the historic Kennedy Hill Farm; here it was that local builder and joiner Thomas Kennedy lived. Among the buildings he built or worked on in the area were two churches in Bedford, the 1832-built Presbyterian Church and the 1835-built brick Universalist meetinghouse. He built himself the Presbyterian Church, hired by the town's building committee at an agreed upon cost of $3,700, while for the Universalist structure, he did all the woodwork. Kennedy's connection with neighboring Bedford is understandable, as he likely gained his skills through an apprenticeship with Bedford's renowned furniture and pulpit-maker, Major John Dunlap. In the town of Sullivan, the builders of the Spaulding family had an intimate association with that town's second meetinghouse, it being erected in 1808 by Thomas Spaulding and taken down in 1851 by his grandson, Dauphin Spaulding, while Daniel Page built two meetinghouses in South Sutton in 1794 and 1795, the second being a replacement for the first that burned down just after it was finished. Thomas Spaulding also supplied the lumber, gin poles, and erected the frame of the first meetinghouse in Hancock in 1789, being paid not in hard money, but 6 pounds worth of rye.

Finally, among these local builders, we might wonder what role the town ministers played in the building of these structures—if a minister was already employed, did he have any say regarding its styling, either overall or even interior finish details? The answer is that we do not know for sure as documentation is largely lacking, but it seems logical that a minister's preferences would be considered by local building committees, and that even the minister's wife might have had some influence when it came to interior details and paint schemes. In 1881, when the United Methodist Church in Hampton was moved to its present location near the town center on Lafayette Road, its pastor, Rev. Jacob Franklin Spaulding, carved a beautiful wooden dove to adorn the steeple, an embellishment that although much weathered still remains today. As to the building and finishing of meetinghouses and churches, might the minister have been involved in this work, too? Once again, evidence is largely lacking either way, but is very likely that if the minister were young in age, he may have taken part in the raising or finishing of the structure, as town ministers were sometimes trained in other secular trades.

One very interesting example of a minister's involvement in church building and design comes from the town of Goshen. Here, the young minister, Eleazar Farr, trained as a cabinet-maker as a young man, was ordained in 1850 and was hired to preach to the Baptists, which had had no church building since their society was formed in 1803. Farr was driven to build a church, and though distrusted by some in town, with one man, Virgil Chase, telling anyone who would listen that "Farr isn't worth anything. You will only lose your money," proceeded to get it done in 1851.[4] Farr not only drafted the plan for the church and proposed to pay half the cost, but also did all the planning, hiring the framers, organizing the details, and "Working with the carpenters, doing with his own hands the intricate 'graining' and 'marbleing' [*sic.*] that originally decorated platform-risers and other portions of the interior."[5] Farr was also the artisan responsible for the church's unusual Gothic-styled window trim and door panels, a distinctive embellishment not found on any other period church in the state and one he also used in the furniture he is known to have crafted.

With the continued expansion and growth in New Hampshire, a new class of builders—that of the regional builder—gradually came to the fore by the mid-1700s. While the local builder would reign supreme in the state's small towns throughout the nineteenth century, the regional builders were men—sometimes a single builder, sometimes a partnership between two men, some related and others not—who travelled farther afield to practice their trade, often building more than

Above left: Hampton, United Methodist Church, steeple detail. The steeple of this church features a dove carved by the church pastor. Though worn by time and weather, it is one of the most charming of the steeple-toppers to be found in the state.

Above right: Portrait, Rev. Eleazar Farr, Goshen Community Church. Farr was a trained woodworker-turned-minister who was the leading figure in designing and organizing the efforts to get this church built. (*Photo courtesy of the Goshen Historical Society and Beatrice Jillette*)

An Eleazar Farr-crafted desk, Goshen. This desk, perhaps the only known surviving piece of furniture attributable to Farr, features Gothic-arched compartments (filled with inkwells at far left) that are identical in form to the distinctive Gothic-arched window trim on the Goshen Community Church. (*Photo courtesy of the Goshen Historical Society and Beatrice Jillette*)

one meetinghouse during the course of their career, as well as other buildings such as private homes and schools. The first known builder in this category, and probably the most prolific meetinghouse builder of them all, was Ephraim Barker (no relation to the Barkers in Rindge), first of Stratham, later of Amherst. He built the Pembroke meetinghouse in 1759, worked with Josiah Clark on the Stratham meetinghouse in 1767, built the Amherst meetinghouse in 1771, the Wilton meetinghouse in 1773 (during which he was injured when the frame collapsed), and the Hillsboro meetinghouse in 1789. Where Barker served his apprenticeship is unknown, but he was an ambitious builder who had a long career.

Other men in this group of regional builders include the following: Jacob Spofford and Samuel Adams built the meetinghouse in Jaffrey in 1775, with Spofford, called "an ingenious mechanic," a member of a well-known building family in Essex County, Massachusetts;[6] the aptly named Church Tabor built the Nelson meetinghouse in 1776, and in 1787, along with his father, Joseph Tabor, he was not only one of the "first-class men" hired to frame the meetinghouse in Washington, he also helped procure the building materials and made the window frames for the structure; directing the work in Washington was Capt. Samuel Comings of Nelson (then known as Packersfield), and it may be that the two had worked together earlier in 1776. Church Tabor had served in the Revolution prior to arriving in New Hampshire, and later on would move to South Hero, Vermont. In 1793, Philip Tabor, also a Revolutionary War veteran, and Cornish resident, built Trinity Church in that town. His exact relationship to Church Tabor is uncertain, as is the date of his arrival in town. He was said by town historians to be "a carpenter and a builder and a generally useful man" and that "he erected several of the important buildings in this and in adjoining towns."[7] On the Seacoast, most notable are Ebenezer Clifford, a native of Kensington, and Bradbury Johnson of Exeter. These two men, along with James Folsom, built that town's elaborate Congregational meetinghouse in 1798, having previously collaborated on the beautifully designed Philip's Exeter Academy building in 1794. Clifford was an extremely talented joiner and architect/builder whose influence in the area cannot be overstated, he being involved in nearly every public and private building project of significance, while Johnson was also a devout student of architecture and may have actually been the designer of the meetinghouse they built together. Later on, in 1803, Bradbury Johnson built the meetinghouse in Saco, Maine, without Clifford.

Another man who was an important builder, though often given but scant attention by most meetinghouse scholars, is Moses Johnson (1752–1842) of Enfield, NH. Nothing is known of his early life, but by the age of thirty, he, along with his wife and three children, joined the Shaker Community that was founded in Enfield in 1782, being one of the original covenant signers. Within three years, Johnson's talents and expertise as a builder had become so well known that he was sent by the local elders to the Mount Lebanon Shaker Society in New York, the sect's seat of government, to build that Shaker community's meetinghouse, the first ever Shaker building built solely as a house of worship. Based on this successful design, Johnson would go on to build nine more Shaker meetinghouses (as well as other Shaker buildings) in New York and New England between 1791 and 1794, these being in Hancock, MA (lost); Watervliet, NY (lost); Enfield, CT (lost); Harvard, MA (lost); Canterbury, NH; Shirley, MA (moved to Hancock in 1962); Enfield, NH (lost); Alfred, ME (lost); and Sabbathday Lake, ME. These two-story meetinghouses, whose building was superintended by Johnson employing local Shaker carpenters, were all built on a similar plan, noted for their unique gambrel roof that was only allowed by elders for meetinghouses in Shaker communities, as well the wide-open lower floor plan, the weight of the upper floors carried by substantial beams and braces so as not to require vertical columns for support. This open space allowed plenty of room for the Shaker's worship services, which included a dance ritual in which all members participated. The gambrel roof design chosen by Moses Johnson is most commonly associated with Dutch influences, but his interpretation of this form is more closely related to the English form, one that was popular in Connecticut.[8] Johnson, it should be noted, built other buildings in the Shaker communities in New York, including a grist-mill, hog-sty, and blacksmith shop. Upon his completion of this intensive Shaker building program, Moses Johnson returned to Enfield, NH, and lived the remainder of his days there. Whether or not he remained a Shaker is not clear, as he signed two discharge orders for the building services that he provided in Watervliet and Mount Lebanon in 1795.[9] The Shakers became famous in America, and remain so to this day, for their handcrafted objects, such as furniture and baskets, their qualities of good design and simplicity hallmarks of their faith. Of this Shaker meetinghouse designer and builder, one historian has stated that "To Brother Moses Johnson should go the credit for starting that desire for good design."[10]

In the Monadnock region, Samuel Kilborn of Fitzwilliam was quite active in building some important meetinghouses. A native of Lunenburg, Massachusetts, his family joined the Shakers at Shirley in 1785, and though his parents would stay there for the rest of their lives, Samuel and his brother left the Shakers at the age of twenty-one, with Samuel moving to Fitzwilliam about 1799, where he lived all but the last several years of his life before dying in Keene in 1835. He is the attributed builder of three important meetinghouses: that at Fitzwilliam in 1816 with Jonathan Cutting, building the meetinghouse in Dublin, a copy of that in Fitzwilliam, with Cutting in 1818, and building the Hancock meetinghouse with Jacob Ames in 1819–20. We know little of Kilborn's training, but it would not be surprising if he learned his carpentry skills at first while with the Shakers, and perhaps later under Cutting (a resident of Templeton, MA), who worked with Elias Carter of Brimfield to build the influential Templeton meetinghouse in 1811.

Another notable builder was Col. William Abbott (1793–1837) of Boscawen, who built meetinghouses in Somersworth, Wentworth, Webster, Henniker, Cornish, Concord, Unity, and Thornton, possibly more than any other man of his time. Interestingly, during the building of the Webster Congregational Church in 1823, the man who framed the building was master carpenter George Pillsbury, the first builder in town to use the square rule.[11] While working with Abbott in 1835 to build the South Congregational Church in Concord, Pillsbury was badly injured and died the following year. In Walpole, there lived another master builder, Aaron Howland, some of whose buildings, including his own residence, survive to this day. He was a well-known builder in his time throughout the region, among his many works being the brick First Congregational Church in Jaffrey in 1831 and likely the Congregational Church in Winchester in 1834.

All of the previously mentioned men worked with wood, but there is one builder, John Leach, who was known for both his carpentry and skills as a mason, building some fine brick churches that still survive. A native of Manchester, Massachusetts, Leach moved to Dunbarton in 1795, marrying the daughter of the local builder of the Dunbarton Congregational Church, William Tenney, and was active as a housewright. In 1823, he was paid $6 for designing the South Congregational Church in Newport, though how he gained this commission is unknown. He subsequently raised the wood frame for that structure and may have executed the brick work as well. In any case, it is noted as one of the finest brick churches of the period, a part of the Elias Carter-influenced Templeton-run churches. Later that same year, he built the brick and wood Presbyterian Church in New Boston. The following year began an active period of building in Concord, including a number of commercial buildings, some of which still survive, and the fine brick First Baptist Church in 1824–25—the oldest church in the city today. To follow this up, in 1827–28, he designed and built the fine Gothic Revival-styled St. Andrew's Episcopal Church in nearby Hopkinton. He continued building in the area, after a brief period living in Boston, his last house being built by 1850. He later died in Brooklyn, NY. Given this output, and the quality thereof, Leach is one of the least known and underappreciated builders of New Hampshire churches.

Finally, among church builders, there would come the day of the trained architect. Men like Clifford and Johnson in Exeter, and others discussed above, certainly helped to bridge the gap, being devoted students of their craft and ones surely inspired by the likes of James Gibbs, Asher Benjamin, and others. It would be the generation that followed, some of them from outside New Hampshire, who would design some of the finest churches in the state from the 1830s into the twentieth century. Most were formally trained, usually through serving an apprenticeship with an established architect, and perhaps with formal schooling.

Men in this class worked in a wider geographic area, often specialized in ecclesiastical architecture, and had an office and support staff to help coordinate their design activities. Men that fall into this category include Asher Benjamin, Alexander Parris, Ami. B. Young of Lebanon, Richard Upjohn, Frederick Clarke Withers, Henry Vaughan, Ralph Adams Cram of Hampton Falls, and the architect firm of Chickering and O'Connell of Manchester. For most of these men, their careers have been amply documented and information about their activities, both

Newport, South Congregational Church, façade detail. This fine church was designed and built by architect John Leach, a man known for the brick edifices he constructed.

online and in print, is readily available, so only brief details of their careers need be mentioned here.

Asher Benjamin (1773–1845) is easily one of the most recognized names in American architecture, his published works, such as *The Country Builder's Assistant* (1797), being highly influential. Benjamin himself designed and built many buildings during his career. For several years beginning in 1825, Benjamin was an agent for the Nashua Manufacturing Company and designed a number of buildings and helped lay out the industrial town of Nashua. Among his works here were the now-gone Olive Street Meetinghouse and the still-extant Unitarian church.

Alexander Parris (1780–1852) was a native of Halifax, MA, and a founder of the group that would become the American Institute of Architects. He learned the practical trade of a housewright through an apprenticeship, but later became an architect who worked in granite, his most famous designs being those lighthouses, such as Mount Desert Rock and Monhegan Island in Maine, he designed for the U.S. Treasury Department, as well as Quincy Market in Boston. In the granite state of New Hampshire, he designed St. John's Church in Portsmouth in 1807, and he is sometimes attributed as the designer of Portsmouth's South Parish Unitarian Universalist Church, built of granite in 1824–26.

Ami Young (1794–1874) was a native of Lebanon who learned the trade from his father, Samuel Young, a noted builder in the area, and later with Alexander Parris in Boston. His early commissions include the historic 1828-built First Congregational

Church in Lebanon, as well as buildings for Dartmouth College in Hanover. He would later open his own offices in Burlington, Vermont, and he designed the second Vermont Statehouse building and later the Boston Custom House before being appointed the Supervising Architect of the U.S. Treasury Department in Washington, D.C., in 1852.

Richard Upjohn (1802–1878) was a native of Britain who came to the United States with his family in 1829 after serving as an apprentice to a cabinet-maker and builder. He settled in Boston by 1833, and he was in New York by 1839. Upjohn was a founding member of the American Institute of Architects and served as its first president in 1857 and was famous for his Gothic Revival churches, two of which are found in New Hampshire—in Manchester and Charlestown. Upjohn was also influential, like Asher Benjamin, with the publication of *Upjohn's Rural Architecture* (1852), the designs in this book being used by builders all across the country. His son, Richard M. Upjohn, also became a prominent architect and partner in his father's firm, supervising the enlargement of St. Luke's Episcopal Church in Charlestown in 1869, originally designed by his father in 1863.

Frederick Clarke Withers (1828–1901) was a native of Britain and one of a growing number of English architects to make an impact on the American scene. He apprenticed with a local builder in his native country from 1844–49 and came to the United States in 1852 to work for the noted architect Andrew Jackson Downing in Newburgh, NY. Within ten years, he opened his own architectural office and over the years built many notable buildings in the Hudson Valley region. In the 1870s, he was a prominent ecclesiastical architect and published his book *Church Architecture* in 1873. One of the designs published in this work was that for St. Thomas Church in Hanover, NH, which his biographer has said "exemplifies the letter and spirit of the Gothic Revival in America and marks the zenith of Withers' career as a designer of churches."[12] This church was built, but not fully to Withers' design as the corner tower was never finished. Toward the end of his career, Withers designed free of charge St. Matthew's Chapel in Sugar Hill, his only wooden church and one of his final church works before his death.

Henry Vaughan (1845–1917) is yet another important British-born architect who popularized the Gothic Revival style. He came to the U.S. in 1881 and settled in Boston. Among his most notable accomplishments were his contributions to the Cathedral of Saint John the Divine in New York and the Washington National Cathedral in Washington, D.C., but he also designed many churches on the East Coast, including the Chapel of St. Peter and St. Paul at St. Paul's School in Concord, and St. Thomas Episcopal Church in Dover.

Ralph Adams Cram (1863–1942) was born in Hampton Falls, and after gaining his education, he moved to Boston in 1881 to apprentice with an architectural firm for five years. Afterward, he travelled to Rome to study classical architecture for several years before returning to Boston to start his own architectural firm with several noted architects. After several changes, the firm of Cram, Goodhue

& Ferguson became one of the most renowned in the country, designing the U.S. Military Academy building at West Point in 1902, as well the Cathedral of Saint John the Divine in New York, and numerous other church and public buildings. While Cram designed many Gothic Revival-style structures, he is considered a modernist by many scholars. So notable was Cram in his heyday that his picture appeared on the December 13, 1926 edition of *Time* magazine. Among the New Hampshire churches he designed are All Saints Church in Peterborough, the Phillips Church at Phillips Exeter Academy, and a portion of the Chapel of St. Peter and St. Paul at the St. Paul School in Concord.

Finally, among the architect firms working in the state, there was that of Chickering and O'Connell in Manchester. George W. Chickering (1869–1935), the firm's principal, was the son of George Chickering, a native of Andover, MA, graduate of Dartmouth College in 1866, and later a school official in Lawrence, MA. George W. Chickering may have been inspired to become an architect by his grandfather, William Chickering, who was a master-carpenter living in Andover, a long-time town moderator, and served on the jury which examined plans for the new town hall in 1853. Chickering graduated from the Massachusetts Institute of Technology (MIT) and subsequently served as a head draftsman before starting his firm, in partnership with Timothy O'Connell (1868–1955), an architect from Fort Dodge, Iowa, who took classes at MIT but did not graduate, about 1895.[13] They had offices in Manchester, Boston, and Springfield and were widely known for their ecclesiastical buildings, designing mostly Catholic churches, but also some Episcopal churches. They worked mostly in brick and stone, being known for their large brick churches and are best known for their Gothic Revival and Romanesque stylings. One of their first commissions was the Immaculate Conception Church in Penacook, built in 1897. Of their many other church commissions, those built in New Hampshire include St. George Maronite Catholic Church in Dover, St. Mary Church in Hillsborough, St. Kieran Church (now a Community Center for the Arts) in Berlin, and the impressive St. Francis Xavier Church in Nashua. After 1911, O'Connell left the firm and became a noted church architect on his own.

13

The Changing Landscape and Uses of Meetinghouse and Church

In this section, there several interesting aspects of meetinghouse and church history waiting to be explored. The first is an examination of the historic town landscape that has existed around these buildings over the years, while the second takes a brief look at these houses of worship and how some of them have been moved, and others repurposed after their religious life has come to an end.

Early meetinghouses and churches, despite their solitary appearance in many towns today, seldom stood alone in their heyday, usually being a part of a wider landscape that has changed over the years. Whether it be their location on a busy town green or in a now seemingly remote location, they were, and still are in some cases, surrounded by smaller buildings associated with them, as well as such places as town pounds and burial grounds or cemeteries. In fact, despite their timeless appearance, what we see today of meetinghouse and church is not always what it once was.

The most iconic structure associated with meetinghouses and churches are the horse sheds. These utilitarian, barn-like buildings were usually located behind or adjacent to the meetinghouse and were built in a long row with a low slanting roof, with individual stalls—as many as twenty or more in some cases—that were meant to provide shelter for the horse and buggies of select church members who regularly attended Sabbath-day services. In most cases, the individual stalls within the horse sheds, like the pews within the church, were privately owned and ownership could be transferred to other parties by a deed. In some cases, the stalls were numbered, or, as in Jaffrey, the owner's name may have been painted above the doorway. Because these horse sheds were not large enough to provide for use by every family in town, those who could afford to purchase a spot within were usually from among the most wealthy and prominent families in town. Excellent examples of these surviving structures include those found in Jaffrey, Hancock, Lyme, and Melvin Village, to name just a few. While it is probable that many early meetinghouses or churches had these sheds, most were torn down in the early twentieth century as motorized travel replaced the horse and buggy. The Bedford Presbyterian Church, for example, had forty horse sheds standing to the south of the church, all but one of which were torn down in 1932, the final one being removed in 1949, while those in Bradford Center were removed in 1953 after having fallen into disrepair.

Another building that might sometimes be found close to the meetinghouse was the hearse house. This was a small shed or barn that was large enough to accommodate the town-owned, horse-drawn hearse that was used to carry the coffin of the deceased to their final resting place. In early colonial days, the deceased were usually carried to their final resting place within a town or family cemetery on a bier, born on the shoulders of anywhere from six to eight men who were either close friends or family members. However, as New Hampshire towns grew and their populations extended even further in distance from the town center, the prospect of carrying the deceased to their final resting place became more burdensome and, as a result, many towns purchased a hearse for this purpose, building a small shed to store it when it was not in use. The timeframe for such a change in local traditions that caused the purchase of a hearse varied, but often occurred at or near the mid-century mark, between 1840 and 1850. As with horse sheds, few of these small buildings have survived into modern times, though examples can be found in Fremont, Salisbury, and Atkinson, while two towns, Fremont and New London, still own original horse-drawn hearses—that owned by the New London Historical Society coming from neighboring Wilmot.

While hearse houses are relatively rare buildings in New Hampshire today, the town burial grounds and cemeteries they frequented are a ubiquitous part of the landscape and have been now for over 300 years. In many towns, those burying places located directly next to or close-by the meetinghouse were the first to be established, being laid out by the first town-fathers just after the meetinghouse was finished. Burial places like these were established based on ancient funerary customs from England and their churchyard traditions dating back hundreds of years. In earliest times, these places were referred to as the "burying ground," "burial yard," "graveyard," or sometimes just "the yard," as the term "cemetery" (Greek for "sleeping place") did not come into common usage until the 1830s. Those located next to the meetinghouse in New England incorporated customs and traditions that were brought to the new world. While interment here was open to most everyone, there was a social hierarchy within the cemetery, with those most prominent individuals being buried closest to the meetinghouse, while those on the fringes of society, such as slaves, the poor, and those who died of communicable diseases, were buried at the back of the cemetery, as far away from the meetinghouse as possible. In rare cases, prominent or beloved ministers were buried inside the meetinghouse itself, usually under the pulpit, as was done with Rev. William Shurtleff in Portsmouth, while other notables were buried under or near the meetinghouse foundation, as happened in Newington, where John

Lyme Congregational Church horse sheds. These sheds, which featured arched openings and the names of their owners above, were built by the father of the man who built this church.

Hancock Meetinghouse, horse sheds. The extensive nature and curved form of these sheds makes them the finest example of this utilitarian structure to survive in the state.

Downing is buried near the entrance to his private pew. It is also interesting to note that these burying places were not consecrated places and therefore were not treated as sacred ground. Indeed, in some cases, cattle were allowed to graze within and it was not unusual for the gravestone of an individual with no family left in town to be uprooted and reused on another grave. In Exeter, their Congregational church burial ground on Front Street was largely lost with the advent of the automobile and the widening of Front Street in the 1920s.[1] The town decided to just lay the headstones flat and pave right over them, though remnants of this cemetery, including upright gravestones adjacent to the church and several laid flat in the grass close to the sidewalk, still remain. Later on, when Catholic churches were established, as with St. Mary's in Claremont in the 1830s, their cemeteries were consecrated and only those who were full communicants in the church were allowed to be buried in that ground. As meetinghouses and churches were lost by fire or moved over the years in New Hampshire, sometimes the old town cemetery is the only remnant of where they once stood. This is the case for the Turkey Hill Cemetery in Merrimack and the Old Town Cemetery in Rollinsford, to name just a very few. As to remaining meetinghouse and church cemeteries, there are many notable examples remaining in the state with interesting examples of the stonecutter's art and burials of important local personages and war veterans, those in Francestown, Danville, Jaffrey, Rindge, Cornish, Portsmouth, Salisbury, and Sandwich being fine representatives.

Jaffrey Meetinghouse, cemetery. This meetinghouse cemetery is one of the most scenic to be found in New Hampshire and is filled with a wide variety of Colonial-era gravestones.

Other features of the meetinghouse landscape, those less common or now long gone, include the town pound, the town stocks, and noon-houses. Town pounds were simple enclosures made of granite or stone, without a roof, and a strong gate. They look strange to us today and many may wonder what their purpose must have been, but the answer is simple. They were used to hold stray farm animals in town in a day when nearly every family owned varying numbers of cows, chickens, pigs, and horses. Those that strayed from their owner's property were rounded up by the town-pound keeper and were kept there until claimed by their owner, who was forced to pay a fine. Surviving town pounds are found easily throughout the state, though those survivors located adjacent to meetinghouses are less common, with those in Bradford Center, Fremont, and New Durham being excellent examples. While we often associate the meetinghouses of old with their religious functions, it is also important to remember that these meetinghouses were the place where local justice and punishment was meted out in a day before prisons were built. Located just outside its front door were the town stocks (often called a "pillory"), a wooden contraption seen in countless movies about our early colonists, where an individual was forced to stand, head and arms locked into place, for hours on end. This form of punishment was outlawed by federal law in 1839, so none survive today in their original locations. Finally, there was the "noon-house" or the "Sabbath-day house," which was sometimes located right next to the church. Since few meetinghouses or churches in New Hampshire, if any, built before 1800 were heated with central stoves, they were extremely cold places in wintertime. Noon-houses were smaller buildings that featured a large fireplace with a roaring fire and were places where those attending services before, between (often at noon-time, thus their name), and after the long Sabbath-day services could get warm. Here also meals could be prepared and consumed and clothes dried, as well as personal foot-stoves replenished with fuel. In many cases, this building was owned by the town and maintained by one of the church deacons, such as that built in New Boston in 1769 and termed a "session-house," from whose fireplace "glowing fire coals were removed to the foot-stoves which rendered their stay in the fireless meeting-house endurable to the female portion of the congregation."[2] There were also private noon-houses, the Fryer family being granted 20 square feet of land near the meetinghouse in Portsmouth in 1669 to set up such a house and stock it with wood. With the advent of the stove, the noon-house tradition gradually faded away. While no original noon-houses remain today on the meetinghouse landscape, evidence suggests that some of these structures may have later been moved and converted to private residences.

While many meetinghouses and churches today are located in areas of a town that have become built-up and adjacent to heavily travelled roads that always keep the modern world close at hand, even today there are some rural towns that still retain some of the meetinghouse landscape features of olden days and therefore give us a glimpse back in time. The site of the old New Durham meetinghouse features a plain meetinghouse with a town pound nearby and remnants of an old burial yard as well, while the towns of Washington, Jaffrey, Sanbornton, Wentworth, Bradford Center, and Salisbury Heights all have fine collections of historic buildings that give us a picture of a town landscape as it existed in the mid-1800s.

Because of their timeless appearance, many may be inclined to think that these old houses of worship have always stood where they are today; while this is true in many cases, it does not hold true for all of them. Indeed, many a meetinghouse or church has been moved over the years for a variety of reasons. Some were moved as the population in a given town had shifted from what was once the center of town to a different area, while in other cases, they were moved even small distances, perhaps from one side of the town green to the other, so as to be better situated, while in yet other cases they were moved, after the passage of the Toleration Act in 1819, as meetinghouses evolved from publicly-owned structures to ones that were owned by a private religious group. Many such structures have been moved over the years in towns all across New Hampshire, with surviving examples found in Warren, Mont Vernon, Keene, Webster, Middleton, Epsom, Lempster, Westmoreland, Hancock, and Wilmot, to name just a few. One of the more recent moves occurred in 2007 in Epsom, when the 1862-built Baptist Church was moved to a new town complex site via a flatbed trailer pulled by a semi-truck right down busy Route 4. This was an event that was reported throughout New England due to the great effort that was required to make it happen. That move also offers a lesson, perhaps, in what such a move must have entailed in the days before the twentieth century; when period historical records or town histories state in simple fashion that a meetinghouse was moved, seldom does the modern reader fully comprehend how it was accomplished. A visit to the town of North Wilmot will give an idea of the complexity of such a move: the North Union Meetinghouse was built at the top of Tewksbury Hill in 1829, but it moved to its current location just a half a mile away in 1850 so as to make it more readily accessible. Going the distance down the steep hill required the use of wooden log rollers and 30-yoke of oxen (sixty animals altogether), as well as sledges filled with rocks attached to the back of the structure to act as a brake. The whole operation, which must have been impressive to view, cost $400, the equivalent to about $95,000 in today's currency, and involved considerable manpower. In contrast, the 1786-built meetinghouse in Keene was moved a short distance to its current spot, just several hundred feet off the town green, after it was sold. This was accomplished by the use of a windlass, a device—in use since ancient times on land and sea—whose motive power consisted of ropes wrapped around a large cylinder or barrel and turned by either man or animal power.

Finally, we come to those church structures that have been repurposed over the years, once their civic and religious life has ended. As has already been discussed, many unwanted structures in early days were simply torn down once they were no longer needed or their continued maintenance was no longer practical. However, since the early twentieth century and continuing to the present, there are many

Epsom, former Free Will Baptist Church. This historic building was moved to its current location in 2007 to save it from demolition, but to this day stands empty and unused on a town-complex site.

churches in towns throughout the state that have found a new life serving purposes for which they were not originally intended. Because of their size and interesting architectural features, and overall prominence, former churches of many different denominations have been converted to homes or residential housing units, local arts centers, theatres, restaurants, and other places for commercial or retail use. Indeed, there is hardly a town in New Hampshire that does not have such a structure in their midst.

While it would require a separate book to document all these former churches, a few examples will suffice to show that, for some houses of worship, there was, indeed, life after death. In the town of Wolfeboro, there are a number of churches that have been converted to private use, including the former Adventist Church on Union Street (later a private residence, now a bed and breakfast) and the former Universalist church on Glendon Street, which later became a Masonic temple and is now a community theatre. In East Alstead, the Gothic-arched windows of the Fuller Manufacturing Company (established 1952) building belie its earlier life as a Methodist church built in 1839. In Berlin, the 1894–95-built St. Kieran's Church was built to serve an Irish immigrant population; it was closed by the Catholic

Church in the 1990s, but in 2000, it became established as the non-profit St. Kieran Community Center for the Arts. In West Manchester, the former St. Patrick Church was converted to residential housing in 2016, while the impressive, 1875-built former St. John's Methodist Church in Dover was purchased by the city and turned into a senior housing complex in the early 1970s. In Contoocook, the former 1929-built St. Mary's Catholic Church, closed in the early 2000s, is now a private residence. In Center Tuftonboro, the Old White Church now serves as a unique music venue, the home of weekly country jam sessions, as well as hosting performances by musicians in many different genres from Irish music to Gospel and more. While both Protestant and Catholic church buildings maintain an emotional attachment with those who have worshipped there, often for successive generations, the process by which these churches are divested varies widely. Most Protestant churches are locally owned and are not consecrated structures, so the decision to discontinue the use of a given church and sell it off, while often a difficult one, is one that is made at a local level, often with little controversy. However, in the Catholic and Episcopal faiths, their church organizational structure makes these decisions more difficult. Episcopal parish churches, though often established and built at the local level, are property considered to be held in trust for the benefit of the diocese and the Episcopal Church as a whole, and thus the decision to discontinue their use is more involved. In 2007, it was the Episcopal Diocese of New Hampshire that sold the historic 1931-built Ivie Memorial Church in Bethlehem to local developer Jon Baker. While the original stained-glass windows remain, all of the fixtures inside and the memorial plaques for the windows were removed and donated to the Bethlehem Historical Society. The same situation also arose for parish churches in the Catholic church, and while a parish church serves a local population that might have some voice in the fate of a church being considered for closure, ultimately that decision rests with the diocese. This has been a contentious issue in many communities all across New Hampshire since the 1990s; with declining church attendance, many parish churches have been closed, with their members being absorbed by another parish in town. For example, in Dover, the 1933-built St. Charles Boromeo Church was closed in 2009 due to declining attendance and, eventually, in January 2017, after the land was sold to a private developer and the church was deconsecrated and associated artifacts, such as stained-glass windows, pews, and religious statues were found new homes, the old church was demolished. While not all of these discontinued churches have fallen victim to the wrecking ball, some controversy about how these churches have been repurposed has arisen. In Epping, the former 1896-built St. Joseph's Church was closed and sold to restauranteurs David and Maureen Kennedy, who converted the church to an Irish pub-styled restaurant called The Holy Grail. Though remodeled, the restaurant, opened in 2008, retains many aspects of its church architecture, including the original stained-glass windows. While tastefully done, the popular restaurant raised the ire of New Hampshire diocese officials who were offended that alcoholic beverages were being served in a former church building. As a result, the diocese now has deed restrictions in place for selling subsequent churches that prohibit the premises from serving alcohol, as well as other business activities that the Catholic church deems to be inappropriate. Interestingly, the Kennedys sought to expand their church-themed restaurant to the Lakes Region in 2016, but were unable to buy another former Catholic church, so instead purchased the 1836-built Evangelical Baptist Church in Laconia, located on Veteran's Square. Sadly, The Holy Grail of the Lakes restaurant did not achieve the popularity of the original location in Epping and it closed in April 2017. At last check, the church was on the commercial real estate market with an asking price of $975,000. In the end, in most cases the repurposing of these former houses of worship has been a positive development by preserving these distinctive and historic structures within the town landscape.

Dover, former St. John's Methodist Church. This large and historic Gothic Revival structure now serves as a housing unit for the city of Dover.

PART III

Meetinghouses and Churches by Town

14

New Hampshire City, Town, and Village Meetinghouses and Churches

Presented in this section are a number of historic meetinghouses and churches in 125 New Hampshire cities, towns, and villages. The towns are arranged alphabetically for easy reference. Please note that smaller locales which incorporate the name of the larger town entity to which they belong and have a shared history, such as East Alton, North Wilmot, and Center Barnstead, will be found under the entry for the primary town, while villages in some towns that are a census designated place, or an unincorporated community with its own zip code, such as Wonalancet (Tamworth), Sanbornville (Wakefield), and Penacook (Concord), are listed under their own names. Additionally, while many important structures for each of the towns in question are here highlighted, not every existing church in these towns is documented, nor are all of them pictured, due to space constraints.

Acworth

Acworth Congregational Church (Acworth Meetinghouse)
Built: 1821
Location: 16 Town Hall Road

This beautiful church, long known as "The Church on the Hill," has certainly earned its nickname. Situated on the town common at an elevation of 1,489 feet, it is the second highest town center in the state where a meetinghouse or church can be found, as soon becomes evidenced when one takes the steep and winding road that leads into Acworth. Indeed, the first minister to officiate in this church, Rev. Cooke, was nicknamed the "High Priest of New Hampshire" because of his church's lofty location. As has been well documented, this church is one of the finest structures of its type in the state, built in the Federal style at a cost of $6,000, and it is part of the

Templeton run of meetinghouses inspired by the noted Massachusetts builder Elias Carter. While some have attributed this church directly to Carter, all records are lost regarding its builder. While it is possible that Carter did build the structure, it is also just as likely that it was built by a local builder, such as those that built similar churches in Fitzwilliam, Dublin, and Hancock. The question will likely remain a mystery. The town's third settled minister, the first to preach in this church, was the highly esteemed Rev. Phineas Cooke of Hadley, MA, who was studying law in Keene when he had a religious conversion and subsequently became licensed to preach in 1812. When he first came to Acworth to preach a year later, he was confronted by a community that had been devastated by the spotted fever, with sixty-six inhabitants succumbing to the disease. In 1814, Cooke accepted the call to preach in Acworth, though the town vote to choose him was a narrow one, primarily because of a prior political speech he had given in Keene. The church in Acworth under Rev. Cooke prospered mightily and many people were brought into the fold during his tenure during various times of religious revival. However, Rev. Cooke's undoing in Acworth was his views on alcohol and the temperance movement—becoming a firm temperance man, he ardently preached his views to a congregation who did not agree with him. As such, Cooke asked to be dismissed from his position, and while he would preach in other locales, upon his death in 1853 in Amherst, MA, his body was returned to Acworth to be buried among a people he had always held in the highest regard. Future ministers in Acworth, like elsewhere, would experience the ebb and flow of religious life; the year 1838 was a big one for religious revivals, with the town minister, Rev. Joseph Merrill, challenged by an evangelist preacher from Vermont, while forty folks joined the church in August 1847, with another forty-one joining in like manner in the spring of 1853.

Services are still held in the church today and the building was substantially renovated in 2008–09 after suffering from neglect and being placed on the New Hampshire Preservation Alliance's Seven to Save list in 2007. Architecturally speaking, the Acworth Congregational Church is a gem; notable features of this rural structure include its façade, with a double pediment, Ionic pilasters, the central door with a rayed fanlight, and Palladian window, while the four-stage steeple with Palladian window and lantern stage, topped off with a swallow-tail banner weathervane, is one of the finest in the state. No visit here would be complete without taking time to examine the church's other fine woodwork, including the carved molding around the doorframes and the unique triangular-shaped cornice brackets found on the pediment.

Above left: Acworth Congregational Church.

Above right: Pilaster detail, Acworth Congregational Church.

Alton

East Alton Meeting House
Built: *c.* 1807–1820
Location: Gilman's Corner, Drew Hill Road

This structure is the first permanent meetinghouse to be built in town, erected by the Free Will Baptist Church, which was established in 1803. Among its initial seventeen members were Jonathan and Mary Leighton, David and Nancy Wentworth, James and Betty McDuffee, and Susannah Wilkinson. The date of the building of the church is not documented, strangely enough, in the otherwise very detailed church records. Early meetings were usually held at "Bro[ther]" James McDuffee's house, but the notations as to the private homes where church meetings were held largely ceased after 1807, but with a few exceptions even into the 1830s, when the meetinghouse is known to have existed. It is possible the meetinghouse was built sometime as early as 1807, though the meetinghouse is not mentioned in the records until 1821, and then only briefly. Nowhere in the records is the construction of the meetinghouse discussed or celebrated. The earliest pew deeds date from 1822, while a later mid-1800s account states the church was built about 1820. While silent on its meetinghouse origins, the early church records are fascinating for the details they record about both religious and civic life in Alton at the time, oft-times these two aspects of life being intertwined. Despite the move of a number of church members to the "Eastern country" in early 1824, including "our beloved brother John Page and family," others moved to town from Wolfeboro and New Durham and "A spirit of union & fellowship is now prevailing amongst the brethren and trials appear to be done away." However, life in East Alton from late 1824 through July 1825 was difficult, it being recorded that "the state of religion is low amongst us" and "it pleased the Lord to visit this Church & People with a great sickness and mortality," nine people, including three infants, dying during this time. This low state continued until a momentous revival occurred as a result of an incident that took place on August 5, 1825, when "Brother Moses Glidden's wife was killed by a stream of

East Alton Meeting House.

Lightning. The shock was solemn and awful, the people appeared awakened and many who had not prayed many years began to pray the following evening … after this the meetings were very full and crowded and many thought on their ways."[1] At its height in the mid-1800s, the church had 300 members, with the church being remodeled into its present form at a cost of $800 in 1848, but within less than twenty years, membership declined rapidly to less than fifty, the last settled minister left in 1883, and the last church member died in 1907. Since the 1920s, the building has been maintained by local groups, with the East Alton Meeting House Society, formed in 1978, serving as its steward today.

Beautifully maintained, the meetinghouse is notable for its blend of Greek Revival styling, as evidenced by the cross gable roofed belfry topped with a simple arrow weathervane, and vernacular tradition, embodied in the three-bay façade with 8 × 8 windows and twin doorways. Look closely and you can see other Greek Revival details in this seemingly simple structure, including the corner pilasters on both the façade and the square tower above. An interesting related feature at this site is the small free-library, fashioned in the form of the meetinghouse, mounted on a post close to the street, where one can borrow or return a book at any time of year.

Community Church of Alton (former Second Free Baptist Church)
Built: 1853
Location: 101 Main Street

This historic church building, as well as the one listed below, is an outgrowth of the strained religious conditions that existed in Alton village in the early 1850s. The church itself was organized in 1831 to serve Free Will Baptists in the immediate area, and in 1838, they joined with a small Congregational church group to build a union church where both could hold services on alternating Sundays. However, the tensions between the groups were always present. Some of this was over church doctrine, but also over different church practices. Free Will Baptist ministers sometimes preached against those Congregational ministers who received a salary for their services, in accordance with the beliefs of the founder of the Free Will Baptists, Benjamin Randall. However, some in town were critical of the travelling Free Will Baptist preachers who accepted for their ministerial services foodstuffs like butter and cheese. As one story goes, a farmer, upon seeing his wife lay out "an array" of food items in anticipation of a ministerial visit, railed that "I have no kind of sympathy with double dealing, not even in a minister. If he will confess he receives your tub of butter and cheese as pay for ministerial services, I am willing you should give them, but I have no patience with a man who raises such an outcry in his preachings against a paid ministry, denouncing them as 'hirelings', who will at the same time come to my house with long arms and large saddlebags to carry away all we may be induced to give him."[2] In any event, when the Congregationalists decided to abandon the union house, so too did the village Free Will Baptists,

Community Church of Alton (Main Street).

building their church in late 1853 and holding their first meeting here on January 2, 1854. This beautiful building, erected at a cost of about $3,500, is indicative of the wealth of its congregants. It is an early example of the Italianate style and the only such church structure of this style built in Belknap County prior to the Civil War according to historian David Ruell. While there have been side and rear additions to the building, the exterior is largely original. Notable features include the triangular-topped windows, the large triple-louver on the tower above the main entry, the large cornice brackets and those supporting the sill on the tower, as well as the quatrefoil decorative woodwork at the base of the spire. Interestingly, the building since 1968 has been owned by the Community Church of Alton, a federation created at the time between the Baptist and Congregational churches as a way of saving ministerial expenses.

Community Church of Alton (former First Congregational Church)
Built: 1853–54
Location: 20 Church Street

The Congregational church in Alton was always a small entity due to the Free Will Baptist influence. Itinerant preachers served the town from 1800 until a church was formed, consisting of eight members, in 1827. Still, no settled minister was employed until Rev. Franklin Davis came here in 1854, and even by 1856, the church only

Community Church of Alton (Church Street).

had eleven members. As related above, they shared a union house with the Free Will Baptists from 1838 to 1853, when they decided to build their own church, just around the corner from the Baptists. Despite the small size of the congregation, the church they built, which cost about $3,500, was impressive, one of the area's best examples of a Greek Revival structure. As with the other historic church buildings in Alton previously discussed, its builder remains a mystery, though he was certainly skilled at his trade. Notable features include the large 12 × 12 sash windows, the slightly projecting entryway flanked by large square pillars, and the corner pilasters on the steeple. The bell was not installed until 1873, while the weathervane was added in 1875. Other than the building of the vestry in 1895, there have been few other changes to the exterior. It should be noted that the sign above the entry which reads "Congregational Meeting House 1827" refers to the date when the original church was gathered, not when this church was built.

Amherst

The Congregational Church of Amherst (Amherst Meetinghouse)
Built: 1771
Builder: Ephraim Barker
Location: 11 Church Street

This meetinghouse was the second to be built in town, raised by a highly regarded local master-builder who built a number of other meetinghouses throughout New Hampshire. It is interesting to note that, as was typical, eight barrels of rum were procured for workmen on the day the meetinghouse was raised, and that the town minister's son, Samuel Wilkins, won a bet by carrying the chairman of the building committee, the heaviest man in town, around the meetinghouse on his shoulders.[3] The first man to preach here was the first town minister, Rev. Daniel Wilkins, who served the town for thirty-eight years, he being succeeded by colleague pastor Rev. Jeremiah Barnard in 1784, who preached in town from 1779 until his death in 1835. Like Wilkins, Barnard also had a colleague pastor appointed to help him in his old age, this being Rev. Nathan Lord beginning in 1816. The hiring of a town of a colleague pastor was not unheard of in New Hampshire, but few towns could afford the extra expense like Amherst. Unfortunately, Lord lost his voice after a severe cold in 1826 and for several years could not preach due to losing his voice, eventually leaving the town in 1828 to become President of Dartmouth College. It was during the ministry of Silas Aikin that the town saw its greatest religious revivals, with sixty

Above left: Amherst Meetinghouse.

Above right: Tower detail, Amherst Meetinghouse.

people added to the church in 1831, and another 101 people being added to the church in 1835. From 1837 to the early 1840s, the church suffered from "that phase of the Anti-slavery movement called come-out-ism ... then agitating the whole region."[4] This consisted of ministers, such as the two in Amherst, who left churches that refused to take a stand on abolition and come out against slavery. The church building itself was moved to its present location from the town common in 1836 after the building was sold by the town in to the Congregational Society in 1832, thereby transitioning from a public meetinghouse to a privately-owned church. In order to accommodate this move, the horse sheds owned by parish members had to be torn down. The structure today is one of the finest of its kind in the area, its steeple being the oldest in New Hampshire and one that is beautifully proportioned. The weathercock weathervane, which tops off the steeple, is a beautiful example of the vane-maker's art. It was crafted by Thomas Drowne of Boston, a man noted for his animated weathercocks, and the son of the man who created Faneuil Hall's grasshopper vane, Shem Drowne. This meetinghouse is also notable for its triple entryways with transom windows and decorative molding, and the tall pilasters on its three-bayed façade featuring 12 × 12 sash windows.

Andover

Andover Congregational Church
Built: 1797, remodeled 1840
Location: State Route 11 at Chase Hill Road

This church was built, finally, in 1796–97 as the town's second meetinghouse, it taking fourteen years to agree on a location once a new meetinghouse was decided on. The town was originally Congregationalist, with Rev. Josiah Babcock being hired in 1782. He officiated at the raising of the meetinghouse, his ornate and overlong sermon ended by a loud blow on the timbers by the foreman in a hurry to get the job done. Babcock served as town minister until his dismissal in 1809. Despite this, Babcock remained in Andover, serving on a number of town committees over the years. While the building would eventually become a Congregational church, this would take time as the state of the Congregational Church in town over the next sixty years was precarious. When Rev. Samuel Kingsbury was hired by the First Congregational Society in 1828 for a period of five years, his service ended in 1831 when the society asked to terminate his contract. The minister gladly accepted, as he had received little pay over the years, with Kingsbury and his wife, Mary, the daughter of Rev. Babcock, likely being financially supported, at least in part, by his father-in-law. The meetinghouse was occupied by the Free Will Baptists at varying times from 1810 into the 1820s, but in 1840, the town relinquished ownership of the meetinghouse to the Christian Church of Andover, providing that they repaired

Andover Congregational Church.

the building; this they did in 1840, the work being finished by December at a cost of $2,162. This is when the church was remodeled into its present Greek Revival form. In 1869, regular Congregational services were once again established here and have remained ever since. The church is distinguished by its portico with pilasters and double entryway, flanked by large 20 × 20 sash windows, and its tower with Greek Revival-styled corner pilasters combined with Gothic spires. Behind the church is a small cemetery with many interesting stones, the variety of their motifs making them worthy of a closer look.

Antrim

First Presbyterian Church
Built: 1893–94
Location: 73 Main Street

For the time between the town's founding and the 1880s, the geographical center of Antrim at Meetinghouse Hill was also the center of the town's settlement. Here is where the Grange Hall is located, and it was here, in 1826, where a brick Presbyterian Church was built. However, by the 1890s, more and more families were settled in the southern part of Antrim, where the current downtown is today, primarily due to the mills and factories operating in this area that offered employment. When discussions began in the early 1890s about building a new Presbyterian Church in this growing part of town, a problem arose; the governing body of the Presbyterian Church in Boston ruled that towns could only have one Presbyterian Church. The church moved ahead with a plan to build a new church, despite protests from congregants who lived in the Center, with the intention of tearing down the old church. The new church was dedicated in July 1894, but the congregation was split. Despite being reprimanded by the Boston Presbytery, the Center Church adherents had formed their own congregation in December 1893 and even changed the locks on the old Center Church so that those from the South Village could not enter. Efforts to tear down the old church were blocked by Eben Bass, who lived in the Center, and others who took the South Village group to court. The Center Church group, however, lost their case, and in 1896 the brick church at the Center was torn down, its pews and other fixtures, including a Holbrook Bell (not a Revere bell as is often reported) that was cast in 1865, having been moved to the new church. This church, born in changing times, is noted for its Gothic styling, including the impressive corner bell and clock tower, its shingled siding, and the large arched stained-glass window on its façade, as well as the rosette and quatrefoil-themed stained-glass windows on the south side facing the Maplehurst Inn.

First Presbyterian Church, Antrim.

The Stone Church (former First Congregational Church)
Built: 1897–98
Builder: Eben Bass
Location: 223 Clinton Road

The building of this church continues the story of the dispute that arose when the new Presbyterian Church was built in Antrim in 1894. Having lost their court case to save the old Presbyterian Church at the Center, Eben Bass and his followers were determined to have their own church in the Center. After the old church was torn down, they formed a building committee and construction began in the spring of 1897. The stone for the church, hence its nickname, was obtained locally, with stone contributed by its parishioners. The church was completed in 1898, its corner bell tower housing a 1,640-lb bell donated by Bass, with the stipulation that it be rung every Fourth of July at dawn and sunset. This church served the area residents well for over fifty years, having 200 members at one time. However, by 1960, membership had dwindled and services were offered in the summer only. Eventually, the church closed and was sold to private parties. It was offered by its owners to the Antrim Historical Society in 2007, but these efforts fell through. In 2017, the church was donated to At The Cross, a grassroots Christian Church that now holds regular services. Notable

The Stone Church, Antrim.

features include the combination stone and shingle siding, bracketed cornices, and the beautiful stained-glass windows, as well as the previously mentioned open bell tower. Not far from this structure is the old Bass farm, which includes the house that served as a parsonage for the old meetinghouse, while just a short distance away is the old Grange Hall, built from parts of the old meetinghouse and former town hall and just up Meetinghouse Hill Road is the old town cemetery.

Antrim Baptist Church
Built: 1871
Location: 85 Main Street

The organization that became the Antrim Baptist church was formed in 1805 at the house of Joseph Eaton in nearby Greenfield and served a wide area, including Society Land (Bennington), Hancock, and Peterborough. In 1857, it was renamed the Antrim Baptist Church, replacing a previous Baptist church that had disbanded in 1841. Its first church was built before 1826 in Society Land, but after the group moved to Antrim, they met in Woodbury's Hall, at the prominent home built by Judge Luke Woodbury, until the present church was built at a cost of $6,200. One of the church's biggest supporters was David Goodell, who operated a prosperous cutlery manufacturing firm in Antrim

Antrim Baptist Church.

and served as New Hampshire's forty-second governor from 1889–91. Located at a prominent intersection in town, this striking church is a good example of a Victorian-era eclectic church. The distinctive corner tower and bracketed eaves show an Italianate influence, while the prominent arched louver and rosette decoration between the entryways, along with the arched and pointed windows above the entries, demonstrates Gothic Revival influences. The gold cross atop the church is a recent addition, dedicated in 2000 in memory of best-selling author and motivational speaker Augustine "Og" Mandino, who resided in town and always wanted such a cross on his church. On the Baptist Church common is located the Antrim Soldier's Monument, which was erected in 1892, with the permission of the church by unanimous vote of its members, by the local Grand Army of the Republic (GAR) veteran's post.

Ashland

Ashland Community Church (former First Free Will Baptist Church)
Built: 1834
Builder: Unknown
Location: 57 Main Street

The First Free Will Baptist Church was built at a time when the village and its population was growing and home-held meetings were no longer suitable. The land for the structure was purchased from church member and building committee member Moses Cheney, who sold it for the price he paid for the land, making no profit on the transaction. Nothing is known of who built the brick structure, nor is its cost known, though pew sales in early 1835 raised $1,159 to help pay for part of the cost. The church as it is seen today is very different from its original appearance. While the basic brick building is much the same, the adjacent brick and wood vestry buildings connected to it were added at a later date, and the simple two-stage tower was increased in size with Victorian-era modifications and the addition of a town clock in 1893, resulting in a taller roof. The windows were once simple rectangular sash windows, but they were lengthened in 1872 and given their arched tops and matching molding. The church today is really a complex of three connected buildings; the original brick vestry, located close to Main Street, was built in 1835, and the vestry building behind that connects it to the original church was built of wood in 1899. The 1835-built vestry is an important structure in and of itself: though the land it sits on has always been owned by the church, they did not own the building. By 1836, this building was the home of a private high school operated by Miss Nancy Perkins until her marriage in 1847. Afterwards, it continued to serve as a school for Holderness Academy and the High School Association into the 1870s, but the building was also home to a millinery shop and an undertaker at one time until the church purchased the building outright in 1878 from the local bank. Sitting on a prominent knoll, the

Ashland Community Church.

church is one of the most visible buildings in town, but with subsequent buildings, including the Odd Fellows Block (built on land purchased from the church) erected in later years, which block the view of the front of the church, it is sometimes lost in plain sight. With the modifications, it is, as historian David Ruell states, "a fine example of the simpler Victorian churches. This style of church architecture has often been neglected by architectural historians." Notable features include the multi-stage tower, the arched stained-glass windows, and their arched hood moldings.

Barnstead

Parade Congregational Church
Built: 1799
Builder: Richard Sinclair
Location: 5 Parade Road

This church, the oldest in the Lakes Region, was built as a simple Type II meetinghouse, without a bell tower, which was added in 1866. Earlier, in 1851, the form of the church had been altered and new windows installed, so the building has evolved over the years as tastes and preferences in church architecture have changed. Other changes include the addition of memorial stained-glass windows and the removal of Gothic arched shutters. While the church today is, perhaps, not as striking in its features as other historic churches in town, its very age and location on the Parade make it well worth a visit. Indeed, entering the Parade area, despite all the changes over the years, really takes one back in time and it still has the air of an old New England village. Nearby is the old Barnstead Parade Cemetery, where lies Rev. Enos George (1781–1859). His monument, erected by his parishioners and friends, documents the fact that this South Hampton, NH, native and Atkinson Academy graduate preached 6,965 sermons, attended 1,000 funerals, and solemnized 693 marriages during his fifty-six years in Barnstead. In addition to his ministerial duties, he served as town clerk for forty-four years, as well as one year as a state legislator and legislate chaplain. Given all these feats, this church really stands as a memorial to one of the most influential and beloved men of his time.

South Barnstead Congregational Church (formerly the Clark Meeting House)
Built: *c.* 1814–1821
Location: South Barnstead Road (Route 126)

This, the next oldest house of worship in Barnstead, was built for a small group of Free Will Baptists, eight of them members of the Clark family, who also donated the land. This family, descended from Revolutionary War soldier John Clark (died 1799), were so numerous in the southeast part of Barnstead that the area was nicknamed Clark Town. It is unknown who built the church, though a member of the Clark family is likely, nor is it known what prompted its building—perhaps it was a religious revival spurred on by the death of Mrs. J. Clark, who died after being struck by lightning in 1820. In any case, the church was a simple country building whose use evolved over time. By 1833, a society was established to maintain the church, but as the number of Free Will Baptist members declined, the church began to be a shared one, they alternating services with an Adventist group beginning in 1857. The last Free Will Baptist meeting was held in 1867, after which the Adventists used the church until about 1891, when they split over a religious dispute. The remaining group, the South Barnstead Christian Association, remodeled the church in late 1891, and the following year, the group became the South Barnstead Congregational Society. The church building saw great change in 1912 when a Barnstead-native, Lewis Hanson of Cambridge, MA, offered the church a bell if a tower for it was built. Barnstead-native Everett Clark, now living in Boston, subsequently gifted a clock, following which the church raised the funds to build the tower, dedicated in December 1912, thus transforming the church into its present form. Today, this beautiful country church, which holds only periodic services in the summer, is distinguished by its bell and clock tower with diamond-paned sash windows and the 12 × 12 sash windows on the sides of the original meetinghouse. Adjacent to the church is the well-maintained South Barnstead Cemetery, in which many members of the Clark family are buried.

Above: Parade Congregational Church, Barnstead.

Below: South Barnstead Congregational Church.

Center Barnstead Christian Church
Built: 1839
Location: 116 South Barnstead Road

This, the youngest of the historic churches in Barnstead, had a rocky beginning. It was built as a private venture by a group of Free Will Baptists led by Rev. David Garland, possibly the son or grandson of the early Barnstead settler Isaac Garland. However, the sale of pews failed to raise enough money to finance the building and all involved, especially Elder Garland, lost heavily. A number of Congregationalists bought pews and eventually they gained control of the building in a strange twist of fate. Other groups have also preached here in the distant past, though the Congregationalists remained dominant until 1960, when the church became an independent one, which status it retains today. Architecturally, the church is a nice blend of Greek and Gothic revival styles, as shown by its full portico supported by Doric columns and the pinnacles on the spire. The steeple is topped by a simple yet distinctive wooden arrow weathervane; while not the original, not surprising given its exposed position, it is a close match to that shown on late nineteenth-century views of the church. The one feature that has been lost since the late 1990s was an unusual and large inverted V-shaped louvre in the pediment area, which seems to have been covered by vinyl siding. Just in front of the church is the town's Civil War monument, which placed the church at the center of many patriotic celebrations over the years.

Center Barnstead Christian Church.

Bath

Bath Congregational Church
Built: 1873–74
Builder: Mr. Mason
Location: 6 West Bath Road

This church is located in the center of Bath Village and is the only church in town. It was built at a cost of $7,000, replacing the original church which burned down in February 1872 during a disastrous fire that destroyed the Bath Hotel and several homes. This church was not just important as a religious institution, but also for civic and social reasons, as the town's first lending library was established here. The church itself is a simple Gothic Revival structure, as evidenced by its arched doorways and windows and trefoil decorated spire. The asymmetrical form of the church, with a corner tower, is also Gothic inspired and fits in well with the surrounding landscape, sitting on a slight rise with the covered bridge and the Ammonoosuc River at the bottom of the hill but a short distance away. Stones for the sill of the church came from an island in the river, just downstream from the Bath Village Bridge. The Bath Village Bridge itself, built in 1832 and the longest such bridge located entirely in New Hampshire, was vital to church-goers, and not just in getting across the river, as it was inside the bridge where parishioners tied up their horses during Sunday services. It is said that you can still see where the horses made cribbing (chewing) marks on the timbers while tethered inside. An additional point of interest is the 1824-built Brick Store directly across the street, claimed to be the oldest continually operating general store in America. Efforts to build the church were put into motion in early 1873, with an architect hired (name unknown) and plans drawn up and construction underway by July 1873. Its building was a true community effort: one merchant donated 40,000 shingles for the roof, while a "bee" was held, comprising about thirty people, to help dig the foundation. As has been typical in North Country towns over the years, efforts to hire and retain ministers has been sporadic over the years, especially early on: in 1883, only $750 could be raised to pay a minister, while in all of 1887, there was no settled minister, while from the 1930s to the 1950s, the church was served by a "farmer-preacher" from Vermont. For some years since this time, this church has joined with other area churches at different periods, including Lisbon, Haverhill, and Wells River, Vermont, so as to be able to jointly hire a minister to their mutual benefit, a situation that continues to this day.

Bath Congregational Church.

Bedford

Bedford Presbyterian Church
Built: 1832
Builder: Thomas Kennedy
Location: 4 Church Road

The Presbyterian Church has roots dating back to 1750 in this community, known early on for its farming (supplying thousands of gallons of milk to Manchester by the 1870s) and brick-making activities. Religious services in town originally took place in the 1755-built meetinghouse, but that structure became the town house for Bedford when the Presbyterians decided to build a new church of their own. Unlike many churches in New Hampshire, much is known about the building of this structure. For example, the underpinning of the church cost $418, and the church was raised without the customary barrels of rum, or any liquor for that matter, doled out to the workers as had been customary in times past. The town history also informs us that the church was originally built with a furnace, perhaps one of the earliest churches to be so equipped, but that this was replaced by several stoves in 1850, which lasted until a new furnace system was installed in 1873. The pastor at the time the church was built was Rev. Thomas Savage, a Boston native who had previously preached in Baton Rouge, LA before coming to Bedford in

1826. In 1856 he lamented the diminishing number of church members, citing as causes "emigration to the west-removal to manufacturing towns-deaths, and the absence of any special religious interest," but noted that "there is a general state of harmony."[5] This church was built in the Federal style, but it has changed over the years—it did not have the beautiful Greek Revival portico it now has. A covered porch was added to the façade in 1881, but by 1894, the building was in overall need of repair. Interestingly, but perhaps not surprising, the ladies of the town Social Circle stated that they would see to the interior remodel if the men of the town saw to the outside of the building. However, this was not fully the case, for it was Frances McGaw Woodbury, the wife of New York City lawyer and Bedford-native Charles Woodbury, who paid entirely for the new portico, designed by Boston architect Wadsworth Longfellow, the nephew of poet Henry Wadsworth Longfellow. The ladies of Bedford, in fact, have always supported their church, and they were not yet done, architecturally speaking, for it is they who raised the $450 for the E. Howard clock that was installed in the tower in 1898. This church is not only distinguished by the impressive portico, but also by its handsome three-stage tower, topped off with an astronomical-themed weathervane crafted by local blacksmith Nathan Kendall back in 1832. Inside, the church retains much of its original woodwork, including box pews with cherry moldings, likely executed by master wood-worker Thomas Kennedy.

Bedford Presbyterian Church.

Belmont

Province Road Meetinghouse
Built: *c.* 1792
Location: 251 Province Road

This structure was once a typical, two-story Type II-style meetinghouse when it was originally built, but it has undergone many changes over the years. The locale was once known as the Upper Parish of Gilmanton but did not become a separate town until 1859, subsequently being renamed Belmont in 1869. Early residents were taxed proportionately for the preaching and support of the two town ministers in center Gilmanton and Gilmanton Iron Works to the south and east. Early worship here was both Congregational and Baptist in form, as Rev. Isaac Smith was ordained here in 1774 and preached throughout Gilmanton for the next forty-three years, perhaps performing the dedication ceremony for this meetinghouse. However, Rev. Walter Powers, ordained in 1786 by the Baptist Society in Gilmanton, was also active in town and preached here on alternating Sundays. By 1816, the meetinghouse became a Free Will Baptist edifice, their group led by Elder Richard Martin. Thirty years later, it was the home of the newly organized Third Free Will Baptist Church, who sometime in 1835–36 remodeled the structure, cutting it down to one story and removing the gallery

Province Road Meetinghouse, Belmont.

and box pews, while in 1853 further modifications were made, including turning the building to face the road. Further change came in 1910 with the addition of the belfry and its bell. After years of declining membership and the church's subsequent closure, the building sat unused for many years before being gifted to the Belmont Historical Society in 1981. The Province Road Meetinghouse is a fine example of rural church with a touch of Greek Revival styling, as is seen in its clapboarded pediment with a semi-circular louver. The meetinghouse is also distinguished by its large 15 × 15 sash windows and the twin entryway's transom windows.

Bennington

Bennington Congregational Church
Built: 1839
Builder: Amos Whittemore
Location: 5 Main Street

The community this church serves was originally known as Hancock Factory village and Society Land and was settled by the 1780s. It was incorporated under its current name in 1842, but before this, in 1839, a Congregational church was formed on July 6, and it was decided to build a church, which was finished later that same year. The man who took the contract for its building, Amos Whittemore, was one of Bennington's most influential early citizens, being active in building the town hall, as well as a boarding house for the local cotton factory and his own home. His brother, John Whittemore, was also active in the church, serving as its first deacon, and years later, his eldest son, John, also served as a deacon. Yet another brother, George Whittemore, was the town's first postmaster and an avid supporter of the church, helping to raise money to build the parsonage and contributing funds to support the town minister. The first minister here was Rev. Ebenezer Coleman, but he served for only a few years. Due to the small size of the town and a corresponding lack of suitable funds for support, few pastors labored here for more than two or three years; Rev. James Holmes, who served from 1869–1883, likely holds the record for having the longest tenure. Even today, the church is a small one that struggles financially, a problem not uncommon in New Hampshire. In 2017, the church had but twenty members and had to close for all activities except Sunday services as expensive repairs to the building were needed. Additionally, the problem of retaining a minister had not changed and they could not afford a full-time position, instead employing three different pastors at varying times. Despite this, the church, the only one in town, is important to the community, both spiritually and architecturally. The church has always been involved in charitable activities, both locally and further afield; in 1904, the church even made monetary contributions to the Boston Seaman's Friend Society. The building is of the Federal style with a hint of Gothic Revival, as evidenced by the arched fan louvre

Bennington Congregational Church.

above its pediment window. Notable features include the twin-entries with sidelights and decorative trim above, as well as the wide corner pilasters. Overall, the structure is a nice example of a period New Hampshire village church.

Berlin

The Congregational Church (former United Church of Christ)
Built: 1882
Location: 921 Main Street

This structure is significant as the oldest surviving church building to be built in Berlin, though it is currently closed and no longer serving in that capacity as of this writing. Originally called Maynesborough, Berlin was first granted in 1771, but no settlers would come to this remote area until 1823. When it was incorporated in 1829, sixty-five people were living here. While the town became prominent in the lumber business, early prayer services were conducted by the inhabitants themselves until the first minister, Rev. Thomas Wheeler, came to town in 1837, followed later that year by Elizah Griffith. Periodic services were conducted in private homes until about 1852, when the upper part of a local store, H. Winslow and Co., was

Former Congregational Church, Berlin.

used, this situation lasting for some twenty years. The land this church sits on was donated by the Berlin Mills Co. (later the Brown Company), one of the city's most prominent and long-time employers in the logging, lumber, and paper industry, and is said to have been built by men working for the mill. Many of the parishioners at the Congregational Church were employed at the mill, so the donation of land was beneficial to both Berlin Mills and its workers. The church design, with its prominent corner bell tower, was inspired by the brick Williston-West Church in Portland, Maine. The wood church is a beautiful example of the Stick Style form, this being most visible in the decorative curved stick work on the façade and on the bell tower. Also noteworthy is the combination clapboard and shingle siding and the arched doorways and windows. The fate of this church remains to be seen, it being for sale on the open marker currently, with no immediate plans for its future use as of yet.

St. Anne Roman Catholic Church
Built: 1900
Architect/Builder: Archibald Lawrence and M. H. Roy
Location: 345 Pleasant Street

This impressive structure was built to serve the large population of French-Canadian immigrants who came to Berlin to work in its mills and in the logging industry. Catholic services were first held in town in 1867 by Father Isadore Noiseux of Lancaster, who at first only came here once a year. The first St. Anne's Church was built of wood in 1881 and was served by visiting pastors until the appointment of Rev. Cournoyer in 1885. At his death in 1899, he was succeeded by Rev. Louis LaPlante, who caused this church to be built very soon afterward, the original church building being moved and turned into a parish school. The architect of the present church was a local man, Archibald Lawrence, who designed many other area buildings, including the Berlin Public Library and the Lisbon Town Hall, while the builder, M. H. Roy, was from Lewiston, Maine. St. Anne is most significant for its largely original interior, including finely detailed pews, a beautiful vaulted roof supported by columns with intricately detailed capitals, decorated ceiling, and an important pipe organ made by Casavant Freres in Sainte-Hyacinthe, Quebec. The interior is so rich that one historian has stated that "the fact that it was executed with such quality of craftsmanship appears to be a minor miracle: a beautiful cathedral in a rural mill town."[6] Just who did this work is unknown, but it may have been executed by local craftsmen. The church's Romanesque-style brick exterior, with its twin towers, triple-arched entryway, and the tall, rounded-arch windows, though less elaborate than the interior, is also eye-catching and is one of the city's most prominent landmarks. The statue of St. Anne, the mother of Mary and grandmother of Jesus, on the shorter tower is also a local landmark in and of

St. Anne Roman Catholic Church, Berlin.

itself, and one that has, quite literally, had its ups and downs. Degraded by pollution from the nearby mills, the statue was removed in the late 1970s for a period of time, but is now fully restored and gilded and back in place. Overall, St. Anne Church is a fitting tribute to the French-Canadian immigrants who helped build Berlin into an important industrial town, as well as their descendants who today are the largest ethnic group in the city.

Holy Resurrection Orthodox Church (Russian Orthodox Church)
Built: 1915
Architect: John Bergeson
Location: 20 Petrograd Street

This eclectic structure, with its six golden onion domes, is one of the most interesting churches in the state from an architectural standpoint, but one with an interesting history to match as well. Russian immigrants first arrived in Berlin in 1900, coming from the provinces of Minsk, Wolensk (now split between the Ukraine and Poland), and Grodnensk (now in Belarus), to work in the mills. Their arrival coincided with the greatest period of Russian migration to the U.S., due to economic reasons, as well as religious persecution. By 1915, there were about 300 Russian immigrants working in the city, most of them men, and only a small number had families. Life for these immigrants in a new land was hard, and they lacked a church of their own for spiritual comfort. However, Russian Orthodox church officials from New York and Massachusetts who visited Berlin suggested to local companies that perhaps a church of their own could be built. The prominent Brown Company and others were willing to help, and with the arrival of Rev. Arkady Piotrowsky in Berlin from Cleveland, Ohio, in 1915, the idea of forming and building a church quickly became a reality. Land was purchased at the base of Mt. Forist and the land was cleared with the help of the Brown Company, while services themselves were held in the local Episcopal church. The Most Reverend Evodkim, the Archbishop of North America, who had visited Berlin, likely helped procure architect John Bergeson, a member of the board of directors for the New York Society of Architects, to design the church, and construction, which began on May 1, 1915, was completed by that October. The church is notable as being one of the last Russian Orthodox churches whose charter was granted by Russia's Tsar Nicholas II before the 1917 Russian Revolution and his subsequent execution, along with his family, by the Bolsheviks. The structure is an eye-catching one, an unexpected sight in a New England mill town. The triple-entry doors with a double pediment above and triple-arched windows on the façade are interesting, as are the small, triple-arched windows on the side pediment facing the parking area. Of course, it is the golden onion domes with the crosses mounted above that really highlight this church and make it a tourist destination. The church would prosper for less than a decade before national and international events intervened. After World War I ended in 1919 and American soldiers were returning

Holy Resurrection Orthodox Church, Berlin.

Dome detail, Holy Resurrection Orthodox Church, Berlin.

home, unemployment rose as the booming wartime economy came to a halt. This event, combined with a growing anti-immigrant movement directed at Russians after the 1918 Bolshevik Revolution in that country, subsequently called the First Red Scare, hit home even in New Hampshire. During the raids organized nationwide by President Wilson's U.S. Attorney General A. Mitchell Palmer, with the help of a young man named J. Edgar Hoover, beginning in late 1919, some 260 individuals in New Hampshire were summarily rounded up, including eight men in Berlin, and deported. Though the number was small, out of the 300 Russian immigrants in town at the time, there soon grew around them an uncomfortable atmosphere of distrust and many of them left town, their numbers substantially decreased in less than ten years. By 1929, the town could not even recognize the church properly, a book published for the town's centennial calling the church a Greek Orthodox one almost certainly by design. The final blow came during the Great Depression in 1931, when a strike by workers at the former Glen Manufacturing Co., now owned by International Paper, resulted in the mill's closure, throwing many men out of work. Other mills were also affected by the strike, and though they survived the business downturn, among the first workers let go in the ensuing layoffs were the Russian immigrants, many of whom returned to their homeland, or went elsewhere to seek opportunities. The Russian Orthodox Church subsequently suffered a decline in the parish and for many years there was no resident priest. The church ebbed and flowed after World War II, receiving some renovations in 1956, but by the 1960s, it was temporarily closed. However, the church persevered and today offers regular services, being a parish of the Orthodox Church in America, an Eastern Orthodox Church.

Bethlehem

Bethlehem Hebrew Congregation Temple
Built: 1877, open for Jewish services *c.* 1929
Location: 39 Strawberry Hill Road

This historic temple was originally built as the Protestant Episcopal Church, but was sold in the 1920s to the Bethlehem Hebrew Congregation. Prior to the purchase of this structure, Jewish services beginning in the early twentieth century were held in a storefront on Main Street. The Jewish presence in Bethlehem has been strong since about 1916, when families from New York, on advice of their doctors, began coming here during the summer months because of the clean mountain air that offered relief to those suffering from hay fever. By the 1920s, thousands of people were coming to Bethlehem and hotels were established that catered to the Jewish families. However, there was no formal place of worship until the old Episcopal church became available. Purchased in 1925, it was probably first used for services in 1929 and from that time forth has held regular services in the summer, but would not provide year-round services until 1990. Interestingly, though the land the structure sits on was purchased by Jewish parties (Maxwell and Birdie Littwin and Harold Goldfarb) from Brooklyn in 1925 for $3,000, the Episcopal church on the site continued to hold services into 1926. In 1928, the property owners transferred ownership to the Bethlehem Hebrew Congregation for $1 and subsequent conversion of the church into a synagogue began. The temple is important as the home of one of the oldest Jewish congregations in New Hampshire, as well as for the unique contributions Jews have made to the economic and cultural heritage of Bethlehem. Indeed, while members of the congregation were desirous of having their own house of worship, they were also very conscious of the need to fit in with the general New Hampshire community. While this entailed some difficulties off and on over the years, the Jewish community achieved this goal to such an extent that it is now part of the bedrock of this mountain village. This unique structure is notable for its board and batten construction, as well as for the tall and narrow Gothic window beside the stone chimney facing Strawberry Hill Road. The entrance on the north side of the structure is highlighted by a portico supported by four columns and the fanlight over the entryway. Inside, there are two stained-glass windows in the sanctuary dedicated to Celia Chinitz Schnapp (1902–1928).[7] These windows were likely placed when the

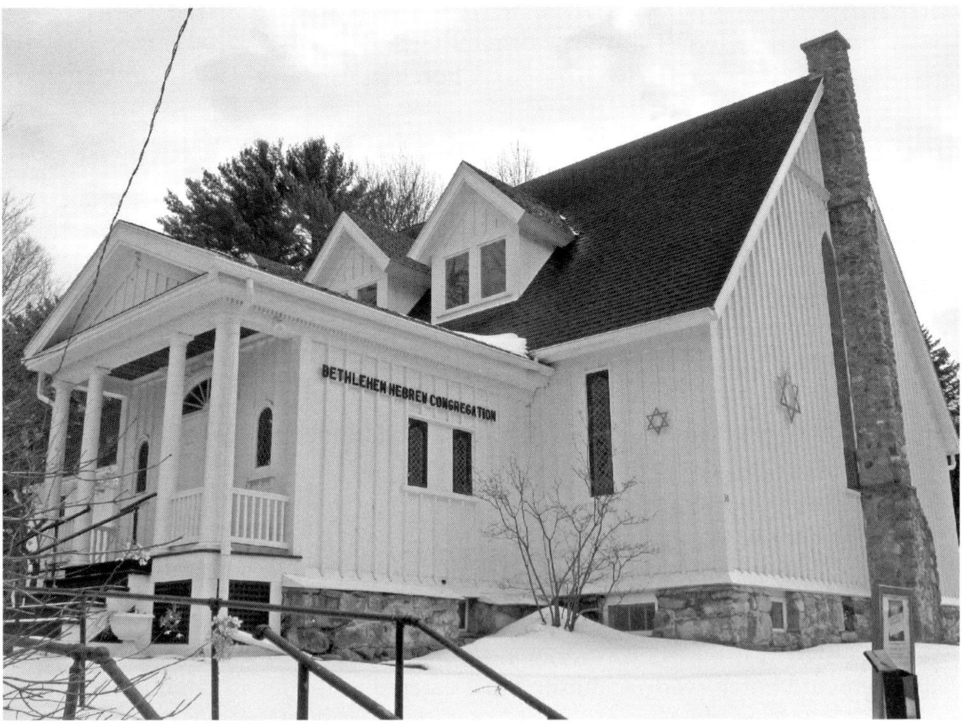

Bethlehem Hebrew Congregation Temple.

church was renovated into a synagogue and were donated by Celia's parents, Aaron and Rose Chinitz, who emigrated from Russia and lived in Manhattan. They bought a cottage property on Strawberry Hill in 1927, and it was perhaps in the summer of that year that Celia spent time in Bethlehem to regain her health, perhaps in a failed effort, for family lore describes her as being "sickly"—though this is not certain.

Ivie Memorial Church of the Messiah
Built: 1930
Architect: Jens Frederick Larson
Location: 2312 Main Street

This Episcopal chapel was commissioned by Alvin Ivie, in memory of his daughter Florence Ivie Abbot. She was a native of Brooklyn, prominent in social circles there, but her father had had a fine house built in Bethlehem in 1908, and it was her summer visits to New Hampshire that brought her into contact with Karl Abbott, a well-known hotel owner and operator who learned the trade from his father, with hotels in Bethlehem (the Upland Terrace Hotel), Franconia (The Profile House), as well as Boston, Florida, and South Carolina. The couple were married in Brooklyn, NY, in April 1918 and had two children, Frank and Emma, but Florence died from consumption (tuberculosis) at the age of twenty-seven, her loss a shock to the family.

Ivie Memorial Church of the Messiah, Bethlehem.

Not only was Florence an Episcopalian, but so were most members of her family, including her uncles, Rev. William Ivie, a pastor and police chaplain in Brooklyn, and Rev. Joseph Ivie, a Brooklyn Fire Department chaplain. The imposing stone chapel—which has never truly functioned as a church—with a designated pastor, was designed in the Gothic Style and is representative of the perpendicular churches found in medieval England. Notable features include the elaborate Gothic stained-glass windows, including a large circular rosette window above the entrance facing Main Street, as well as the crenellated tower and the large wooden doors, with the elaborate wrought-iron hinges and stone molding surrounding them. The architect may have been inspired by All Saints Episcopal Church, built on a similar plan in Peterborough from 1916–20. Sadly, the chapel, which used to be used for local weddings, was sold by the Episcopal Diocese about 2006 and is now owned privately and no longer open. The fate of the chapel remains in doubt as questions about its possible use remain unknown and some repairs to the structure are needed.

Boscawen

Boscawen Congregational Church
Built: 1799–1800
Location: 12 High Street

Located at a prominent junction of U.S. Route 3 and Route 4, this wood church is notable for its long religious and civil service to the town. It was built on the plains in the eastern part of the town on the site of an earlier meetinghouse that burned down in 1798—an act of arson. In fact, there was much lawlessness in Boscawen at this time and "deeds of violence were frequent. Bridges were taken up, young orchards destroyed, horses killed in the pastures, the houses of individuals assailed and life endangered."[8] The resulting efforts to build a new meetinghouse in this part of town resulted in conflict; when residents in this part of town petitioned for the building of a new meetinghouse, the vote was deadlocked and no decision to rebuild was made. Then, the citizens in the east offered a deal: they would build a meetinghouse, as long as the town would accept it for public use. This effort was also denied, so, in 1799, the residents decided to build their own church, the funds obtained by voluntary donations. The decision by the majority of the town not to support rebuilding efforts was no doubt due to the fact that a meetinghouse had been erected in the western part of the town (now in Webster, see the entry for that town) and they were not willing to expend the money to build another. The resulting structure was a typical period meetinghouse with twin enclosed porches, a belfry and spire, and an entry on the long side of the building. The spire was topped by a weathervane in the form of a wooden weathercock, but one that was apparently done quite poorly, "The country joiner who fashioned it never having studied the rules of art, the cock was not regarded as a fitting adornment."[9] It was soon taken down and replaced with a gilded vane of unnamed form, which lasted until the building was remodeled in 1839, while the weathercock was mounted on the signpost of the Ambrose Tavern and was still flying there in 1878. It is also said of this church that the bell mounted in its belfry was the first in the Merrimack Valley north of Dunstable (Nashua). When the news of George Washington's death reached town in early 1800, the bell was rung and townsfolk gathered at the church to hear the news. Rev. Samuel Wood, who was ordained in the town in 1781, alternated services between the western and eastern meetinghouses, but when dismissed by the town in 1802, he became the pastor of this church, a position he would hold until his death in December 1836. In 1839, the church was extensively remodeled into its present form, being turned on the site and a new steeple built, and the entrance changed to the narrow side of the building, as well as stained-glass windows installed. As a result of these changes, the church became a Greek Revival structure, as is shown in the columns flanking the entryway, the wide corner pilasters on the main block of the building and those on the two lower stages of its steeple. Town meetings were held here until this remodel, but resumed in 1847 when the building was raised 4 feet and a town hall built in the new basement. During the 1938 hurricane, the stained-glass windows were blown out, replaced with clear glass windows similar to the 1799 originals. In 1940, when the intersection was reconfigured, the church was again turned and the town hall in the basement remodeled. Though the church is no longer the site of the town hall, it served as such well into the 1980s.

Boscawen Congregational Church.

Bradford

Bradford Center Meetinghouse
Built: 1837–38
Location: 18 Rowe Mountain Road

This Gothic Revival meetinghouse was built close to the site of the town's first meetinghouse, located, as its name implies, in the geographical center of town. The site is notable for its surroundings on the town green, including an early school house, the town pound, and the first burial ground, and offers a quintessential view of a period New Hampshire village. The structure was built by the Congregationalists in town on land purchased by James Presbury and adjacent to the town's first meetinghouse built in 1797. Nathaniel Presbury is another of that family associated with this area, having built the stone-wall around the cemetery about 1801. The first town meetinghouse stood here until 1863, when it was taken down and rebuilt as the Bradford Town Hall at its current location (undergoing renovation as of late 2018). The total cost for this Congregational Church building and land was about $1,328, it being considered a quite elegant church at the time, fitted out with a bell, gallery clock, and lamps inside for illumination in a time before the advent of electricity. The builder of this church, likely a local carpenter, is not known for certain, though Stephen Hoyt, who built a number of homes and mills in Bradford during that time, is a good candidate, while local cabinet-maker David Hawks, who built his own home, may also have been involved in its building or finishing details. The rural church, which is well-maintained and in good condition, is notable for its two-stage tower with pinnacles and crenellation details and its twin-entryways, which feature sidelights and unique decorative trim. Services were held here regularly through 1958, but since this time have only been held twice a year, though the building, owned by the Union Congregational Society since 1986, is open for worship services and community events.

Bridgewater

Bridgewater Town House
Built: 1804
Location: Bridgewater Hill Road

In 1790, a Congregational Church was organized at Bridgewater Hill, which was a branch of the church in nearby Hebron. Services for some years after were held in barns and homes, sometimes by a hired minister, but often by Deacon Joshua Fletcher, who preached in the area through 1818. In October 1799, the town voted to build a meetinghouse, but these efforts came to naught. In 1802, the First Religious Society

Right: Bradford Center Meetinghouse.

Below: Bridgewater Town House.

of Bridgewater was formed, with the intention of building a meetinghouse, and in 1803, a building committee was formed. The man who presented the plan for the 49 × 38 meetinghouse was James Sargent, who may also have built the structure. The meetinghouse was subsequently raised over two days in 1804; when vendors set up booths to sell spirits to the workers, selectman were embarrassed by this and purchased the liquor at the expense of the town to distribute to the gathered crowd free of charge. Eventually, four denominations shared the meetinghouse—Congregationalists, Free Will Baptists, Methodists, and Universalists—each given a number of Sundays based on what they had paid to help build the structure. The Congregationalists predominated with fifteen Sundays, while the Universalists only had it for five Sundays from April through December. The original structure was a typical Type II meetinghouse, though in 1849, the upper story was converted to the town hall. Later, in the 1860s, the town was required to clapboard and paint only the upper part of the building that they used. In 1881, the former meetinghouse was cut down to its present one-story size, reduced 20 feet in length, and the roof turned around. From that time to 1916, the building served as the town hall and for occasional religious services, but after this time, it has largely been used for sporadic services. Interestingly, the greatest prosperity of the church, from a spiritual standpoint, came during the years 1825–1830, when Rev. Charles Bowles preached here. He was an African-American, born a slave, who served as a soldier in the American Revolution for both Massachusetts and New Hampshire and, afterward, while working as a sailor, had a religious awakening and became a devout Baptist who served as a traveling preacher throughout New Hampshire and Vermont. He only left Bridgewater because the town could not afford to pay him a salary. During various points in time, the structure has fallen into disrepair and been threatened, but the citizens have always come through and the historic building is now in fine condition. It is one of the more difficult meetinghouses to find in New Hampshire, located in what is now a remote area of town and accessed by long and winding dirt roads, but the drive is a scenic one. Just down the road from the meetinghouse is the beautiful and well-kept Old Home Cemetery, where some of the first settlers are buried. The town center now lies to the west along Newfound Lake, so this survivor is a perfect example of the changing population centers in New Hampshire, as well as an example of a meetinghouse whose form has evolved over the years to fit the changing needs of the community.

Campton

Campton Congregational Church
Built: 1824
Location: 495 Rte. 175

This church was founded in 1774, but did not build a meetinghouse for many years, instead holding services in private homes. After the first pastor departed in 1791, for many years there was no settled minister, though a meetinghouse was built in 1802 that saw use until 1858. The West Meetinghouse was built on the west side of the Pemigewasset River in 1824 to serve a population who formerly had to travel to Plymouth for services. Under newly settled minister Jonathan Hale, this event inspired many to religion and the church added twenty-seven new members that summer alone. It would remain in its westerly locale until 1858, when it was moved across the river to its present location. The whole building was taken apart at a cost of $1,725 and reassembled in its current location, given a new and steeper roof over its original, as well as new pews and other furnishings inside. The bell in the steeple was donated by Sylvester Marsh, the man who built the Mount Washington Cog Railway. Horse sheds were also constructed behind the church by individual parishioners, but after years of up and down maintenance, they were removed in 1946. The church was also equipped with two wood stoves, but even these could not warm the building in the dead of winter, so services were not held during these months for many years. Architecturally, the church is one of the finest of the early meetinghouses surviving in the area north of Concord, its Greek Revival form highlighted in its double entryway, wide corner pilasters, as well as the columns on the louvered belfry. The windows, too, offer a distinctive look, being standard 12 × 12 sash windows with dual sets of shutters for the upper and lower sashes. Not far away is the Blair Covered Bridge, at which crossing the first bridge was built in 1829, making this area of town more accessible and the later moving of this meetinghouse an easier task.

Campton Congregational Church.

Campton Baptist Church
Built: 1826
Location: 1345 Main Street

The Baptist Society of Campton was first organized in 1811 and, like the Congregationalists, first held their meetings in private homes. In 1824, it became a part of the Baptist Church in Woodstock (then called "Peeling"), but became an independent church just three years later. Before this time, in 1826, the church built its own building; the structure cost $600 and all the bricks were made locally. In keeping with tradition, pews in this church, too, were individually owned, their sale helping to fund the building and furnishing of the structure. Interestingly, the parsonage for the church, which is still in use in that capacity, was built behind and to the right of the church in 1868 at the request of Rev. Joseph Breed so that "people could not hear his wife scold."[10] The vestry to the left was built in 1873. The building's Federal-style exterior is largely original, notable for its dual entryways with fan louvers above, as well as the compass-headed window on the façade.

Campton Baptist Church.

Canaan

Canaan Meetinghouse (Canaan Town Hall)
Built: 1792–96
Builder: William Parkhurst (finished by Robert and John Barber)
Location: Canaan Street Historic District

Granted in 1761, settlement in this town, named after Canaan, Connecticut, began in 1766. However, no meetinghouse was constructed for many years and sporadic religious services were held in local homes and barns. While many were desirous of a meetinghouse, the idea was rejected as being too costly. In 1788, it was voted unanimously to build one, but even then, numerous delays ensued. The eventual building of Canaan's first and only meetinghouse was tied up with the development of the Broad Street (now known as Canaan Street) area and the purchase of land for the town common. Of course, the usual delays as to where to locate the meetinghouse were had, but finally the structure was built; even then, difficulties arose when the builder, Parkhurst, was severely injured on the job, as has previously been discussed. Even after the meetinghouse was complete, difficulties continued and many details were not built to the satisfaction of the town's building committee, especially much of the pews and other seating inside, but also the basic underpinning of the building. It fell to Capt. Robert Barber, William Parkhurst's father-in-law, and his son, John, to finish the building, which they finally did in 1796. Since its building, the structure has always been a town building, though a formal deed to the building was not obtained by the town until 1829. Not only were town meetings and voting conducted here, but the town's various religious denominations took turns using the building on the Sabbath (though Baptists predominated), and many social activities took place here as well. In 1841, the Baptists gained permission to lay a floor across the upper gallery and fit that space for worship services. In 1884, the Canaan Lyceum Hall Association was formed and a hardwood floor was laid in the upper hall over that the Baptists had laid for use as a roller-skating rink, the only known example of such a use for a New Hampshire meetinghouse. As it was originally built, the meetinghouse was a typical Type II period meetinghouse with twin porches. In 1829, the eastern porch was replaced with a Federal-style bell tower, though the original entrance on the long side was retained. The clock in the tower was added in 1894. Despite being a bit weatherworn as of this writing, it remains an impressive structure, as demonstrated by its long side featuring seven bays and a total of twenty 20 × 20 sash windows, as well as its distinctive open cupola.

Canaan Meetinghouse.

Old North Church
Built: 1828
Builder: Bailey Welch
Location: 588 Canaan Street, Canaan Street Historic District

This Gothic Revival structure anchors the north end of the Canaan Historic District and was the first dedicated home of the town's Congregationalists. The church was first organized in 1799 as a branch of the church in Hanover and received only periodic visits from a minister for many years until 1825, when Rev. Amos Foster was ordained and served for nine years. A young man from Hanover, a native of Salisbury, Foster was at first met with some skepticism by the older members and with outright rudeness by those younger members, but he soon won them over. It was under his leadership that this church was built. While he first conducted services in the old meetinghouse (see above), the Baptists dominated in the use of that building, so the Congregationalists decided to buy the needed land and build their own edifice. The builder, Bailey Welch, fell from the steeple during its construction, but survived the ordeal and was paid $100 for his services, the church being dedicated in January 1829. Among the members of this church who were a driving force in gaining their own house of worship was Jacob Trussell. Just seven years later in 1836, for his having taken part two years earlier in the destruction of Canaan's Noyes Academy, a prep-school whose enrollment was open to black students, Trussell was ex-communicated from the church, but was reinstated as a member,

Above: Old North Church, Canaan.

Right: Entryway detail, Old North Church, Canaan.

despite expressing no remorse for his actions, in 1854. In 1853, the plain church was renovated into a Gothic Revival structure with the addition of pointed arched windows and tower louvers, as well as the tower pinnacles and crenellation details. In later years, the church fell into disrepair and membership declined in numbers. In 1869, the church closed, having dwindled down to twenty-one members, and remained closed into the first decades of the twentieth century. The Catholic Church attempted to buy the building for $100 in 1885, but their offer was declined. Today, annual services are held at the church, which has been fully restored and is well maintained.

Former Canaan Methodist Church
Built: 1844
Location: 486 Canaan Street, Canaan Street Historic District

This beautiful structure, now a privately-owned home, was built under unusual conditions. Methodists were among the first settlers that came here, but services seem to have been sporadic until after 1800. Camp meetings along Hart Pond were held in 1806 and a preacher was here by 1809, the church having 170 members by 1810. A Methodist meetinghouse was first built on South Road in the southern part of town, mainly to accommodate members of the church from Enfield, but it was a small structure and one that eventually fell out of disfavor due to its location. In the summer of 1842, camp meetings were held in the woods near the Wells Cemetery and a great religious revival occurred, resulting in eighty converts and 132 people baptized in the faith. Most inspirational were the sermons of Rev. John Newton Mars (1804–84), a black man from Norfolk, CT, the son of former slaves Jupiter and Fanny Mars. He is called by one historian a "Celebrated Standard Bearer in the Wesleyan Tradition" and was famous for his animated sermons and his ability to organize the efforts against slavery.[11] His impact on Canaan was mightily felt and, full of religious zeal and desirous of being closer to their fellow townsmen, the Methodists decided to build a church on Canaan Street, which was completed by October 1844 and was dedicated debt free. Even before the church was built, difficulties in the congregation arose over Rev. Erasmus Morgan, a man described as "neither humble or charitable."[12] Fully one half of the church membership refused Morgan's services, and instead chose their own pastor, he being Rev. Charles Caples, a black man. Morgan somehow had Caples' preaching license revoked, but a divide ensued in town among the religious denominations; the Baptist minister in Canaan supported Morgan, while the Congregationalist supported Caples. Ultimately, both Caples and Morgan left Canaan, leaving Rev. Reuben Dearborn to officiate at the opening of the new church. For many years, the church had men that might preach for a year or less before moving on and, with the natural ebb and flow of religious feelings, the church slowly dwindled. By the 1880s, there was one Methodist preacher in town, with him splitting duties between this church and the main one

Former Canaan Methodist Church.

at East Canaan, a village that became the economic center of town with the coming of the railroad and the rise in manufacturing pursuits. Eventually closed, the church was later sold and has become a private residence. Nonetheless, it is a fine example of a blend between the Greek Revival and Federal styles, notable for its triple entryway and three-bayed façade with center pilasters and its two-stage, topped off with an octagonal cupola. Photos from the late 1970s show that the steeple had an additional stage, a small section below the domed roof that had simulated windows, but this has subsequently been removed for unknown reasons.

Canterbury

Shaker Meetinghouse (Church Family Meeting House)
Built: 1792
Builder: Moses Johnson
Location: 288 Shaker Road, Canterbury Shaker Village

The Shaker community in this town had its beginnings in 1782, when members of the Mount Lebanon Shaker community in New York visited here and found fertile ground for new converts. Eventually, the land for the Shaker village was donated by three prominent families and the village was formally founded in 1792 under Father Job Bishop. The first building built by the Shakers was this distinctive gambrel-roofed meetinghouse, done so under the guidance of Shaker master-builder Moses Johnson from Enfield, NH. As with regular New England meetinghouses, this structure was built through the labor of local carpenters under Johnson's guidance, the frame raised on May 9, 1792, with completion of the meetinghouse in full on September 20 that same year. However, at the raising, the Shakers observed vastly different customs than were generally common at the time, their workmen not supplied with alcohol and the whole work done in reverent silence and humility, as befitted the raising of such an important religious structure. This meetinghouse was closely based on Johnson's design for the first Shaker meetinghouse in Mount Lebanon, its lower floor used for worship services, while the upper floor was used as sleeping quarters for the Brothers and Sisters (as Shakers called themselves). The 3 × 5 bayed meetinghouse is also known for its twin entryways—one for the men and one for women members. As to the interior, which is open to the public, notable features are the wide-open floor space on the lower level, deliberately designed so as not to require supporting vertical columns that would be an obstruction to the Shaker's worship and dancing rituals. One interesting feature of the floor are the eight diagonal rows of flush nails and dowel pegs, four on the Sister's side (west), four on the Brother's side (east) and running from the back wall to the front. It is thought these were used to help the Shakers properly align themselves for their ritual dancing, but it is unknown who originated this marking system, perhaps Johnson, or maybe the sect's elders. Either way, it was a simple yet effective method that helped to maintain order in the meetinghouse. The interior was also painted a distinctive Prussian blue, a dark shade that became the prescribed color for meetinghouse interiors by the Shaker Millennial Laws. The exterior was painted a gleaming white, the only structure in their community that, by law, could be painted this color. The meetinghouse in Canterbury saw continuous use for nearly 200 years by Shaker members, with Eldress Bertha Lindsay (1897–1990) and Sister Ethel Hudson (1896–1992) being the last of the sect, which once had 300 members at the height of its popularity in 1850. Today, the meetinghouse is one component of the beautifully preserved Shaker Village, open to the public since about 1980 when Shakers were still living here and designated a National Historic Landmark in 1993.

Shaker Meetinghouse, Canterbury.

Center Harbor

Center Harbor Congregational Church
Built: 1837
Location: 52 Main Street

First settled in 1765 as part of the town of New Hampton, it was set off from that town in 1797. At the time, the Free Will Baptists were predominant and they built a church edifice in 1812, which remained standing until the mid-1850s. The Congregational church here was organized in 1815 with thirteen members, nine of whom were living in town, while services alternated between Meredith Village and Center Harbor. In the 1830s, the town became a destination for summer tourists and travelers heading to the White Mountains, they being inconvenienced when it came to Sabbath Day services by having to travel to a neighboring town. As a result of this, a church was built in the summer of 1837 at a cost of $1,700, the structure built by local men. The land was donated by John Coe, a shipbuilder from Durham who later became Center Harbor's postmaster, his home reputed to be a stop on the Underground Railroad for runaway slaves. The following year, the Congregational Church of Center Harbor was formed. Several pastors were employed here for a short time before the arrival of Rev. Almon Benson, who preached here beginning in 1840, retired in 1863, and remained in town, dying here in 1884. He is buried in the village cemetery in front of the church he led for many years. Because his salary during his pastorate was not enough to live on, Rev.

Center Harbor Congregational Church.

Benson was also a farmer who ploughed the soil four days a week, did minister work on Fridays and Saturdays, and preached on Sundays. He also owned a bit of land and after his retirement made a living boarding summer tourists. The church structure is of the Greek Revival style, modified in 1885 with the addition of the front vestibule and the raising of the church to add a large basement. Today, all that is left of the original façade are the two upper-story windows and the corner pilasters. The three-stage steeple maintains its original design, housing a bell that was installed in 1856. Though substantially altered and sheathed in vinyl siding, the church is nonetheless a pleasing sight and occupies a prominent position near Lake Winnipesaukee.

Charlestown

South Parish Unitarian Church
Built: 1842–43
Builder: Stephen Hasham
Location: 252 Main Street

The first meetinghouse in Charlestown was built of logs in 1760, with a framed meetinghouse following in 1768. Congregational minister Rev. Bulkley Olcott was ordained in 1761 and would preach there until his death in 1793. After that time, the town had no regular religious services, but they resumed when the South Parish of Charlestown was established in 1810. Its members, who lived in the southern part of the town, were motivated to form the parish because of the difficulties of traveling some 8 miles distant to the original town meetinghouse. Once formed, the parish hired Hebron native and Exeter and Harvard graduate Rev. Jaazaniah Crosby as their pastor, who would subsequently serve the church for the next fifty-four years and become one of Charleston's most distinguished and beloved citizens. Many details about his life and anecdotes about his ministry are found in the town history, one of the most humorous concerning a couple he was marrying; after the ceremony, he stated to the couple "You are now married and I hope you will always live in love and unity," after which the new husband, mistaking an ideal for a nearby town, "straightening himself up into a very erect and magisterial position said 'Doctor, we are married to be sure, as you say, and I hope that we shall always live in love, but as to living in Unity, Dr. Crosby, I never will, for its the rockiest place that ever I see.'"[13] Originally, Crosby was a Congregationalist, but over time, his views changed and he became a Unitarian; this distressed some members of his flock, who were more orthodox in their views, and eventually, in 1835, a split in the once-harmonious church resulted when twenty-three members departed to form the Evangelical Congregational Church. This was just one instance of the Unitarian Controversy

South Parish Unitarian Church, Charlestown.

that spread throughout New England and beyond during the years 1805–1840. The South Parish built their first church about 1819, but it was the last structure destroyed by the Great Fire of 1842, begun when a prisoner is the town jail hoped to make his escape by setting fire to the town jail. The new church was commenced later in 1842 and was completed in 1843, attributed to local builder, hotel-operator, and clockmaker Stephen Hasham. The church is a fine example of a brick Gothic Revival structure and is notable for its arched windows with matching arched hoods, as well as the delicate wood tracery around the Gothic-arched entryway and the open belfry. The steeple itself is also striking, with a square first stage decorated on the corners with octagonal columns. The brick church was painted a buff color for much of its early life, from at least 1876, but was restored to its original brick in 1952.

St. Luke's Episcopal Church
Built: 1863
Architect: Richard Upjohn
Location: 188 Main Street

The Episcopal Church got its start in 1822 when the First Religious Episcopal Society of Charlestown was established. In 1829, the name was changed to St. Luke's Episcopal Church, with services first being held in the town's Union Meetinghouse, but by 1837, the building was in such poor condition that services were held in several schools in the area. Services ceased in Charlestown by 1841 after the membership declined steeply, and would not begin again until 1859, at the behest of several members of the original congregation. Once again, the services were held in the town hall or a local hall, but a parish organization was established in early 1863 and a building fund established soon thereafter. The noted architect Richard Upjohn of New York was hired as the architect, while Bullard and Buzzell, contractors from Alstead, were hired to build the structure. It is notable as one of the few churches designed by Upjohn built in New Hampshire, and the only one built of wood. It may be wondered how such a small organization could afford to hire a famed New York architect, but the officials give us the answer, for among them were Porter Spencer, George Olcott, Jr., and Richardson Robertson, all prominent and well-to-do men whose families were among the original settlers in town. The church was consecrated in December 1863, and over the next few years, its membership grew, with it soon becoming clear that more space was needed. As a result, the church was enlarged in 1869, this time under the guidance of the original architect's son, Richard M. Upjohn. The small yet elegant structure is a perfect example of the country churches featured in its architect's popular book, *Upjohn's Rural Architecture*, and is of board and batten construction, featuring Gothic Revival styling. In addition to its siding, which has been beautifully preserved, the structure is noted for its multicolored slate roof, pointed Gothic windows with diamond panes, quatrefoil trim on the gable ends, corner tower, and steeply-pitched roof.

St. Luke's Episcopal Church, Charlestown.

St. Catherine of Sienna Catholic Church
Built: 1880
Location: 285 Main Street

The Catholic church in this part of New Hampshire got its start in neighboring Claremont in the 1830s, but would experience little growth until the rise of mill manufacturing in the area, and the subsequent arrival of the Irish immigrants in the 1850s. The first Catholic services in town, under the control of St. Mary's in Claremont, took place in private homes, local businesses, and the old town hall by the 1870s. St. Catherine Church's beginnings came in 1879 when Sherman Paris donated the land located behind his Main Street home for the establishment of a church, as well as paying for the construction of the building and its furnishings, including four Tiffany stained-glass windows, which are a valued and cherished part of the church to this day. Paris and his wife, Catherine, were New Yorkers, inspired to move here after making a stop here in 1867 while on the way north to the White Mountains. Paris soon purchased the homestead of Henry Hubbard, Jr. (son of a New Hampshire governor), and though intending it to be merely a summer home, eventually moved here year-round. While he was not Catholic, Catherine was, so the church, though open to the public, was built for her and its name is not

Saint Catherine of Sienna Catholic Church, Charlestown.

surprising given these circumstances. The church remained a Mission Church until 1904, when it was designated a parish. In 1905, a rectory was purchased on Main Street an inconvenient distance from the church, so the lot next to the rectory was also purchased and the church was cut in two sections, the main body and the bell tower, and was moved with the use of wooden rollers to its current location. The church was subsequently refurbished and rededicated in 1915. The well-kept church was renovated again, nearly a century later, in 2012, and is in excellent shape. The pleasing structure is an eclectic mixture of the Stick, Gothic Revival, and late Victorian styles. The former is seen in the distinctive diagonal stick-work above the entrance to the church, as well as the front gable above and on the tower's upper-stage, while the pointed top windows with diamond glass panes and the circular window on the façade are Gothic Revival touches. The subtle Victorian influence may be seen in the scalloped trim and the scalloped edge louvers on the tower.

Chatham

Chatham Congregational Church
Built: 1871
Location: 177 Chatham Road (Route 113B)

Located on New Hampshire's eastern border with Maine, this town was first granted in 1767 but not settled until after 1770. It has always been a small community, having a population of 516 in 1850, and 337 in 2010. As far as can be ascertained, religious services were held in local homes, and there was no town supported ministry, though it is possible that itinerant preachers may have come from nearby Fryeburg or other Maine towns. No church was established here until this one was built in 1871, town native Ithiel Clay (1819–1901) being the man who donated the land, provided the funds for its building, and helped support a minister. His grandfather, Jonathan Clay, was a Free Will Baptist minister in Buxton, ME. Clay was one of the most prominent men of his time in Chatham and the entire White Mountain area, and it was once suggested that he run for state governor. Early on, Clay served as a school teacher, but later worked in the logging industry (where he employed over 100 men) and as a farmer who owned considerable land; he also has many other achievements to his name. In short, he was an intellect who was used to hard work. He was also said to be a temperance man who was also anti-slavery, so his leadership in causing a church to be built here is not surprising. He

Chatham Congregational Church.

was equally aided in his efforts to bring a church to town by his wife, Caroline, to whom he was wed in 1862. The simple yet attractive church is a nice example of a late Greek Revival structure, noted for its corner pilasters and steeply pitched roof, as well as its 9 × 9 sash windows with dual shutters. The three-stage steeple, topped off with a church-style weathervane that was likely purchased via catalog, is attractive yet unassuming, as is typical of rural churches in the state. The bell housed in the belfry was purchased from the Revere factory in Massachusetts and shipped to Portsmouth; from there, according to oral history, it was hauled on a sled by six-yoke of oxen in the middle of the winter. Located in North Chatham, this church is also unique in that it is the only church in the state that can be reached only by going through a neighboring state, in this case Maine. While South Chatham can be reached from East Conway, the northern part of town can only be accessed via Route 113B from Stow, Maine, to the east, the road connecting South and North Chatham having washed out years ago.

Chester

Chester Congregational Church
Built: 1773
Location: 4 Chester Street

Found in a charming, yet bustling village center, with the ancient village cemetery just across the street, this structure was the town's second meetinghouse. As originally built, it measured 45 × 60, with a porch at one end, and a bell tower and spire at the other, which measured over 100 feet tall and was crowned with a gilded weathercock. The standing order in Chester was Congregational, and change here, as elsewhere in New Hampshire, was slow to come; when in 1806 Samuel Graham carried his bass viol into the meetinghouse to play music on Thanksgiving Day services, "no sooner did he begin to sound it, then Deacon William Wilson took his hat and left in hot haste."[14] In 1809, a petition was presented to the town to let other denominations preach in the meetinghouse; this was subsequently allowed for Methodists, Baptists, and Free Will Baptists, but only for those preachers approved of by the town. One of the longest-serving ministers in the town was Rev. Nathan Bradstreet, who was ordained in this structure in 1793 and continued without apparent difficulties for the next twenty-one years. However, by 1815, the church's male membership had dropped from thirty to eleven in number and the vast majority of the congregation was no longer happy with Bradstreet and the performance of his duties. What followed was a legal and religious mess—councils were called for to mediate the dispute and outside ministers were called in to smooth matters over, but neither side could agree. Eventually, the Chester Congregational Church, with the exception of a few members who supported Bradstreet, excommunicated their minister, a

Right: Chester Congregational Church.

Below: Woodcut view of original Chester Meetinghouse before its 1839 remodel, from Chase's *History of Old Chester*, 1869.

very unusual step. More councils were convened and the excommunication was eventually lifted, with the town and Bradstreet parting ways in October 1817. Ten years later, Bradstreet committed suicide in Westford, MA, having never worked as a settled minister again. By 1837, the old meetinghouse, now the Congregational Church, needed repairs, and efforts began to either sell or alter the building. Finally, in 1839, it was decided by the parish to alter the structure, the work to be completed by the end of the year. The church was turned, its spire cut down, and the end porch removed. The interior was also significantly altered, and today, it is just the frame and roof timbers that remain from the original meetinghouse. The E. Howard clock was added to the steeple in 1881, but otherwise the church is unchanged from its 1839 remodeling. Today, the church is a nice rural interpretation of the Greek Revival style. Most prominent and unusual are the very wide center and corner pilasters, these consisting of flush vertical boards without capitals. A more traditional feature is the wide pediment decorated with a triangular louver. The three-stage tower is simple in design, with a Greek Revival touch found in the pedimented middle stage.

Chichester

Chichester Methodist Church
Built: 1833
Builder: Caleb Beede
Location: 45 Main Street

The Methodists got their start in this town in 1819 when a Methodist circuit rider, Rev. John Lord, preached to a group near a local spring. In 1829, Rev. Ezekiel Stickney came here, organizing religious instruction and services in local homes and schools. In 1830, under the influence of circuit rider Rev. Orlando Hinds, a Methodist Society was formed; members were added to the church after a four-day religious meeting was held at the old Congregational meetinghouse, and sixty church members were added after a meeting at the Centre School House. With this fervor, a building committee was formed, and by November 1833, the present church was built, the second religious edifice in town after the 1791-built meetinghouse. Rev. Hinds helped lead the funding efforts, raising $100 of the cost from a citizen of Boston, while master-workman Caleb Beede, said to be a local preacher, led local men in the construction, aided by True Sanborn and Hiram Chase. In the summer of 1834, a large religious revival was held on the Batchelder farm on Bear Hill, with 354 new members professing their faith. The church continued to be served by circuit riders until 1847 when Rev. F. A. Hewes became the first settled Methodist minister. The church remains an active and vital part of the town to this day, and occupies a prominent part in the village landscape on Main Street. Though uncertain, the church building appears to be largely original, though it is

Chichester Methodist Church.

possible that some of the renovations mentioned in records as having been made in 1847 changed the character of the building. Readily evident changes include the stained-glass windows and the modern vinyl siding. The church is a nice example of a Gothic Revival building, as evidenced by the pinnacles above the twin entryways and on the spire, as well as the Gothic-arched fan louvers above the windows. The side window trim, in the form of columns, is a unique feature that matches the trim for the front entryways.

Chichester Congregational Church
Built: 1838
Location: 153 Main Street

The Congregational Church in town was formed in 1791, with the ordination of Rev. Josiah Carpenter and the building of the first meetinghouse soon to follow. After the Toleration Act of 1819, and the later dismissal of Carpenter in 1827, the Congregational influence in town waned as Free Will Baptists and the Methodists gained converts. Rev. Rufus Putnam became the minister in 1832 and a series of revivals occurred. By 1838, the old meetinghouse was no longer suitable, so that year, a new church was erected after much debate. Virtually nothing is known of its builder, though the building bears some resemblance to that erected in Dunbarton

Chichester Congregational Church.

a short time before. Some records state that the Congregational meetinghouse was burned in 1840, but this almost certainly refers to the original 1791 meetinghouse. The church is a blend of the Gothic and Greek Revival styles, the former evidenced by the arched louvers on the upper stages of its tower, while the latter is evidenced by the portico and pediment above. The features of the church have changed over the years, as early photos show Gothic-arched louvers over the windows and twin entryways, and spires above the door trim just like that on the town's Methodist Church. Whether this lost feature was removed due to deteriorated woodwork, or when the structure was clad in vinyl siding is unknown. Despite these changes, the church remains an impressive building, sited on the town's historic and scenic Main Street.

Claremont

Union Episcopal Church (The English Church)
Built: 1773
Builder: Ebenezer Rice
Location: 133 Old Church Road

The Episcopal church got its start in Claremont in 1771 when Connecticut clergyman Rev. Samuel Peters came here as a missionary from the Vermont church, with the first parish records dating from 1773. It was Peters who gave Vermont its name after viewing its mountain scenery from Killington Peak and, as a Loyalist, he was imprisoned during the Revolutionary War. Because of the association of the Anglican Church with the Royal government in the New Hampshire colony and elsewhere, many church officials were viewed with suspicion regarding their political views or even imprisoned. However, before the war New Hampshire's Royal Governor John Wentworth took great pains to support the expansion of the church in New Hampshire. He not only provided the plans for this church, but also pledged to supply nails, glass, as well as a bell and an organ when the church was finished. However, once the war began, Wentworth was forced to flee the state and these pledges went for naught. In fact, once the frame was raised, the building sheathed, and a floor and a roof were in place, work on the building ceased due to the war and it would not be finished until at least 1789, and possibly a few years later, the needed funds procured by the sale of the pews. As originally built, the structure was a simple one with four bays, but in 1800, the bell tower was added, and in 1820, the building was lengthened by 25 feet, the two sections rather unevenly matched, the divide between old and new clearly visible today. No matter what changes in the structure may have taken place, there can be no doubt that it was a solidly built one; in the early 1800s, "a tornado swept over the country while the people were assembled for divine worship. Among them was a Mr. Dodge, who had been employed as a carpenter when the frame was raised. He was a very large and strong man and had a seat near the door. When the trees began to fall about the building, many were greatly alarmed and rushed for the door, where they found Mr. Dodge defending the passage, denying all egress, and with his brawny arm pushing back the crowd, saying 'I know this frame. No wind can demolish it. Your only safety lies in keeping beneath its shelter.'"[15] The most prominent rector of this church was probably Rev. Daniel Barber, who served from 1795–1818. Though said to have been a rather strange man with but little dignity, he grew the church and provided solid leadership during his tenure. However, his time at the church came to an end when he embraced the Roman Catholic faith, following in the footsteps of his son, the Rev. Virgil Barber, founder of the first Catholic church in the state in Claremont (see below). The church would remain the only one of the Episcopal faith in town until the 1830s. The growth of the village area due to the rise in manufacturing would soon result in the creation of a second parish in town. The Union Church is well-kept today and in excellent repair, a beautiful example of a period meetinghouse that still hosts services. Notable features include the impressive bell tower with octagonal cupola, as well as the six bays on the long sides (four original, two that are later additions) that feature compass-headed windows. The surrounding area, too, is historic in nature, with the old cemetery across the street, as well as Old St. Mary Church, while behind and to the right of the church is a surviving horse-shed building used for storage.

Union Episcopal Church, Claremont.

Old St. Mary Roman Catholic Church
Built: 1823
Location: Old Church Road

Simply put, this eclectic structure is perhaps the most historic Catholic Church building in the state of New Hampshire, its building coinciding with the first organization of that faith in the state. The early history of this church is synonymous with the life of Rev. Virgil Barber, the son of the Episcopal minister in Claremont, Rev. Daniel Barber (see above), it being stated by one historian that the events in Claremont "have no parallel in the history of Catholicism in the United States."[16] Virgil Barber, like his father, became an episcopal minister, and was principle of the Episcopal Academy in Fairfield, NY, when he visited his father in Claremont in the summer of 1816. The two men subsequently discussed some of the problematical doctrines of their faith, and later that year, after some consultation, studies, and much soul searching, Rev. Virgil Barber converted to Catholicism, and by 1817, he had moved to New York along with his family, his wife, Jerusha, and five children, to begin the conversion process. While Episcopal ministers could be married, Catholic priests, of course, could not be, and things were further complicated by the fact that Barber's wife was pregnant. In the end, a solution was reached, with Virgil Barber entering the Jesuit Order, his wife and three oldest daughters were accepted as nuns, while the two youngest children (a boy and a girl) would be cared for by friends, the boy going to a Catholic school and the girl becoming a nun when the proper age was reached. After studying in Rome, Barber returned to Claremont in the fall of 1818 and helped celebrate the first masses ever in the town, when seven people, including his mother, were baptized. After his conversion to Catholicism, Rev. Daniel Barber studied the faith and returned to Claremont in 1822 to do missionary work on behalf of his church, and it was also at this time that he donated the land on which the first Catholic Church would eventually be built. Rev Virgil Barber followed his father back to Claremont soon after, in December 1822, after being ordained in Boston. He would later travel to Three Rivers, Canada, to solicit funds for the building of a church here, likely because this area "was the closest source of Catholic sympathy and help" to Catholics in New England.[17] Subsequent visits the following year, 1824, helped further the building of the church, which included not only the structure that survives today, but also a building that served as a home and a school, which was torn down many years ago. Barber would remain a force in Claremont for five years before his recall to Boston in 1828 due to the financial difficulties of the church, as well as financial disputes within his family. With his absence, the mission church of St. Mary would languish for many years, and did not become a regular parish in town until 1870, though the old church by this time was dilapidated and services were held in the new St. Mary Church built that same year. There is much more to tell about the life of the Barbers outside of Claremont, and their life story would make a compelling movie, but the impact they had on Catholicism in New Hampshire is indelible. The church structure that is Old St. Mary, which holds periodic services on special occasions, is a striking one to say the least. Nominally, it is built in the Federal style, but has a touch of early Gothic Revival with the pointed brickwork above the windows. Also unique are the circular windows on the upper portion of the projecting tower, as well as the wooden urns on the roof corners (probably a later addition). The left side of the church was once attached to an older structure that served as a school academy below, open to all students, not just Catholics, and the Barber's residence above, and the place where the two buildings were joined is clearly visible. The church is also notable as the site of the first consecrated Catholic cemetery in New Hampshire, with the earliest burials being closest to the church, many of them unmarked. A walk through its grounds demonstrates that many of the parishioners here were Irish Immigrants.

Old St. Mary's Roman Catholic Church, Claremont.

Universalist-Unitarian Church
Built: 1832
Location: 106 Broad Street

This much neglected church has received little attention compared to Claremont's other historic houses of worship. The Universalist faith was first practiced here as early as 1815, but the number of adherents was small. They united with the Methodists and Baptists to build a small round brick church on the site of the present Trinity Episcopal Church by 1818, and here held services at alternating times before they built their own church in 1832. In that year, the First Universalist Society was given permission by the town to build a church on the common next to the town cemetery, at a site decided by the selectman, at a cost of $500 per acre. The church was formally dedicated in October 1832, though a formally established Universalist church (as opposed to a society) was not established until 1834. The church was built in the late Federal style, but was remodeled in 1883, with the bell tower added. Finally, in 1972, the land beneath the church was deed to the Universalist Church. The structure is now primarily an eclectic one, combining late Victorian, Stick style, and Gothic Revival elements, its most notable feature being its pyramidal spire topped off with

Former Universalist-Unitarian Church, Claremont.

an elaborate weathervane. Squeezed in between the library and the firehouse, the most distinctive part of its surrounding landscape is the town cemetery directly behind it, well worth a close inspection for the many interesting gravestones it contains for some of the town's most noted citizens. The church has been closed for religious services for about thirty years, with ownership reacquired by the city in 1989. Since then, the building has deteriorated and has become a heavy financial burden to the city. In 2017, the church was purchased by the Lake Sunapee Baptist Church in Newport at a cost of $700, though the assessed value was placed at $271,000. If all goes well, they hope to use it for their student and after-school programs, thereby breathing new life into this endangered structure. The church was subsequently prepared for its new role in 2018, though the town still maintains ownership of the structure's bell and weathervane.

First Congregational Church
Built: 1835–36
Location: 72 Pleasant Street

The Congregational Church was established in Claremont in 1771, about the same time as the Episcopalians, but was not nearly as robust in its early years and it had no dedicated meetinghouse until 1785. Despite this, the town had a problem maintaining ministers of this denomination for years—some preached for just a short time before moving on, another was deemed unfit overall as a church member, while another was released because he was in favor of the temperance movement. The current church building as erected during the tenure of Rev. Tertius Southworth, who served from 1834–38, deemed to have been a good man but was dismissed because he opposed the methods of a revivalist minister working in the area and dismissed some members of his own church because of their association with him. The most prominent minister of this church in the early years was Rev. Robert Lawrence, who was pastor here for twenty-one years beginning in 1839 and is noted as the compiler of the noted book *New Hampshire Churches* (1856), an authoritative publication that is the source of much information in this work. This church was built when the first meetinghouse was converted to a town house; situated in downtown Claremont, it is a hidden gem and one of the finest Gothic Revival churches in this part of New Hampshire. Most notable is the crenellated tower decorated with corner pinnacles and the quatrefoil incised woodwork panels surrounding the arched louvers on each side of the tower.

Trinity Episcopal Church
Built: 1852
Architects: Wills & Dudley
Location: 120 Broad Street

This church got its start when there was a division in the Episcopal parish in town, primarily due to the fact that those living and working in the busy village area found it inconvenient to travel to the Union Church in West Claremont for services. Though a small round union church was built in the village in 1818 on the site of the present Trinity Church, it was not a separate entity and eventually would be outgrown. The parish of Trinity Church was organized in 1843, they also holding an interest in the old Union Church, where services continued to be held, and in 1852, a new and more substantial church was erected. The architects of the building were Frank Wills and Henry Dudley, Englishman known for their Gothic Revival churches who worked out of New York City. The builders were Washburn and Nichols of Albany, NY, and the building cost was originally $7,000, but with subsequent alterations cost considerably more, the final price not cited. It originally was constructed with a corner bell tower, but this was lost during the hurricane of 1938 and never rebuilt. The building is an outstanding example of the Stick style, noted for its irregular form and steeply pitched roof.

Right: First Congregational Church, Claremont.

Below: Trinity Episcopal Church, Claremont.

Colebrook

Monadnock Congregational Church
Built: 1829–31
Location: 147 Main Street

Formed in 1802, the Monadnock Congregational Church was organized by missionary minister Rev. John Willard from Lancaster and was the first church in town. The group would continue to be served by travelling ministers until 1810, when Rev. Dyer Burge, active in this area of Vermont and New Hampshire, was hired and held services in local schoolhouses around Colebrook and Columbia up to 1815, after which the church was without a pastor for a time. The siting of this church, when it was finally built, is quite interesting. The land was donated by the Smith & Pratt company of Colebrook in about 1826, the owners being John Smith of Hartford, CT, and Samuel Pratt of Marshfield, VT. The two first came to town in 1809, purchased many lots of land, and subsequently built a sawmill and a cotton factory and employed many men in the village. John Smith, a "*mulatto*" (black man), was nicknamed "Guinea" Smith but seems to have been well accepted in Colebrook.[18] His donation of land is a rare early example of African-American involvement in a North Country town. Despite the donation, things did not go smoothly as Colebrook's factory village was devastated by a fire in 1820, and while Smith & Pratt rebuilt some of their enterprises, they went bankrupt in 1826. The deed for the land they donated to the church actually passed to a Boston bank, but was quit-claimed to the church in 1836. After initial fundraising efforts, the frame of the church was raised in 1829, but the church was not fully finished until early 1831. Today, it stands as the oldest church structure in the North Country and, as the town of Colebrook has grown, so too has this church. As originally built, it was a small building with a low square tower without a bell, but in 1858, it was enlarged and fully painted. In 1873, the church gained most of its present form when the square tower was removed, a second story was added, and the vestibule and steeple, as well as the town clock and bell, as well as a furnace, were added at a cost of $6,000. The church did suffer a fire in 1967, but was subsequently repaired with slight changes to its details. Interestingly, the church was subject to some disputes with other denominations in the town almost from the start; when pews were sold to complete the structure, many were purchased by individuals who were not members of the congregation, perhaps with an eye towards gaining control of the building. In January 1845, the Universalists requested the use of the church for a two-day meeting, but were rejected by the church members, stating that this "cannot be consistently be assented to by us inasmuch as we honestly believe that Universalist preaching has a pernicious influence on society, especially on the rising generation."[19] The church building was subsequently closed and locked, but the Universalists, led by one Seth Tirrell of Stewartstown, broke in and held their services anyway. The Congregationalists

Monadnock Congregational Church, Colebrook.

subsequently locked the church again that night, only to have it broken into again the next day. Afterwards, cooler heads prevailed and nothing further happened. In fact, by the 1880s, nearly all the denominations in town had used the church at one time or another. Today, the church and its building, distinguished by its Victorian-styled steeple and a façade with an open pediment and single rounded-arch stained-glass window, remains an important town institution.

Concord

CenterPoint Church (former First Baptist Church)
Built: 1824–25
Builder: John Leach
Location: 20 North State Street

Of this notable church, one historian states that "It is doubtful if any public edifice in Concord has been more changed in its interior and exterior appearance."[20] The Baptist church got its start here in 1771 when missionaries first preached the faith, but a formal church was not established until 1818. This plan for building this so-called "downtown" meetinghouse was begun in 1823 when land was donated by William Kent, and a building committee was subsequently formed and plans laid. The church constructed by the talented John Leach was an impressive one, costing considerably more than planned, with the cornerstone being laid in May 1824. Oral tradition states that when the orientation of the church was being discussed, a local man, an old sea-captain, proclaimed "why brethren, place her broadside to the wharf-that's the way we always took on passengers."[21] With such a placement, passersby could not just walk past the front door, but would walk close-by the church windows overlooking the sidewalk and be able to hear the singing and sermon being preached within. As originally constructed, the church, which cost $7,000 and was dedicated in December 1825, was a Federal-style building that was a simplified version of the magnificent brick church Leach had constructed in Newport (see below). Up to 1850, many members of the church were low on the economic ladder, but by the early 1900s, many prominent Concord citizens were members. In 1845, the church was enlarged by 20 feet on the north end and "modern" windows were installed. In 1875, the church was renovated into the form it retains to this day, the projecting costing about $12,000. These changes turned this building into a Victorian-era church with elements of Greek Revival. On the street side, the church has four bays, the tall stained-glass windows notable for their Victorian trim, while the short end façade is highlighted by a portico with a heavily bracketed pediment, within which is a diamond-shaped woodwork panel. The five-stage tower is an eye-catching one that is heavily bracketed in several stages and highlighted by decorative woodwork that reflects both Victorian and Greek Revival elements. This church, though it has often been overshadowed over the years by its neighboring churches (see below) of impressive size, including the now-gone White Memorial Universalist Church, is notable as the oldest religious structure in Concord.

The Chapel of St. Peter and St. Paul
Built: 1886–1894
Architect: Henry Vaughan
Location: St. Paul's School Campus, 325 Pleasant Street

This late Gothic Revival chapel, known on campus as the "New Chapel," was built under the influence of this prep school's first rector, Rev. Dr. Henry Augustus Coit. The school was established in 1856, but by 1881, Coit envisioned an even more impressive house of worship for the school's growing student body. To that end, the Alumni Association raised $100,000 in four years, a large amount for the day, with the result that Coit's dream would soon become a reality. In 1886, with building funds now available, the school, modeled after an English private school, hired the noted English architect and Gothic Revival specialist Henry Vaughan to design their vision. The resulting chapel is not only considered Vaughan's finest architectural

Right: CenterPoint Church, Concord.

Below: The Chapel of St. Peter and St. Paul, Concord.

achievement, but the Chapel of St. Peter and St. Paul is also considered one of the finest Gothic Revival churches built in America. Later sections were added by noted architects Bertram Goodhue (a new cloister in 1919–20) and Ralph Adams Cram (1929–30). The imposing 124-foot tower of the chapel was completed in 1894, its pinnacles topping it off on a grand scale, while the steeply-pitched roof, buttresses, pointed arch windows, and stone tracery are all equally impressive features. Though the school is affiliated with the Episcopal Church and follows its traditions, interfaith services are held here at the chapel to start every day, with student acolytes leading a procession, carrying banners, torches, and crosses. It is in this chapel, perhaps, that the school's motto, "learn those things on earth the knowledge of which continues in Heaven" is spiritually embodied.

First Church of Christ, Scientist
Built: 1903–04
Architect: Francis Allen and Charles Collens, Boston
Location: 33 School Street

This church is intimately connected with the founder of the Church of Christ, Scientist denomination, Mary Baker Eddy (1821–1910), a native of nearby Bow. A controversial figure in American religious history, Eddy founded the church in Boston in 1879, based on her own experiences and study, its mission being to commemorate the words and works of Jesus Christ and bring back early Christianity and its lost art of healing through prayer. She wrote the central text of the church, *Science and Health*, beginning in 1872, it being first published in 1875, and revised it throughout the rest of her life. The book is considered one of the most influential works ever written by a woman, and, in short, claims that sickness is just a belief, not a property of matter, and that prayer can remove that negative belief and bring about healing. The first church for this faith was built in Boston in 1894. Eddy moved to Concord in 1899, living at her Pleasant View estate (now the site of the former Christian Science Pleasant View Home) and soon the idea of building a church in Concord was brought to her attention by locals, not an idea she had originally entertained. The site chosen was that where the Christian Science Hall (a home she purchased and renovated into a church in 1897), now deemed too small for its congregation, was located. The cornerstone for the church was laid in July 1903 and Eddy was very involved in the details, gifting the Concord Church $100,000 for its construction, choosing Concord granite for the building material, consulting with the building's architect, and visiting regularly to view its progress. The church was dedicated in July 1904. Mary Baker Eddy was very much involved in Concord on a philanthropic basis, donating funds to pave streets and buy shoes for the town's poor children, but she only once attended her own church, preferring services at her home because of her widespread fame and the crowds of people that followed her everywhere. When she did attend the church, she entered through a separate door into the Mary Baker Eddy Room, which was

Right: First Church of Christ Scientist, Concord. Postcard view, *c.* 1920.

Below: Door detail, First Church of Christ Scientist, Concord.

decorated to her tastes and today is one of the highlights of the church's interior. The church is an imposing example of a Romanesque Revival structure, noted for its asymmetrical form with varying roof lines, massive 165-foot corner tower, stone tracery, and the Corinthian columns carved in stone flanking its massive wooden main entrance doors. The north and south transept stained-glass windows were executed by John Hardiman & Co. in Birmingham, England, and were designed especially with the healing tenets of the church in mind. From 2014–17, the church was renovated at a cost of $2.5 million, some of that cost funded by donations from other Christian Science churches all around the world due to the historical importance of the Concord church to the faith. In 2012, the church received media attention when its tower was found to be the home of a Peregrine falcon, an endangered bird and a rare site in an urban setting. In 2013 and 2014, a pair of falcons nested in the tower, aided with the building of a nesting box by the Audubon Society, their presence highly beneficial in keeping the stone structure clean by preying on the pigeons that roosted in the area.

Cornish

First Baptist Church of Cornish
Built: 1803
Location: 29 Cornish Stage Road, near Junction of Rte. 120

This church was originally located southwest of its present location, at the junction of Harrington Hill and Parsonage roads, being moved to its current location in Cornish Flat in 1818 due to changing settlement patterns. The church was organized in 1789 and held early services in barns and homes of its members. Early on the Baptist Society was often short on funds and could not afford to pay travelling ministers for their services; in 1799, they attempted to unite with the Congregationalists in town so that they share the costs of joint worship, but these efforts were unsuccessful. The building of this church in 1803 signified a period of prosperity and a rise in membership. The builder of this church is unknown, but the possibilities are intriguing as the structure's Federal-style details, as demonstrated by its beautifully constructed façade featuring a Palladian window and triple-entry doorways with fan-lights above and diamond-patterned trim, demonstrate the influence of the noted Connecticut architect Asher Benjamin, who practiced his trade in Windsor, Vermont, just across the river from Cornish from 1796–1800 and tried to establish there a school for architects and builders. The church was renovated in 1845 with many original interior features, such as the pulpit and sounding board, removed, while the exterior was slightly changed at the rear and stained-glass installed in the front Palladian window. The steeple was also altered, its open belfry boxed in and a spire added. This church is also notable for much of its interesting and colorful history that has been recorded. In the early 1830s, the church united with the Universalists in town and shared the Baptist meetinghouse with them, the understanding being that whoever first occupied the pulpit after the church doors were unlocked on the Sabbath would have the use of the church for that day. Rev. Oliver Barron vigorously denounced Universalism, however, and was clearly unhappy with this arrangement, it being noted that on one occasion one man represented each group and, after the doors were unlocked, began their race to the pulpit, the Baptist representative winning out by shoving his rival aside into the deacon's bench at the foot of the pulpit. The town historian states that "So that day they had Baptist services, but how profitable they were spiritually, the writer cannot say."[22] In many towns in New Hampshire beginning in the 1830s, the issue of slavery and its abolition became a frequent subject expanded on by local ministers, and Cornish was no different. Rev. David Burroughs, who was pastor here from 1837–42, preached many anti-slavery sermons, and while many in his flock shared his views, there were some opposed, with the result that on one occasion the white church doors were painted black. In another example of opposing views, Burroughs, upon entering the church one Sabbath Day, found a black ram standing in his pulpit. He calmly left his pulpit and gave his sermon from the deacon's desk below, while the out-of-place farm animal above "occasionally responded during the service, beside occasionally rising and standing on his hind legs, looking over the pulpit at the audience and causing much amusement for the children."[23]

First Baptist Church of Cornish.

Trinity Church
Built: 1804–08
Builder: Philip Tabor
Location: 833 Rte. 12A

This church is notable not just as an outstanding example of rural architecture, but also for its historical associations. The Episcopal faith in Cornish traces its origins back to 1793, when an Episcopal association was formed under the influence of Dartmouth College student Philander Chase, the son of Congregational Church deacon Dudley Chase. While at school, the young man came across a copy of *The Book of Common Prayer*, a book used in Anglican church services, and quickly became a convert to that form of religion, espousing its virtues to his family members and friends. Soon, Episcopal missionaries made their way to Cornish to offer services to this small but growing group, with the result that a new church was formed. Philander Chase would remain an Episcopalian for the remainder of his life, moving to Ohio, where he founded Kenyon College, and later Illinois, serving as a bishop in both states, and later became the bishop of the Episcopal Church in the U.S. One of his Cornish relatives, Salmon P. Chase, gained an even wider fame after his move to Ohio, serving as a senator and governor from that state before becoming Secretary of the Treasury under Abraham Lincoln, and afterwards a Chief Justice of the U.S. Supreme Court. The land that Trinity Church stands on was donated by General Jonathan Chase, a noted Revolutionary War soldier, so the Chase legacy in town and on this church is a strong one. Religious services were first held in the 1773-built town meetinghouse, which was abandoned by the Congregationalists after their original church was dissolved in the 1780s over doctrinal issues, but that structure was in need of serious repair by 1801, so Trinity Church voted to tear it down and build a new church based on plans submitted by Philip Tabor, a well-known local carpenter. The old meetinghouse was subsequently torn down in 1804 and a new one on the same spot begun that same year. While the building was likely framed in 1804, it was not fully finished until 1808 due to a lack of funds. As originally built, the church had a porch on each end, as well as a belfry and steeple, but was later altered, the belfry and steeple removed, and the porch to the rear removed and first replaced with a semi-circular chancel (possibly influenced by the same feature on the church in Claremont), which was also later removed. The interior has also been altered over the years, but the building nonetheless is a simple yet elegant example of the local builder's art. Most striking is its simple square tower and the unusual 25 × 20 sash windows. Equally notable is the cemetery, which is adjacent to this church, the earliest burials predating both Trinity Church and the earlier meetinghouse that was once here. A stroll through its grounds is a must, for here you will see a fine collection of slate and early marble gravestones, the white and gray stones offering an interesting contrast from afar, while a close examination of the stones will reveal interesting epitaphs and decorative motifs marking the final resting place of early

Trinity Church, Cornish.

town notables. This church remained in active service from its building to 1875, after which, for a period of twenty years, declining membership caused a cessation of services, which resumed by the late 1890s. In modern times, the structure ceased its religious associations and was privately owned at various times. In 1984–85, the church was renovated by Cornish resident and then-State Representative Peter Hoe Burling, remaining in private hands until after 2004, when it again became a house of worship, providing regular Episcopal services in the summer months.

Croydon

First Congregational Church
Built: 1854
Location: 883 Route 10

This church is located in the Croydon Village area, also called the East Village, and was first built as a Methodist Church. Though circuit riders had often visited here and conducted services and held classes, a church was not formed in Croydon until

First Congregational Church, Croydon.

1853, their church being built the following year. The church remained a Methodist one until 1881, when it merged with the Congregationalist Church. The structure is a nice example of a largely Greek Revival church, noted for its center and corner pilasters, steep pediment, and simple two-stage tower with Gothic pinnacles. The pedimented windows are also a nice feature, being of the more unusual triple-sash variety. The church has been restored and well-maintained over the years and fits in beautifully in its rural village setting. When the metal roof was installed several years ago, it offered a unique opportunity to view the large roof timbers and see how the structure was put together.

Croydon Flat Church-United Church of Christ (former Universalist Church)
Built: 1854
Builder: Paul Jacobs
Location: 29 Croydon Turnpike

Now a Congregationalist church, this structure was originally built for the newly organized Universalist Church in Croydon in late 1854. The Universalists were prevalent in Croydon, first forming their own society in 1832, and holding meetings in the town hall, but had no settled minister. This changed in 1853, when a formal

Croydon Flat Church.

Universalist Church was organized and Paul Jacobs (1783–1854) financed and built a church for them at a cost of $2,000. Jacobs was one of Croydon's most prominent citizens; he served as town selectman and representative to the New Hampshire House of Representatives, was a dairy and sheep farmer, built a manufactory for potato starch (used in home cooking), and was instrumental in getting the road that connected Croydon Flat to the East Village constructed. At the time of his death on September 16, 1854, the church was not yet completed. An early deacon in the church was Col. Otis Cooper, who served the town as Justice of the Peace for twenty years. Little seems to be known about those that preached here, but the most notable, Rev. Robert Stinson, was its only settled minister. During the Civil War, he served as the chaplain of the 6th New Hampshire Regiment and died shortly after the war's end. As seen today, the church is a fine example of a period rural church, but with a few unique features. Most notable is its wide pediment, within which is featured a large circle mounted on a pediment. While the green-painted star within this circle is believed to be a modern addition, the circular decoration looks to be original to the church. Another feature that catches the eye is the linear trim around the upper part of the doors, window frames, and the openings on the upper stage of its steeple. These elements elevate the church from an ordinary one to one that is both distinctive and visually appealing.

Dalton

First Congregational Church of Dalton
Built: 1830
Location: 735 Dalton Road

This church is significant as the first ever to have been built in town, and the only house of worship for fifty years thereafter. The Congregational church here was founded in 1816, originally consisting of nine members, but it was Rev. Luke Spofford of Lancaster who seems to have been the driving force in the building of the church. Once framed, the church was not finished for several years and was a simple affair, without a steeple or the front porch that it has today. No matter how simple the structure may have been, the building was no doubt an inspiration, as in 1833–34, the town experienced its greatest season of religious revival, adding sixteen members under the guidance of Rev. William Hutchinson's preaching. In fact, for much of the church's early existence, it had no settled pastor until the tenure of Rev. Horace Wood, which lasted from 1839–45. Afterwards, settled ministers were few and far between. However, the closely-knit members were adamant about holding services every Sunday, with a respected deacon leading the prayers and giving a sermon when a minister was not available. In 1879, the church gained its present form with the addition of the front vestibule, steeple, and weathervane, all at a cost of $768, with a rededication taking place in 1880. As it stands today, the church is a pleasing example of rural architecture, plain in appearance with a late

First Congregational Church of Dalton.

Victorian influence. The façade features twin entryways with fine molding around the doorways, while the steeple is a delight, featuring dentil work and triangular block trim around the open belfry. The weathervane is a period scroll type typically sold as a church vane, likely purchased by catalog from a manufacturer in New York or the Boston area.

Danville

Danville Meetinghouse (Hawke Meetinghouse)
Built: 1755
Location: 470 North Main Street, Route 111A

Located in an area that was once the western parish in the town of Kingston, this meetinghouse is one of the most significant in all of New England, and the oldest meetinghouse in New Hampshire today surviving in its original eighteenth-century form. It was built in 1755 by a group of local citizens desirous of having their own meetinghouse, rather than travel the far distance to center Kingston for religious services. When the parish was set off in 1760 as the town of Hawke (its name changed to Danville in 1836), the meetinghouse was presented to the town and became the town meetinghouse. Nothing is known of its builder, but it was likely a local man. The building was not fully outfitted with pews or interior woodwork until 1760, after it became town owned, and subsequent pew sales helped to finish the structure, the town therefore bearing no expense for its meetinghouse, a rather unusual situation for the times. The cemetery that lies adjacent to the meetinghouse was formally deeded in 1817 as the old cemetery filled up and fell out of use, though some burials are recorded here in the first years after the structure was built. The meetinghouse was for many years a vital part of the community, being used for town meetings until 1887, though religious services were less frequent as the Congregational Church here, never very strong, eventually faded away and other denominations, such as the Free Will Baptists, built their own churches in Danville. Indeed, by 1856, the Congregational form of worship had, as one historian wrote, "become one of the things that were, very little religious influence is felt in the place," and only Free Will Baptist and Methodist congregations existed here in the early 1870s.[24] However, the first and only minister settled in the town, Harvard-educated Rev. John Page, has a well-earned place in the town's history. He served the town from 1763 until his death in 1783 and was a well-respected figure. Page died after a smallpox epidemic struck the Tuckertown section of Hawke, close to the meetinghouse. Despite the risks, Page ministered to members of the Tucker family in the winter of 1782 and subsequently contracted the disease himself. Instead of returning to his home next to the meetinghouse, Page quarantined himself in a cabin in the woods of Tuckertown and there died alone, his body subsequently

Danville Meetinghouse, west gable-end view.

Interior timber and pew details, Danville Meetinghouse.

removed and hauled to the town cemetery by sled. Interestingly, while many period meetinghouses in New Hampshire were altered over the years to accommodate changing architectural tastes, the Danville Meetinghouse remained largely unchanged, and even as early as 1817, it was considered by some to be an "ancient" structure. Of the few changes in this meetinghouse, the interior was altered with the removal of the box pews in the 1860s so that dances could be held on the main floor. The pew components were stored in the gallery and some may have been reused when the box pews were reconstructed during restoration efforts. From about 1890 to the first decade of the twentieth century, the meetinghouse saw little use and was eventually acquired by a private group in 1911, the newly formed Old Meetinghouse Association. To this day, the association has not only preserved the old meetinghouse, but also restored the interior to its original appearance. These efforts took place in 1936 when the box pews were restored, much of the work done by Danville farmer and carpenter Arthur Tuck, as well as an immigrant English woodworker living in nearby Kensington, Harold Greenwood. The expert work they did in fashioning the pews has made it difficult for modern historians to determine which of the pews are original and which are restorations. The building is impressive for both its size and simple form. Notable features include the clapboard exterior, the majority of which is original, the same being true for most of the 12 × 12 sash windows; the main entrance, which features twin Tuscan-style pilasters (an indication they are a later addition, dating after 1830), and the doors of the entryway facing the road feature paneling that likely dates from 1800–1830. The back (north) side of the meetinghouse is interesting for its view of the elevated pulpit window, measuring 16 × 16 and larger than the rest of the structures windows so as to allow more light to illuminate the pulpit desk. No visit to this meetinghouse would be complete without a tour of its interior, which is open to the public at several times during the year or by special arrangement. Inside, one is almost taken back in time by the elegant wood-paneled pulpit with sounding aboard above, the old exposed timbers, and, of course, the distinctive box pews.

Derry

First Parish Meetinghouse
Built: 1769
Location: 47 East Derry Road

Now at the end of an eight-year restoration and preservation project that began in 2011 and will cost close to $1.5 million, this meetinghouse is one of the most historic structures of its kind in southern New Hampshire, and is notable as being the home of the first Presbyterian church to be gathered in New England. The church dates its founding to 1719, when Rev. James McGregore, a native of Derry (Londonderry) in Northern Ireland who immigrated to America in 1718 along with members of his congregation, held the first services here under a large oak tree on Beaver Pond in April 1719. This church grew quickly as the number of Scotch-Irish immigrants grew and by 1721 built its first meetinghouse. By 1734, 700 people attended the church for communion services, most of them town residents, and the church continued to grow, necessitating a new and larger meetinghouse, built in 1769. Known originally as Nutfield, in 1722, the town was incorporated as Londonderry. In 1827, the church congregation split, with many going to the western parish in town—that portion of town retained the original name of Londonderry, while the eastern portion took the name of Derry. The first minister in this meetinghouse was Rev. William Davidson, who married the widow of his predecessor and served the town from 1740 to 1791. He has been called "mild," "amiable," and "greatly beloved" by one historian, but also criticized as "not an exact theologian, nor a very effective preacher."[25] Interestingly, the parish this church served, once Presbyterian in form, united with the town's Third Parish, a Congregational one, in 1809–10, and thereafter became essentially Congregationalist in form, though some of the older Presbyterian Church members would leave over this change. In the historic Forest Hill Cemetery, located adjacent to the church, there are burials dating back to 1729, including those for the town's first five ministers who served from 1719 to 1850, an uncommon occurrence in most New Hampshire towns with such a long history. The meetinghouse itself has undergone many changes over the years—as originally constructed, it was a Type II meetinghouse with a steep roof and twin porches at either end of the structure. Sometime in the late 1700s, a slender steeple was added to the west end, and in 1822, the building was cut in half and enlarged by 24 feet, with the substantial bell tower built to replace the steeple. The bell hung in its belfry was the first in Londonderry. Though the original builder of the meetinghouse is unknown, church Deacon Nehemiah Choate, a noted builder in the area at the time, built the magnificent bell tower, distinguished by its octagonal upper stages and its open-arched belfry surrounded by finial topped balustrades. In 1845, the interior was remodeled, the upper half used as a sanctuary, the lower half for town offices, the tower clock was installed in 1876, and in 1884, stained-glass windows were installed. In the intervening years, the church had deteriorated to a point where it was added to the New Hampshire Preservation Alliance's Seven to Save list in 2009. Renovations began in earnest in 2011, with the uppermost portion of the bell tower, 40 feet above the clock stage, removed in September 2015 for renovation and scheduled for reinstallation in 2019 in time to celebrate the 300th anniversary of the town's founding. Among the town members who have attended this church over the years is the famed naval aviator and astronaut, Alan Shephard, an East Derry native.

First Parish Meetinghouse, Derry.

Dorchester

Dorchester Community Church
Built: 1828
Location: North Dorchester Road

Originally known as the South Meetinghouse, this structure was originally located in the Thompson Hill area of Dorchester and was built by subscription. By the 1880s, few families were living in this area, so it was decided to move the church to its current location on the town green and near the Town Hall. The church was originally larger in size, but when it was decided to move it in 1883, its timbers were cut down in size at a local mill, resulting in a somewhat smaller building. The only remnant of the meetinghouse left at its original location is its foundation. The church as it stands today is a simple yet attractive example of a rural, mostly Greek Revival building, its most notable features being the columns flanking its central entryway, corner pilasters, while the round pediment window is more of a Victorian-era influenced feature. The two-stage rooftop tower, which dates from its 1883 rebuild, has an open hexagonal belfry that is topped off by a church scroll weathervane, the tower having originally projected off the front of the structure. Though the church had periods of lesser religious activity in the early twentieth

Dorchester Community Church.

century, in 1940, it was restored and electrified, and since that time has been used regularly for services. The site around this church, the Dorchester Common Historic District, is also of note, being the home of not only the old town hall, church, and the Town House Cemetery, but also the town historical museum, which is located in an 1808-built schoolhouse that moved here from another location in town and was one of the first such buildings in town.

Cheever Chapel
Built: *c.* 1870
Location: State Route 118 at Groton-Dorchester town line

This private chapel was originally built as a schoolhouse and was once situated on the North Dorchester Road before its move here and conversion to a chapel *c.* 1905. Its name comes from the fact that it is sited in an area of town that was once known as Cheever Village, likely named after Nathan Cheever, who came here with his wife, Mehitable, from Danvers, Massachusetts, after 1800. Their daughter,

Cheever Chapel, Dorchester.

Sally Cheever Blodgett, became a school teacher and is said to have "had a natural fondness for literature and great facility for expression."[26] She was first a member of the Congregational Church in Dorchester, but later joined the faith of her husband, Ebenezer Blodgett, and became a Baptist. The couple after 1848 lived in Rumney and were members of the Baptist Church there (see below). This chapel has hosted religious services for many years and is distinguished by its small corner tower and beautiful arched stained-glass window, featuring a dove and floral elements, with Federal-style keystone trim on its façade. Since 2018, the fate and status of this chapel is in doubt; as of this writing, the chapel has been offered to the town as a gift, but there has been some reluctance in accepting it due to the building's condition, as well as other issues regarding taxation. However, the chapel is loved by many in town for its unique form, historical nature, and its stained-glass window, so it is hopeful that the building will be preserved. Over the years, the chapel has been home to various denominations to use for their Sunday church services, the current occupant, the Apostolic Lighthouse United Pentecostal Church, calling it home for most of the time from 2008.

Dover

Religious Society of Friends (Quaker) Meetinghouse
Built: 1768
Location: 141 Central Avenue

The religious group that built this meetinghouse was once the most persecuted in all of New Hampshire, as previously discussed, as well as one of the most numerous. The Quakers first came here as missionaries in the early 1660s, and though driven out of town, the fortitude and grace shown by them during harsh times struck a chord with many in Dover. Within twenty years, a third of the town consisted of Quakers, they building their first meeting house at Dover Point in 1700, and one closer to the current center of town in 1720. This structure is the Friend's third meetinghouse in Dover and is important as the oldest remaining Quaker meetinghouse in New Hampshire. Regular monthly meetings and Sunday services were held here from 1702 to about 1912 until declining numbers reduced the use of the meetinghouse to once yearly services. In 1952, the meetinghouse was reopened and has been used for monthly and business meetings on a regular basis. Notable among the worshipers here was the poet John Greenleaf Whittier (1807–1892), who was a practicing Quaker, his parents were married in this meetinghouse, and he attended services here as a child. This five-bayed meetinghouse is typical of the eighteenth-century meetinghouses built in New England, notable for its 12 × 8 sash windows on the upper floor and its more typical 12 × 12 sash windows on the lower level. On the facade of the meetinghouse, facing Pine Pill Cemetery, is the vestibule with its two entryways, the entryways being a standard feature of Quaker meetinghouses, while the vestibule was added in the early 1800s and features a center and corner pilasters. These entryways were segregated, one for men, the other for women, each of them entering into their half of the meetinghouse, the interior meeting space being separated by a wall, which is how the structure remains today. Men and women were equal in the church, but their meetings were once separate. Today, all the members, men and women, meet in just one half of the meeting space, the other half is now used to house a kitchen and office space. In 1989, the structure was raised so that a basement could be added, but otherwise the meetinghouse appears in its largely original form. It is interesting to note that the Friends early on did not employ ministers to preach their faith, and that services, or meetings as they are termed, were (and still are) held in contemplative silence, sometimes lasting over and hour, without music or sermons, though any member who feels the spirit of God within them may speak to the other members about the messages they have received. Today, the forms of Quaker worship in America vary and some meetings employ a pastor. The meetings Quakers hold consist of two types, those held on a weekly basis on Sundays for religious observation and those held on a monthly, quarterly, or yearly basis that are either business or doctrine related. The Friends Meeting in Dover was once one of the most important in New

Quaker Meetinghouse, Dover.

England, drawing members far and wide from New Hampshire and Maine, making this meetinghouse one of its more important structures.

First Parish Church
Built: 1825
Builder: Captain James Davis
Location: 218 Central Avenue

The Congregational Church was the established denomination in Dover from about 1631, though the church was not formally established until 1638, making it the second oldest church in the state behind that in Hampton. The early ministers in this then frontier town had troubling tenures, with Rev. John Reyner, pastor from 1655–1669, dealing harshly with the Quaker missionaries. One of the church's most distinguished pastors was Rev. Jeremiah Belknap, from 1767–1786; his sermons prior to the Revolutionary War led some members of his congregation to manumit their slaves, pointing out the incongruity of holding people in bondage at a time when the colonists were seeking freedom from British oppressors. He later became a noted historian, penning the first authoritative history of New Hampshire. The current First Parish Church, built by a well-known local builder, is considered a local example of a brick Federal-style church, with broad influences from Asher Benjamin and Charles Bullfinch, but also inspired by well-known churches in nearby towns. Historians believe its immediate influence was the 1807-built St. John's Church in nearby Portsmouth designed by Alexander Parris,

First Parish Church, Dover.

while the beautiful four-stage steeple is a variant of the 1801-built First Religious Society Church in Newburyport, MA. Such outside influences were not unusual, but local craftsmen also put their mark on this church; local carpenters George Pendexter and Samuel Drew are recorded as the church's designers and doing the joiner's work, while metal-worker William Gerrish crafted the 5-foot-long copper weathercock that still flies above the church today. The first clock installed in the tower in 1835 was crafted by Benjamin Morrill of Boscawen, but later replaced after it fell into disrepair. This structure's highly visible location on Central Avenue, not far from City Hall, makes it a crown jewel on the city's skyscape, the recently renovated steeple, distinguished by the octagonal belfry and lantern in its upper stages, offering a pleasing sight. The façade of the building, with triple-entry doors and compass-headed windows beneath the massive pediment of the slightly projecting facade is an impressive sight and indicative of the talents of its designers and builders alike.

St. Mary's Roman Catholic Church
Built: 1872
Location: 25 Chestnut Street

This church is most notable for being the home of the oldest Catholic parish in the state of New Hampshire. The church got its start here beginning with the arrival of Irish immigrants to work in the town's growing textile mill and manufacturing

St. Mary's Roman Catholic Church, Dover.

industry in 1819. Indeed, it was their need for a local priest to conduct Catholic services that led Bishop Fenwick of the Archdiocese in Boston to send missionary Rev. Virgil Barber of Claremont (see above) here in 1826, celebrating the first Mass in the town courthouse on October 22, 1826.[27] As a result of these efforts, an Irish Dominican priest, Rev. Charles Ffrench, was sent here to build a church, which was dedicated in 1830 as St. Aloysius Church. For many years thereafter, the Dover church served Catholics from southern Maine to northern Massachusetts. The neighborhood around Chestnut Street was known locally as "Dublin" because of its large Irish population. It was on the current site of the church that St. Aloysius was located, but in 1870, the wood church was moved to the back of the lot and a new brick addition to the front was begun, spurred on by the efforts of Father James Drummond. However, a fire on Halloween destroyed the wood church and the new construction just after it was roofed, so a new church had to be constructed from the ground up. This was completed and dedicated as St. Mary's in 1872. The imposing brick church is a Gothic Revival one, distinguished by its triple-arched entryways and the rosette window above the central doorway. The central tower is distinguished by the alcove above the rosette window which houses a statue of Mary, and the arched louvers of the bell tower above. Originally, the tower was taller, being capped off with a pyramidal roof surrounded by four Gothic spires, but this was removed during renovations in 1947, as were spires at the corner of the façade.

St. Thomas Episcopal Church
Built: 1891–92
Architect: Henry Vaughan
Location: 5 Hale Street

The Church of St. Thomas was formally organized in Dover in 1839 after the first services conducted in town by Rev. Thomas Lambert. Their first church was a wooden Gothic Revival structure built on the land now occupied by the City Hall, the property also including the historic Hale House, an impressive mansion built by the well-known regional architect and builder Bradbury Johnson. This land was taken by the city by eminent domain in the late 1880s, with the old Episcopal Church being torn down in 1891 and the Hale House moved to its present site on Hale Street. The church found a new home very close by, purchasing the current lot on Hale Street and hiring famed architect Henry Vaughan to design their new church in the Gothic Revival style. Construction began in 1901 and religious services were first held in September 1902, though the church, on the National Historic Register since 1984, was not formally consecrated until 1916. Some of the stones in the wall of the church were donated from far and wide, including many local parishioners, while much of the green-tinged granite came from a quarry in neighboring Durham.

St. Thomas Episcopal Church, Dover.

Built in the style of English Perpendicular churches that was favored by Vaughan, the rectangular structure is distinguished by its buttress-supported tower with battlements at the top and the adjacent circular turret tower which is 70 feet tall. Vaughan, known for his Episcopalian church architecture, had gained much fame for his Chapel of St. Peter and St. Paul built in Concord beginning in 1886, so his choice for St. Thomas is not surprising. The price for this church was a modest $26,000, about a quarter of the cost of Vaughan's church in Concord. This church is amongst a group of seven stone churches designed with similar features by Vaughan from 1890–1913, one of which, the proposed St. Martin's in New Bedford, MA, was a mirror image of St. Thomas, but was never built. St. Thomas Church today is little changed from its original appearance with the exception of the addition of memorial stained-glass windows to replace some of the original diamond-glass panes.

St. Joseph Roman Catholic Church
Built: 1946–48
Architect: James O'Shaughnessy
Location: 150 Central Avenue

Another distinctive feature on the Dover skyline, this mid-century stone church sits on land once owned by Quakers Stephen and Lydia Hanson. After their deaths by 1849, there were several owners, as well as millinery shop located here. With the overall growth of the city of Dover and its large number of Catholics, the need for a church in the southern part of the city became very apparent. The house on the site had been rented to local women in its last ten years before the site was donated to the church for the building of St. Joseph. Construction began in May 1946, with the church being formally dedicated in October 1948. Its architect was active in building churches in New Hampshire, also responsible for the unusual St. Paul Church in Franklin and another St. Joseph church in Laconia (see below). This St. Joseph is notable as a beautiful example of a Stripped Classicism-type structure, a form that became popular in the early twentieth century, though by the time this church was built, it had largely fallen out of favor. Buildings of this style are known for employing classical building elements, such as columns or a prominent pediment, but are stripped bare of most traditional decorative details. Too, such buildings were built of stone, and usually on a monumental scale, most of them being government buildings, many built in America in the 1930s by the Works Progress Administration (WPA). Unfortunately, this building style was also popular worldwide with notorious totalitarian dictators like Hitler and Stalin, so fell out of favor after World War II in America. However, the style as it is used in this church is both pleasing and imposing at the same time, the church distinguished by its six-stage set-back steeple and its massive portico with a steep pediment, beautifully decorated in relief, supported by massive square columns.

St. Joseph Roman Catholic Church, Laconia.

Dublin

Dublin Community Church, United Church of Christ
Built: 1852
Location: 1125 Main Street

Located in the Dublin Historic Village District, this church is also important as marking the final break between the church and town that had existed from its founding and incorporation in 1771. The prior structure built on this site was the town's second meetinghouse, erected in 1818 and once part of the Templeton Run of meetinghouse directly inspired by Massachusetts builder Elias Carter. Interestingly, this site on a hill was opposed by the town's second settled minister, Rev. Edward Sprague, "on account of its bleak position. He is reported to have said that he never would preach in a house placed there."[28] In fact, his words were prophetic; thrown from his carriage in December 1817, he died a week later, the meetinghouse subsequently erected afterwards in 1818. This fine meetinghouse, however, had a relatively short life and must not have been well cared for, as by 1847, it was in disrepair and discussions were made as to its fate. That year, the town sold the meetinghouse at auction to a local citizen, who in turn sold it to the First Congregational Society for exactly what he had paid for it, the meetinghouse, some twenty-eight years after the passage of the Toleration Act, passing into private hands. Debate about how to proceed took several years, but by 1852, the definite decision to take down the old meetinghouse was finally made, with this new

Dublin Community Church.

church built in its place that same year, subsequently dedicated in March 1853. Though a privately-owned structure, this church, which is the focal point of the historic district, was still the site of town meetings until 1882. A pleasing example of a Greek Revival rural church, its most notable feature is its façade, with a recessed entryway and two splendid Composite Order columns and the twin-entryways with sidelights and transom windows. The three-stage steeple is less elaborate than its Templeton-inspired predecessor, possibly because of the location's high and windy summit, which made maintenance and repairs difficult. The original tower in the clock was placed about 1894–95, being purchased by subscription from its original owners, the Unitarian Church in Keene, who had torn down their old church in 1894 to build another and had no home for the clock, which, ironically enough, had originally been donated to that church by Dublin native John Elliot. However, at least through the early twentieth century, this clock was notoriously unreliable and did not work well. I have not been able to ascertain whether it was simply repaired, or replaced altogether.

Emmanuel Episcopal Church
Built: 1888
Architects: Robert Andrews and Herbert Jacques
Location: 94 Dublin Road, Dublin School Campus

This charming and diminutive church was originally built as a summer house of worship for visiting Episcopalians who came from Boston to Dublin in the 1880s.

Emmanuel Episcopal Church, Dublin.

This site, now on the built-up campus of the Dublin School, was once heavily wooded on one side, while on the other, the hillside stretched for miles below and offered a pleasing view of the distant hills and valleys. One of the few Shingle-style churches in New Hampshire, it is noted for the shingled siding on its lantern-style turret (which provided excellent ventilation during the summer) and front gable end, as well as for its complex and appealing roof lines. Also notable are the bands of small windows that are located just below the eaves, some of them of the memorial stained-glass variety, including those in the chancel for Elizabeth Crowninshield (died in Dublin in 1885), the wife of noted Union Army Officer Caspar Crowninshield, a member of one of Boston's most prominent families, while others have small diamond panes of glass reminiscent of very early Colonial churches. So notable was this church when it was built that it was featured in both architectural and religious publications of the day, and is considered by one historian "Dublin's most important ecclesiastical structure."[29] Today, the church remains a summer house of worship.

Dunbarton

First Congregational Church of Dunbarton
Built: 1836
Builder: Captain Samuel Kimball
Location: 6 Stark Highway North

The church in this town, founded in 1765, was organized in 1789, its first meetinghouse built that same year by Archibald Stinson and William Tenney. When that structure became the town hall (destroyed by fire in 1908) after the passage of the Toleration Act of 1819, the church built a new building just opposite the town green. Its architectural style is a combination of the Greek and Gothic Revival styles, along with some Federal elements, and is overall a pleasing structure. Most notable are its 20 × 20 sash windows on the façade and its three-stage tower featuring an octagonal domed upper stage with Gothic spires. After its completion, Rev. John Putnam, the town's second minister, states that "During the next ten years this church enjoyed some precious seasons of refreshing from the Lord, though no extensive outpouring of the Spirit has been realized. In 1842 a revival was enjoyed of a limited extent, which brought twelve new members into the church in the course of a year."[30] Such were the ups and downs of many churches throughout the years in New Hampshire.

First Congregational Church of Dunbarton.

St. John the Evangelist Episcopal Church
Built: 1866–69
Location: 270 Stark Highway North

This church is notable for its affiliation with one of New Hampshire's most famous families, the Starks. John Stark was a member of Roberts Rangers during the French and Indian War and a famed officer in the Revolutionary War, known for his fighting qualities and outstanding leadership at the Battle of Bunker Hill and the Battle of Bennington, among many others, rising to the rank of brigadier general, while his son, Caleb Stark, who lived in Dunbarton and was prominent in town affairs, also served as an officer during the war. It was John Stark who coined New Hampshire's famous motto "Live Free or Die" in 1809. This church has origins dating to 1865, when Episcopal services were first conducted at the old Stark schoolhouse in Dunbarton. The following year, John Stark's great-granddaughter, Miss Mary Stark, donated a piece of her own land close to the Caleb Stark mansion in Dunbarton for the building of a private chapel for the family. This church was constructed from 1866–69 by local builders, the church's beautiful Gothic chancel window and organ donated by Rev. Henry Coit, the first rector at the St. Paul's School in nearby Concord. The church was moved to its present location in 1890 by teams of oxen, placed on land donated by David Sargent. Since that time, the church has been open

St. John the Evangelist Episcopal Church, Dunbarton.

to the public, no longer operating as a private chapel. The charming rectangular church is notable for its Gothic pointed windows, trefoil cut-out trim panels along the eaves on its south end and over the main entryway, as well as its wood-shingled cupola housing a bell.

Eaton

The Little White Church (Eaton Center Free Will Baptist Church)
Built: 1879
Builders: Robert, Henry, and Charles Robertson
Location: 2371 Eaton Road (Rte. 153)

This church, located in a scenic rural area near Crystal Lake in Eaton Center, may be the most photographed house of worship in the state of New Hampshire. Though now owned by an association whose membership is open to all and operated as a community church with no affiliation to any one denomination, the church was once the Conway Church, which was organized in 1826 by a Free Will Baptist minister from Conway, and later the Eaton and Conway Church, finally becoming the Third Eaton Free Will Baptist Church after the congregation split in 1834. Still later, it became the Second or Eaton Center Free Will Baptist Church after the town was divided in 1854. Despite these confusing beginnings, the church was strong through the 1850s, but by 1879, its membership had declined steeply. Early meetings were held in private homes, barns, and later Edwin Snow's store, but in 1878, Charles and Emma Robertson offered land for the church next to the town cemetery, with the stipulation that a church be maintained on the property or else the deed would be void. The Robertson family subsequently built the church at an agreed upon price of $1,200, with forty pews sold at $25 apiece to help fund the costs. A bell was purchased in 1904, but it is unclear if the church had a bell prior to this. Despite the fine new church, membership in the church continued to decline, though it always remained a center of community life, as well as providing a place for worship for boys and girls who attended summer camps, and was well maintained. By the end of World War II, with membership in the church down to one individual, the church was subsequently sold by the Free Will Baptists to a local association for just $1, thereby becoming the Community Church of Eaton. Beautifully maintained to this day, The Little White Church still holds regular religious services, but is also a popular wedding venue. The rural church is notable for its steep roof and three-stage steeple, visible from across Crystal Lake, as well its plain but elegant façade, with double-doors in a single entryway, flanked by 4 × 4 sash windows with shutters, the open pediment above containing a single diamond-shaped window.

The Little White Church, Eaton.

Effingham

Effingham Congregational Church (Lord's Hill Meetinghouse)
Built: 1798
Builder: Isaac Lord
Location: Province Lake Road, near junction with Hobbs Road

This meetinghouse owes its existence to its namesake, Isaac Lord, whose tavern stands just across the street and whose mansion sits just a short distance away up on Hobbs Road. Though not an original town founder, Lord was certainly one its most important citizens—it was through his efforts that the meetinghouse was built, and through his efforts that it was sited where it is today, advantageous to him in every regard. Lord arrived in town by the early 1790s, building a toll bridge across the Great Ossipee River in town in 1792, which he maintained until 1820. At this time, he made a deal with the town of Effingham: if they would buy his bridge, the price said to be $750, he would purchase a bell for the meetinghouse. This deal was indeed concluded, the only known bridge for bell swap ever in the state of New Hampshire, resulting in the placement of a 929-lb. bell (as recorded by the manufacturer, though one historian lists it as 1,100 lb.) in the meetinghouse in 1821 that came from the original Paul Revere bell foundry. Lord also served as town treasurer in 1797, as well as several terms as state representative, was a wealthy merchant who built the

Effingham Congregational Church.

first store in town, and just before his death in 1838 owned over 1,100 acres of land in town and possessed large numbers of cattle and sheep. The meetinghouse he built was typical for the times, with a bell tower at one end, but in 1845, it was remodeled in the Greek Revival style, with a simple belfry, the steeple built to its current state in 1898 by George Beal, with the addition of the spire and topped off with a triple-arrow weathervane, likely made by a local metalsmith, nearly identical to those found on two churches in nearby Cornish, Maine. Sited in the beautiful Lord's Hill Historic District, the church is distinguished by its large 25 × 20 sash windows and overall fine proportions. Services are no longer held here regularly and, in fact, the Congregational church in Effingham was never a strong one, being organized about 1800 by Rev. Samuel Hidden of Tamworth and extinct by the 1830s. Though reorganized in 1836, the church remained small into the twentieth century, with no regular preaching, the Congregationalists often uniting with the Free Will Baptists in their services.

Center Effingham Baptist Church
Built: 1844
Location: 1027 Route 153 (Drake's Corner)

The area of Effingham known as Drake's Corner, originally vied with Lord's Hill for the building of the first meetinghouse in town. Though it lost that battle, the church built at Drake's Corner would soon prove to be the primary house of worship in Effingham as the Baptist faith seemed to hold more appeal than that of the Congregationalists and has always had regular preaching. The area where this church was built is named after one of Effingham's founding families, with Weare Drake being a town leader early on. The Calvinist Baptist Church was founded in Effingham in 1807 by two ministers from Maine, among its members were many from the Drake family. Meetings were held in private homes or the Lord's Hill Meetinghouse early on, but in 1822, the Baptists built their own church on this site, likely a simple Type II meetinghouse. This church was subsequently torn down in 1844 and a new church built on the same site according to most historical accounts, though this is disputed by Effingham town historian Eric Potter, who believes that the original meetinghouse was simply rebuilt into its new form, with the original frame still used. Pictures of the church prior to 1880, while not definitive, lend credence to this assertion. Whatever the case may be, the church was rebuilt in the Gothic Revival style in 1844, given a two-stage square steeple topped off with towering pinnacles at each corner. When remodeled into its present form in 1880, the roof-mounted steeple was removed and a bell tower added to the façade, replacing its double entryways with a single entrance. It is also during this remodel that all of the windows were likely replaced with 2 × 2 × 2 triple sash windows. While the details of its building are lacking, it remains a nice example of a rural New Hampshire church. The site is also notable for its adjacent cemetery, which was established at least as early as 1791, over three decades before the first church was built here, and is one of the oldest in town.

Center Effingham Baptist Church.

Epsom

Epsom Baptist Church (former Free Will Baptist Church)
Built: 1861
Builder: James B. Stanton
Location: 1606 Dover Road

Originally built as a Free Will Baptist Church, this building was their second in Epsom, the original having been built in 1833, seven years after the church was organized. The pastor at the time of its building, which cost $2,200, in 1861 was Rev. Moses Quimby, who preached in town during four separate tenures at the church. Part of the inspiration for the building of this larger church was the fact that, in April 1861, the church experienced a season of revival and added more members. The master builder, also a Free Will Baptist, was James Stanton of West Lebanon, Maine, who was noted for his work and management in the building process. The new church was ready for use and dedicated in December 1861. It is interesting that the old church on the site where this was originally constructed was sold and moved, later altered to become the town post office. However, the move did not go so well; hauled by teams of oxen, the structure became stuck and tilted sharply to one side, and remained that way when worshippers used it the following Sunday, some becoming seasick. Luckily, when the current church was moved to its present location by tractor-trailer truck in February 2007, no such problems occurred. The church served the community for many years before declining membership forced its closure. When the land on which it stood, at the junction of Black Hall Road and Rte. 4, was acquired by a national convenience store chain and the building threatened with demolition, the town of Epsom accepted the building and moved it to the present town complex site. However, as of this writing, nearly eleven years later, the fate of the old church remains in limbo. The original hope was that it could be converted to town offices, but the monetary outlay was too great and was not approved by taxpayers. Serious upgrades in its electrical system would be required, as well as updated plumbing, and generally the building still requires much interior work. The church is an eclectic mix of elements. The façade features a vestibule with quoining on its corner, an Italianate-style feature, with an entryway on each side, the pediments of the vestibule and the roof above offering a Greek Revival temple-like view, while the rickrack trim on the top edge of the belfry is a delightful Victorian touch.

Former Epsom Baptist Church.

Exeter

The Congregational Church, United Church of Christ (The First Church)
Built: 1798–1800
Builders: Ebenezer Clifford and Bradbury Johnson
Location: 21 Front Street

Regarded as one of the most historically significant meetinghouses ever to be built in New Hampshire, this large church is an architectural gem. The church it serves was formed in 1638 by Rev. John Wheelwright, an Englishman who was a schoolmate and friend of Oliver Cromwell. After his arrival in Massachusetts in 1636, he was soon banished by the Puritans, along with his sister-in-law, Anne Hutchinson, due to differences in doctrine. Wheelwright travelled north with his followers, founding the town of Exeter in 1638 and forming the first church there. This meetinghouse is the fifth for the church and its building took nearly three years to complete and cost £10,000, the equivalent of about $1 million in today's currency. The result was a truly masterful structure unlike any meetinghouse of its time, distinguished by a number of features; its hipped roof design was a throwback to the first meetinghouses built in New England, while the fact that its entryways were only located on one side of the structure, as opposed to the typical meetinghouses with entrances on three sides, signified the coming change in function from meetinghouse to church. A Federal-style structure, the meetinghouse is also notable for its elaborate façade highlighted by a two-story pavilion with triple entryways below and compass-headed windows above, each framed with keystone trim and Doric pilasters. Equally impressive, and imposing, is the three-stage tower above the pavilion, with an octagonal open belfry and an octagonal lantern, topped off with a harvest-themed weathervane directly inspired by plans in Asher Benjamin's *Country Builder's Assistant* (Plate 33), a work very likely owned by the builders of this meetinghouse. A hand-wound clock was placed in the tower in 1848, but was replaced by an electric clock in 1956. As to coloring, the meetinghouse is thought to have been unpainted, except around the windows, but was painted white in the 1830s. However, the color was changed to tan sometime thereafter, and it remained that color for many years before being painted white again in 1940. This meetinghouse is not just noted for its architectural form, but also for those who have entered the building over the years; the famed orator and lawyer Daniel Webster litigated a case here in the 1830s when the building was still used for civic and town functions, and was present for a fiftieth anniversary gathering for the founding of Phillip's Exeter Academy, while Abraham Lincoln attended services here, the pew that he used one of the church's prized artifacts, when visiting his son, Robert

The Congregational Church, Exeter.

Façade detail, The Congregational Church, Exeter.

Todd Lincoln, who attended Phillip's Exeter Academy. Finally, this meetinghouse is also part of Exeter's Front Street Historic District, with many fine late eighteenth- and early nineteenth-century homes in the immediate vicinity, while the remnants of the meetinghouse cemetery, which was deliberately paved over as Front Street was expanded in the early 1900s, can be seen close to the right side of church. Its most notable stone is that for the Rev. Ward Clark of Kingston, the son of Exeter's Rev John Clark, who died as a result of the Great Throat Distemper epidemic that began in 1735 and ravaged New Hampshire's seacoast towns for three years.

Fitzwilliam

Third Fitzwilliam Meetinghouse
Built: 1817
Builder: Samuel Kendall
Location: 13 Templeton Turnpike, on the Village Green

The historic meetinghouse in this town was born out of the ashes of its predecessor, being the second meetinghouse built in Fitzwilliam in less than thirteen months.

The second Fitzwilliam Meetinghouse, as previously discussed, was built on this site in 1816, but within months, it burned down after being hit by lightning during a violent storm in January 1817. Very soon thereafter, the town set about to build its replacement, laying the cornerstone in May 1817 and dedicating it for use in November of that same year. The two structures are said to have been nearly identical in form, except that the current meetinghouse is 20 feet longer. The building of two such important and sizeable structures in 1816–17 is all the more remarkable, considering that 1816 was known as "The Year Without a Summer," when temperatures dropped below 40 degrees during July and August and frost or snow was experienced every month of the year, adversely affecting crops and the fall harvest, resulting in higher prices that and the following year for most farm produce and food items. Despite the tough economic climate, Fitzwilliam seems to have weathered the storm. Beginning in 1827, the meetinghouse weathered storms of a different type when disputes arose over matters of doctrine between Congregationalists and Unitarians. The minister, Rev. John Sabin, and his followers formed an Orthodox Society, while those with more liberal views formed their own society. Rev. Sabin refused this society use of the meetinghouse, though at the annual town meeting in March 1831, selectman allowed the liberal society eight Sundays a year for services, and the Baptists two, the remainder going to the Orthodox Society. Not content with this arrangement, the Orthodox Society, under Rev. Sabin, built their own church in 1832, while the Baptist Society built their own in 1841. After this time, the Third Fitzwilliam Meetinghouse reverted to town use, though the Unitarian Society paid rent to use the meetinghouse for their services and did so for many years until about 1860, when religious services in the townhouse ended. The 1816-built meetinghouse had a Revere bell, and so too did its replacement, which shipped from the Revere foundry in the fall of 1817. This bell cracked in 1881 and had to be recast, the work done by William Blake & Co., tradition holding that 300 silver dollars were used in the forging of the new bell to enhance its tone. The clock in the steeple was installed in 1861, purchased by subscription funds from the E. Howard Clock Company. The meetinghouse, as previously mentioned, is part of the Templeton run of meetinghouses inspired by the work of Massachusetts builder Elias Carter, and though the interior has changed as the structure's use has evolved, the outside of the building remains much the same as it did in 1817. The towering steeple, distinguished by the open belfry stage decorated with Federal details and Gothic points on the corner and the lantern stage above, is eye-catching and visible for some distance. The town debated removing some of its upper stages during the time interior renovations were made in the 1860s, but this was never done, though, as of this writing, the steeple requires some restoration work. The façade of the meetinghouse is notable for its elegant columns, the Palladian window above the center entryway, as well as the fine pediment with an oval window surrounded by floral and decorative elements that is the hallmark of all the Templeton Run meetinghouses in New Hampshire.

Third Fitzwilliam Meetinghouse.

Francestown

Francestown Meetinghouse
Built: 1801–03
Builders: Isaac and William Patch (1834)
Location: 1 New Boston Road (Rte. 136)

Originally known as New Boston Addition, Francestown was not incorporated until 1772 and built its first meetinghouse in June 1775, just as the Revolutionary War began; as a result, it would take many years to finish. By 1796, it was decided to build a new meetinghouse, which was eventually done on essentially the same site, building it 6 feet further south. The Congregational church in Francestown was first organized in 1773, but had no settled minister until Rev. Moses Bradford arrived here in 1790, his tenure lasting for nearly forty years. The builder of the 1801 meetinghouse is unknown, but the structure is described as having two towers, one at each end, and cost $5,274. The first town meeting here was held in March 1803, while the following month, the old meetinghouse that stood next to it was taken down, with the timber sold and used to build a barn elsewhere in town. The current meetinghouse dates from 1834, when the structure was turned and totally rebuilt in its present Greek Revival style by Isaac and William Patch at a cost of $4,952, though the current three-stage steeple was constructed in 1855 when a new bell was installed to replace the 1808 original, with the town clock added in 1912. The meetinghouse is distinguished today by its three-bayed façade that features triple entryways with transom windows, stately pilasters on the corners and flanking the central doorway, as well as the dentils used to decorate the fine pediment. Further, the meetinghouse is located at a prominent junction between Rte. 136 and Main Street, which used to be part of the Second New Hampshire Turnpike, near the center of town, and across the street from the Town Common Historic District. This district includes the 1847-built Francestown Town Hall and Academy building, which succeeded the meetinghouse as a home for the town's civic functions. Directly adjacent to the meetinghouse is the historic town burial ground, the oldest cemetery in town, which contains gravestones that predate the meetinghouse by many decades. The Francestown Meetinghouse passed from town ownership to the Independent Congregational Church after a New Hampshire Supreme Court decision in 1884 and was subsequently repaired at a cost of $2,800. It later became the Unitarian Church and remained owned by them until 1987, when the meetinghouse was sold for $1 to a local group formed to preserve the structure. Today, it is the site of many cultural and social events in town, including weddings, religious services, lectures, and concerts.

Francestown Meetinghouse.

Fremont

Fremont Meetinghouse (Poplin Meetinghouse)
Built: 1800
Location: 464 Main Street

This five-bay meetinghouse is notable for both its form and unusual degree of preservation and, along with the meetinghouses in nearby Danville and Sandown, is part of a group of related historic rural meetinghouses in southeastern New Hampshire. Originally part of Brentwood, the town was incorporated as Poplin in 1764, its name subsequently changed to Fremont in 1854. Despite the fact that its separation came about because of settler's complaints about the distance they had to travel to attend meetings, the town of Poplin is unusual in that it never had a settled minister, nor did it build a meetinghouse until thirty-six years after the town was incorporated. While a meetinghouse frame had been erected on Sand Hill (now Main Street) in 1764, it was never finished and was subsequently torn down in 1768. When a new meetinghouse was finally approved in 1800, it was voted that it resemble the Baptist meetinghouse in Brentwood, and that the Baptists in Poplin would complete and furnish the meetinghouse without any expense to the town.[31] As was typical, the meetinghouse was used for both civic and religious services, these later performed by itinerant ministers of the Baptist (likely Calvinistic), Congregational, Free Will Baptist, Methodist, and Unitarian denominations, with the Methodists probably the most successful, if that term can be used to describe a town in which, as one historian commented in the 1850s, "some evangelical influence seems very desirable to be brought into vigorous action for the moral and religious improvement of the people."[32] That the people of the town were hardworking and industrious farmers is without question, but it is also likely that they were somewhat independent-minded when it came to religious matters—the Fremont Meetinghouse may be the only one in the state from which licensed tavern keepers were allowed by the town to sell liquor or "intoxicating beverages" from the side porches of the meetinghouse during the annual Muster Day festivities, a practice that ended in 1853.[33] In 1857, a traveler wrote to the *Exeter Newsletter* that "the meeting (church services) at the old meetinghouse is not very fully attended. The house is large reminding one of Noah's Ark."[34] The meetinghouse continued in regular use up to 1912, when it was abandoned and used to store lumber and farm equipment. It returned to use in 1922 when it was refurbished and used for Old Home Day services, an annual event that continues to be held to this day. Architecturally, though this meetinghouse does not attract the same attention that older examples in neighboring towns garnish, it is no less important and equally worthy of attention. The Fremont Meetinghouse, a late but typical example of a Type II meetinghouse, is significant as the only structure of its type remaining in New Hampshire with its twin porches intact, and one of only two such survivors of its kind in all of New England. The meetinghouse

Fremont Meetinghouse.

largely resembles its original form except for several details; the structure was likely unpainted early on, its first documented painting dating to 1841, while in that same year, the building was re-clapboarded and given new doorway trim and window casings, which detailing, while quite plain, is more in keeping with the Greek Revival style then prevailing. At the rear of the meetinghouse may be seen the elevated pulpit window, which had been removed during repairs in 1881, but was restored in 1992–93 during a renovation project that also restored the entire interior, including the box pews. The site of this meetinghouse also offers some historical features of interest, including a hearse house, built in 1849, and a town pound that is a replica of that which stood at this same site from 1802–1820, likely removed due to the smells generated by the animals penned in there, as well as the Village Cemetery across the street.

Gilford

Union Meetinghouse (The Universalist Church)
Built: 1834
Location: 24 Belknap Mountain Road

Located in a historic village area, this church was built by the Universalist Society, but was only used by them for a short time. Nothing is known of the builder or any further early details about the church and its organization. For some period of time, the church was unoccupied, but in 1874, it was bought by the Methodist

Society and used by them until about 1922, after which time it was shared by them with the Free Will Baptists for several years until it was again abandoned. In 1941, it was twice sold to private individuals, and services resumed again for a short time. In 1943, the building was sold to George Ames, who subsequently donated the structure to the Gilford Historical Society, on the condition that the society be renamed in his father's name. Since 1943, the church has been the meeting place and museum for the Thompson Ames Historical Society. While under Methodist control, the church was extensively renovated inside and out in 1889, getting a bell and the 25-foot pyramidal spire, as well as new doors and stained-glass windows. It was probably also at this time that the meetinghouse was painted beige, with red trim, though it is now painted white. The interior of the church was remodeled at the time in a distinctive Carpenter Gothic style, notable for its barrel-vaulted ceiling and wood-trimmed alcove (where the choir loft once was) at the front and the wooden panel design on the opposite wall behind where the pulpit was once located. This meetinghouse's exterior is interesting for its blend of subtle Gothic Revival styling, as evidenced by its belfry and spire, as well a touch of the Greek Revival, as seen in the façade's corner pilasters. The first stage of the tower, too, is notable for its decorative Gothic point trim-work, which forms a triangle at its center and is a quite unusual touch added by a rural carpenter.

Union Meeting House, Gilford.

First United Methodist Church of Gilford-Laconia
Built: 1968–69
Architect: Daniel Tully
Builder: Robert Caron, Manchester, NH
Location: 18 Wesley Way

This space-age structure was dedicated for service in October 1969, just three months after the Apollo 11 moon landing. Today, over fifty years after its building, it is still an eye-catching structure and one of the most unusual of the modern churches built in New Hampshire in the last half of the twentieth century. The designer of this church building, Daniel Tully, was an architect and engineer who pioneered the use of "hyperbolic paraboloid concrete shells" in buildings in New Hampshire and elsewhere in New England, which were both "an economical way to achieve large spans for … public structures, but was also embraced as a unique means of architectural expression."[35] Tully, who virtually cornered the market for this type of structure in New Hampshire in the 1960s and 1970s, built many structures of this type during his career and was especially known for using such designs in a number of college athletic buildings and facilities throughout the region. The structure and shape of the roof offers not only large and open spaces within, but also a pleasing exterior perspective that varies depending upon the angle from which it is viewed. The view of the façade from the main entryway shows a pyramid form that is cathedral-esque in its modernity, while the side views show the true size, beauty, and scope of its sweeping form, representative of a modern sculpture, a futuristic jet airplane or spaceship, or whatever else one might care to imagine.

First United Methodist Church of Gilford-Laconia, Gilford.

Gilmanton

Centre Congregational Church
Built: 1826–27
Location: 503 Province Road

This town from its earliest beginnings had several widely spaced areas of settlement, including Gilmanton Ironworks to the east, lower Gilmanton to the south, upper Gilmanton (later Belmont) to the north, as well as Center Gilmanton. The first meetinghouse was built near the geographic center of town beginning in 1774 (not completed until 1790) in an area that remained quite rural, and was no longer used for town meetings by 1797, these being held at the Gilmanton Academy building beginning that same year. By the mid-1820s, worshippers in Gilmanton's several areas desired houses of worship of their own, with the result that, in 1826–27, two new churches were built in town, this one in this growing center of town activity, and another at the Ironworks. Nothing is known of the builder of this structure nor any of its construction details, except for the fact that it cost $3,500. The resulting church has been called by one historian "the finest Federal style church in the county, unrivalled in its state of preservation and architectural quality."[36] This is not surprising, because its early members included some of the most notable men of the day in Gilmanton, including a future New Hampshire governor, William Badger, most of whom were involved with the prestigious Gilmanton Academy. This private school was established in the center in 1797, but there was no dedicated place where religious services could be held for both its students and the population in the growing village center that surrounded the school. The chosen site for the church is adjacent to the academy building, which now serves as town offices, and after its completion the school, which in the 1830s also became a theological seminary, had pews reserved for its student body. The exterior of the building is largely unchanged, with the exception of a basement addition in 1984. Most notable is its façade, with a center entryway with double-doors flanked by a pair of slender columns and compass-headed windows, while above the doorway is a rectangular recessed area with a decorative swag giving the date of the building's construction. The side of the four-bayed church is distinguished by its 20 × 20 compass-headed sash windows trimmed with keystone molding. Overall, it is a beautiful building that readily coveys the prominence and wealth of the community it served.

First Baptist Church (Lower Gilmanton Church)
Built: 1842
Builder: Silvester French
Location: Province Road (Rte. 107) near junction with Stage Road

This denomination was formed in Lower Gilmanton in 1773 and built their meetinghouse the following year. It was subsequently moved to this site in 1788.

Above left: Centre Congregational Church, Gilmanton.

Above right: First Baptist Church, Gilmanton.

After a division within the church, the sect had its ups and downs, but maintained ownership of the building and continued services there. However, by 1841, it was in such poor condition that debates within the church were held as to either repairing the old structure or building a new church, the latter option being chosen by its members. When it came to the new church that was to be built, it was voted to build a new church, on the recommendation of the building committee, based largely on the building erected the year before in Northwood (see below), one of the finest Greek Revival structures in the state. This was done in early 1842, with committee member Silvester French chosen to superintend the framing on the church, with the stipulation that each shareholder in the church was required to provide two men to help in the building efforts. The building was completed by the fall of that same year at a cost of about $1,500, with money raised from pew sales used to finish the structure. The finished church, while not as elegant as the church it copied, is nonetheless one of the finest Greek Revival churches in Belknap County, its tower very close to that in Northwood and distinguished by the pedimented gables on its upper stage. The façade is distinguished by its twin entryways with small 7 × 7 sash windows above and a central 20 × 20 sash window flanked by pilasters. Each of the windows and doors are framed by molding featuring blocks on the upper corners. The property is also notable for the original horse-sheds that are still in existence, rare survivals in this part of New Hampshire.

Gorham

Gorham Congregational Church
Built: 1861–62
Builder: Valentine Styles
Location: 143 Main Street

The Congregationalists in this North Country town, formerly known as Shelburne Addition until its incorporation in 1836, gained their church under very unusual circumstances. No Congregational preaching was even conducted here until 1856, and that by a minister of the New Hampshire Missionary Society. Three years later, Oxford, Maine, native Rev. George Tewksbury arrived here as a missionary, at first holding services in the village school and then in Ingalls Hall, a public building erected by noted local builder Valentine Styles. Services were held here for several years, but the Congregationalists first entertained the idea of having their own church when Styles offered to build one at his own expense. This is not surprising, as Styles, who arrived here from Shelburne about 1854, was important to the growing town, laying out Exchange Street for the town and building several commercial buildings, a boarding house, as well as private homes on Mechanic and Church streets. Styles approached Rev. Tewksbury, proposing to build a church on speculation, he retaining ownership of the building until the Congregationalists could raise $600 to help pay for it, though he would bear the rest of the building's $3,350 cost. This agreement was concluded, with the result that in just over a year after it was built, the Congregationalists raised the needed funds to take ownership and proceeded to finish the building in 1862. A bell was purchased and the pews were furnished at a cost of $350, this money raised by the Ladies' Society in Gorham, a group founded by the first minister's wife, Sarah Tewksbury. The speculative arrangement with Styles to build the church was a highly unusual one, the method seldom used elsewhere in New Hampshire. Rev. Tewksbury continued here until his resignation in 1865, but at the town's urging, returned here in 1869 to preach until 1876. The church built by Styles is a pleasing one that has stood the test of time. Its three-stage tower is notable for its open, octagonal belfry that features Italianate-style brackets, the whole topped off with a distinctive scallop-tailed weathervane that was probably crafted by a local blacksmith. The church's façade features an open pediment with Italianate brackets and distinctive circular window, as well as twin entryways with a large circular-headed stained-glass window in between.

Gorham Congregational Church.

Goshen

Goshen Community Church (formerly Goshen Baptist Church)
Built: 1851
Architect: Rev. Eleazar Farr
Builders: Lovell Baker and Daniel Stearns
Location: 34 Brook Road (Route 10)

One of the most interesting of the rural churches in New Hampshire, the Goshen Community Church was originally a Baptist Church built under the influence of its pastor, Rev. Eleazar Farr, a native of Marlow, NH. Farr had studied theology at Brown University, as well as the New Hampton Institute, and had previously worked as a city missionary in Lowell, Massachusetts, and was preaching in Unity when he received a call to come to Goshen. His wife, Charity Tandy Farr, was a native of Goshen, and her aunt offered some financial inducement for Rev. Farr to come to Goshen, so the offer was accepted in 1850. Farr would immediately proceed to the building of a church in the growing village area, as Baptist services had first been held in private homes when the church was formed in 1803, and since 1816 were alternately held in the town meetinghouse or a local schoolhouse. As previously recounted, some doubted he could get the church built, but others were sure he would follow through on his efforts, one of the Marlow men hired to finish the meetinghouse once it was built, John Quincy Jones, stating that "I have known Eleazar Farr ever since he was a boy, and he will do as he agrees."[37] In fact, Farr did get the church built, with the frame being up by August 1851, the spruce timber coming from Lovell Baker's property and finished into lumber at the nearby Chandler sawmill, while the stone for the foundation came from the side of Page Hill, gotten out by Hyland Dodge. Farr supervised all this work on the framing and the steeple and did much of the delicate interior finishing and was responsible for the painting of the church, while the Marlow builders Jones and his partner, Daniel Buss, did much of the finish work. The result was a beautiful church, built at a final cost of $1,095, four-bays on the front, combining elements of Gothic and Greek Revival styling, its most impressive feature being the Gothic arch window treatment and door panels (details almost certainly executed or influenced by Farr), as well as the steep pediment with decorative circular louvered woodwork surrounding a star at center. The original bell in the belfry was cast by Blake & Richardson in Boston and is said to have a letter "F" engraved on it in honor of Eleazar Farr. The good reverend would continue in Goshen until accepting a call to preach in New Jersey in 1858. A short time later, the Baptists would join with the Congregationalists, an arrangement that held until 1878, when it became a Baptist church again, which arrangement continued well into modern times. The church had its first female pastor, Rev. Miss Ethel Lombard, in 1924, she being known for her musical ability and "her strong personality ... assets of unquestioned value."[38] Today, the church built by Eleazar Farr remains a vital institution in the religious and social life of Goshen.

Goshen Community Church.

Grafton

Grafton Center Meetinghouse (former Congregational Church)
Built: 1796–97
Location: 860 Main Street (U.S. Route 4)

Battered and bruised by time and neglect, and burned by fire, this former meetinghouse is, as of this writing, the most endangered in New Hampshire. If efforts are not undertaken for its renovation, the church will soon be but a memory. Located on the Grafton town common, the meetinghouse was built by the town and was open for all denominations to share, later called a "union" meetinghouse after the passage of the Toleration Act of 1819, as no one group—Baptists, Congregationalists, and Methodists—had the funds to build their own building. The first meeting was held here in June 1797, the cost of the building financed by pew sales to fifteen families, payment being made in cash, lumber, grain, and stock over two years. As originally built, this large structure had no steeple and was a Type II meetinghouse, and remained a shared structure, used by both town and church for many years, though questions about who would pay for its maintenance were a common source of contention. In 1856, the town voted to divide the structure, the upper-story gallery being fully floored over to create a second-floor sanctuary for the church, with town offices on the ground floor. It was also at this time that the three-stage steeple was added to the structure to give it its current form. This arrangement between church and state prevailed until 1963, when the town abandoned the meetinghouse for newer offices in the former East Grafton School. The Congregational Church took over the entire structure and had pews added to create a ground level sanctuary, which was known for its chestnut trim. Though a church organization was first formed here in 1800, with Rev. Oliver Williams as first pastor, the church has never been a strong one here over the years in terms of numbers, despite the large size of the structure, which could originally seat 300 people. In 1856, it was reported that there was no church in town using the building, while in 1886, a church with but twenty-five members existed, with them sharing a pastor with the Union Church in East Grafton. The meetinghouse served as a Congregationalist church for most of the twentieth century and remained so until it was sold in 2010 to John Connell, a private citizen, formerly of Salem, Massachusetts. At this same time, the town common was purchased by the town (having once been church property), while the old parsonage was sold as a private residence. Connell moved here as part of the controversial Free State Project and felt called to buy the old meetinghouse, not only residing there, but also forming the Peaceful Assembly Church, though he had no prior background as a minister and did not call himself one. He was soon enough embroiled with the town in a legal dispute about tax payments because his church had no affiliation with a recognized denomination. It was during this period that the character of the meetinghouse and surroundings changed for the worse. Already in disrepair, the church's entryway was painted a garish purple color, while the property around the church accumulated a large amount of household items and debris, the unsightly spot right in the center of town angering many residents. When the church caught fire and was partially burned on January 12, 2016, Connell tragically lost his life in the blaze, and the legal dispute remained unresolved. Eventually, in 2017, the town agreed to abate the large tax bill if the church would meet deadlines in repairing the fire damage by December of that same year. Despite the initial excitement over its restoration, including its placement on the New Hampshire Preservation Alliance's Seven to Save List for 2017, this work was never fully completed, and a tarp remains in place to cover portions of the burnt-out building. The status and timetable for any repairs to this structure, if there is one, remains uncertain as of this writing, and today the meetinghouse and surrounding property remain in a sad state of disrepair and neglect, the building now in receivership status, in the custody of the state of New Hampshire. Despite the depressing scene, the impressive nature of the original meetinghouse can be still be gleaned through all the exterior damage. While severely altered by circumstances both planned and unforeseen, it is a structure worthy of being saved given its prominent location and lengthy history. Whether the resources, probably in the millions of dollars range, can be mustered to achieve this goal is doubted by many in town.

Grafton Center Meetinghouse.

Greenland

Greenland Community Congregational Church
Built: 1756
Location: 4 Church Lane, junction Post Road (Rte. 151) and Portsmouth Avenue

The Congregational church that stands at this location today is vastly different than when it was originally built, having undergone several extensive remodels over more than 250 years. Once the South Parish of Portsmouth, the town of Greenland was formed, with Congregationalism as the standing order, in 1721. The first meetinghouse had been built in 1706, but by the mid-1700s, the structure was an old one in need of repair. Town legend also considered the meetinghouse to be jinxed, as in its earliest days two men were killed outside its doors during an Indian raid, while in the 1750s, a woman named Sarah Fox fell through the floor in the steeple, but survived her fall. Whatever the case may have been, it was time for a new meetinghouse. The new meetinghouse was built during the last years of the ministry of Rev. William Allen, the town's first settled minister, and during the time when his eventual successor, Rev. Samuel McClintock was hired as an associate pastor, helping Rev. Allen in his duties before becoming town minister after Allen's death in 1760. As originally constructed, seen today only in the main block of the church building, the meetinghouse was of the typical Type II design, with a bell tower added in 1801. However, during the 1800s, it would be extensively remodeled to give it an entirely new look. The first remodel took place in 1834 during the ministry of Rev. Samuel Clark, a graduate of Dartmouth whose initial salary in 1829 was $450 yearly, as well as a supply of 20 cords of pine wood. Though uncertain, the church's unusually large 30 × 30 sash windows may have been installed at this time. Nearly fifty years later, a second major remodel took place in 1881 during the ministry of Rev. Edward Robie. During this time, the church was remodeled in a late Victorian-era style, given a new steeple featuring a tall, shingled spire, topped off with a lyre and tulip styled weathervane, symbols of Christian joy and charity. The church also gained its elaborate and finely decorated Greek Revival portico during this remodel. Rev. Robie was a native of Gorham, Maine, and graduate of Bowdoin College, after which he studied at Phillip's Andover Seminary and overseas in Germany before returning to teach Hebrew at Phillips before his call to Greenland. He was ordained here in 1852 and ministered to the town for sixty-five years, thought to be a record in the United States at the time of his death in 1917 due to a fall at the age of ninety-six. Robie was beloved in town, but early on rankled some with his abolitionist preaching, some members in 1863 resolving "That our minister be requested to let the negro and politics alone in the pulpit" and "That we are entirely opposed to negro equality."[39] The love and respect the people in Greenland had for Robie is unquestioned; one anecdote states that while he was teaching a girl's Sunday school class, he asked the question of his pupils whether there ever was a perfect man. While he expected a negative answer from the girls, they replied with an emphatic "Yes—Dr. Robie."

Greenland Community Congregational Church.

Hampstead

Hampstead Meetinghouse
Built: 1749
Location: 20 Emerson Avenue

This border town was once part of Amesbury and Haverhill in Massachusetts and known as Timberlane Parish due to the many trees in the area. Once the long-standing border dispute between New Hampshire and Massachusetts was solved in 1740, the town was incorporated in 1749 under its present name. Even before its incorporation, the parish had begun procuring timber for a meetinghouse, and by January 1749, a foundation had been laid. The central site for the meetinghouse was chosen on a high eminence of land owned by Capt. George Little, he deeding the land in return for always having a place for a pew in the meetinghouse. While the frame of the meetinghouse was erected in 1749, the exterior was not fully clapboarded, though meetings were held within until 1752, and the interior was not fully completed until 1768. Up to 1792, the Hampstead Meetinghouse, the second oldest meetinghouse in the state, was a typical Type II meetinghouse, in the same class as those younger survivors in Danville, Fremont, and Sandown. However, by this time, the building was in need of repair and painting, and a 98-foot-tall bell tower was also added to the structure, built by Col. Thomas Reed and Abner Rogers, each of whom received as partial payment for the work a pew in the meetinghouse. The town paid for these repairs and addition by raising the ministerial tax on its residents. One of the highlights of the new bell tower was the golden weathercock, which was fashioned by a young woodworking apprentice named Stephen Colby. This style of weathervane, once common in the area, is a rare survivor in New Hampshire today and well worth a close look. The original by Colby was replaced in 1882, and that replacement is now in the town's Historic Library Museum after being replaced by an exact replica, also made of wood. While the bell tower was built in 1792, it would not gain a bell until 1809 after one was deeded to the town by Deacon Thomas Huse. The bell, which cost $600, is a rare one, made by Paul Revere, Jr., in collaboration with George Holbrook at Holbrook's foundry in Brookfield, MA. Town lore states that only a few people knew about the bell, and that when it was first brought to town, it was hung from the limb of an old oak tree and subsequently rung to the surprise of all within hearing.[40] The Hampstead Meetinghouse remained a house of worship for the Congregationalists in town until 1837, when they relinquished the building and built their own church. After that time, it served as Hampstead's Town Hall for many years and remains a town building to this day used for many civic and social functions. While the exterior of the church largely dates to its 1792 remodel, the interior has been much changed, a reflection of its change in purpose, including the removal of the box pews and replacement of the upper gallery with a floor supported by columns in 1856 to create a complete second-story space suitable for town functions.

Hampstead Meetinghouse.

Hampton Falls

First Baptist Church
Built: 1836
Location: 2 Lincoln Avenue

The denomination for which this church was built was the most conservative of the religious denominations in Hampton Falls, formed during the changing times of the early nineteenth century. Eight members of the Dodge family who worshipped in Exeter withdrew from that church in 1828 and formed the Baptist Church of Seabrook and Hampton Falls, worshipping first at the house of Richard Dodge in Hampton Falls and soon thereafter at the old meetinghouse in Seabrook until 1834, when they worshipped at the newly-formed Rockingham Academy in Hampton Falls, located near the town green. This solution was temporary, for the growing church soon established a building committee, including Richard Dodge and George H. Dodge, and resolved to build a church of their own in 1836. It was a simple rectangular structure with a tower, very close in size to the altered Hampstead Meetinghouse (see above). The structure cost $2,118 to build and though details as to its builder and exact form are not known, it is possible that George Dodge was the builder. Dedicated in September 1836, the first minister to preach here was Rev. Samuel Cook, who after 1838 became chaplain at the New Hampshire State Prison in Concord. In 1859, the structure gained most of its current look when it was closed to services for the year and heavily remodeled inside and out at a cost of $2,000, the bell tower replaced with a simple spire. Perhaps because of this remodel, twenty-three of its members asked to be dismissed from the church, forming their own in Seabrook. More changes came for the church in 1892, when it was moved back from the village green to its present location and raised so a vestry could be built beneath it. Horse sheds were also built at this time. In 1894, the unusual memorial clock, as previously discussed, was gifted to the church and placed in its steeple. The church today is best known for its memorial clock, but is also distinguished by its single entryway with sidelights and simple yet elegant steeple. The building is also notable for its setting on the town green and the two historic homes nearby, including that for Meshech Weare, a native of the town who served as New Hampshire's first president (a title later changed to "governor") in 1784.

Unitarian Church (formerly First Congregational Church-Unitarian)
Built: 1838
Location: 143 Exeter Road

Despite the fact that this church is one of the most important religious buildings of its kind in New Hampshire, nothing is known of its designer or builder, nor anything about its construction details. The church is the direct descendant of the

Right: First Baptist Church, Hampton Falls.

Below: Unitarian Church, Hampton Falls.

first Congregational church denomination in Hampton Falls, which underwent great changes in the early 1800s. Its last settled minister was Rev. Jacob Abbott, who was ordained in 1798 and served until 1827, but by about 1809, he had come to accept Unitarian views, with the result that many people who were not in accord with his liberal doctrine left the church. After Abbott's departure, the old order in Hampton Falls was largely gone, many members departing to join other denominations such as the Baptists, leaving behind the more liberal members of the old church. In 1827, the successor organization to the first church established in 1712, the First Congregational Society, was organized and worshipped in the old Hampton Falls meetinghouse before building this church in 1838. Despite its name, and the fact that it inherited the artifacts of the original church, including three silver communion cups presented to the church by its first minister in 1726, this society was Unitarian in its doctrine. From its formation, most ministers served here for only a short period of time, several years or less, and often the church relied on ministers from the Unitarian Society in neighboring Exeter. One notable exception to this was the pastorate of Rev. A. M. Bridge, who labored here for fourteen years from 1851–1865. Among the many worshippers here over the years have been two native sons: the noted architect Ralph Adams Cram and Franklin Sanborn, a journalist, author, and abolitionist who was one of six men to fund John Brown's raid on Harper's Ferry in 1859. However, by 1900, the society had greatly declined in numbers, and ever since that time, it has only been open during the summer months. The church was severely damaged by a hurricane in 1949 but was subsequently re-roofed and repaired over the course of several years. Despite its limited use, the church is now a well preserved and most excellent example of a Greek Revival-style house of worship, the only steeple-less church of its type in Rockingham County, and possibly the only *in antis*-style church remaining in the state. The whole façade makes for a stunning representation of a Greek temple, quite unusual given its rural surrounding, distinguished by its elaborately decorated full entablature, central columns, and antae decorated with unusual trefoil insets. Equally distinctive are the recessed entryways with a central 9 × 9 sash window flanked by 3 × 3 sidelights. Earlier views and descriptions of this central window show that it once was flanked by shutters, but these were removed at some time after 1984. Whoever the architect or builder for this church may have been, he knew what he was doing and likely borrowed some of his ideas from the books of Asher Benjamin to create this pleasing structure. He also, as was common with New Hampshire Greek Revival structures, gave the church a slightly steeper roof than is normally associated with this style to help reduce its snow load in the wintertime, a subtle but practical design variation. Finally, this church is also notable for its relatively unaltered interior as well, including its notable wall paintings, which were said to have been executed about 1839 by itinerant Italian painters and are remarkably well preserved, having been repaired in 1951. Located in a rural setting that has seen but little change, this church is indeed a historical and architectural treasure.

Hancock

Hancock Meetinghouse
Built: 1820
Builders: Jacob Ames and Samuel Kilborn
Location: 47 Main Street

Considered to be one of the finest examples of early nineteenth-century church architecture in the state, this meetinghouse was originally located across the street. One of the Elias Carter-inspired Templeton run of New Hampshire meetinghouses, its spire in particular is a close match to the meetinghouse built in Fitzwilliam in the previous year. Given its remarkable state of preservation and location in a village area known for its collection of late eighteenth- and early nineteenth-century structures, the Hancock meetinghouse is also a contender for the distinction of being the most photographed church structures in the state. The original meetinghouse in town stood until it was burned in October 1819, the town soon thereafter planning to build another meetinghouse. Despite the passing of the Toleration Act, the new meetinghouse, which was first located on land provided by the town very close to its original location and finished by late October 1820, would be a collaboration between Hancock and the First Congregational Society. The town provided the land and $1,000 towards the cost of the structure, providing that the structure be built of wood and in nearly the same size and form as the recently built Dublin meetinghouse. The town also retained the right for however long the building should stand to use it for town purposes. To this day, the Hancock Meetinghouse is owned by both entities, with the church sanctuary located on the second floor, while the lower area is used as a public space administered by the town and open to all for a wide variety of functions throughout the years. The structure is well cared for, receiving an $850,000 renovation in 2015, and is noted for its fine façade and steeple. The steeple houses a 1,193-lb. Revere bell from the company's original foundry and an E. Howard clock that was installed in the 1872 at a total cost of $650, the clock itself costing $475—town natives Augustus Clark and Darwin Fogg were among the main contributors. In the early years, as was customary in New England, the job of ringing the bell was put up for public bid; in 1822, the job fell to one Cristy Duncan for the sum of $11.75, he being required to sweep the meetinghouse four times a year and ring the bell daily at noon and 9 p.m., as well as at any funeral or other public occasions. By 1831, the price paid by the town for these same services in the meetinghouse rose to $30. To get back to the features of the meetinghouse, its beautiful façade features triple-entryways with a Palladian-style window above, flanked by elegant towering pilasters. The pediment of the structure is also finely executed featuring an oval window with Federal-style beading and olive branch décor beneath. Equally striking, albeit on a different level, is the row of curved horse sheds behind the meetinghouse, perhaps the most elaborate survivor of this once-common type of service structure. The first minister to preach in this meetinghouse was Rev. Archibald Burgess, who was ordained in 1822. For over a year prior to that time, the church and town had disagreed over whom to settle, the man whom the town had called being a Unitarian, perhaps a bit eccentric, and not to the liking of the First Congregational Society, and no services were held in town for over a year. Burgess accepted the call and was a stalwart in Hancock for over two decades before his resignation in late 1849 due to poor health. It was also in this meetinghouse that the first Sunday school was established in Hancock in the early 1820s, this form of religious teaching being something of a new idea at the time in New England. The meetinghouse was moved to its current location and changed to its current interior configuration in 1851 after the town and the church came to an agreement; the town had originally decided it was best to leave it in its old location and repair the building, but the church wanted the move so as to position it closer to its 1836-built brick rectory that also served as the Hancock Academy school building. The town agreed, as long it was done at no expense to them, and upon the stipulation that the building be partitioned to give the town a separate space from the pew-holders. It is no doubt because of the long-standing amiable relations between the town and the church that this meetinghouse has survived in its largely original form and function. Finally, no account of this meetinghouse would be complete without an account of its clock caretakers or agent. The first was John Newell, a well-known miller, local builder, and inventor, but his tenure beginning in 1872 was short in years in comparison to Robert "Bob" Fogg, Sr., who began his tenure in 1965 after being requested to take a look at the malfunctioning clock by a town selectman. Fogg, who moved to town in 1962 from Albany, NY, was employed as a mechanic and agreed, finding that the gears in the clock were jammed and was able to fix it in a timely fashion. From that time until early 2016, Fogg served as the caretaker of the clock, climbing the long and narrow steps to the clock on a regular basis, usually twice a week (several times more as he got older), to wind the clock and make minor repairs as needed, as well as giving tours and talks about the clock. While many town clocks have become electrified over the years to eliminate the need for winding, this has not been the case in Hancock. Indeed, since 1965, the clock has seldom failed to work and keep accurate time due to Fogg's devotion; he kept the time accurate through the use of an atomic clock he purchased, and whenever he noticed that something was amiss, he was quickly on the scene to provide a fix. Since 2016, the job of winding the clock has passed into the hands of his son, Bobby Fogg, Jr., who was raised in Hancock, and carries on the job in the footsteps of, and still watchful eyes of, his father, a venerable man and beloved figure in town.

Above left: Hancock Meetinghouse.

Above right: Façade detail, Hancock Meetinghouse.

Haverhill

First Congregational Church
Built: 1827–28
Location: 122 School Street

Located in the historic Haverhill Corner district, this church edifice embodies the spirit of the original religious conflicts that once existed in this town and the surrounding area. The church was originally built by the town's Methodist Society, its foundation laid on June 4, 1827, and was the first "meetinghouse" in this area of town, prior religious meetings being held in homes and the local courthouse. Despite the fact that the Methodists were encouraged to build here, and were fervent in their desire to have a church building, they accomplished the feat only by heavy borrowing. The finished structure was completed by early 1828, with Methodists appealing to townsmen for funds to pay the debt, but their efforts went for naught, and in 1829, they sold the building to the Congregational Church for $3,000. This sale must have been a bitter pill for the Methodists to swallow, and a sad irony besides, as it was the town's Congregationalist minister, Rev. Grant Powers, who opposed Methodism's rise in Haverhill. Stern and Calvinistic in his beliefs, Powers, who was related to some of the town and area's first founders, called Methodism "unscriptural and dangerous to the prosperity of Zion" and vigorously confronted anyone who held their beliefs.[41] His influence in combatting the Methodists held for some time, but his undoing began in 1824 after he penned an anonymous letter regarding reports of a miracle that occurred at a Methodist camp meeting in Warren, where a young woman by the name of Narcissa Griffin was said to have had a face that shone like an angel and that her skin was unnaturally smooth. Powers, in a satirical reply, wrote that he believed the story, as he felt the skin of the woman "had felt a hundred of them and they all felt exactly so-smooth as a bone."[42] The phrase "smooth as a bone" not only became a popular local saying, but also implied a sense of sexual indecency that offended many. Powers eventually confessed to having written the letter and his influence waned thereafter, but he remained in his Haverhill pastorate until 1829, long enough to see his denomination take over the fine edifice built by his enemies. To conclude the story, despite the temporary monetary setback, the Haverhill Methodists did rebound, worshipping at the courthouse before building another church building in 1836. The town of Haverhill, indeed, has an interesting and combative history in regards to the Congregationalists and their affairs. Though too long to give in full here, the saga of the bell, which stood above the old meetinghouse located on Ladd Street north of Haverhill Corner, is an interesting one, the members of the church in that area refusing to give up possession of the historic bell, even in the face of force, for use in this newly-acquired Methodist church. Architecturally, the church is a fine example of a Federal-style brick edifice, noted for its twin entryways topped off with fan louvers and decorative wood molding in a diamond pattern, while in the pediment there is a Palladian window planked by quarter-round sunburst-styled louvers. The three-stage tower is nicely done, with lower stages topped off by balustrades featuring urn-shaped finials at the corner, the whole tower capped by an octagonal belfry and dome. The town clock was added at a later point, but as of this writing, one side is boarded over and in the process of being restored. One of the interesting interior features of this church is a gallery clock, which was made by the prolific clockmaker John Osgood. A native of Boxford, MA, and trained as a clockmaker, he moved to Haverhill about 1793 to set up shop and was very active. One of his last creations was the clock he made for this church, the only one of its kind known among his output, and presented to the church just two years before his death in 1840.

First Congregational Church, Haverhill.

Henniker

Congregational Church of Henniker
Built: 1834
Builder: Col. William Abbott
Location: 43 Maple Street

Like so many other New Hampshire church edifices, this house of worship was built out of the ashes of its predecessor, which burned to the ground in August 1833. Rev. Jacob Scales, who ministered here from 1827–39, was minister when the church was built and was notable for the high number of infant baptisms he conducted during his tenure, close to 200 in number amongst the town's inhabitants. Indeed, Scales was an enthusiastic and active supporter of the gospel in Henniker, with several religious revivals occurring in his years here, including the year this church was built when forty-seven people joined the flock. The new church built by Col. Abbott was dedicated in August 1834, almost exactly a year after the old church was burned, and is similar in construction to the church he built in Webster (see below). It cost about $5,000 and is notable for its three-stage tower capped off by a golden dome. The bell in the tower was made by the Revere Copper Company, while the original clock was made in Boscawen by Benjamin Morrill, though it was later replaced in 1949 and has been on display at the American Clock & Watch

Congregational Church of Henniker.

Museum in Bristol, CT, since 1983. The upper portion of the exterior is largely original, though the façade was altered, probably in the 1880s, having its original triple entryways replaced by a single door with an elongated roof overhead mounted between the two side windows. This church was the fourth in the town's history, the first being a log house without glass windows, which was also burned. On the eve of the Civil War, one historian stated about the town's inhabitants that "It is thought that church members are more active than they were forty years ago. There is not so much open wickedness, by far, among adults now as then. At that time, there was a vast amount of intemperance, open opposition to truth and righteousness, and blasphemous conversation."[43]

Holderness

Trinity Church
Built: 1797
Location: 933 Rte. 175

This diminutive house of worship, around which has grown up a churchyard cemetery over the years, was built as a private structure and is notable has one of just two surviving church (as opposed to meetinghouse) buildings to have been built in the eighteenth century in New Hampshire. Though records regarding its building details have been lost, Trinity was built at the behest and majority financial contribution of Samuel Livermore (1732–1803), a native of Massachusetts who first bought property in Holderness in 1761 and moved here for good in 1775. By this time, Livermore was a well-known figure in New Hampshire, having been a representative to the colonial legislature and an Attorney General of New Hampshire in the royal government on the eve of the American Revolution. Livermore was also a prominent Episcopalian, being married to Jane Browne, the daughter of Rev. Arthur Browne of Portsmouth, the dean of New Hampshire's Anglican clerics. Some have speculated that Livermore moved to Holderness to avoid the politics of the Revolutionary War era; if so, he was successful, for he remained a prominent figure, serving as New Hampshire's Chief Justice from 1782–1790 in the post-Revolutionary War era and played a vital role in New Hampshire's ratification of the U.S. Constitution, his motion on the vote making the state the ninth and final vote to enshrine the Constitution into law. It was, of course, by Livermore's influence that the Episcopal Church was established in Holderness, one of only four towns to establish the church early on. Indeed, the town's first Episcopal minister, Rev. Robert Fowle, was initially brought here to tutor the Livermore children, being hired on as town minister in 1789 under Livermore's direct influence. Church services were first conducted in Livermore's home until Trinity Church was built on land owned by Livermore and near to his home. Though essentially a private church, public services were held here for a time, but the active life of the church lasted less than fifty years. By the 1840s, the Episcopal church had declined and was nearly extinguished after Fowle's death in 1847. The church remained in the Livermore family until 1854, when it was deeded to the Churchyard Cemetery Association for the sum of $1. It remains in their possession today and has been well maintained over the years. From 1879–84, it saw regular service as the chapel for the students of the Holderness School, but once they built their own chapel on campus, the church has only been sporadically used on special occasions. Trinity Church is an unassuming, yet attractive structure, single-story, three bays wide featuring 12 × 12 sash windows, with a single entryway on the west end through a small vestibule with a small hipped roof. Its exterior is probably unchanged from when it was first built, the same being true inside, the original box pews remaining, except for some of its wood paneling details. Equally fascinating here is the churchyard that surrounds Trinity Church, an American version of an English churchyard in many ways, the most notable and early markers being the distinctive table stones for Livermore and his family located on the north side of the church and close to the building itself, a continuation of old English burial customs, where those who were most prominent in society and church life were buried closest to the church.

Trinity Church, Holderness.

Hopkinton

First Congregational Church
Built: 1789
Location: 1548 Hopkinton Road

This church was borne out of stormy beginnings and has been much altered over the years, bearing little resemblance to its original form. As previously stated, the previous Congregational meetinghouse in Hopkinton was deliberately destroyed by fire in 1789 due to a long-standing controversy about where to site the meetinghouse. This structure was its replacement, erected the same year, in its original form having twin porches and a seven-bay façade with triple-entryways. Among the committee of five men chosen to draw up plans for the meetinghouse, as well as to supervise its building, was Aaron Greely, known for his surveying work, and Moses Hill, known for building a home and mill at Contoocook. It was likely that Hill was the master-builder on this project. A two-stage tower with an open belfry was added when the church was moved a short distance to its present location in 1807, though a bell was not procured until 1811. The 1,158-lb. bell is an original Paul Revere bell, the twenty-fifth to come from their foundry, and came to town from Concord by way of Dimond Hill, stopping along the way to be rung at the home of Daniel Chase, who was the main benefactor of the bell. It was also in 1811 that the town failed to vote on a measure to raise pay for the town minister, Rev. Ethan Smith. While the days of town-supported religion in Hopkinton were nearing an end, it was in that same year

First Congregational Church, Hopkinton.

that more people, 192 in number, were added to the church during a great period of revival, than at any other time. In 1829, the church gained its current form when it was extensively remodeled in the rural Greek Revival style and was rededicated in December 1829. One interesting aspect of the new church was its weathercock weathervane, which was replaced with the simple church-scroll type vane it now has probably by the 1880s or even earlier. Today, this church is noted for its temple-like façade with twin pediments above a slightly projecting vestibule. The pilasters on the vestibule are interesting and indicative of the rural craftsmen that executed the work, they consisting of a series of horizontal boards, while the pediments above the twin entryways exhibit the same simplicity.

St. Andrew's Episcopal Church
Built: 1827–28
Builder: John Leach
Location: 354 Main Street

The Episcopal church in Hopkinton was founded in 1803 under the name Christ's Church and for many years worshipped in the local courthouse. Visiting clergy usually supplied the pulpit until 1826, when Rev. Moses Chase became rector, a position he would hold until 1841. The following year, a new Episcopal parish was formed, taking the name of St. Andrew's, with a fine church structure also built just a stone's throw away from the old meetinghouse in the center of Hopkinton. The

St. Andrew's Episcopal Church, Hopkinton.

wood and stone Gothic Revival style of St. Andrew's was executed by architect/builder John Leach, who was in high demand at the time, having built many notable brick buildings in nearby Concord. As originally built, the church had a square bell tower that was crenellated and adorned with finials. This stood until 1930, when the tower was redesigned by the famed architects Ralph Adams Cram and Frank Ferguson and given an octagonal belfry and spire so as to impart a colonial-era look that would fit in with its surroundings more perfectly. The structure is also noted for its granite exterior, the Gothic-arch windows with tracery and trefoil trim, as well as the Gothic pinnacles flanking the single entryway. It is interesting to note that Hopkinton for a time was one of the most important towns in the state and many of those who were its most prominent or wealthy individuals belonged to this church. The state legislature occasionally met here from 1798–1807 and the town vied for the honor of becoming the state capital, but lost out to Concord, thereby diminishing the town's importance and business over time.

Jaffrey

Jaffrey Meetinghouse
Built: 1775
Builders: Captain Samuel Adams, Jeremiah Spofford, and Jacob Spofford
Location: 38 Blackberry Lane

This meetinghouse is one of the most celebrated buildings in New Hampshire, its reputation certainly enhanced by the history with which it is associated. This was the first meetinghouse built in town, its timbers being cut near Thorndike Pond over the winter of 1774–75 and dragged to the town common over the snow. Though uncertain, the frame of the meetinghouse was likely raised by Captain Adams, a young man from Rindge, on Thursday, June 15, 1775, as Fridays were deemed to be bad luck for such a start. Town tradition states that the meetinghouse was raised on Saturday, June 17, the day of the Battle of Bunker Hill in Charlestown, MA, and that the roar of the cannon could be heard. It is quite probable that work on the meetinghouse continued on the day of the battle, as no follow-up work would have been allowed on the Sabbath. Whatever the case may be, once raised, the meetinghouse would not be finished until after the Revolutionary War, an understandable reason for a delay if ever there was one. Indeed, as late as 1789, the town was still voting on whether or not to accept in full the meetinghouse built by Samuel Adams, and it was not until 1801 that it was fully painted, likely in the same straw-yellow color that the Rindge meetinghouse used and was so popular in the Monadnock region. The meetinghouse remained unheated until about 1820, when a stove was installed in front of the pulpit by public subscription, though the town would not pay for the firewood required as fuel until 1825. The original form of the meetinghouse was that of a typical Type II: rectangular in size, seven bays wide with a porch at each end. This form was altered, as was quite common, in 1822, with the addition of a bell tower at the west end in 1823, built entirely by private subscription, though the town did pay to procure the bell. The resulting tower, built by Joel Patrick, is masterfully done, featuring largely Federal-style elements, though the pinnacles on the lower stage give it a hint of Gothic Revival. The whole is topped off by an exquisite scrolled weathervane with a heart-shaped body and star tail. It is not known who crafted this fine example of the vane-maker's art. Perhaps it was a local blacksmith, of which there were many in Jaffrey, though the most likely candidates may be members of the Haywood family: patriarch Benjamin Haywood, a blacksmith, and his son, Joseph Haywood, a goldsmith with a wider expertise in the art of metallurgy. No account of this meetinghouse would be complete without giving due to the town's first and only settled minister, Rev. Laban Ainsworth. He was a native of Woodstock, Connecticut, a graduate of Dartmouth, and served briefly as an army chaplain during the Revolutionary War. He first preached in Jaffrey in 1781, and the following year, he was hired by the town. He would grow to become

Jaffrey's most respected citizen, known not just for his religious activities, but for his ministrations to the sick and ill in town, his involvement in the local schools, and his overall wisdom in town affairs. As he grew older, associate pastors were hired to help in the regular activities of a minister, but Ainsworth remained the town's senior pastor until his death in 1858, his tenure lasting an incredible seventy-six years. He is buried in the historic cemetery that is located behind the meetinghouse—take a look at the back of the meetinghouse, too, and you will see the central rounded-arch, 34 × 15 sash window that provided the light for his many sermons in the early years. However, the time of this meetinghouse would pass by the 1830s, as the various denominations in town, one by one, left the building, unwilling to share the space and desirous of a building all their own. The Universalists eventually became the sole occupants, against the desire of many taxpayers, and soon enough, they also left, with the building unused except for the annual March meeting and at election time. In 1855, the meetinghouse was officially designated as Jaffrey's Townhouse, though few have ever accepted the new designation, but it was not until 1870 that the interior was remodeled, completely doing away with its original colonial interior, which seemed to bother nobody at the time. In 1922, the Village Improvement Society in Jaffrey worked with the town to restore the interior to its original design and ever since this time the meetinghouse has been well cared for, including a newly shingled roof in 2017.

As to its surroundings, the Jaffrey Meetinghouse has much to offer that is original to the site, including one of the finest late Colonial-era burial grounds, its horse sheds, the Ainsworth homestead, or "Manse" as it is referred to locally, as well as the First Church which replaced the meetinghouse as a house of worship. The Ainsworth Manse is just around the corner from the meeting house and was built in 1788, replacing an earlier residence for Rev. Laban Ainsworth and his wife that had burned down earlier that year, severely injuring Mrs. Ainsworth and taking the life of young Isaac Spofford, a deacon's son who was staying with the them on that fateful night in February 1787. The house remains in the hands of Ainsworth descendants to this day. The eleven horse sheds behind the meetinghouse were authorized by the town in 1808 and likely built that same year, being in existence by 1810 when the town granted to twelve shed owners the rights to the ground, as long it was only used for this purpose and that the sheds be well-maintained. Only these twelve were authorized, though the first was later taken down to allow better access to the town cemetery, and are likely the oldest such structures of their kind surviving in New Hampshire. Finally, no visit to this meetinghouse would be complete without a tour of its burial ground, which offers a fine collection of slate gravestones from the late Colonial-era marking the final resting place of many of Jaffrey's most prominent citizens. Most notable are the gravestones for Isaac Spofford, son of Deacon Eleazer and his wife, Mary, "a brand plucked from the ashes of Rev. Laban Ainsworth's house 13 Feb. 1788" and those for Jaffrey's early African-American residents, Amos and Violet Fortune, he "born free in Africa, a slave in America," dying in 1801, and

Above: Jaffrey Meetinghouse.

Right: Tower and steeple detail, Jaffrey Meetinghouse.

she "by Marriage his wife, by her fidelity his friend and solace," dying in 1802. Of the more modern burials, many are interesting, the most notable being the final resting site of the famed American author Willa Cather (1873–1947).

St. Patrick's Roman Catholic Church
Built: 1915–17
Architect: Frank Joseph Untersee
Location: 87 Main Street

This church is indicative of the wave of Irish and French-Canadian immigrants that settled in New Hampshire and Jaffrey beginning in the 1830s and continuing to the end of the century. By the late 1860s, there were about twenty Catholic families living in Jaffrey, but they had no local church in which to worship. In 1869, the missionary Rev. Daniel Murphy came from Keene and began to celebrate a monthly Mass in Jaffrey Center, holding services in the town firehouse. Services continued as the population grew, many of them French-Canadian immigrants who were Catholics. When a parish church was established in Peterborough, Jaffrey became a mission of that parish and Rev. John Holahan would travel here from Peterborough by train to offer services on a weekly basis. This continued until 1885, when Jaffrey gained its first Catholic priest, Rev. Patrick McEvoy, a native of Ireland. It was under his guidance that the first Catholic church, a wooden structure, was built here by 1888. Interestingly, the church in Jaffrey

St. Patrick's Roman Catholic Church, Jaffrey.

grew so much, now counting about 350 parishioners, that the tables were turned, and the church in Peterborough became a mission church to the newly established St. Patrick's Parish, named by its founding immigrant pastor in honor of the patron saint of his homeland. By 1915, the parish had grown even more, and with 1,200 parishioners, the old wooden church was no longer suitable. Under the guidance of Rev. Herbert Hennon, the parish engaged the noted Swiss-born, German-educated, ecclesiastical architect Frank Untersee from Boston to design a new church that would be made of stone. Much of the stone was brought to the building site over the course of several years by local parishioners, though Father Hennon also combed the local countryside for pieces of granite and carried them by his buggy to the building site. The foundation for the church was laid in 1915 and it was finally dedicated in September 1917. The beautiful Gothic Revival church is notable for its stone exterior consisting of thousands of pieces of granite in varying sizes, shapes, and colors, as well as for its bell tower topped off with four Celtic crosses at the corners, and its Gothic-arch windows.

Jefferson

Former St. John's United Methodist Church
Built: 1868
Location: 900 Presidential Highway (U.S. Rte. 2)

Now the home of the Jefferson Historical Society Museum, this large church was the second to be built in town, the first being for the Baptists in 1835 (lost by fire in 1907). The town was first granted in 1765 under the name of Dartmouth, but the unexplored wilderness area attracted few settlers other than Col. Joseph Whipple. In 1796, the town was granted again under the name of Jefferson. The first religious activity in the locale took place in the summer of 1784 when Rev. Jeremy Belknap of Dover, Rev. Daniel Little of Kennebunk, Maine, and Rev. Manasseh Cutler of Ipswich, Massachusetts, held services in Whipple's barn during a thunderstorm. Despite these Congregational services, the denominations that really gained a foothold here were the Baptists and the Methodists, the first Methodist preaching coming at the arrival of circuit riders from Vermont in 1820. The Methodist church in Jefferson was organized in 1860 and preaching continued in local homes until this church was built at a cost of $4,000 on land donated by Joshua Plaisted, the son of the builder of the Waumbeck Hotel in Jefferson in 1860, Benjamin Plaisted. The church was likely built by a member of the Plaisted family, as Jared Plaisted built a store in Jefferson in 1861. Postcard views show that this church was at first painted a brick-red color, it being said that Nate Perkins, who was a "liberal" contributor to the church and donated the land for the parsonage, "had a mania for red paint."[44] The four-bayed vernacular structure is notable for its tall and slender stained-glass windows with simple hoods above, steep pediment, and single entryway with a

Former St. John's United Methodist Church, Jefferson.

window above featuring an oval hood. The steeple is a simple one of two-stages with an open belfry. The church remained in use until the 1970s, by which time it had fallen into disrepair. The church found another building for their services, with the result that it became the home of the Jefferson Historical Society in 1979.

St. Agnes Roman Catholic Church
Built: 1900–01
Builder: Sam Samson
Location: 796 Presidential Highway (U.S. Rte. 2)

This small church has been a mission church of All Saints Parish of nearby Lancaster since 1936, and holds services on a rotating basis during most of the year, with more frequent services in the summer. By the late 1890s, four Catholic families, all Irish immigrants, had settled in Jefferson, but had no church of their own, being forced to travel to Whitefield, though services were also held outdoors in a local meadow in the summer. Later, with the influx of French-Canadian immigrants, the need for a Catholic church in Jefferson grew. The church was first a mission church for St. Matthews's in Whitefield, remaining as such until it became a part of All Saints Parish. In addition to serving local families, St. Agnes also served as a place of worship for many summer tourists from May to October, including the Waumbeck Hotel. The church is notable

St. Agnes Roman Catholic Church, Jefferson.

for its shingled exterior and prominent use of flying buttresses, while the interior has a beautiful barrel-vault ceiling finished in carpenter Gothic-style woodwork, a particularly pleasing and suitable feature in this heavily forested region of the North Country. The building of the church is credited to a local man, Samuel Samson, but whether he designed the church is unknown. Members of the Samson family were heavily involved with St. Agnes, including Louis and Ida Samson, who sponsored the Sacrament of Confirmation event in 1937 and raising funds for a new altar in 1959. The church remains much the same as when it was first built; the interior was refurbished in 1960 with a new altar made by Roger Guay of Concord, NH, while the exterior was repaired and painted in 2000–2001 in advance of its centennial celebration.

Keene

United Church of Christ in Keene (The First Church)
Built: 1786
Builder: Benjamin Archer
Location: 23 Central Square

This, the fourth and final meetinghouse to be built in the town of Keene, is one of the most interesting and eclectic church buildings in all of New Hampshire. As originally built by Revolutionary War and Battle of Bunker Hill veteran Benjamin Archer, the structure was 50 × 70 feet, rectangular in shape as was common in the day, with a porch on the eastern end and a bell tower and steeple on the west end. The glass for its windows came from Boston and Wrentham, Massachusetts, as well as Providence, Rhode Island, while the weathervane came from Boston. The structure was eventually painted a pale yellow or straw color and had green doors. These details are interesting and serve to give us an idea as to how the meetinghouse once appeared, even if they have all disappeared over time. The meetinghouse has always been the home of the Congregational Church in Keene, the first minster to preach a sermon here being Rev. Aaron Hall, a Yale- and Dartmouth-educated cleric who served the town until his death in 1814 after serving the town for thirty-seven years. After a brief interim pastor, Rev. Z.S. Barstow (also a Yale graduate) was installed as minister in 1818, being the last to be settled by the town before the advent of the Toleration Act of 1819. Following this time, the relationship between the town, its minister, and the old meetinghouse gradually came to an end. In 1823, the town reduced the salary of Rev. Barstow because of the many citizens who withdrew their tax support, though his salary was restored in 1824. In 1825, Barlow's salary again was reduced and 1826 was the final year in which the town paid his salary, the amount being assumed by the First Congregational Society. It was also in 1824 that the town put the meetinghouse, the land it stood upon, and the town bell up for auction, but had no bids. The real separation of church and town occurred in 1828 when the town conveyed their rights to the meetinghouse to the First Congregational Society in full in return for retaining the rights to the bell and use of the structure on "public" occasions, the society agreeing to move the church off the green to its present location within eighteen months with no expense to the town, as well as their payment of $750 to the Keene Congregational Society to cede their rights to the meetinghouse. These terms were agreed to by the First Congregational Society and the move was completed in 1829, this being done via the use of a windlass, with the church turned one-quarter round so as to face the street. It was also at this time that the old meetinghouse was thoroughly remodeled in the Greek Revival style, given a portico supported by four large Corinthian columns and a towering 130-foot five-stage steeple, said to be inspired by that in Fitzwilliam, built by townsman William Wilson, while the demolition of the old bell tower was supervised by Capt. Samuel Bassett.[45] Eleven years later, in 1840, the final separation of church and town occurred when the town voted to relinquish all rights to the meetinghouse. In 1859–60, the church was again remodeled and gained its present form when it was moved back on the lot it occupies, the building raised to give it a vestry beneath, the beautifully decorated façade was added, and the steeple was rebuilt with added height, now soaring 152 feet in the air. The new work was done to the plans of the Worcester, Massachusetts, architectural firm Boyden & Ball, while the work was done by Joel Bullard of Alstead, also known for his work on St. Luke's Episcopal Church in Charlestown (see above). The net result of this continued evolution for over seventy years is a church rich in architectural detail that few others in the state can match.

Right: United Church of Christ in Keene.

Below: Column and Corinthian capital detail, United Church of Christ in Keene.

St. James Episcopal Church
Built: 1863–69
Architect: Charles E. Parker
Location: 44 West Street

Designed by a native of Keene, St. James Episcopal is notable not just for its architect, but also for its historical association with the Civil Rights era in America during the 1960s. The Gothic Revival church was designed by noted architect Charles Parker (1826–1890), a native son who moved to Boston as a teenager and opened his own office there in 1846. One of his first notable buildings was Keene's Town Hall in 1848, though Parker would go on to design ten churches from 1857–1881, eight of them in Massachusetts and Vermont, and two in New Hampshire, St. James, and the South Congregational Church (1859) in Concord, which is still extant. St. James is notable for its stone construction, imposing corner tower, and narrow arched windows. The parish of St. James was formed in 1859 and construction of the church began in 1863, with the main structure first used for church services in August 1864. St. James gained its current form in 1869 when the corner tower and steeple were built. Despite its important architectural history, however, St. James is more important as the home church of Jonathan Myrick Daniels (1939–1965), a native of Keene and civil rights activist and martyr. Jonathan, the son of Phillip and Constance Daniels (both members of the Congregationalist church in Keene), became an Episcopalian when a young man. Upon graduation from the local high school, he attended the Virginia Military Institute, graduating as class valedictorian, following which he attended Harvard in the fall of 1961. Prior to this time, perhaps due to the death of his father, Jonathan had begun to question his faith, but experienced a renewal after attending an Easter service at a Boston church in 1962. Following this, he felt a call to serve God and enrolled in the Episcopal Theological Seminary in Cambridge, Massachusetts, in 1963. In 1965, while still a student, Daniels and several other members of the seminary, no doubt moved by Dr. Martin Luther King's call for students and religious leaders to join the Civil Rights movement, travelled to Selma, Alabama, to take part in protests there. After a brief return to school, Daniels returned to Alabama, taking part in such events as voter registration, tutoring children, helping poor families to gain government aid, and also tried to integrate the local Episcopal church there, while at the same time working on his independent studies. After a brief return to Cambridge to take exams, Daniels returned to Selma in August. On August 14, 1965, he was part of a group of several dozen protestors who picketed a whites-only store in Fort Deposit, all of whom were subsequently arrested, with Daniels and others held for six-days. Upon their release on August 20, Daniels, along with a white Catholic priest and two black activists, including teenager Ruby Sales, walked to a nearby store to get a cold drink, but found their entry into the store blocked by a local deputy armed with a shotgun who subsequently fired on the group. Daniels pushed Ruby Sale to the ground and was hit by the gunfire and

St. James Episcopal Church, Keene.

killed instantly. The Catholic priest also took fire, but survived, as did the rest of the group. The deputy was subsequently tried and acquitted by an all-white jury, claiming self-defense. Daniel's body was subsequently returned to Keene for burial in Monadnock View Cemetery, his funeral services being held at St. James and attended by many people. Twenty-six years after his death, in 1991, Daniels was designated by the Episcopal Church as a martyr for his selfless actions and dedication to the Civil Rights movement; inside St. James, there is a memorial display for Daniels, and a New Hampshire State Historical Marker on the grounds of the church outside.

Kensington

Universalist Church (former Union Meetinghouse)
Built: 1839–40
Builders: Josiah Sanborn and Dearborn Blake
Location: 97 Amesbury Road

Sited in a compact village setting and adjacent to Kensington's Upper Yard burying ground, this rural church was originally built to serve several different denominations. Known originally as the Union Meetinghouse, it was built on the site of the town's first meetinghouse for use by the Congregationalists, Universalists, and Unitarians and as originally built had no belfry, this being added about 1860. The men that built the church were prominent carpenters in Kensington and built many of the surviving Greek Revival historic buildings in the area. While the meetinghouse was a privately-owned structure, it sat on land owned by the town, which situation continued until 1915, when the town formally deeded the land to the Universalist Society. As a union house, the building was used on alternating Sundays by each group who, when they could not meet here, met in the town house located just a short distance away. This changed in 1865 when the structure became the Universalist Church, the Congregationalists building their church that same year just a short distance away. Regular services were held here for many years, but by the 1920s, religious services were held in the summer months only. The structure is distinguished by its façade, featuring corner pilasters, twin entryways with sidelights and flanking columns, and its steep pediment with fan louver. The pinnacles on the belfry add a note of the Greek Revival style to the structure, very popular during that time period. Though the Universalist Church is weatherworn and in need of attention, it last seeing an overhaul in the 1990s, it nonetheless remains a dignified and pleasing structure, the adjoining Upper Yard burying ground, filled with many gravestones created by stonecutter Jeremiah Lane from neighboring Hampton Falls, adding an even more ancient atmosphere to the historic surroundings.

Universalist Church, Kensington.

Laconia

Evangelical Baptist Church (former Meredith Bridge Congregational Church)
Built: 1836
Location: 12 Veteran's Square

Now abandoned and up for sale as of this writing, this Lakes Region church has undergone many changes and has been a true survivor over the years. When built, it was in the town of Meredith Bridge, this changing in 1855 when the town of Laconia was incorporated and encompassed the land of several surrounding communities. Originally a Congregational church, the structure was the second in Meredith Bridge after the first church was destroyed by fire in early 1836. Plans began immediately to build a new church, the cost being $6,000, some of which was raised by the sale of pews. As originally constructed, it was Greek Revival structure with a three-stage steeple, its name changing to the Laconia Congregational Church once the new town was incorporated. In 1871, the character of the church was changed when it was renovated under the guidance of local architect and builder Arthur Davis. A new tower and steeple were constructed which, at 170 feet in height, made it the tallest building on the Laconia skyline at the time. The building was also raised 6 feet to provide for a vestry and other service spaces below, while the façade was also redesigned, the large arched windows being added. By the time the church was rededicated in 1872, it had been transformed into a Victorian- and Italianate-styled structure that was more in keeping with the tastes of the time. While these changes were voluntary, the church underwent other changes that were a result of unfortunate circumstances; in 1902, a nearby fire in the downtown area engulfed a nearby hardware store, setting off its store of gunpowder. The church suffered blown out windows and so much damage to its walls that the Congregationalists sold the land to the city and built a new church elsewhere. The damaged church was subsequently sold to the People's Christian Church (later the Evangelical Baptist Church) for $1,000 and moved to its current site just hundreds of feet away and repaired. Years later, the steeple of the church was blown down during the hurricane of 1938, it being replaced the following year with a shorter steeple. The church remained in religious service until the Evangelical Baptist Church found a new home in 2013, the old building in need of costly repairs and increasingly expensive to repair and maintain. The church building subsequently went on the real estate market, being acquired by the Kennedy family in 2014 for use as a restaurant, Holy Grail of the Lakes, based on the successful model of their original Holy Grail church-turned restaurant in Epping. The interior subsequently underwent a $2.3-million renovation to convert it for restaurant use, though many unique aspects were retained. Despite the high hopes for this new phase of the structure's life, they were never realized and the restaurant closed in early 2017. As of this writing, the church has remained vacant and is up for sale, its future quite uncertain.

Former Evangelical Baptist Church, Laconia.

South Baptist Church
Built: 1877
Location: 85 Court Street

This fine Victorian-era church serves as the home of a Baptist Church that can trace its history back over 180 years. Originally organized in Meredith Bridge as the First Free Will Baptist Church in 1838, they built their first meetinghouse on this site in 1841. When that structure was deliberately burned in October 1876, plans were soon launched to build its replacement, and by November 1877, the newly-built church was up and running. Later renamed the South Baptist Church, regular services are still held in this venerable building to this day. The building is notable for its eclectic blend of Italianate and Gothic details; located in close proximity to a busy street, a mere drive-by view of this structure will not suffice to give one a full appreciation of its beautiful façade, highlighted by a projecting tower, with a large arched central window above its arched entryway, flanked by tall and narrow arched windows. The steeply pitched roof, with its prominent brackets, is pure Italianate, as is the wooden quoining treatment on the buttressed lower corners of the tower, while the miniature gables that top off the buttresses, as well as the pinnacles on the upper tower, offer a touch of Victorian Gothic. The whole makes for an interesting combination that is pleasing to the eye.

South Baptist Church, Laconia.

United Baptist Church of Lakeport
Built: 1891–92
Architect: George Guernsey
Location: 23 Park Street

This beautifully eclectic church, built on the ashes of its predecessor, is a wonderful reminder of the once-vibrant nature of Lakeport during the late Victorian era. This small village area, first settled in the 1760s, was known for the many steamboats, including the colorfully-named *Wangan*, *Belle of the Wave*, and *Maid of the Isles*, which brought freight and summer tourists to the area immediately surrounding this church, followed by the railroads, with the Lakeport railroad station also located within sight of the church. Indeed, it was the steamboats and railroad that brought many worshippers to this church in the summer seasons. However, this church was not just built for tourists—the Free Will Baptist Church of Lakeport was organized in 1838 and built its first church on this Park Street location in 1852. When this structure was destroyed by fire in December 1890, plans were made for its successor, which was largely completed in one year's time. The man chosen to design and build this church was the dynamic George Guernsey of Montpelier, Vermont, a Civil War veteran, later mayor of Montpelier, and a leading architect in that state who designed eleven churches from 1878–92, including one in Lancaster (see below). Guernsey

United Baptist Church of Lakeport, Laconia.

was paid $12,358 for his work, the entire church coming in a cost of nearly $20,000, the building completed in April 1892 when its pews were installed. While there have been some changes in the structure inside and out, these have been minor and the church appears much the same as it did when it was first built. Deemed as the finest structure of its kind in Belknap County by historian David Ruell, and perhaps in all of New Hampshire, this Victorian structure combines ornamental and structural elements of the Gothic and Romanesque Revival styles, the former demonstrated by its large arched rose windows and soaring tower with buttresses and pinnacled spire (featuring an illuminated clock, the first in the state north of Concord), while the shorter corner tower is a highlight of the later. The many interesting features of this church, combined with its historic location between Opeechee Bay to the south and Paugus Bay to the north makes it a must-see destination.

St. Joseph's Roman Catholic Church
Built: 1929–30
Architect: James O'Shaughnessy
Location: 30 Church Street

The Irish influence in Laconia and the surrounding area is embodied in the building of this church. Once known as the "Irish" Catholic church in town (Sacred Heart was the town's "French" Catholic church), the structure was built to accommodate

St. Joseph's Roman Catholic Church, Laconia.

a growing parish. The Catholic presence in Laconia began as a mission church, with priests such as Father John Daly, an Irish Franciscan from Dover, and Father Isidore Noiseux, a French-Canadian, visiting here beginning in 1856. The local parish was subsequently established in 1871, the church growing rapidly due to the influx of Irish and French-Canadian immigrants to work in the local mills and factories that were thriving in this manufacturing town. The first Catholic Church was built in Laconia in 1867, but was destroyed by a lightning strike and resulting fire in 1877. A new church was completed by 1881, but by the 1920s, it proved to be too small for the growing numbers it served. The current location of the future church was determined in 1904 when the church purchased the prominent Busiel mansion for use as a rectory. The former owner of this property, John Busiel, was a prominent mill owner in Laconia and employed many Irish and French-Canadian immigrants. When a new church was decided upon, plans were drawn up by a Boston architect, James O'Shaughnessy, known for his designs for a number of churches, including a later example in Dover (see above). It is said that O'Shaughnessy worked in the offices of the noted architect Ralph Adams Cram, and that perhaps St. Joseph Church is indicative of Cram's influence.[46] Whatever the case may be, as originally designed, the church was to be built of granite, but brick was chosen in order to save the parish about $9,000 in costs. However, a benefactor stepped forward to donate this sum, so the original granite construction plan was executed. The result is an excellent example of a twentieth-century Gothic Revival church, noted for its soaring façade with buttresses and a large Gothic arch stained-glass window with tracery above the entryway. Despite its fine construction and historic past, as of this writing the church must be considered an endangered one whose future is uncertain. Faced with dwindling numbers, the New Hampshire Diocese has here, like elsewhere in the state, been forced to consolidate its parishes and deconsecrate and sell or demolish buildings it no longer needs or can afford to maintain. Such a decision was made in Laconia in 2010, though the new Laconia parish, St. Andre Bessette, has no firm timeline for doing anything as of this writing, nor has the church yet been put up for sale. Ultimately, however, the plan will eventually be followed to either sell or demolish St. Joseph, the last option one that would result in a significant loss to Laconia's ethnic and architectural heritage.

Lancaster

Lancaster Congregational Church (former Lancaster Orthodox Congregational Church)
Built: 1840–41
Location: 142 Main Street

The Congregational church in this town, as in many others in New Hampshire, went through periods of great upheaval in the 1820s and 1830s. Originally established in 1794, it was first led by Rev. Joseph Willard, the town's first settled minister. However, after the passage of the Toleration Act of 1819, difficulties arose among several factions in the church, prompting Willard to offer his resignation in 1822. His replacement being deemed too severe in his beliefs, Willard returned as minister in late 1824, serving until his sudden death in 1826. Preaching after this was sporadic due to the conflicts in the church between those who were liberal in their beliefs, and those who were more conservative. Finally, a break occurred in late 1836 when thirty-eight conservative members left the church to form the Orthodox Congregational Church. In 1840, a building committee was formed, and later that year a church was raised, it being finished the following year. Eventually, by December 1843, the members of the old church were unified with this breakaway group, thus ending the existence of the original Congregational church in town. This church is still active today, though it is no longer an orthodox one, instead being an open and affirming church. The church structure remains largely unchanged from its original Gothic Revival form, though unspecified improvements were made in 1886–87 at a cost of $1,400, with the church being remodeled in 1898 with an addition placed on the north side of the building. This fine building is most notable for its projecting front tower, built in three stages, its lower columns, as well as the building's corner pilasters with their Gothic arch inset treatment.

Lancaster
Congregational Church.

St. Paul's Episcopal Church
Built: 1875–76
Location: 113 Main Street

The Episcopal faith was first practiced in this North Country town in 1856 by missionaries, with services held in local homes and, in the summer, at tourist resorts, until this church was built. The board and batten structure cost $9,000, including the land upon which it was sited, with efforts to build the church led by William Haywood and his wife, she being the first to be confirmed in the faith in Lancaster. Unfortunately, nothing is known about the designer or builder of this simple yet elegant church, which remains largely unchanged from its original appearance. Built in the Gothic Revival style, the church's most distinctive features beyond its siding are its arched doorway and narrow arched windows, and steeply pitched roof.

St. Paul's Episcopal Church, Lancaster.

Christ United Methodist Church
Built: 1888–89
Architect: George Guernsey
Location: 135 Main Street

The Methodist church in Lancaster got its start in the summer of 1800 when travelling ministers stopped here to preach at a local residence. Their reception was not a warm one, as a group of locals attacked them, grabbing one of them and giving him a ducking in the Connecticut River, telling him not to hold any further meetings here. Despite this contentious beginning, circuit riders continued to visit Lancaster quite regularly, with the result that a Methodist Episcopal Society was formed here in 1831. In 1834, the Methodists built their first church in the village on the site of the current church and adjacent to the hill-top Wilder Cemetery at a cost of $1,000. This church gave good service until the current church was built at a cost of $7,800. George Guernsey, a noted Vermont architect, designed the structure, one

Right: Christ United Methodist Church, Lancaster.

Below: Eyebrow window detail, Christ United Methodist Church, Lancaster.

of several New Hampshire churches he designed or built, including one in Laconia (see above) and one in Manchester (see below). Interestingly, the church was able to save considerable money in its building through the use of donated labor by local workers. This church is a fine example of an eclectic Victorian structure, one of the most notable in the North Country. The large rose window is a Romanesque Revival feature; it was crafted by Redding, Baird & Company of Boston, who advertised their "cathedral glass" during this time period before going out of business about 1905. Some of the other windows, including the stained-glass memorial windows and perhaps the stained-glass eyebrow window on the south side of the structure at street level, were made by the Ecclesiastical Glass Works of Boston, founded by Englishman Samuel West and in operation from about 1850 until his death in 1891, making these windows among his last productions. The arched windows and arched belfry opening are Gothic Revival features, as is the towering spire of the church. The whole is topped off by a now-unusual period weathervane featuring the Angel Gabriel in female form, complete with trumpet. This form of weathervane was once common, but survivors of this type are now rare. The overall details and composition of this church, as is typical with Guernsey's work, have resulted in a unique structure that is pleasing to the eye. Finally, though located on Lancaster's busy Main Street, an unusual view of this church may be seen from the hilltop site of Wilder Cemetery next door, the oldest burying place in Lancaster, which features gravestones for the town's earliest inhabitants, as well as that for Col. Edward Cross, the famed commander of 5th New Hampshire Regiment during the Civil War who was mortally wounded at the Battle of Gettysburg in July 1863.

Lebanon

First Congregational Church
Built: 1828
Architect and Builder: Ammi B. Young
Location: 10 South Park Street

Nestled in downtown Lebanon, just off the town green, this beautiful structure was designed and built by a hometown boy who went on to become a famous regional and national architect. As with many other towns, this church was built by the town's Congregationalists because they grew tired of sharing the old town meetinghouse with the other religious denominations in town in the aftermath of the Toleration Act of 1819. The frame was raised by Ammi Young (1798–1874) and his crew on April 24, 1828, and the church was dedicated for service later that year on August 13, the cost of the structure being $3,162. It is not surprising that Ammi Young was chosen as the builder of this edifice; his father, Samuel, was prominent in town affairs and practiced the trade of a builder, passing his skills on down to his son. At the time when this church was built, Ammi Young was a busy man, designing Wentworth and Thornton halls on the campus of Dartmouth College in neighboring Hanover in 1828–29. This church, however, was not Young's first, for across the river he built the Congregational Church in Norwich, Vermont, in 1817 at the age of nineteen. However, this church surpasses that in Norwich for the fineness of its design and is known as his most important early work before he went on to design dozens of other federal buildings as the first Supervising Architect of the U.S. Treasury Department beginning in 1852. Built in the Federal style, this church was clearly inspired, at least in part, on the designs of the noted architect Asher Benjamin. However, the façade treatment of the First Congregational Church, with its narrow portico, the pavilion above featuring a compass-headed window, the whole topped off by a three-stage tower, is what makes this edifice stand out. In addition, the unusually tall windows on the side of the church which illuminate the sanctuary were also a nice design touch and unique for the time period. The church has changed but little over the years, being twice lengthened on the south side over the years, beginning in 1866. Today, the church, now heading towards its 200th birthday, is one of the architectural treasures of the area and has been very well preserved and maintained over the years.

First Congregational Church, Lebanon.

Façade detail, First Congregational Church, Lebanon.

Lempster

Lempster Meetinghouse
Built: 1794
Builder: James Bingham and Elijah Frink
Location: 112 Lempster Street

This survivor is important as one of the few remaining examples of eighteenth-century meetinghouses in southwestern New Hampshire. The meetinghouse served both civic and religious duties from its building until 1822, when it was moved to its current village location on what was then the bustling 2nd New Hampshire Turnpike route to Vermont and Canada. The original site of the meetinghouse, about a mile southeast of the current site, took some years to decide, even though the town was first settled in 1770 and the Congregational Church organized in 1781. One of the big events in the meetinghouse's history was a revival that followed a town funeral in 1798, probably that for Deacon Elijah Bingham (father of the builder of the meetinghouse), at which Psalm 12:1 was read, beginning with the cry "Help, Lord, for the godly man ceaseth; for the faithful fail from among the children of men." This revival subsequently added many people to the church and resulted in forty children being baptized in one day. Little is known about the details of the meetinghouse and its building as the church records were lost by fire in 1844 when the old parsonage was burned. However, both the Bingham and Frink families were early and prominent citizens in Lempster. James Bingham was the son of Deacon Elijah and is said to have built the most expensive house in town, while Frink was an innkeeper, at whose home the first town meeting was held. His home was near to this meetinghouse's original location and was used as a noon-house during the winter months so that members could get warm. Prior to its move, the Lempster Meetinghouse was a Type II meetinghouse with twin porches, like that built in Fremont (see above) and other southern New Hampshire towns, with the 100-foot bell tower added after its move in 1822. An original bell from the Paul Revere foundry once hung in its belfry, purchased in 1824, but it cracked at some point, subsequently being melted down and recast by another bell foundry in 1844. Once its time hosting religious services was over, the meetinghouse has served as a town hall, a high school academy (1835), library (1893), as well as hosting activities for the Silver Mountain Grange No. 96 (1897–1990s) and the Lempster Dramatic Union beginning in 1854. The exterior of the meetinghouse remains largely intact from its 1822 move and alterations. The original windows were replaced in 1910, but were fully restored in 2013 to their original configuration. The interior was greatly changed beginning in 1835 when it was used as a school, the gallery replaced

Lempster Meetinghouse.

with a full floor to create a second-story space. From 2006–2015, the meetinghouse underwent a full stabilization, repair, and exterior restoration project, with the result that this historic structure will continue to serve as a local landmark and institution for many years to come.

Lisbon

Lisbon-Landaff Shared Ministry Church (former First Methodist Episcopal Church of Lisbon)
Built: 1842
Location: 49 South Main Street

This church was the first ever to be built in the limits of modern-day Lisbon (an earlier one was built in what is now Sugar Hill). In its earliest days, it served as a Methodist Episcopal Church and was originally built as a simple, one-story structure at a cost of $3,000, with a simple belfry but no spire. In 1887, the church was renovated at a cost of $4,528, with the sanctuary raised to its second-story location and meeting room and class space added below, in keeping with the Methodist traditions of religious education. The clock was added to the tower in 1888, an important feature not only for the town citizens, but also those who were passing through on the train, the tracks running just behind the church. Horse sheds were built in two rows, the first in 1869, and another added in 1902, this last being short-lived as they were destroyed by heavy snow loads in 1906. The 1869 horse sheds stood until their removal in 1942. The Methodist church was established here in Lisbon village in 1839 under the leadership of Rev. John Smith, this church built at a time when there were still but few houses in the village area. The church, with its four-faced illuminated clock, has been a familiar part of the local skyline for over 100 years now. It is notable for its tall and narrow three-bay façade, with a clapboarded pediment featuring late Victorian-era trim in triangular form. The recessed entryway features a fanlight above the door and is notable for its paneled woodwork. Finally, the stained-glass windows are also a nice feature of this village church. The churches in Lisbon had their greatest period of growth in January 1895 when Rev. Ralph Gillam of Boston's Union Church preached here and inspired many, with ninety people moved to pledge that they would "lead a Christian life" after the very first sermon.[47] The revival lasted a full two weeks, during which, on several days, local schools, as well as businesses and mills closed early so that students and workers could attend prayer meetings. In all, some 300 people joined local churches, this one being the main benefactor, as a result of this revival.

Lisbon-Llandaff Shared Ministry Church, Lisbon.

The Church of the Epiphany (former St. Margaret's Guild)
Built: 1911
Architect: Edmund Quincy Sylvester, Jr.
Location: 90 School Street

Nestled within the confines of a small neighborhood, this wooden church is a hidden architectural gem. The Episcopal faith first gained traction in Lisbon in the late 1880s when missionary priests from All Saints Church in nearby Littleton conducted periodic services. In 1906, services began to be conducted on a regular weekly basis by Rev. Frederick Cowper of Woodsville, with a guild established that same year. In 1908, the guild took the name of St. Margaret, with the mission formally attached to All Saints Church in 1911. Prior to the building of this church, services were held in member's homes and local hotels and halls, but in 1911, St. Margaret's Guild put into motion their plans to build a small church of their own. The architect chosen for its design was a well-known Massachusetts ecclesiastical architect, a graduate of MIT who opened his own office in 1900. Sylvester was known regionally for his Episcopal church designs from 1902–1915, including six churches in Massachusetts and Maine, and three in New Hampshire, these being in Manchester, Berlin, and Lisbon. The building of the church, however, was truly a local affair, with the well-known Parker & Young firm of Lisbon, at one time the

The Church of the Epiphany, Lisbon.

largest manufacturer of piano sounding boards in the world, supplying over 4,300 feet of hemlock, spruce, and pine boards at a cost of about $150, while its windows were donated by the Church of the Transfiguration in Bretton Woods. Building funds were raised through many activities, including a cake sale in 1909 that netted $46, a hefty sum at the time. Construction began in May 1911 when its granite foundation was laid, with the church opened for Christmas Eve services that same year. The church went by the name of St. Margaret's Guild until 1945, when it took its current name, and has been very active over the years in its charitable practices both locally and worldwide, including contributions to restore church libraries in war-torn Japan in 1948. Built in the Shingle style, the church is distinguished by its wooden shake-siding, which gives the building an aged air, a hallmark of this style meant to hearken back to early colonial times, as well as its steeply pitched roof. The distinctive smaller side windows, with their diamond-shaped glass panes are also a hallmark of this style.

Littleton

First Congregational Church
Built: 1832–33, remodeled 1874
Builders: Capt. Andrew Tenney, Jonathan Nurs, and Jonathan Lovejoy
Location: 189 West Main Street

This church replaced Littleton's 1815-built meetinghouse, and though it was built years after the Toleration Act of 1819, it was a town-owned structure whose cost was borne by those who purchased the pews within. The Sunday services were originally to be split proportionately among the denominations of those who purchased the fifty-two pews, but while the Methodists early on would occasionally preach here, the Congregationalists remained firmly in control of the church. As in many towns, there was much dispute about where to build this church—the old meetinghouse located in the town's geographical center was in poor condition, but town votes to repair the structure failed. Those in the fast-rising village area of Littleton wanted the church in their area, and Rev. Drury Fairbank agreed, believing it was what was best for the largest group of worshippers, even if his support might cost him his job as town minister, one which he had held since 1820. Consequences be damned, Fairbank pushed for the new location, causing one resident who opposed the move to comment that "a new meeting-house meant a new minister."[48] Fairbank would ask to be dismissed from his position just two years after the church was built, believing it was best for his congregation in the wake of the events surrounding the building of the church. As originally constructed, the church was a typical Gothic Revival edifice, with a square, two-stage bell tower. Twenty-two subscribers committed to contributing funds, materials, and labor worth $943 in 1830 to help in building the church, including carpenter/builders Jonathan Lovejoy and Jonathan Nurs. Lovejoy provided a $10 donation in the form of physical labor, while Nurs provided $2 in labor, though the town history specifically lists him as aiding the professional builder and architect overseeing the project, Capt. Andrew Tenney of Lebanon. The building remained in its original form for forty years, but was substantially remodeled into its current form in 1874 when it was enlarged and its old tower replaced with its prominent twin spires, the taller being 110 feet tall with a weathervane, the shorter being 70 feet in height. The church remains a Gothic Revival structure, as can be seen in its arched windows and the pointed buttresses on the corners of both towers though the embellished louvers on the tower's belfries offer a touch of Victorian styling. The cost of the 1874 remodel was $8,000 and was perhaps influenced by an overall revival of religion in the town in 1874 inspired by union meetings and services involving all the denominations in town. The twin spires are also indicative of the growth and prosperity of Littleton at the time, but who was responsible for their construction is not certain. The most likely candidates are the builder Ellery Dunn, of whom it is stated "Nearly all the buildings on Main

First Congregational Church, Littleton.

Street erected between 1860 and 1890 were constructed by Captain Dunn" or the Simpson Brothers, John and Samuel, who were prominent builders in Littleton from 1868 to 1890.[49]

First United Methodist Church
Built: 1850–51
Builders: Levi Ranlet
Location: 18 Main Street

This prominently sited church was built as a cooperative venture between Levi Ranlet and the First Methodist Episcopal Church. Ranlet purchased the land the church is sited upon for $500, it formerly famous as the location of the "red store," a mercantile operation run by Major Ephraim Curtis from 1804–41. Ranlet offered the church, of which he was a member, an arrangement in which he would design and build the structure at his own cost, recouping his expenses by selling the pews within at a total amount which would equal his costs. The final amount he received was $4,659. As originally constructed, it was a Greek Revival structure with twin entryways, a portico and two Doric columns; the lumber came from the local sawmill of Philip Paddleford, the son of Littleton's well-known covered bridge builder, Peter Paddleford, while the timbers for the rafters were cut in the local woods in April 1850 and hauled to the sawmill over a foot of newly-fallen snow by Alexander McIntyre, for which work he received from Ranlet a pew in the church. The church was dedicated for service on January 8, 1851, the bell in its three-stage tower being the first of its kind in Littleton. Interestingly, Ranlet was accused of financial irregularities in this church's building, but a thorough examination of his records and receipts soon proved otherwise, the builder actually suffering financial loss because some who promised to buy pews reneged and paid nothing. Early on, the Methodists were in danger of losing control of the church, as some pews were purchased by Unitarians and Spiritualists (the denomination with the most pews holding control), but within a year the threat was overcome. Notably, during the intense national debates surrounding the issue of slavery from the 1840s up to the Civil War, the Methodists in Littleton and the surrounding area were firmly against the evils of slavery, even though they did not agree with the extremist activities of the abolitionists, this being in contrast to the Congregational Church in town, which was split on the issue. The Methodists thrived in their new home, its prominent location in the growing town making it the spiritual home of many prominent individuals, including Henry Thayer, whose grand hotel, one of the most noted establishments in the state, was (and still is) just across the street. This wealth and success are demonstrated by the heavy investment they made in their building and property; in 1875 and 1881, the interior was remodeled at the cost of several thousand dollars, but it was in 1888 that the church gained the form that we see today. At a cost of $4,000, the structure was raised some 6 feet to provide for meeting space below and the façade was entirely redone, its Doric columns eliminated and twin entryways replaced with a single one, with a large compass-headed window placed above. The town was probably split in their opinions on these changes; while the Methodists obviously liked their new edifice, many in town, including period historians, lamented the loss of the old façade, claiming the only noble part of the building left was its steeple. The façade is interesting, an eclectic one with a touch of the Greek Revival element surviving in its pilasters, while the narrow clapboard siding is a hallmark of the rural builder. The large central window is Federal (not Palladian as is stated on the historic plaque) in form, except for its huge proportions, while the hood and brackets above it offer a small Victorian touch. All of the church's windows were originally of clear glass, but those on the sides were replaced with stained-glass memorial windows in 1900–01 when the interior was once again refurbished at a cost of $3,000. Seven of these windows were paid for by subscription, memorializing individual family members, while one honors the early founders of the church, and its builder, Levi Ranlet. While one town historian claims that these windows were produced by Tiffany, records show that they were made by Redding & Baird of Boston.

First United Methodist Church, Littleton.

Loudon

Loudon Town Hall
Built: 1779
Location: 433 Clough Hill Road

This structure, originally constructed as a Type II meetinghouse, was built six years after the town's separation from Canterbury in 1773. Of course, folks in what is now Loudon objected to having to travel so far to meeting in Center Canterbury, but when they became an entity of their own, they were then faced with the decision as to where to locate their first meetinghouse. Eventually, the geographic center of Loudon was chosen and the frame was raised and enclosed in 1779, costing about $700 to frame and $1,000 in labor. At the raising, an additional $108 in rum was purchased for the event, as well as two quarts of snake root (to treat possible snake bites). Twin porches were added to the gable ends in 1789, but otherwise the building remained unfinished until 1794. Efforts to paint the exterior failed at town meeting in 1795 and apparently for many years after. The structure gained its current form in 1847, when the porches were removed and a new façade was built, as was the three-stage tower, transforming it into a Greek Revival-style edifice. Especially notable are the towering corner pilasters and those flanking the central entryway. It was also in 1847 that the interior was changed, the gallery floored over to create a second-story space for the Free Will Baptist Church, while the lower level was used as town offices

Loudon Town Hall.

and a polling place. The structure continued as shared space between the town and the church until 1976, when new town offices were built. There was apparently no bell in the belfry until a local citizen donated one in 1878, made by William Blake in Boston. Today, the town hall looks much the same as it did after 1847, though the bold lettering on its façade was added beginning in 1973 and stained-glass was added to the upper-story windows during minor renovations in 1922–23. The Congregationalists were the standing order in Loudon early on in this structure's life, but by the first decade of the nineteenth century, the Free Will Baptists were gaining precedence, forming their own society in 1817 and sharing the town hall until 1823, when the Congregationalists gave up the town hall altogether. Since that time, the town hall has been the continuous home of the Free Will Baptist Church.

Loudon Congregational Church
Built: 1826–27
Location: 7018 Church Street

The story of this church edifice begins when the Congregationalists in town decided to abandon the use of the old town hall (see above) in 1823. Dissatisfied with having to share that building with other denominations, they gave over its use to the Free Will Baptists and, at least at first, resorted to private homes and public schoolhouses as settings for their worship services. In addition, many individuals had left the church, deciding to join the Free Will Baptists instead, so the Congregational church was weakened after 1817, and in 1821, they had to reduce their minister's salary. Initially, efforts to build a new church in 1823, about a mile from the old town hall, failed, but in 1826, those efforts to build began again. However, the congregation could not agree, some wanting to stay in the neighborhood of the old town hall in the geographic center of town, while others wanted it built at the rapidly growing village area of town, some 4 miles to the south. Neither side could agree, and there was much ill-will, but those in the village area proceeded to build this church on their own, further increasing the divide among the Congregationalists. The town minister, Rev. Enoch Corser, did preach the dedication service for the new structure, but would not perform any other services in the new church. Those in the village subsequently asked to be dismissed from the old church to form their own church society and were fought on this matter too, but eventually won out and formed the Second Congregational Church in September 1828. From that time forth, both societies were weakened in Loudon, both barely able to afford a full-time minister and sometimes relying on missionary aid for many years, though today the church is the sole Congregational one in town and is a vital part of the community. Though weatherworn, the church is still a nice example of Federal-style architecture in a rural setting, the columns flanking its twin entry-ways, the fan louvers above the windows, and the octagonal belfry of the two-stage tower its most distinguishing features. The church appears to have undergone only minor changes, with the original sash windows replaced by stained-glass windows sometime in the

Loudon Congregational Church.

late nineteenth century. Behind the church, there are two cemeteries, the older Moore Cemetery to the right, established by a local citizen initially as a private burying place, and the more modern Mount Hope Cemetery to the left.

Lyme

Lyme Congregational Church
Built: 1808–11
Builder: John Thompson, Jr.
Location: 1 Dorchester Road, on the town green

Located in a quiet town with a population of 1,700, this meetinghouse is one of the finest to be found in the Connecticut River Valley area of New Hampshire. The town was first granted to John Thompson and others in 1761, with settlement beginning several years later. The Congregational church was established here in 1771, with the first meetinghouse built ten years later. However, by the early 1800s, a larger meetinghouse was needed and plans were commenced by the Lyme Meeting House Society to finance its building through pew sales, its location just a very short distance from the old meetinghouse on common land. The master-builder who supervised the construction of this ambitious building, John Thompson, Jr., was a local man, son of one of the town's original grantees, who built a number of other homes and buildings in Lyme and was very skilled at his craft. The design of the church is credited to Salmon Washburn, also a Lyme native, the son of Libeus Washburn, a prominent citizen who served as a selectman but worked as a carpenter, joiner, and furniture maker. Upon completion, the church cost about $6,000, a large sum for the day, but not surprising given its size and design features. While the younger Thompson built this structure, his father, John Thompson, built the many horse sheds from about 1810–14, about fifty in number originally, which feature a salt-box shingled roof and arched openings, and were built in three different rows, two of which are no longer extant. The surviving row of sheds, twenty-seven in number, is the longest line of horse sheds in New England, and probably in all of America. As was common, each shed was individually owned and ownership could be transferred by deed, but the land on which they sat remained in town control.

While this structure serves as a community church today, it has been a meetinghouse in the truest sense of the word for much of its life; when first built, it served both as a house of worship and as a place where town business was conducted. In addition to being the home of the Congregational Church, it has also been the home to the town's social library (1858–1909), a meeting place for the Morning Star Grange (1899–1980s), and as the place where town meetings were once again held from 1920–1957. To accommodate these changes in use, the interior was altered in 1847 when a second story was created at the gallery level. As for the

Lyme Congregational Church.

exterior, it has changed but little since it was first built, the major change being the E. Howard clock added to the tower in 1921. Built in the Federal style, the structure is distinguished by its projecting vestibule and façade, which features triple entryways, the central one being larger than those flanking it, each with a fanlight and flanking columns. Above the central doorway is a Palladian window, with a small pediment above that. Above the vestibule is an unusual tower, three-stages in height, each of which is square, topped off with a domed roof with pinnacles at each corner. Overall, the church is both a beautiful and imposing structure, made even more so by its close location next to Route 10 on the town green. Adding to the setting are the previously-discussed surviving horse sheds to the east side of the church, as well as the Old Lyme Cemetery just across the street, which is the final resting place for many of the town's earliest settlers and is noted for its nice collection of gravestones.

Madison

The Madison Church
Built: 1885
Location: 53 Conway Road

This Victorian-era church has always been associated with the Baptist faith, first serving the Free Will Baptists. That denomination got its start in the area in 1789,

The Madison Church.

when the territory that would eventually become the town of Madison in 1853 was part of Eaton and Albany and was served by many itinerant preachers, a previous church having been built in 1825. Less than three years after this church was built, the structure "was thoroughly renovated and retrofitted, and a fine bell hung in the tower," while in 1913, the interior was renovated.[50] What prompted the 1888 renovation so soon after the church was built is unknown. At one time, horse sheds stood behind the church, they being built on land donated to the church in 1911 by Irving and Rita Kennett and built in 1912. In the severe winter of 1919–20, the sheds collapsed due to heavy snow loads and were a complete loss, but were rebuilt the following summer with money from the Ladies Aid organization, as well as by private subscription. Apparently tired of maintaining the sheds, they were auctioned off in 1931 and removed. The church structure is a beautiful one, dignified in its simplicity, its most notable features being the three-stage tower and the decorative pediment, scroll work and brackets above the entryway. The church, now a member of the American Baptist Churches, is the only one in Madison today and plays a vital role in the small community it serves.

Manchester

Grace Episcopal Church
Built: 1860
Architect: Richard Upjohn
Location: 106 Lowell Street

The Episcopal faith got its start in Manchester in 1841 when the first services were held, conducted by the rector of the Saint Paul School in Concord. Later that year, the first Episcopal parish in the city was formed, taking the name St. Michael's. Their first church was built at a cost of about $2,000 on the current site of the church, the land donated by the Amoskeag Mills. However, by the late 1850s, the church had grown considerably in numbers and provisions were made to build a new structure. The prosperity of the church is demonstrated by the fact that they hired the most prominent ecclesiastical architect in America at the time, Richard Upjohn of New York, to design their new home. The old church was cut in half and moved off the site, with construction beginning in June 1860 and the new church consecrated under its new name, Grace Episcopal, in December of that same year. The church is built of stone in the signature Gothic Revival style favored by Upjohn, notable for its imposing corner tower, Gothic-arched windows, and steeply-pitched roof. When an addition to the north side of the church facing Pine Street in the form of a parish house was made in 1886, Richard Upjohn, Jr., was hired as its designer to

Grace Episcopal Church, Manchester.

ensure the addition matched the original structure. This addition later on, in 1913, became a chapel dedicated to St. Michael, who is represented in charming statue form in an alcove above the entryway. On the west side of the church along Lowell Street, a new parish house was built in 1913, designed by the prestigious Boston firm of Cram, Goodhue, and Ferguson. Overall, the whole complex of buildings represents a small slice of medieval England in the heart of a major New England manufacturing city. Grace Episcopal has been a major presence in the city for many years and has had but few rectors over the years as those who have served in that position have had long tenures. One of the most interesting of these men was Rev. Lorin B. Young, who served from 1941 until his retirement in 1967, a man beloved in the city for his devotion to social causes (he was also known for the same in his previous position in Brooklyn, NY), as well as his presence about the city, he being called "Manchester's Good Shepherd on a bicycle." Grace Episcopal is also notable for its assistant clergy, Rev. Ann Webb, who, upon her ordination in 1978, was only the second female priest to attain the position in the New Hampshire Diocese.

Saint Joseph Roman Catholic Cathedral
Built: 1867–69
Architects: Patrick Keely and Patrick W. Ford
Location: 145 Lowell Street

This large brick church was the second Roman Catholic edifice built in the city of Manchester after St. Anne's, and was built because of the large influx of Irish and French-Canadian immigrants and the resulting crowded conditions at the older church. First built as a parish church, it is notable as being the successive work of two Irish-born American architects who were well-known for their Roman Catholic architecture. The primary architect, Patrick Keely, was born in County Tipperary and immigrated to Brooklyn, NY, in 1842, having been trained in building and design by his father in Ireland. During the course of his career, he designed over 600 Roman Catholic churches in America, including every Roman Catholic Cathedral in New England, Saint Joseph being his only New Hampshire church. When Saint Joseph was enlarged in 1892, the architect was Patrick Ford, who arrived in New York in 1866 from County Cork, having been educated at Queen's College. He had worked with Keely for a short time before eventually moving to Boston to open his own firm, designing dozens of Roman Catholic church buildings and structures, including Saint Anselm College's Alumni Hall in Goffstown, and one no-longer extant church in Exeter, before his sudden death in 1900. Constructed in the Gothic Revival style, the cathedral is noted for its corner tower, which soars to a height of 165 feet. The church gained cathedral status in 1884 with the creation of the Roman Catholic Diocese of Manchester, with Bishop Denis Bradley choosing Saint Joseph as his seat. This is not surprising, as Bradley prior to his elevation, had been the pastor of Saint Joseph since 1881. The church, which originally had seating for

St. Joseph Roman Catholic Cathedral, Manchester.

1,300 people, has a vaulted ceiling supported by twelve pillars and the side-walls featuring twelve double stained-glass windows. The church was enlarged at its eastern end in 1892–93 on designs by Patrick Ford, including a transept and chancel and the Sacred Heart Chapel, the work done by noted Manchester builder Alpheus Gay. The nave windows of Saint Joseph are among the many notable details of this cathedral inside and out, having been crafted by the Tyrolese Art Glass Company of Innsbruck, Austria, about 1891 and exhibited at the 1893 World's Fair in Chicago before their installation. In the last few years, the cathedral has undertaken an ongoing interior restoration project, including the installation of a large marble reredos (altarpiece) from the now deconsecrated Holy Trinity Church in Boston (also designed by Patrick Keely), the original in Manchester being destroyed during renovations in 1969.

Gethsemane Lutheran Church
Built: 1886–87
Location: 65 Sagamore Street

The immigration wave into Manchester in the mid- to late-nineteenth century to provide the manpower for its mill and manufacturing enterprises was comprised not just of the Irish and French-Canadians, but many other ethnic groups as well,

Gethsemane Lutheran Church, Manchester.

as is amply demonstrated by this pleasing church. Many Swedish immigrants also made Manchester their new home and Lutheran services were first held in a mission chapel located on the corner of Beech and Merrimack Street, but eventually membership grew to the point that in 1885, it was decided to build a more substantial church, the land donated by Amoskeag Mills, proof positive that mill owners had a desire to keep their immigrant workers spiritually engaged. The church was dedicated in 1887, having been built and finished inside by Swedish carpenters and craftsmen. Built in the Gothic Revival style, the wooden church, now clad in vinyl siding, features arched windows and a narrow two-stage tower. Most interesting are the row of four small, arched windows at the base of the tower, and the large Gothic-arched double-doored entryway. As originally constructed, the church was symmetrical in its plan, but this changed in 1990 when the church was connected to the adjacent St. James Hall, a Methodist building built in 1891. Other changes include the addition of the stained-glass windows on the nave and over the doorway, commissioned in 1946 and installed in 1947, designed by William Jack of Boston. That over the doorway denotes the founding date of the church, while others are memorial windows, including those for two men who were killed during World War II. Interestingly, services in the church were conducted in Swedish until the practice was ended in 1907 as later generations no longer spoke the language of the home country.

Saint Marie Roman Catholic Church
Built: 1891, 1898–99
Architect: J. A. Baserick
Builders: George Guernsey and Napoleon Dubuque
Location: 378 Notre Dame Avenue

The parish of Ste. Marie was founded in West Manchester in 1880 to serving the growing population of French-Canadian immigrants to the city. The first church, a wooden structure, was built in 1880, but the parish truly flourished when Monsignor Pierre Hevey arrived in 1882. He had a vision of how Ste. Marie should be, with the church perched on Rimmon Heights, visible to the workers at the mills below, their houses in close proximity to the church to form a parish neighborhood. Not only would the neighborhood of Notre Dame become a reality, with the parish comprising some 6,000 parishioners by 1889, but Hevey also was the founder of many of the neighborhood's institutions, including Notre Dame Hospital (Now Catholic Medical Center), St. Mary's Bank, the Notre Dame Orphanage for Girls, and Saint Peter's Orphanage for Boys. When the original church was burned in October 1890, plans to rebuild were begun within months in 1891, with the basement of the future church serving as the site for early services with the ability to seat 800 people and fully finished with an altar. Further construction would not be resumed once the basement chapel was completed until early 1898, but by November 1899, Ste. Marie Church was finished. Of the men who completed St. Marie, Guernsey, was a well-known ecclesiastical architect and builder from Montpelier, Vermont, while Napoleon Dubuque was a local carpenter, perhaps responsible for some of the interior work. The result was one of the finest Gothic Revival churches in the state and one of the city's most visible landmarks, its spire and cross rising 240 feet skyward. Constructed of brick, the symmetrical church is distinguished by its elaborate façade, with triple entryways, a tower featuring Gothic-arched windows soaring above the central doorway. Within the bell tower are four bells that call to the faithful and can be heard throughout the city, the largest weighing in at 7,150 lb., the smallest, dedicated to the church's namesake saint, weighing 1,795 lb. In addition to the church, there is a whole complex of period buildings surrounding it that are related to the activities and administration of the parish. Today, Ste. Marie Church remains a prominent institution in Manchester, serving the spiritual needs of the community, many of them descendants of its first immigrant parishioners.

Saint Marie Roman Catholic Church, Manchester.

Saint George Greek Orthodox Cathedral
Built: 1964–70
Architect: Christopher Kantiaris
Location: 650 Hanover Street

Described as "an excellent example of the concept of architecture as a piece of sculpture," this unusual cathedral is representative of the large influence of Greek immigrants of the Queen City beginning about 1893 and ending in 1924, though a second wave of immigrants followed the devastation of World War II.[51] The first acknowledged Greek immigrant here was a Doctor Zervoudakes, a Cretan who arrived here from Montreal, but many others would follow. It is no coincidence this cathedral is located where it is, for just a short distance away is Spruce Street, where many of the Greek immigrants first lived. Though there were just a handful of Greeks here by 1900; by 1910, there were over 1,300; and by 1920, there were nearly 3,800 in Manchester. Saint George Church was founded in 1905 in response to this increase in numbers, there being not only the need for a church of their own, but also the will to get one built. Despite a schism in the local church which occurred in 1936, Saint George is the oldest and most distinguished Greek Orthodox Church in the state. Their unusual cathedral, designed by a Springfield, Massachusetts, architect of Greek descent who built Greek Orthodox churches throughout New England, is truly a work of art that reflects the modernity and space-age style of

Saint George Greek Orthodox Cathedral, Manchester.

the 1960s. This cathedral must be seen in person to appreciate, the main domed body highlighted by its vertical rows of colored circular windows that illuminate the interior.

Marlborough

The Federated Church of Marlborough (former Trinitarian Congregational Church)
Built: 1834
Location: 16 Pleasant Street

This simple yet elegant church, constructed out of bricks that were made locally, was first the home of Marlborough's third Congregational organization, the Trinitarian Congregational Church established in 1833, and the second formed after the original relationship between town and church ended in 1824 with the death of its last settled pastor, Rev. Halloway Fish. As in other towns, the Trinitarians found it inconvenient to share the old town meetinghouse with other denominations, so became determined to build a church of their own. There was some concern about building the church in the village area of Marlborough (away from the geographic center of town) because there were few homes and only a few businesses here at the time. However, its proponents prevailed, said to have been helped in part by neighboring churches. In October 1834, the new building was dedicated for service, its presence helping in the coming years to the build-up of the village. The brick church that was built is Gothic Revival in style, distinguished by its twin arched-entryways and the series of three arches on its façade, referred to as a "blind arcade" in architectural terms because the arches are merely decorative elements as opposed to having a load-bearing function. The short tower, which results in a broken pediment, is also unusual for the times. The church has expanded in size over the years: in 1851, more space was needed, so it was lengthened to accommodate twenty more pews, and in 1869, the church was again altered after a period of revival added over forty new members, with $1,428 raised to build a recess on the east end of the church with fourteen pews added. In addition to the Trinitarians, the Baptists (who disbanded in 1862), Universalists, and Methodists were also active in town, but by the 1920s, the size of each of the remaining congregations were declining in numbers, making it difficult for each denomination to support and maintain its own church building. As a result, in 1927, the Congregationalists, Universalists, and Methodists united to form The Federated Church of Marlborough, choosing as their home this church in 1929. Today, it is the only church in Marlborough, sustaining its nearly 100-year mission of honoring the town's religious traditions, while at the same time acknowledging its diversity.

The Federated Church of Marlborough.

Melvin Village

Melvin Village Community Church
Built: 1866
Location: 476 Governor Wentworth Highway (Rte. 109)

Located on the northern shore of Lake Winnipesaukee, this small church is known both for its beautiful setting and for its nearby historic literary association. The First Free Will Baptist Church of Moultonborough and Tuftonborough in Melvin Village, a part of the town of Tuftonboro, was formally organized in 1837. The church would have its ups and downs over the next fifteen years, but was reorganized in 1852 and began a steady rise in membership, so much so that this church was built to serve its needs. It is a simply built and pleasing structure, the work of a country builder, with little architectural adornment beyond its corner pilasters, fitted with a simple three-stage tower. Originally the belfry was fully open, but diagonal braces now occupy some of this space and leave it less exposed. The weathervane of this church is a common but interesting design, its body in the form of lyre, a Christian symbol of joy, while its tail features an open tulip bud, a symbol of Christian charity. The church is beautifully sited on a point of land overlooking the lake, which is visible from its chancel window, and right next to the spot where Melvin Stream empties into the lake. It is at this spot, now marked by a sign depicting a Native American and denoting it as "The Grave by the Lake," that the skeletal remains of a large man, said to be about 7 feet tall and probably a tribal chief, were unearthed in 1808. This find was made famous by John Greenleaf Whittier's poem "The Grave by the Lake" when it was first published in 1865, and it was the following year that this church was built close to the site, one that has been visited by countless summer tourists ever since. Soon after the church was built, a cemetery behind it, overlooking the lake, was also established. Here, you will find many interesting stones, including that for John Rollins, who "passed to the Summer land" in 1869. While the original church exterior has changed but little, a modern addition was added, and the adjacent horse sheds were likely built after 1910, based on period views. Once a Free Will Baptist Church, this church became a community Baptist church in 1940 with the merging of two different Baptist groups and remains affiliated with the American Baptists today. The church not only carries on its historic lineage, but even conducts modern baptisms in the waters of Lake Winnipesaukee, just as was done in the days of old.

Melvin Village Community Church.

Meredith

First Congregational Church
Built: 1832
Builder: Jonathan Crane
Location: 4 Highland Street

Located near the center of Meredith and a presence on the local skyline due to its hilltop location, this church serves a congregation that was originally formed in 1815. The church first served the towns of Center Harbor and Meredith, but eventually the members in Center Harbor left to form their own society. This structure was built to replace an earlier one located near the town line and was originally located close to the shore of Lake Winnipesaukee on Meredith Bay until its move to its current site by 1843. Built in the Federal style at an original cost of $940, it has seen many changes over the years. In 1871, the church was remodeled and enlarged at a cost of $4,369, but the nature of this work is unknown, while the adjacent chapel was built in 1878, but not connected to the church until the 1920s. In that same time period, the façade was also remodeled into its current form, its twin entryways replaced with windows and replaced with a central entryway, thereby completing the architectural evolution of the church from its original Federal style to one that more closely matches the Colonial Revival style that was popular in the 1920s. Previously, in 1903, Miss Virginia Ladd, the invalid daughter of Seneca Ladd, donated to the church its tower clock, therefore adding another stage to its steeple. The association of the church with the Ladd family, whose house was on Highland Street, is an interesting one. While his daughter, Virginia, was a churchgoer, Seneca Ladd was not; known as a bit of a freethinker and philosopher, he came to Meredith about 1837, first practicing the trade of a carriage-maker, and within several years going into partnership to open his own carriage manufacturing business. When his factory burned down in 1850, he immediately leased another mill and started a piano and melodeon manufacturing plant, operating out of Meredith and Boston in partnership with his brother. After his retirement in 1869, he went on to found the Meredith Village Savings Bank (still in business today), and also had a deep interest in science, geology, and history, being a member of the New Hampshire Antiquarian Society and discoverer of a famed artifact, what would later be called the Mystery Stone, an egg-shaped stone object with carvings on it said to have been done by Native Americans, which is now on display at the New Hampshire Historical Society Museum in Concord. As for Virginia Ladd, she was very much involved in community affairs for most her adult life until her untimely death in 1927.

First Baptist Church of Meredith
Built: 1833–34
Location: 89 Main Street

Originally named the Second Baptist Church of Meredith, this church was formed in 1831 after a period of great religious revival in town, its members coming from the First Baptist Church. Its first minister, Rev. William Taylor, was a well-known Baptist evangelical in New Hampshire, he being the one to choose its location "upon a rock" in Meredith Village.[52] Unfortunately, nothing is known of its building, except that it was paid for in full within a short time after its building. The structure is an unusual one, being constructed of brick at a time when the vast majority of area buildings were built of wood. Designed in the Federal style, the flat-topped pediment, which supports the tower above, is an unusual departure from the norm. The façade is the most drastically changed part of the church, resulting from a fire caused by a lightning strike in 1902. Severely damaged, the church was altered during its subsequent renovation, the original twin entryways replaced with a one-story wooden vestibule with a central doorway, while the center window above was bricked in. The vestibule was originally finished in asphalt siding that had a brick pattern, since replaced by white vinyl siding. The result of these changes today is a quirky but pleasing house of worship, with the look of a residential porch added onto an otherwise stately brick edifice. In addition to these changes, the tower itself has also changed, the belfry formerly being open, but enclosed by the 1890s, while a rear addition was built in the 1970s. When the other Baptist church organizations in Meredith went extinct, this church later went by the name of the Meredith Village Baptist Church before subsequently gaining its current name. Like many other Baptist churches in New Hampshire, it has had many

Above left: First Congregational Church, Meredith.

Above right: First Baptist Church of Meredith.

ministers over the years, and has also had many years where preaching from a settled minister was hard to come by. Early on, students at the New Hampton Academy, sponsored by the New Hampshire Baptist Society for many years, supplied the pulpit when the need arose. From 1856–58, disputes between the congregation and Rev. George Daland, a native of Massachusetts, arose over the issue of slavery, while in the 1870s, naval chaplain Rev. William Stewart was a successful minister who energized the church for two years until he was ordered to report for duty in 1877.

Merrimack

Merrimack Valley Baptist Church (former Second Congregational Church)
Built: 1829
Location: 517 Boston Post Road

The building of this church may be seen, perhaps, as the one of the tangible results of the Toleration Act of 1819 in Merrimack. After the death of the town's long settled pastor, Rev. Jacob Burnap, in 1821, the Congregational Church fell on hard times here. This church, later called the Union Evangelical Church of Merrimack, was organized to serve the needs of those in the southern part of Merrimack, as well as those in neighboring Hollis, Amherst, Milford, and Nashua. Services were first held in a local school house in 1828, but in May 1829, the frame of a meetinghouse was raised, its builder unknown now due to a lack of records, with the structure dedicated for service on October 7 of that same year. Built in the Greek Revival style, it is notable for its recessed entryway with twin Doric columns and corner pilasters, and has a tower consisting of three, square stages, the upper one adorned with scallop-edged shingles and a circular louvered vent. This tower, or at least its upper stage, may have been added later, or underwent alterations as its details reflect a Victorian influence. The church's first pastor, Rev. Samuel Tolman, manned the pulpit, supported by the New Hampshire Missionary Society, and was quite successful, growing the church from a handful of members to over eighty, though after his dismissal in 1836, there was no settled pastor and the membership dropped by half. Rev. John Shepard arrived in 1844 and lasted three years, but excommunicated more members than he added to the church. Rev. Tolman subsequently returned in 1848 and again built the congregation and proved a stabilizing force for the next five years. For many years, the church labored under many societal concerns, including "the suppression of intemperance, Sabbath breaking, and their attendant vices."[53] To support the activities and mission of the current church, a large complex of modern buildings has been built around, and connecting to, the original church building.

First Church of Merrimack (former First Congregational Church of Merrimack)
Built: 1837
Location: 7 Baboosic Lake Road

The Congregational church in Merrimack was formed in 1771, with its first minister, Rev. Jacob Burnap, ordained the following year. He would serve the church and town as a settled minister for an incredible fifty years until his death in 1821. Afterwards, the Congregational church in town fell on hard times; for the next four years, there was no settled minister, largely due to a lack of funds now that the newly formed Merrimack Religious Society had but little funds to its name. A minister was again hired in 1825 but lasted just three years, mainly due to a lack of support, though the establishment of a Sabbath-school during this time was a major achievement. Missionary preachers were subsequently hired for short periods of time as the congregation could afford, with services held at the old meetinghouse in the center of town at Turkey Hill. However, by the 1830s, the center of the town's business activities had moved closer to the Merrimack River. As a result of a small revival and new Christian families moving to town, the church decided to build a new home in 1837, while reorganizing their church organization at the same time.

Right: Merrimack Valley Baptist Church, Merrimack.

Below: First Church of Merrimack.

The site they chose was a central one and remains so to this day, located on an impressive site. Built by a rural builder or builders whose identity is not known for certain, the church is an eclectic one, combining elements of the Greek Revival style, as seen in its corner pilasters, pediment, and the molding around its twin entryways, while elements of the Federal style are also prominent, most notably in its Palladian window and the louvered vent in the pediment.

Over the years, the structure has been greatly altered, most notably with the large addition to the rear, as well as the change in side windows in the original main block of the building. With this move to a new home from the town-owned meetinghouse, the fortunes of the church subsequently improved, with a new pastor, Rev. Stephen Allen, hired in 1839 and serving for ten years. This church remained a Congregational one for many years, but in 1965, it became more conservative in its doctrine, which, according to the church's own history, upset many in town. The conservative nature of services here gained further traction with the arrival of the conservative Presbyterian minister Pastor Bruce Gordon in 1967, and continued under Pastor Allen Tomlinson, who came to the church in 1988. In December 2014, the church gained its present affiliation when it was accepted into the Orthodox Presbyterian Church Presbytery of New York and New England, thus changing its name.

Middleton

Old Middleton Town Hall
Built: 1795–96
Location: 180 King's Highway Road

Perhaps more so than any other structure discussed in this work, the old saying "You can't judge a book by its cover" applies to Middleton's Old Town Hall. On the outside, it looks like a typical "old" building that could be found in any New England town, one that has been altered and added to over the years as its uses have changed—not an ugly building by any means, but also one that might not catch one's attention either. However, enter the Old Town Hall and head upstairs via the narrow staircase and your mind will be changed and you will feel like you have been carried back in time some 150 years ago. Granted in 1778, the town's early religious history is varied, and the fact that there never was a standing order in Middleton is the reason that its first meetinghouse was not built until nearly twenty years after its founding. While a Congregational preacher did minister here for several years, his efforts to gather a church failed, and by the late 1700s, the Free Will Baptists, founded by Benjamin Randall in neighboring New Durham, were the most successful when it came to gathering religious adherents. This meetinghouse was originally located just a mile away on Ridge Road and was a one-story structure,

Middleton Town Hall.

Wall mural detail, Middleton Town Hall.

plain in nature and similar to other rural meetinghouse in the Lakes Region such as that in New Hampton (see below). In 1812, the meetinghouse was moved to its current location by many teams of oxen, with the original meeting space moved upstairs when the building was enlarged into a two-story structure, the lower space used for town functions. Though Middleton is a quiet town today, back in the mid-1800s, it was an important stage stop on the busy road from Dover to Sandwich, so the buildings at this important intersection saw much use in addition to its originally designed function as a place where town affairs were conducted, including annual town meetings and election voting. The upstairs sanctuary in the Old Town Hall was used by the Free Will Baptists for many years, it being formally designated as their church space in 1841, there being no other church in town until 1954. This upstairs space is distinguished by its original raised pulpit and boxed pews, but is most notable for the finely painted wall murals which feature an all-surrounding arboreal theme, as well as a harp and an angel's trumpet on the wall behind the choir gallery. This work is thought to have been executed in 1841 by mural artist John Avery of Wolfeboro and is one of the few surviving examples of his work in the area. The structure remains town-owned, and while today no church organization uses the upper space in the Old Town Hall, it still sees occasional use through special services and weddings throughout the year. By the early 2000s, this structure was endangered, badly in need of shoring up its supporting timbers, and in 2011, it was named by the New Hampshire Preservation Alliance to its Seven to Save List. As of 2018, the repairs the Old Town Hall needed have largely been accomplished, with some finishing details left to be completed and the Old Town Hall, as has been the case for years, is available to anyone who may wish to book it for any variety of functions.

Milford

Eagle Hall (former Milford Meetinghouse and Congregational Church)
Built: 1784
Location: Union Square

This structure is notable for its long history and the evolution of its varied use over the years. As originally constructed, this building was Milford's first (and only) meetinghouse; its frame was raised in the summer of 1784, but it would take many years to finish. There was no floor until 1785, while money for window glass and frames, as well as clapboards, was not raised until the winter of 1784–85. In March 1785, it was also decided to add porches to the meetinghouse, which was of the common Type II form. The meetinghouse was not finally finished until 1796, but further changes came in 1803, when a bell tower, modelled after that in Francestown, was added to the structure. The bell that once occupied its belfry, until being moved to the current town hall when it was opened for use in 1870, was a gift from a friend of Milford's first settled minister, Rev. Humphrey Moore. Cast in the Revere bell foundry in 1802, it weighs in at 802 lb. and is one of the oldest Revere bells in existence and one of the town's most important historic artifacts. The meetinghouse was used as a house of worship by the Congregationalists up to 1832, when the relationship between church and town ended at Rev. Moore's request. The Congregationalists offered the town $500 for the structure, but were turned down after a very close town vote. For the next year, it was decided by the town that each denomination in town would share the building, but this did not sit well with the Congregationalists and they subsequently built their own church in 1834 (see below). This structure remained town-owned for many years after, first used as a townhouse, it being turned on its original site in the town green ("the oval" as it is known today) and remodeled in 1847. It was in 1846 that the gilded eagle atop the structure's cupola was erected at a cost of $65. This eagle flew over the newly-named Eagle Hall until 1996 when it was brought down due to its aged state and replaced with a newly crafted one, with a wing-span of nearly 9 feet, made by John Weidman of Brookline and installed in 1999. The building was moved to its current site, originally called the "factory lot" in 1869, and after this time, it has been used as community and commercial structure. Many important town events have taken place here over the years, including the hosting of an anti-slavery convention in January 1843 attended by such notables as Frederick Douglass and abolitionist

Eagle Hall, Milford.

William Lloyd Garrison. From 1866 to 1870, Eagle Hall was also the home of the town clock, it being mounted in the octagonal belfry. Since 1920, the building has been owned by the Odd Fellows, an international fraternal organization that has had a presence in New Hampshire since the early 1800s. Eagle Hall today, with its many architectural changes, may best be classified as an eclectic structure which offers many interesting details—the broad pediment with its large circular window is a combination of the Greek Revival and Victorian styles, while the octagonal belfry topped with a dome and the gilded eagle is reminiscent of the Federal style.

First Congregational Church
Built: 1834
Location: 10 Union Street

This pleasing church building continues the religious history of the Congregationalists after their use of the town meetinghouse (see above) was ended in 1833. The funds to build the structure were raised by subscription, with the frame of the church raised in May 1834, it being subsequently finished in an attractive manner that is a mix of the Federal and Greek Revival styles. Notable features include its triple doorways with transom windows above and Federal-style trim, and the towering corner pilasters, with identical ones flanking the central doorway. The pediment is notable for its central eight-paned window flanked by quarter-round louvers, while the three-stage tower that rises above is beautiful in its simplicity, featuring corner pilasters at each stage. The building has seen some revisions over the years, most notably in 1850s when the church was enlarged with the addition of twenty-eight pews. Located just outside the current downtown area of Milford, its spire visible from the oval, the church has played a central role in the community since its founding in 1788. As in other New Hampshire towns, the pre-Civil War period from the 1830s to the 1860s was fraught with debate and anxiety over the issue of slavery. However, under the leadership of reverends Abner Warner (1839–1846) and E. N. Hidden (1849–1857), Milford's Congregational church was bolder than most in the area when it came to their stance against slavery. While the church did not go so far as to break their fellowship with other area churches who were lukewarm about abolition, they were adamant in their preaching and sermons about the evils of slavery. Rev. Hidden is also known to have performed the marriage ceremony for Harriet Adams and George Wilson, an African-American couple, in October 1851; eight years later, in 1859, Harriet Wilson published a novel entitled *Our Nig: Sketches from the Life of a Free Black*, one of the very first novels published by an African-American woman in America.

Above left: First Congregational Church, Milford.

Above right: Façade detail, First Congregational Church, Milford.

Milton

Milton Townhouse
Built: 1803–1804
Builders: Caleb Wingate, Gilman Jewett, and Daniel Hayes
Location: Corner of Rte. 125 and Townhouse Road

Once the Third Parish of Rochester with settlers arriving here in the 1760s, Milton was incorporated as a separate town in 1802, soon after building their own meetinghouse as was customary. The building of this meetinghouse was contracted out to three men, with Caleb Wingate raising and constructing the frame, Gilman Jewett doing the outside finish work, and Daniel Hayes finishing the interior. The structure cost $2,352 when all was said and done, including the rum that was consumed on the day of its raising. The meetinghouse was first used in August 1804, and would remain an important structure for the next four decades. As originally constructed, the building was a Type

II meetinghouse, but was distinguished by having three porches, one over the entryway on the long side, and a porch on each gable end, this at a time when twin-porch meetinghouses were more common. Almost from the beginning, town support for the ministry in these changing times was small; in 1803, and again in 1805, a 50-cent tax was approved on those who could vote or owned property to help support the ministry, though in 1805 such taxpayers were allowed to designate to which denomination their money would be allocated. After 1813, it appears that taxes were no longer raised for ministerial support. Preaching in town was sporadic until 1815, when the First Congregational Church was formed. This group used the meetinghouse until 1835, when they built their own church at the Three Ponds area of Milton. Thereafter, the old meetinghouse was used by other religious groups in town, but after 1841, it saw sporadic use only when the First Christian Church built their own structure. Finally, in 1855, the town of Milton took full control of the building, cutting it down to its current one-story configuration, removing the porches, reconfiguring the windows, and entirely altering the interior for secular use, all vestiges of its pulpit and pews removed. Thus, the building that is seen today really dates from 1855, except for some of its original timbers. In 1965, a pulpit was reconstructed inside, though its placement or form do not match the original. One other notable aspect of the townhouse's history is the adjacent historic town pound, directly across Rte. 125. It is an unusual round town pound, one

Milton Town House.

of only three remaining in New Hampshire, originally built in 1804, reconstructed in 1823, and moved back from the road in 1928.

Milton Mills

Liberty Congregational Church (former Methodist Church at Milton Mills)
Built: 1871
Location: 5 Highland Avenue

Located in the northern part of Milton, along the Salmon Falls River, which serves as the border between New Hampshire and Maine, this village was known throughout the 1800s for its many mill and manufacturing concerns. The first mill established using the locale's water power was built here in the 1780s and business grew steadily from there, reaching its peak by the 1890s. The Methodist church was established here in June 1869, with their church edifice built in 1871. Prominently sited and with its towering spire, the church was highly visible to those who worked in the mills during the week and attended services here on Sundays. Little is known of its building, except that the hand with its finger pointing skyward, which tops off the steeple was carved by Erasmus Shaw. He was likely related to A. B. Shaw, a church steward and trustee who owned a box and lumber mill in Milton Mills and was also a local builder, perhaps the builder of the church as he is listed in multiple local records as both a carpenter and a builder. This type of steeple adornment is very uncommon, with no other known examples in New Hampshire. This same kind of symbolism, the hand pointing skyward to God, was also a very popular gravestone motif in the 1870s, so examples for Shaw's inspiration were readily available locally, but his work carved in wood is indeed a unique and interesting feature. The original hand is now preserved and on display at the Milton Historical Society, with a modern replica taking its place. This church is an eclectic blend of the Gothic and Greek Revival styles, as well as Victorian-era styling, upon its completion, though the design details are subtle, indicative of its rural construction. The middle stage of the tower and steeple originally had Gothic pinnacles at each corner, while the Victorian influence is seen in the building's stained-glass windows and the scallop-shingled spire, as well as the wooden trim-work that adorns the eaves of the main block of the building as well as the two main stages of the tower and the hoods over the windows, doorway, and tower louver openings. The Greek Revival style may be seen in the corner pilasters on the building's main block and tower. The church was recognized fairly early on for its beauty, being uniquely described by one early historian as "a very neat and tasty house of worship."[54] The building is still a functioning church to this day and looks to be well maintained and appears much as it did when first built, with the exception of a rear addition and the loss of its Gothic pinnacles.

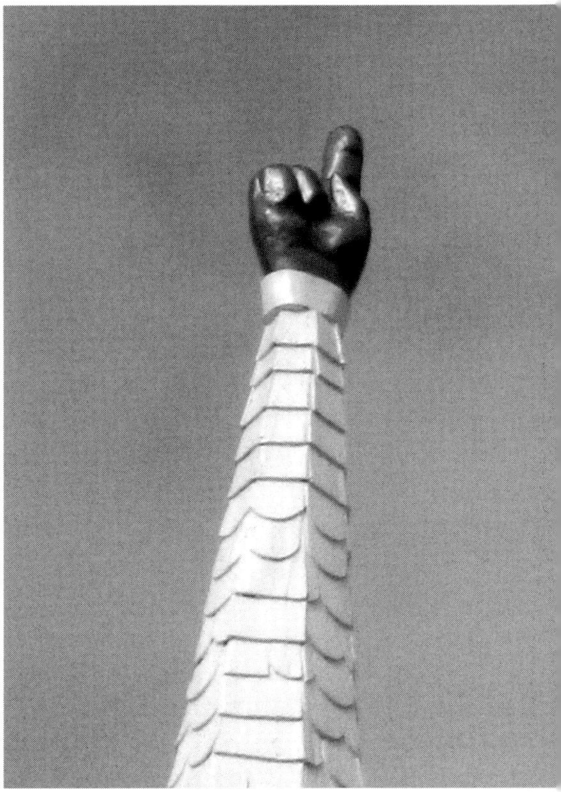

Above left: Liberty Congregational Church, Milton Mills.

Above right: Steeple detail, Liberty Congregational Church, Milton Mills.

Mont Vernon

Mont Vernon Town Hall (former Mont Vernon Meetinghouse)
Built: 1781
Location: 1 South Main Street

The town that is today Mont Vernon was formerly a part of the town of Amherst, but by 1779, its inhabitants had begun their quest to be set off as a separate parish. The town of Amherst opposed these efforts, but residents nonetheless formed their own church, called the Second Church of Amherst, in 1780, and were encouraged by visiting clergy to build their own meetinghouse straight away. This they did, beginning in early 1781, with each family in the parish donating their share of timber for the frame, which was drawn over the crusted snow to the site of the meetinghouse, the last timber being gathered in April. Meanwhile, the inhabitants sent a petition to the New Hampshire legislature in March 1781 asking to be set off as a separate parish, and by the time the petition was granted in July 1781, the meetinghouse was raised and enclosed, the first parish meeting held inside on July 24, 1781. Those who attended sat on rough benches and the meetinghouse would not be fully finished inside until 1792, though it would not be until 1803 that the parish was set off as the town of Mont Vernon. In 1821, the meetinghouse was repaired, given a new front door that was painted a mahogany color, and the entire building painted a bright yellow. In the winter of 1833–34, the meetinghouse caught fire but was saved, being repaired the following spring. As originally constructed, the structure was a Type II meetinghouse with twin porches, but it was altered in 1837 when it was moved to its current location from the town common, new windows placed, and the steeple added. At this time, town offices were established on the ground floor at the rear and it was here that town meetings have continued, maintaining the governing traditions that existed from the very start. The meetinghouse continued as a house of worship for the Congregationalists until 1897, when the entire building was taken over for town offices, the church moving to a new home across the street, which it still occupies today. The town hall gained its final form in 1897 when $500 was spent to provide for additional changes inside and out. This included new windows, they being in the same frame but the smaller panes replaced with 6 × 6 sash windows on the side and 2 × 2 sash windows on the façade. The twin entryways on the façade were also eliminated, replaced with a single center entryway. Notable features of the structure include its octagonal belfry and the corner pilasters on the façade, as well as the prominent pediment over the entrance. In essence, nearly every important decision that has been made by and for the town has been formulated within this venerable structure. This includes the decision to name the town, named after George Washington's Mount Vernon estate but incorrectly spelled due to a clerical error when the act of incorporation was recorded by the state.

The town had many Congregational ministers who preached in this building during the first 116 years of its existence, and was a largely successful group. Rev. John Bruce was a beloved figure who served from 1784–1809 as the first settled pastor, while Rev. Nathaniel Kingsbury served from 1823–36 when the town experienced two major revivals. One pastor, however, had his tenure cut short when his actions caused a break with the community. Rev. Stephen Chapin served from 1809–1818, and though conservative in his views (those who failed to attend church were called to account for their reasons in not doing so every year), he added 115 new members and was well-liked by the people. He was dismissed in 1818 when he refused to baptize a child, having changed his views on the subject. Despite meetings on the subject and outside help from Rev. Moore of Milford, the people of Mont Vernon refused to renounce the idea of infant baptism and terminated their relationship with Chapin.

Mont Vernon Town Hall.

Nashua

Unitarian-Universalist Church of Nashua (former First Unitarian Congregational Society of Dunstable)
Built: 1827
Architect: Asher Benjamin
Location: 58 Lowell Street

This church is famed not only for its beauty, but also for the prominent architect who not only likely designed it, but also designed the early layout of this manufacturing town. The First Unitarian Congregational Society got its start in Nashua (formerly called Dunstable) in 1824, and as its numbers grew, it rented out the Olive Street Church, which was built and owned by the Nashua Manufacturing Company and designed by Asher Benjamin, for services from 1825–26. The following year, they built their own church "in a pretty grove of oaks on the north side of the river."[55] Given Asher Benjamin's high-profile activity and position in Nashua at the time, it is not surprising that the society would choose him as the architect. While there is no extant document that names Benjamin as such, the form and beauty of the Unitarian structure, combined with the factors mentioned above, makes it fairly certain that

Unitarian-Universalist Church of Nashua.

this building is one of his creations. It is notable for its hill-top location and Greek Revival design and Federal-style elements, highlighted by the six-columned portico, perhaps the finest in the state for its time period, and its broad pediment featuring an arched window with keystone molding. Asher Benjamin first gained fame as the author of *The Country Builder's Assistant* in 1797 and later worked in Boston, designing and building a number of prominent houses and churches. From 1825–1827, he worked in Nashua as an agent for the Nashua Manufacturing Company, supervising the construction of their canals, locks, mill buildings, and roads. The cemetery next to this church, the Nashua Cemetery, was established by the society in 1835 and was later enlarged with subsequent land purchases, with many of the city's earliest prominent individuals buried here.

St. Aloysius of Gonzaga Roman Catholic Church
Built: 1873, 1979
Location: 50 West Hollis Street

The original church on this site was built not long after the end of the Civil War to accommodate the city's steadily increasing French-Canadian immigrant population. With a population of 1,500-such immigrants by 1871, a new parish was organized

Above: St. Aloysius of Gonzaga Roman Catholic Church, Nashua.

Left: Postcard view, former St. Aloysius of Gonzaga, Nashua.

here that same year, the first parish priest being Quebec native Father J. B. Milette. Prior to his arrival, land for the church had been procured on Hollis Street, and in May 1872, the cornerstone of St. Aloysius was laid. The church was dedicated for service in June 1873. As the parish grew, a bell was purchased for the belfry about 1881, it weighing some 2,500 lb. As originally built, the Gothic Revival brick church was noted for its twin towers and a triple-arch Gothic window, and was large enough to seat 1,150 people. This church structure served the town well for 103 years until it was severely damaged by fire on July 20, 1976, with the roof collapsing. So damaged was the church that the parish decided to raze what remained and build a new church on the site, which was ready for service in 1979. However, many artifacts from the old church were saved and are on display inside the new church. Most notable is the fact that the parish preserved the shorter of St. Aloysius' two towers, with the new church, which features Gothic windows, built adjacent to the tower, occupying the same space as the original church. The decision to save the original tower was an inspired one and offers a unique view of past and present combined on one site. Once built to serve French-Canadian immigrants, this new church building follows in this same tradition, now serving Nashua's growing Hispanic population.

The First Church Congregational
Built: 1893–94
Architect: Amos F. Cutting
Location: 1 Concord Street

This imposing structure, built in the Romanesque Revival style, was designed by a Worcester, Massachusetts, architect who also designed the State Library in Concord. He was influenced by the famed architect Henry Hobson Richardson and his American version of this style. These features include the impressive, 118-foot tower, the rounded corners with conical roofs, as well as the varied texture of the granite walls, the stone for the building quarried in Marlborough, NH. Other notable features, and there are many to catch the eye here, include the large circular windows with blue stained-glass, one on the main façade between the two entryways, and that on the west gable end, as well as the rounded arch doorways, the doorway on the west end flanked by pairs of polished stone columns. The Congregational church was established in this town, then called Dunstable, in 1685, making it one of the oldest in the state. This building is the tenth that the church has occupied since its formation, it being located on a prominent hill in the center of town on the site of the old Indian Head Tavern and, later, Coffee House, which was a prominent stop on the stage-coach route between Boston and Concord.

The First Church Congregational, Nashua.

St. Mary & Archangel Michael Coptic Orthodox Church (former St. Francois Xavier Roman Catholic Church)
Built: 1896–98
Architects: Chickering & O'Connell
Location: 39 Chandler Street

As with St. Aloysius, this church too was built to serve the city's large French-Canadian population, which reached nearly 10,000 by 1900. The St. Francois Xavier Parish was formed in 1885, its territory, lying north of the Nashua River, taken from that of St. Aloysius, with Father Henri Lessard, a native of Quebec, its first parish priest. Services were first held in a small chapel, built on land donated by the Jackson Mill Company, with a Roman Catholic infrastructure built in the area in the succeeding years, including a convent for the Sisters of the Holy Cross, a school attached to the convent, as well as a rectory and a cemetery established on the old Amherst road. The cornerstone for this church was laid in July 1896, with it being dedicated for service in May 1898, its final cost being about $80,000. Part of the building expenses were contributed by local parishioners from their weekly wages, many of them employed in the local mills. The building was designed by a Manchester firm known for their ecclesiastical structures, including that in

Penacook (see below). Some 8,000 people attended its dedication service, the first sermon delivered in the French language, as they were here for many years. Situated on a hill overlooking the city, and with its towering form, St. Francois Xavier was soon noted as one of the finest church edifices in New Hampshire and remains so to this day. It was built in the Norman style, a specific type of the Romanesque Revival style in America, noted for its use of elaborate rounded archways in its entryways and windows and the geometric carved patterns used in molding and trim, each modelled after those features commonly found on Norman buildings of twelfth-century Europe. The patterns in stone for this church are in checkerboard form, visible above the central entryway and in panels at the top of the central tower and in the upper wall of the transept. One of the most notable features of this church are its many buttresses, each topped by a copper turret, which surround its three domed towers. The stone used in this structure's construction is largely Vermont blue marble with a rock-faced texture and cut in ashlar (square or cubed) form, while the stone arches over the central doorway and Norman windows are of white marble. It is claimed that the church was the first in New Hampshire to be built entirely in marble. For years, St. Francois Xavier was a vital part of Nashua's religious life, but, as has been common throughout New England with the Roman Catholic Church, the number of congregants began to dwindle as the manufacturing base in Nashua gradually dwindled and the character of industry in the city changed. The New Hampshire Diocese by the late 1990s decided that the city could not support all of the parish churches in town, while St. Francois Xavier was particularly problematic due to the costly repairs it required, estimated to be around $1 million. The church was subsequently closed in 2003 and put up for sale by the diocese, but sat empty for three years until it was finally sold to a local developer who originally intended to donate it to the Armenian Orthodox Church. However, that transaction failed and the church sat empty for several more years until its sale to St. Mark Coptic Orthodox Church of Natick, Massachusetts, in early 2009. Coptic Christian services were being held here by November 2008 even before the sale was finalized, and once the sale was finalized, St. Francois Xavier's name was changed to St. Mary & Archangel Michael Coptic Orthodox Church. In the beginning, the church served about 140 Coptic Christian families who lived nearby, they previously having to make the long-distance journey to Natick to attend services. Though purchased and used again as a religious structure by 2009, the fate of the building was still in doubt for many years, so much so that it was placed on the New Hampshire Preservation Alliance's Seven to Save List for 2016. However, because of this designation and the resulting publicity surrounding the historic church, the church has since qualified for grant funding to begin the process of restoration and preservation, with the stated goal of maintaining its historical character.

Left: St. Mary & Archangel Michael Coptic Orthodox Church.

Below: Side view, St. Mary & Archangel Michael Coptic Orthodox Church.

New Boston

Community Church of New Boston (former First Presbyterian Church)
Built: 1888
Builder: George P. Bennett
Location: 2 Meetinghouse Hill Road, Central Square

This pleasing structure, built in the Victorian style with a touch of Gothic Revival, is the fourth in the history of the church. The first functioning meetinghouse in town was built in 1764 (an earlier meetinghouse was started in 1740 but burned before it was completed) on the hill in the center of town. After the Toleration Act of 1819, the Presbyterian Church, which had been the predominant religion in town since its organization about 1768, decided to build a new meetinghouse, the so-called Church on the Hill in the Upper Village area of town, completing their edifice in 1823. This structure, built by John Leach, served the church for a half century, but when it fell into disrepair, the church decided to build a new chapel in the Lower Village area in 1874 due to its rapidly growing population. This new chapel had a short life, being burned to the ground along with the other surrounding buildings, including the town hall and Baptist Church, in the fire of 1887 that destroyed much of the Lower Village. After the fire, plans to rebuild on the same site were immediately begun, with the old Church on the Hill serving as a temporary house of worship for both the Presbyterians and Baptists until their churches could be rebuilt. The Presbyterian Church was rebuilt in 1888 by George Bennett, an experienced carpenter whose career began in Lyndeborough in 1866. He built not only this structure, but also a schoolhouse, twelve residences, and four barns and other farm buildings. The church has had some interior changes over the years, while in 1897 an addition was built on the west end, encouraged and paid for in part by a woman's sewing group known as the Mizpah Circle. The structure's exterior is distinguished by a corner tower and steeple, notable for the Victorian trim that decorates the belfry opening, as well as the triple-arch, stained-glass window on the façade. Hidden from view is the church's Revere Bell, which was cast in 1826 and weighs in at a massive 1,446 lb. This bell originally hung in the 1823 meetinghouse, and it was this bell that was rung by Lottie Adams and Marcy Dale to warn the town of the fire in 1887. It was transferred to the new church in 1892 when the old Church on the Hill was abandoned and sold—later destroyed by fire in 1900. The church, as its name implies, has been a mainstay in New Boston ever since its rebuilding, giving up its Presbyterian denomination and becoming a community church in 1949. The relationship between the church and the community was characterized by Rev. Louis Swanson at the time, stating that New Boston was "Happytown, a church and state uniting voluntarily in true democratic form," and so it remains to this day.[56]

Community Church of New Boston.

Newbury

Center Meetinghouse
Built: 1832
Location: 945 Rte. 103

This meetinghouse is the third in the history of the town, originally named Fishersfield from its granting in 1772 up to 1837 when it was changed to Newbury. It was built for the Religious Toleration Society and was used by several different denominations, including the Free Will Baptists, Methodists, and Universalists. The Free Will Baptist denomination had the largest number of members over the years, while the Congregationalists, who were prominent elsewhere in New Hampshire, never established an organization. The Center Meetinghouse, however, is most notable for its form and interior layout, which was directly inspired by the designs of the famed architect Asher Benjamin. While most churches being built at this time period were of the Greek Revival style, which was then very popular, this structure was more conservative in design, built in the once-popular Federal style that were depicted in Benjamin's published works used as guides by local builders. This Federal detailing can be seen in the projecting front pavilion, which is where the twin-entryways are located and supports the forward part of the two-stage tower. According to one noted historian, the structure "displays excellent workmanship," and it is also evident that "The architectural conservatism of the Newbury building ... suggests either that its builder was elderly and fully wedded to familiar older building types and details of joinery, or that the Lake Sunapee area was sufficiently rural that new ideas from urban centers had not yet penetrated the region by 1830."[57] The interior is also unusual in its layout, in that the pulpit location is at the front of the auditorium close to the front entryways, rather than on the back wall opposite the entryways. There is no stated reason for this so-called "reversed" plan, though it was a quite common in rural church design from about 1820–1860, the theory being, according to historian Philip Zimmerman, that this departure furthered the traditional Puritan ideal that no part of a meetinghouse structure was sacred.[58] While Zimmerman rejects the popular notions that the evolution of the front-located pulpit came about so as to discourage latecomers to church services and possibly give the minister a better view of his congregation, there can be no doubt that such practicalities were a resulting benefit. The Center Meetinghouse has undergone periods of decline and revival over the years, its fortunes tied to both religious and commercial activity in this Lake Sunapee town. By 1880, Newbury was in a period of decline, with a decreased population and the Center Meetinghouse in a dilapidated state, having seen but little preaching over the preceding years

Center Meetinghouse, Newbury.

and seldom used. It was first restored in 1892, this accomplished by the efforts of John Hay, a man who summered here and was famed for being President Abraham Lincoln's personal secretary, and, later, serving as the Assistant Secretary of State and then Secretary of State under presidents William McKinley and Theodore Roosevelt. It was he who provided the impetus and most of the funds to restore the meetinghouse so that it could once again be used as a house of worship for summer tourists. By the 1920s and '30s, the Center Meetinghouse was again in decline and was battered by the Hurricane of 1938, losing its banner-style weathervane (which was saved and can still be seen today), though the Board of Trustees who now held title to the building did their best and made periodic repairs. The meetinghouse was fully renovated again beginning in 2005 and now is in excellent condition, it being a centerpiece in the town and a venue not just for religious services, but also for a wide range of community events and activities.

New Castle

New Castle Congregational Church
Built: 1828
Location: 65 Main Street

The church organization in this town underwent great changes from the 1790s to the 1820s. Its last settled minister was Rev. Oliver Noble, whose tenure ended with his death in 1792. After this time, there was no regular preaching in town and the church membership dwindled to one member by 1821, with the old 1704-built meetinghouse being seldom used and slowly falling into decay. The old meetinghouse was subsequently torn down and a new one built in 1828. It is unclear if regular services were resumed in New Castle, though services were conducted by either neighboring or itinerant ministers from time to time until Rev. James Hobart was finally settled here in 1839, employed by the New Hampshire Missionary Society. The status of the building early on is also unclear: records vaguely state that it was not finished and dedicated until 1836, but whether it was complete enough to host any meetings prior to this time is not known. One early historian has said of this church building that "our carpenter built a new church which is not remarkable, but it is not pretentious, and it has a simple and rather well-proportioned interior."[59] In fact, the structure is a nice example of a vernacular building built in the Federal style, highlighted by its octagonal belfry, triple entryways with transom lights, and the row of three windows above, each topped with a fan louver. The original dome above the belfry was replaced in 2006, with the original subsequently turned in a gazebo, which is placed on the church grounds and hosts community concerts and other events. This church's surroundings are also significant, it being located in the center of historic New Castle and across the street from the ancient Frost Cemetery,

New Castle Congregational Church.

a small but exquisite Colonial-era cemetery with gravestones dating back to 1732, including that for Abigail Frost, a poetess and daughter of one of the town's most prominent citizens, John Frost.

New Durham

New Durham Meetinghouse
Built: 1770
Location: Old Bay Road

Located in a spot that is now seemingly remote, this area, known as New Durham Corner, was once the town center in terms of social and economic activity. The town was first granted in 1749, but it was not until the early 1760s that the town saw its first settlers, with New Durham finally incorporated in 1762. This, the first and only meetinghouse in town, would not be built for another eight years, likely due to the French and Indian War, and even after it was built, no meetings were held here until 1772, which is reflected in the signing on the historic property today. This site is unusual in that it is an intact early town center, complete with meetinghouse, the original town pound built in 1809, as well as the town's first cemetery, all contained in a now-designated historic area called Meetinghouse Park. The original structure was a standard Type II meetinghouse, two stories high and built on a large rock ledge, with a foundation of loose stone. The town only had one settled minister in its history, the Congregationalist minister Rev. Nathaniel Porter, whose tenure lasted from 1773–1777. Religious matters in New Durham, and throughout the Lakes Region, would change in 1780 when Benjamin Randall came here and established the Free Will Baptist Church (see below), the denomination growing by leaps and bounds through the preaching of Randall and his associates. Randall and his successors would preach in this meetinghouse, as well as local homes, for some years, until they built their own church in 1819. After this time, the meetinghouse was no longer used as a house of worship and was used only several times a year. To reduce maintenance and repair costs for the neglected building, the meetinghouse was cut down to its current one-story configuration in 1838. The use of the meetinghouse continued to decline, especially after the center of town activities shifted to the Plains area of town in the 1850s, but remained town-owned until 1908. In that year, the new town hall was completed and, now, New Durham no longer needed the old meetinghouse, so it was sold to a local man, who used it as a barn, with the pound also actively used. Located in a heavily wooded area, the meetinghouse saw hard use and then was neglected for many years, and by the time the site was donated back to the town in 1979 by descendants of the original family that had bought it, it was badly in need of preservation. Efforts began fairly soon after by those interested in preserving this aspect of the town's history, though there were those in town who thought the building should be torn down. However, after many years and being approved for funding to aid in restoration, the building and site were largely renovated by 2017. Though the meetinghouse has been severely altered over the years, it is attractive in its simplicity, one of its most interesting exterior features being the stone foundation, while inside most of the old pulpit has remained intact. This survivor and the surrounding area highlight the age of the town like no other place can. Indeed, any visit here should include a short walk through the old cemetery, where burials are marked by simple fieldstones, as well to the town pound, which is 30 feet square with walls that are nearly 6 feet wide at its base.

First Free Will Baptist Church
Built: 1818–19
Location: 56 Ridge Road South

This church, one of the most beautifully sited churches in all of New Hampshire, is notable for its historic association as the mother church of the Free Will Baptist denomination in America. While there are several lines of the Free Will Baptist faith that originated independent of one another, including that established in North Carolina by Paul Palmer in 1702, the most robust, perhaps, was that established in northern New England by Benjamin Randall (1749–1808), right here in New

New Durham Meetinghouse.

First Free Will Baptist Church, New Durham.

Durham, in 1780. Through the itinerant preaching of Randall and his associates in Maine and New Hampshire, the Free Will Baptist Church became the fastest growing religious denomination in New Hampshire in the early decades of the nineteenth century, as is well documented in the accounts of many other church buildings found in this work. Though Randall died eleven years before this church was built, New Durham was, and remained so for many years, the epicenter of the spread of the Free Will Baptist religion and today is a historic site for Free Will Baptists, a place of pilgrimage for many in the faith who not only wish to see Randall's final resting place, but also worship in the New Durham Ridge church that his followers built in his memory after having used the town meetinghouse (see above) and local homes for many years as places to conduct their services. Plans to build the church began in 1818, with the building completed in 1819, it built on a large rock ledge. As originally constructed, the building was a simple mixture of the Greek Revival and Italianate style, and had no tower. The broad pediment and corner pilasters, as well as those flanking its doorway, are rural interpretations of the Greek Revival, while the paired brackets on the eaves of the building are Italianate features, an indicator that even local builders were up on then current building trends. The tower was added in 1869 and carries on this same mix of styles in its details, though the pinnacles on the upper-stage are a Gothic Revival feature. Today, this historic church is still owned and used by the First Free Will Baptist Church in New Durham, and has been excellently preserved over the years.

New Hampton

New Hampton Town House
Built: 1798
Builder: Samuel Kelley, Jr.
Location: Junction of Town House and Dana Hill Road

The town of New Hampton was granted in 1765 and incorporated in 1777, but plans for a meetinghouse were not put into motion until two decades later. This was not uncommon in Lakes Region towns, and town meetings were conducted in local homes and taverns prior to this building's construction. Finally, in April 1778, the town voted to build a meetinghouse and finish it at town expense. Five men were chosen to design and plan the building's construction, which was to be a twin-porch meetinghouse of the Type II variety. The meetinghouse was built by a local carpenter, Samuel Kelley, Jr., who received $333 for his work. His father was also a carpenter by trade and was an early settler, arriving here in 1775 from Brentwood. The meetinghouse seems to have been finished by September 1798, with the first town meeting held inside in March 1799. The first town minister, Rev. Salmon Hebard, was subsequently settled in June 1800, his pastorate lasting about

New Hampton Town House.

fifteen years. After this time, the meetinghouse saw little use as a house of worship, though the Congregationalists still used it before finally disbanding in 1842. While the Free Will Baptists likely used the church on occasion early on, they had their own building by 1802 (see below). Little used except for annual town meetings, the structure slowly fell into disrepair over the intervening decades and there was some discussion about moving the meetinghouse down to the current village area, but this failed. In 1872, the town voted to repair and renovate the old meetinghouse rather than build a new town hall. This work was completed that summer by a local carpenter at a cost of $1,196, resulting in the building that we see today. The building was at this time reduced to one-story, with its twin porches removed. The only other exterior changes of note include some additions to the rear in about 1940. One notable interior change at this time was the addition of a stage, complete with a painted theater curtain, which depicts the Town House itself, created by artist and sign-painter George Thompson of Holderness. While this meetinghouse has seen architectural and functional changes over the years, one of its original functions remains the same, as every year since 1799, annual town meetings and elections have been held here, a fine record indeed. Notable features of this meetinghouse include its 20 × 15 sash windows with board and batten-style shutters and its corner pilasters.

Dana Meeting House (former First Free Will Baptist Meeting House)
Built: 1801–02
Location: 288 Dana Hill Road

This church, now owned by the New Hampton Community Church (see below), is notable as the only intact one-story meetinghouse remaining in New Hampshire. Meetinghouse of this diminutive size were rarely built to begin with, except by the Quakers, with the Dana Meeting House distinguished by its high level of preservation and historic integrity. The First Free Will Baptist Church was founded in New Hampton in 1800, and they soon began to plan for their own meetinghouse, holding meetings in the interim, as was typical of this denomination, in private homes. The builder of this meetinghouse is unknown, though it is interesting that Josiah Magoon, who was on the building committee, was also on the building committee for the New Hampton Town House (see above), while it is recorded that his son, Stephen, was a cabinet-maker who made its pews and finished the interior in 1810. The surviving box pews and original pulpit are among this meetinghouse's original outstanding features. Though likely finished beforehand, the first meeting inside this building was held in December 1802, when its first elders and deacons were ordained. Among these men was Dr. Simeon Dana, a native of Lebanon, NH, and a graduate of Dartmouth College prior to his arrival. One of the most noted men of his time in New Hampton, he was an early convert to the Free Will Baptist faith and served as its clerk prior to his ordination and subsequent preaching duties. In the medical field, he was both town doctor and town dentist and had a large practice, charging 25 cents per visit, while treating the poor for free, and at his death he was "universally respected and lamented."[60] This meetinghouse remained in steady use for many years, but with the shift toward the village area of town and the establishment of neighboring Free Will Baptist churches, it gradually declined in membership, and by the 1880s, it was largely abandoned, though remaining untouched. Its savior came in the form of Rev. Dr. Adoniram Judson Gordon, a native son, Boston minister, and founder of Gordon College in Wenham, Massachusetts. When he returned to New Hampton for a visit in 1888, he found the Dana Meeting House in poor condition and immediately began a campaign for its restoration. Services were held at the church for the first time in years and funds were solicited to raise money for repairs, which were completed over the next two years. Today, the Dana Meeting House is well maintained and in excellent condition, the only change to the exterior over the years, and this probably in the mid-1800s, being the roofed porch over the entryway. Interesting features of this simple structure include its stone foundation, as well as the elevated pulpit window on the rear wall.

Dana Meeting House, New Hampton.

New Hampton Community Church
Built: 1854
Builders: Zelotes and John Gordon
Location: 14 Church Lane

Recognized as one of the architectural treasures of New Hampshire, this structure was built by the New Hampton Village Free Will Baptist Church. Their organization was formed in 1853 when two Free Will Baptist churches based in New Hampton and Meredith united, inspired by the establishment that same year of the New Hampton Institute in the village, a Free Will Baptist school that later became a theological seminary. The newly formed church voted to build their own house of worship in September 1853, and by June 1854, the new structure was dedicated. It was built by the clerk of the church, Zelotes Gordon, along with his brother, John Gordon, both local carpenters. It is unknown for certain who designed the church, but it was likely Gordon himself, as his house on Main Street is also a Greek Revival structure. During the course of its building, carpenter James Hodgdon fell 75 feet from the steeple to the ground, hitting the roof first, and though seriously injured, he survived the fall. The church has had many pastors over the years and has been well sustained with preaching throughout its history. The first to preach in this structure was Rev. Porter Burbank, followed by Rev. Isaac Stewart, who later wrote a history of the Free Will Baptists. Several pastors, Rev. Arthur Cox and Rev. Elijah Prescott, served the church for extended periods of fifteen years. During those intervals when there was no minister, sermons were given by students and professors of the New Hampton Institution up to 1870, when the theological seminary moved elsewhere.

New Hampton Community Church.

In the early 1900s, the church would begin to see changes when the New Hampton Institute became a secular school and this church became, in effect, a chapel for all its students, no matter what their denomination, continuing on the historic connection between the church and the school. In 1951, the organization gained its current name when it was reorganized as a community church. While the interior of the building has changed over the years, the exterior has largely remained the same as when it was first constructed, with the exception of a rear addition, the installation of a tower clock in the 1960s, and some other minor details. According to one historian, this church must be ranked among the best and most sophisticated Greek Revival-style churches in New Hampshire, while another goes even further, calling it "one of the finest examples of its style in New England."[61, 62] What first catches the eye here is the recessed entry porch, supported by two massive Doric columns, above which is a three-stage tower. Add to this the deep pediments and the well-executed pilasters and antae and the result is an outstanding example of a monumental Greek Revival-style structure, the effect heightened even more by its prominent location facing Main Street.

Newington

Newington Town Church (former Newington Meetinghouse)
Built: 1712
Location: 316 Nimble Hill Road

Significant as the oldest meetinghouse in New Hampshire, this church is also the oldest structure which has remained in continual use by Congregationalists in America. The town was once part of Dover, being established as a separate parish in 1713 and incorporated as an independent town in 1764. The meetinghouse was raised in 1712, but would not be completed for several years once pew sales began in 1714. As originally constructed, this was a Type II meetinghouse and had a private pew entrance on the east end for Col. John Downing, Jr., who after his death was buried at the corner of the church near this entrance, where the gravestone can still be seen today. The structure also had a bell tower, but it is unclear if it was original or was added later on, with repairs made on the tower in 1744. This tower first housed a bell that came from Newington, England, but gained a Revere bell in 1804 when the original was cracked and subsequently sent to the Revere foundry for recasting in 1804. What came back was another bell altogether, one weighing 505 lb. originally intended for Pembroke, Massachusetts, and cast in 1802. The first settled minister for Newington was Rev. Joseph Adams, who was ordained in 1715 and served until January 1783, an incredible sixty-eight-year pastorate that was one of the longest in the state's history. Adams was a native of Braintree, Massachusetts, and was related to presidents John Adams and his son, John Quincy Adams. The meetinghouse gained its current Greek Revival look in about 1830 when it was remodeled, with the new entryway and arched windows added, as well as a two-stage tower with decorative corner finials. Though the interior was also remodeled, the original box pews remain to this day. This meetinghouse served the town as both a religious and civic structure until 1872, when a new town hall was built. The surroundings of this church, as part of the Newington Center Historic District, are also of note. Just up the street is the old town parsonage, a salt-box structure built by church sexton Richard Pomeroy in 1710 and now a historical society museum, as well as remnants of the town forest and several other historic town buildings that date from the late nineteenth century. Next to the church is the old meetinghouse cemetery, though few stones from the eighteenth century remain, while in front of the church is a block of stone known as the Town Horse Block, which was used primarily by the ladies attending church to make it easier for them to mount and dismount from the horse that took them to and from the meetinghouse.

Above left: Newington Town Church, with horse block in foreground.

Above right: Window detail, Newington Town Church.

Newport

First Baptist Church
Built: 1821, 1870
Builder: Col. William Cheney
Location: 85 North Main Street

It may surprise many to know that this grand church is the oldest one remaining in Newport. The Baptists were in Newport early on, establishing a church in 1779, just sixteen years after the town was first settled. They built their first church in 1798 in the

Northville section of town and had their ups and downs over the years, with periods of revival followed by periods where the church struggled to make its presence felt. In 1820, a Baptist Society was established in the village area after an extensive revival had taken place the previous year, they building this church in the summer of 1821. As the town historian states, "In March the materials were in the forest, and in June the building was raised without accident."[63] It measured 64 × 44 feet and seems to have been a twin-porch meetinghouse. Its original builder was one of the town's most distinguished citizens, Col. William Cheney, a deacon of the Baptist Church, who built many other structures in town, including homes, commercial buildings, canals, dams, and mill buildings. As originally constructed, the church would serve the Baptists of Newport for fifty years. In 1870, the church was turned and totally rebuilt on its original site at a cost of $8,800, the foundation laid in July and the new church dedicated in December of that same year. In 1874, the vestry addition was made, further increasing the footprint of this church, prominently sited on the town common. As currently configured, this impressive church bears no resemblance to its original form, and is now an eclectic structure that features elements of the Gothic Revival, Italianate, and Victorian styles. The towering façade of the church faces the common and has twin entryways, between which is a two-story, Gothic-arched stained-glass window. Many other windows of this same type, though smaller in size, adorn the façade, towers, and sides of the church, each featuring a

First Baptist Church, Newport.

window hood in matching rounded form. At the corners are twin spires, that on the western side being square and the tallest, while that on the opposite side being octagonal in form, while the broad eaves around the main block of the building are supported by large Italianate-style brackets. Victorian detailing may be seen in the round window above the large central arch window on the façade, as well as the mini-gables used on the octagonal tower's spire and the decorative applied wave-style trim below the eaves on the larger square tower. The whole makes for an unusual and detailed structure that is pleasing to the eye.

South Congregational Church
Built: 1823
Builder: John Leach
Location: 58 South Main Street

Noted for its beautiful proportions in brick, this edifice is a part of the Templeton run of churches, inspired by the designs of Massachusetts builder Elias Carter, and the most northerly located of the group. A previous meetinghouse had been built in 1791 further west in the geographical center of Newport, but the site of this church was chosen because of its central location in the growing village area, not far from the confluence of two branches of the Sugar River and the mills that were established on them. The pastor of the church at the time of its building was Rev. James Wheelock, the son of Dartmouth College founder Eleazar Wheelock. An enthusiastic and effective minister, he was also said to have been "impulsive," and may have been involved in the design of the church during his time here from 1818–23.[64] The frame of the church is known to have been raised by John Leach, who was also paid to provide plans. He built a church with a similar spire in Concord (see above), but what other work he performed in the building of this church is unknown. The Newport town history specifically credits the building of the church to James Breck, Hubbard Newton, Capt. Elkanah Carpenter, and Caleb Heath, while also noting that they served as the building committee during the planning of the structure.[65] So involved with the Congregational church was Capt. Carpenter that at his death he left funds for the church. While the question of who designed this Federal-style church is in doubt, the results were stunning. Its highlights include towering blind arcades executed in brick on the sides and façade, which has a slightly projecting vestibule, above which is a broad pediment that features an oval window. Other notable details to look for include its triple-entry doorways with fan-lights above, as well as its four-stage tower, with finials on the corner of each stage, the upper two, including the belfry, being octagonal in shape, the whole topped off with a swallow-tail banner weathervane. Significantly, the belfry houses a bell cast at the Revere foundry in 1822, it weighing 1,241 lb. and donated by James Breck. While the exterior of the church has seen little change, the interior of the church was remodeled in the early 1850s, and more extensively in 1869 at a cost of some $8,000 to conform to Victorian ideals, including replacing the original clear windows with stained-glass.

South Congregational Church, Newport.

In 1927, interior revisions again were made, including changing the window glass back to clear panes. It is interesting to note that in 1871 the Congregationalists were the third denomination in town, after the Universalists and the Methodists, to celebrate Christmas, with their church brilliantly lit up for all to see.

The United Methodist Church of the Good Shepherd (former Methodist Episcopal Church)
Built: 1851
Location: 11 Park Street

The Methodist denomination began in Newport about 1829, with Rev. Peter Wakefield preaching the first sermon. He was a former Baptist who had been expelled from that church and subsequently became a Methodist, never having previously heard a Methodist sermon. In 1830, a small class, consisting of but six members, was formed in Newport for study, and it is from these small beginnings that the Methodist Church grew. Initially, the Methodists held services in private homes, and later local schoolhouses. When the practice of using public schools was objected to by some in town about 1840, the denomination built a chapel in the Northville section of town, and later used the Universalist chapel. When a group of dissenters split from the Congregational Church, they formed a bond with the Methodists to form a Methodist Episcopal Society and

The United Methodist Church of the Good Shepherd, Newport.

decided to build their own house of worship, the structure being dedicated in December 1851. The parsonage adjacent to the church was built in 1854 at a cost of $2,000. Built on land facing the town common, it is an attractive and eclectic structure, one that combines elements of the Greek, Gothic Revival, and Stick-style forms; the former is seen in its broad pediment, corner pilasters, and two-stage tower and spire, while the Gothic Revival is evident in its arched windows, and the Stick style is easily recognized on the detailing of the gable of the porch roof over the main entryway on both the main structure and the parsonage. In 1920, the interior of this church had murals painted by a German prisoner of war, a baron, who was trying to earn money so that he could return to his homeland after the end of World War II.

North Conway

First Church of Christ Congregational
Built: 1884
Architect: Erastus Bigelow
Location: 2503 White Mountain Highway

The church organization that worships here was originally founded in 1778 and built their first meetinghouse soon thereafter in Conway. A second was built in the village of North Conway, adjacent to the town cemetery in 1792. The original meetinghouse was used until another was built in North Conway in 1855. This structure served the Congregationalists until 1884, when this church was completed. This church was needed because of the evolution of North Conway's economy from a simple farming town to a White Mountain tourist destination. With many hotels established in the immediate area, summer tourists from Boston, New York, and beyond flooded the area, brought here by the railroads. Those that were churchgoers needed a church that was within close walking distance to attend Sunday services, and thus this church was born. The primary mover was Erastus Bigelow, a noted inventor and a founder of the Massachusetts Institute of Technology (MIT), a summer resident with a large home and farm in the Intervale. It is said that he was the one who planned and funded much of the cost, but he died before the church was completed. Thankfully, other summer residents, led by his daughter, Helen Merriman, and her husband, Rev. Daniel Merriman, a Congregationalist pastor from Worcester, Massachusetts, as well as Rev. S. Gerard Norcross and his family led the charge and the church building was completed, costing about $10,000. Helen Merriman was not only an artist and founder of the Worcester Art Museum, she also dabbled in Spiritualism, and was a major philanthropist in North Conway, donating the land and money to

First Church of Christ Congregational, North Conway.

help found North Conway's Memorial Hospital, and also served as president of the North Conway Public Library. One early historian deemed the church she helped to build "one of the prettiest churches this side of Boston."[66] The church was built in the Gothic Revival style and is distinguished by its corner tower and Gothic-arched windows. The church has changed over the years, with the addition of a parsonage on the south side of the building and a new primary entryway at the base of the tower. The church early on was finished inside and out in earth-tone colors, russet and terra cotta, which is still reflected today in the shingling of its tower roof.

Northumberland

The Meeting House (former Northumberland Meeting House)
Built: 1799
Builder: Capt. Jeremiah Eames
Location: Main Street, Route 3

This structure was the town's first and only meetinghouse, being erected twenty years after the town was incorporated in 1779. Early meetings, mostly conducted by itinerant ministers from New Hampshire or Vermont, were conducted in local homes. The town voted to build a meetinghouse 48 × 36 feet in size in 1796 and again in 1797, but the structure was not built until 1799. The building committee

The Meeting House, Northumberland.

consisted of Capt. Jeremiah Eames, Antipas Marshall, and Joseph Peverly. Eames is notable as a Revolutionary War veteran (as was Marshall) who either built or rebuilt old Fort Wentworth in Northumberland in 1776, not far from the site of where the meetinghouse is now located and where units of Col. Timothy Bedell's Rangers were garrisoned. Less than a year after this meetinghouse was built, famed Methodist circuit-rider Jesse Lee preached here in September 1800, and the custom of employing itinerant ministers became the norm for the next six decades. Eventually, the use of this meetinghouse faded altogether and it was eventually acquired by Judson Potter, a well-known local farmer and lumberman who served both in local government and also as a state representative. The old meeting house and the land it sits on now was donated to the town about 1960 and was subsequently restored and dedicated in 1961. The building is an attractive one-story structure, its most notable features being the columns that flank the central doorway and the broad pediment featuring horizontal board construction.

Northwood

Northwood Baptist Church (former Calvinistic Baptist Church)
Built: 1816–17
Location: 133 First New Hampshire Turnpike (Route 4)

Located on a busy highway and now housing a business rather than a church, this historic building is passed by hundreds of travelers of today, many of whom do not realize that it is the oldest church building remaining in Northwood. Early Northwood residents in the eastern part of town were rather liberal in their religious beliefs and did not have much interest in the Congregational order. A Baptist meetinghouse was built on this site in 1772, but no Baptist minister was settled by the town until Rev. Edmund Pillsbury, ordained in 1779, was hired in 1789 to preach half of the time here, and half of the time in the Congregationalist meetinghouse, receiving in return fifty bushels of corn, 50 pounds of flax, 100 pounds of beef, five barrels of cider, 20 cords of wood, as well as three cows, ten sheep, and one horse.[67] The town history states that the first meetinghouse was rebuilt in 1816 and rededicated in August 1817. Though uncertain, given the time frame involved, over at least eight months, it seems likely that the old meetinghouse was torn down altogether and a new structure built out of what lumber could be salvaged. As originally built, it was a simple church, with twin-entryways and a small, two-stage tower, built largely in the Federal style. The Baptist church always retained regular preachers after about 1804, with Rev. Eliphalet Merrill serving twenty-four years, and it prospered as the eastern part of town grew economically. The building's architectural character was changed again in the 1830s, prior to 1837, when a new steeple was built and a tower clock was purchased, made by Thomas Woolson, Jr.,

Former Northwood Baptist Church.

of Claremont, giving the structure a Gothic Revival-style appearance, as is shown in the mini-gables above the louvered belfry openings. It may also have been at this time that the twin entryways were replaced by a single entryway and that the semicircular louvered vent in the pediment was removed and boarded over. Today, the former church houses an auction business and is dilapidated in appearance, with graffiti spray painted on its side and badly in need of painting and repair.

Free Will Baptist Church
Built: 1838
Location: 545 First New Hampshire Turnpike (Route 4)

This denomination was established in town in 1833, and first met in a local school building, but they soon decided to build their own house of worship in the central part of Northwood on Clark's Hill. The structure was, and is still, an impressive one, originally built as a largely Greek Revival-style building, characterized by the corner and central pilasters on its façade and twin entryways, above each of which was a rectangular window. However, the pinnacles on the corners of its two-stage tower are a Gothic Revival element, which was a very popular feature on rural churches during the time. The Free Will Baptist Church was a prominent one for many years and had nearly 200 members by the 1880s. As a result, in 1888, the church was enlarged, with the original structure raised and a lower level for meeting

Free Will Baptist Church, Northwood.

space added. It was at this time also that the façade of the church gained its current configuration, the twin entryways replaced with a single entryway with a Gothic-arch opening, as well as arched windows placed where the original entryways were located. From the pediment above the structure has largely remained original, except that the louvered belfry replaced the original open belfry. A row of horse sheds once stood where the church parking lot is now located. The status of this structure as of this writing is uncertain as the church is now closed.

Northwood Congregational Church
Built: 1840
Location: 881 First New Hampshire Turnpike (Route 4)

Called "one of northern New England's finest Greek Revival churches," the building of this structure was greatly inspired by a mother's grief and determination.[68] The town's first meetinghouse, in which the Congregational order prevailed, was built in 1780, but by the late 1820s, it was in disrepair, subsequently being remodeled to a small degree. With great periods of revival in the town throughout the 1830s and many new members resulting, a new church would soon be needed. The impetus for a new church came from an unlikely source, the sudden death of Mary Coe's son, David Barker. Now married to Ebenezer Coe of Northwood, Mary had previously been married to David Barker, Jr., who died in 1837. Her son was preparing to enter

Above: Northwood Congregational Church.

Left: Portico detail, Northwood Congregational Church.

college when he died and Mary Coe conceived of a way to honor his memory by contributing the $500 that had been saved to pay for his college to a building fund for a new church. Her current husband, Ebenezer Coe, for whom the Coe-Brown Northwood Academy (established in 1867) would be named, agreed to contribute an additional $500 to the building fund and, with other contributions, a site was chosen and the church was built in 1840, sited on land adjacent to where Coe-Brown is now established. Six years after the building of the church, Mary and Ebenezer Coe would move to Bangor, Maine. The exterior of the church today is largely original, with the exception of a change in widow glass, and is a stunning example of the Greek Revival style then in vogue, its unknown builder going the full measure to create a temple-like structure. While many rural Greek Revival inspired churches merely employ pilasters applied to a façade, this structure is distinguished by its four Doric fluted columns, the recessed wall behind employing corner and central pilasters, while above is a full entablature, finely executed. The three-stage tower is also beautiful in its simplicity, employing a short first stage, while the top of the belfry is distinguished by its parapet decorated with floral scroll-work. This parapet had been removed from the church sometime in the 1960s and stored in the basement, being restored and reinstalled in the 1980s. This church bell was gifted as a memorial in the 1880s, being cast at the foundry of William Blake & Company of Boston. The Congregational Church in town remained strong for many years, but eventually faded away, with the church building subsequently taken over and maintained by the Harvey Lake Woman's Club, who used it as meeting place. Today, the Congregational Church is again established and active and this building is the site of weekly services, as well as other community events. The church sanctuary has also been used for many years by the Coe-Brown Academy for its commencement services, a fitting tribute to Mary Coe and her son, whose memory was meant to be perpetuated with its building.

Orford

Orford Congregational Church
Built: 1854
Architect: Moses G. Wood
Location: 617 State Route 10

Located on the western side of the Orford town common, and once known as the West Church, this unique structure was designed by a local architect. The church was organized in 1822 after difficulties between Rev. Sylvester Dana, settled here in 1801, and some members of his church arose, resulting in twenty-eight members of the town's First Congregational Church withdrawing to form a new church. Dana had previously preached in the town's two meetinghouse on alternating Sabbath days, the west one located here, close to the Connecticut River, and the other located 3 miles to the east and close to the center of town. Dana would continue with the West Church for another decade before leaving in 1833. The original meetinghouse on this site, built in 1797, gradually fell into disrepair and the idea to build a new church edifice was underway by the early 1850s. The architect chosen, Moses Wood, was a local man who made architectural drawings for the new church as early as 1851, now framed and hanging in the sanctuary. Once the needed funds were raised, work on the church began, with final completion likely in 1854, though the records on its construction are conflicting and vague due to a lack of records, some accounts stating it was finished in 1850. Adding to this uncertainty is the clock that graces its tower. It was made by noted clockmaker Benjamin Morrill of Boscawen and may have been the last tower clock he ever made, and to this day, it is still hand-wound and keeps good time. The keeper of this clock for many years was Orford-native Adolphus Phelps, who was paid to clean the clock several times from 1851–1881, and may have even been responsible for winding it on a regular basis. The 1851 record of its cleaning leaves one to believe that it once graced the tower of the prior meetinghouse, but records for this time period are lacking. As to the church bell, the original used here came from the old meetinghouse, lasting until it was cracked in 1862 when being rung for Fourth of July festivities. The bell that replaced it was cast at Henry Hooper's foundry in Boston in 1863. This church is noted as perhaps the most impressive Gothic Revival church made of wood in all of New Hampshire, combining elements of the high Victorian style as well. Originally painted gray, it

Orford Congregational Church.

was painted white early in the twentieth century and has remained that color ever since. The structure is notable for the towering buttresses that are found on the corners of the façade and on the central tower, as well as the unusually tall pinnacles that top them. In keeping with its Gothic Revival styling, the church has tall, lancet-style windows, while the Victorian influence may be seen in the applied wood trim in frieze form on the upper tower above and below the clock, and on the eaves of the façade. It is interesting to note that Wood's original drawings do not depict a clock in the tower, but quatrefoil windows instead, adding further to the mystery. Over the years, the church structure has had its ups and downs: the tower was renovated in 1960 after years of neglect, while the tower clock was removed for a time in the 1960s after it failed and after some poor repair work in the 1980s, and even vandalism, the clock is now performing has it has for over 160 years.

Ossipee

Early Settler's Meeting House (former First Free Will Baptist Church)
Built: *c.* 1811
Builder: Jacob Leighton
Location: Corner of Fogg's Ridge Road and Granite Road

Despite its current historical designation, this structure was always a house of worship during its active period. Built in a location known as Leighton's Corner on land donated by Jacob Leighton, it served a group of Free Will Baptists that was formed here in the summer of 1807. While the exact date of its building is unknown, records indicate it was standing by 1812, likely having taken several years to finish. The timber was said to have been gotten out by Leighton himself about 1804, consisting of pine beams hewn from the entire length of individual trees. It was originally sided with shingles rather than clapboards, they being "from four to six feet long, laid three feet out to the weather" and was originally "placed on common stones set flat on the ground.... The whole building could rise and fall by the action of frost without injury to it."[69] Early in its history, about 1820, a great hailstorm is said to have broken many of the panes of glass in its windows. The impetus for the formation of the church came from the preaching here of Elder Benjamin Randall, the founder of the Free Will Baptists, and Elder John Buzzell, resulting in a great revival. Among the first to be baptized were members of the Leighton, Goudy, and Fogg families, the immersion taking place in a brook which had been dammed, located at the bottom of nearby Leighton Hill.[70] The church was a branch of the Parsonsfield, Maine, church for some time, among the elders preaching here being Jeremiah Bullock. The church was a successful and cohesive one for years, but disputes among its members regarding doctrine eventually arose, perhaps as early as 1843 over the formation of a church temperance society. Those who followed the teachings of Jeremiah Bullock became known as "Bullockites" and were opposed to Sunday schools, temperance movements, and any missionary activity. The two groups within the church formally split about 1856, the more conservative Bullockites remaining in the original meetinghouse, while the more liberal members formed their own society and built a new church a short distance away (see below). Upon taking sole possession of the old meetinghouse, which was now in disrepair, the structure was soon renovated and gained its current configuration, the work done by Jeremiah Leavitt at a cost of $160. The single entryway on the façade, formerly facing Fogg's Ridge Road, was replaced with windows, with twin entryways with transom lights placed on the gable end facing Granite Road. It is a simple yet attractive example of a period rural church. For about twenty years, the meetinghouse remained an active house of worship, but by the 1880s, it had become largely inactive, with no regular services here. What few members remained finally deeded the building to the Ossipee Historical Society in 1928. It stands today not only as a historical monument to the early settlers in this locale, but also as one of the few original meetinghouse structures in New Hampshire directly associated with the prominent Elder Jeremiah Bullock and his interpretation of the Free Will Baptist faith. While the location is a remote one today, it was not always so, once being an active community spot. Directly across the street from the church is a building that once served as a store and grange Hall, adjacent to that being a now-gone horse shed for church members built in 1860.

Early Settler's Meeting House, Ossipee.

First Free Will Baptist Church of Ossipee, Effingham, and Wakefield
Built: 1856–57
Builder: Joseph Nutter
Location: Granite Road

This architectural gem, located off the beaten path, is notable as one of the finest rural Greek Revival churches of its time in the Lakes Region. The Free Will Baptists here originally worshipped at the original meetinghouse at Leighton's Corner (see above) just down the road, but when divisions in the church arose, it split into two factions, the larger of them building this church. Though construction began in 1856, with eight men serving on a building committee, the new church was not formally organized as the First Free Will Baptist Church of Ossipee and Wakefield until April 1857, probably about the same time this church was finished and dedicated, though the date of these events has gone unrecorded. Later on, the church also added the town of Effingham to its name, reflective of where subsequent members resided. The church was built in the Greek Revival style and is three bays in width by three bays in length, featuring 12 × 12 sash windows on the long sides and 6 × 6 sash windows on the front gable end. The façade features twin entryways, each with sidelights and pedimented cornices above, a distinctive feature that is found above all of the church windows. The façade is also distinguished by the circular window in the broken pediment, as well as its finely

First Free Will Baptist Church of Ossipee, Wakefield, and Effingham, Ossipee.

molded corner pilasters. The carpenter in charge of the building, Joseph Nutter, did a fine job and the exterior of the church remains largely the same as when it was built. This church's shared features with the Methodist Church in neighboring Tuftonboro (see below), in which another Nutter was involved in building, may indicate that Joseph Nutter designed this structure himself, and clearly demonstrates the family's building skills. The First Free Will Baptist Church remained prosperous for many years, but was in a slow decline by the 1890s, and by the 1920s, it no longer could afford to settle a minister on a full-time basis. Despite the lack of use over the next thirty years, the church was kept in good repair, and by the 1960s, it again saw regular use, primarily during the summer tourist season, which situation remains largely the same to this day. Located across the street from this church is the First Free Will Baptist Cemetery, the burials in which predate the building of the church by forty years or more.

Water Village Community Church
Built: 1877–78
Location: 370 Water Village Road

Located in an area of town along Beech River, just over 3 miles west of Ossipee village, this attractive church was built to serve a newly-established congregation in a once-thriving mill area bordering North Wolfeboro and Tuftonboro. The Free Will Baptist Church at Water Village was formed in July 1870 with ten members, with services held early on in a local schoolhouse, alternating Sundays with a local Advent Society. As the congregation grew and the school could no longer hold all those who attended worship, the idea of building a church edifice soon took form. It was originally proposed that a union church be built with the Adventists, but that group declined, so the church decided to build on their own. The structure that resulted cost about $2,000 and was paid for by the sale of church pews, which sold anywhere from $45 to $65. The lumber was donated by some of the wealthier members, it being cut at the nearby mill of Stephen Jackson, who was also a pew owner. The frame of the church was raised in September 1877, with the structure dedicated and ready for service on March 6, 1878. Nine of the twelve men who helped in its construction and donated funds were pew owners. Those who helped in its building that were not church members include George O. Bean and George F. Bean, as well as Charles Beacham. It is highly likely that George O. Bean both designed and built this well-proportioned church as he was active in the construction trade in the Water Village area, building, among other structures, the Ossipee Mountain Grange Hall on Pork Hill Road near the intersection with Water Village Road in 1904. The church was built in a modest Greek Revival style featuring a plain, broken pediment and a three-stage steeple above topped off with a simple arrow weathervane, which was at one time damaged by a lightning strike. Both the lower stages of the steeple and the corners of the façade feature simple pilasters. The church has remained unchanged in form to this day and has had little exterior work done, except that performed on the foundation to alleviate

Water Village Community Church, Ossipee.

flooding problems over the years. As with many rural churches in New Hampshire, this church has had periods of great success, followed by periods of inactivity and decline. Due to falling membership a and a resulting lack of funds, no active preaching was conducted here from about 1900 to 1913, and again from 1932–1948, and it was probably in the 1930s that the church gained its present name after merging with the Advent Society, which also had declining membership. Though the church remains Baptist affiliated, the community aspect of the church has been its true focus from that time to the present day. The church was reorganized in the 1950s, and since that time, it has held regular services and has remained active in the community.

Penacook

United Church of Penacook (former First Baptist Church of Fisherville)
Built: 1857–58
Builder: John S. Brown
Location: 21 Merrimack Street

Recognized as one of the finest wooden churches of its time period in all of New Hampshire, this structure stands as a monument to a man who was one of Penacook's most prominent early citizens. Baptist believers in Penacook first attended church in neighboring Boscawen, but in early 1845, brothers John S. and Henry H. Brown purchased a dry-goods store in town and converted it to a church, naming it Union Hall. Later in 1845, the First Baptist Church of Fisherville (Penacook's former name) was formed, and among its first members were the Brown brothers and their wives. Indeed, the Browns were among Penacook's most prominent citizens, coming here from Attleboro, Massachusetts, and involved in the cotton manufacturing business and the building of the Penacook Mill behind the church, as well as in the shoe manufacturing business, all at a time when the village was at the height of its economic development. John S. Brown was not only a businessman, but he was also a hands-on builder and doer, being severely injured when the Brown brothers were transferring equipment from the Contoocook Mill they rented to the Penacook Mill they built in 1849. John Brown was also involved in many community organizations, including serving as a member of the Woodlawn Cemetery Association, a stockholder and founder of the Penacook Academy school, and a founding firefighter member of the Fisherville Fire Engine Company No. 1. However, John Brown was also a devout Baptist, playing the double-bass viol in the church choir, while his wife, Hannah, was one of its singers. One son of John and Hannah Brown was slated to become a minister, but was killed in action during the Civil War at Petersburg, Virginia, in the waning months of the war. Discussions about building a Baptist church began in 1847, but a lack of finances resulted in a decade delay; when the idea was brought to the fore again in 1857, John Brown was the primary mover as a member of the building committee and provided both a large amount of labor and funds to bring the plan to fruition, while the land for the church was donated by the Contoocook Manufacturing Company. Whether a professional architect was engaged in drafting the plans for the church are unknown, but the results were impressive. The church was built in a combination of the Greek Revival and Italianate styles, and when fully complete inside and out, it cost about $18,500, with most of the funds donated by the Brown brothers. Outstanding features include the 150-foot bell and clock tower, which sits atop a beautifully executed pavilion with Ionic pilasters, giving the structure a temple-like façade that is the highlight of Greek Revival styling. The tall and narrow rounded arch windows are an Italianate influence, they being repeated in panel form on the sides of the pavilion and on the belfry above. This community church has been well-maintained over the years and continues as a pleasing and beautiful landmark on the local skyline.

Immaculate Conception Roman Catholic Church
Built: 1897
Architect: Chickering & O'Connell
Location: 9 Bonney Street

The first professed Catholics first arrived in Penacook from Ireland about 1850 and were employed in the local mills, but regular services would not begin until about 1852, with missionary priests visiting the town about once a month, usually in the

Right: United Church of Penacook.

Below: Immaculate Conception Roman Catholic Church, Penacook.

homes of local residents. By the early 1860s, Penacook became a mission church, but the village would not gain its own house of worship until the old Methodist church was purchased in 1867, and from there the church would grow. Under the leadership of Rev. Denis Hurley, a native of County Cork, Ireland, the current church was built. Hurley first arrived here in 1893 from All Saints Church in Lancaster, and within less than a week purchased for $5,000 a private estate located between High Street and what is now Bonney Street and turned the mansion into a rectory, an impressive building in its own right still owned by the Diocese. In 1896, a wooden Romanesque Revival church was built adjacent to the rectory on designs provided by architects in Manchester who were well known for their ecclesiastical structures. The church was begun in early 1897 and dedicated in November of that same year. It is notable for its projecting front tower featuring a pair of narrow arched windows and steeply pitched roof, while the façade features triple-entryways, each crowned with a rounded-arch window. While most Romanesque Revival buildings were constructed of stone, this is a rare and more subdued example made of wood, perhaps dictated by reasons of economy so as not to incur a financial burden the parish could not readily meet. Sited on a hilltop and adjacent to the mansion turned rectory, the church is both a pleasing and impressive sight. In the first decade after the church was built, its congregation was not only the largest in town, but the church and all its property was said to be the most valuable in Penacook. One family with an intimate association with the Catholic Church in Penacook was that of John Linehan. He arrived here in 1852 in the first wave of Irish immigrants and his son, Andrew Linehan, was the first child to be baptized in town in that same year. It was also in the house of John Linehan that early masses were held. One of his sons, Timothy Linehan, later became a Catholic priest, while his only daughter, Margaret, would enter the order of the Sisters of Mercy in Portland, Maine, in 1885.[71]

Peterborough

Unitarian Universalist Church (former First Church of Peterborough)
Built: 1825–26
Builder: Samuel Kilborn
Location: 25 Main Street

This church, directly inspired by the published designs of Asher Benjamin, is one of New Hampshire's finest Federal-style churches. Built by a well-known Monadnock Region builder who also constructed fine churches at Dublin and Fitzwilliam, this church has been the subject of much debate about its possible architect. For many years, the church design was attributed to the noted Boston architect Charles Bullfinch, and while it is very possible, based on town records, that general plans may have been obtained from Bullfinch, he was in no way directly associated with its building as he was in Washington, D.C., working on the Capitol buildings at the time of construction. Perhaps because of this debate, this church seldom seems to get the attention it deserves, often overshadowed by other Monadnock Region churches. Nonetheless, this church is a beautiful and well-proportioned building. The five-stage tower is very similar to Benjamin's designs and features, with urn-style finials on the lower stages and a clock stage that was added in 1856. The façade of the building features triple entryways with Federal-style trim and fan louvers above. The brickwork on the façade, in the form of a blind arcade, is also striking and was executed by local brick-mason Zadoc Chapman using bricks made in the Hadley family brickyard.[72] It is perhaps not surprising that Samuel Kilburn of Fitzwilliam was chosen as the builder, as not only did he have the requisite experience, but he may have been recommended by Nahum Parker of that same town, who was a member of a three-man committee, consisting entirely of non-Peterborough residents, tasked with choosing the site of this new church (though their choice was ultimately rejected). The exterior of the church has changed very little over the years, though behind the semi-elliptical louver in the pediment there is visible a rectangular window which is two-panes in height, perhaps this space being open at one time to allow for ventilation. The original church organization here was

Unitarian Universalist Church, Peterborough.

formed in the 1760s and was Presbyterian in nature, the first minister, Rev. John Morrison, was a native of Scotland, being but twenty-three years of age. His tenure was a short but stormy five years, the town distraught due to his "Profane Swearing, Drunkeness, Lewdness."[73] Afterwards, he joined the British Army and died in South Carolina during the American Revolution. Later notable ministers were Rev. Elijah Dunbar, Jr. (1799–1827), and Rev. Abiel Abbot (1827–1848)—both were among the most respected men in town. It was under Dunbar's tenure that this church was built, and the Presbyterians broke with the church to form their own church in 1822, while Abbot was a Unitarian, which doctrine the church adheres to even today.

Union Congregational Church (former Presbyterian Society and Union Evangelical Church)
Built: 1840
Location: 33 Concord Street

This modest Gothic Revival church structure is representative of the complicated early religious history of Peterborough. As discussed in the history of the town's Unitarian Universalist Church (see above), Peterborough originally had a standing order that was Presbyterian in form. This changed in 1799, when a Congregationalist minister was settled, though upon the condition that a Presbyterian form of communion be conducted once a year. This situation continued until 1822, when a Presbyterian church was organized by those in town who had never accepted the above arrangement. The newly-formed group built their own meetinghouse a short distance from the village in 1825, but once again would have Congregationalists in their midst when the old church organization from which they had separated adopted the liberal Unitarian doctrine in 1827. Both Congregationalists and Presbyterians worshipping here maintained separate groups and, with the beginning of what would become a significant religious revival in town, a new church was built in 1840, closer to the village. Few details about its building are known, except that the brick and lumber from the old meetinghouse, including bricks made in the Hadley family brickyard, were used in building the new edifice. The building is distinguished by its two-stage tower which features Gothic pinnacles on the corners of each stage, perhaps meant to upstage the recently built Methodist Episcopal Church located just up the street. The façade of the structure is plain yet attractive, featuring twin-entryways with sidelights and two pairs of 6 × 6 sash windows, one set above the entryways and the other in the pediment. This building served both groups for many years, but in 1858 both decided to dissolve and reformed again as one body, taking the name of Union Evangelical Church. In 1894, the church gained its current name after its Presbyterian affiliation had been dropped, marking the third, and probably final, separation between Presbyterians and Congregationalists in Peterborough.

Union Congregational Church, Peterborough.

All Saints Episcopal Church
Built: 1916–20
Architects: Ralph Adams Cram and Frank W. Ferguson
Location: 51 Concord Street

Quite simply put, this Norman Revival structure is one of the most important churches ever built in New Hampshire. Not only was All Saints designed by a native son, Ralph Adams Cram, who was one of America's most accomplished architects, but it is also very nearly the ideal embodiment of its design style. The Episcopal Church in Peterborough was first established as a mission church in 1904 and gained parish status in 1914. The design and planning of All Saints Church actually began prior to this, in 1912, as the building was not built by the parish or diocese, but by the efforts of a private donor, Mary Lyon Cheney Schofield (1869–1943). By the time of its building, the town had gained a reputation as a cultural and artistic center and was thus was a destination for many wealthy summer residents and tourists. Mary Lyon was born in New Britain, Connecticut, to wealthy parents and would later attend Wellesley College. Her first husband was Charles Cheney, who died in 1897 and her second husband was William Schofield, both being graduates of Harvard. The Schofields, after their marriage in 1907, built an estate in Peterborough, and with no church of their faith close-by, offered to build one at their own expense, with Mary being intimately involved with Cram during the church's design phase. This should not be surprising, as Mary Lyon Schofield was a woman of many accomplishments, including lecturing on women's financial obligations throughout the state and establishing training courses for women in agriculture at her own estate, establishing a Dairying Course for Women at the University of New Hampshire in Durham, chairing the New Hampshire Woman's Liberty Loan Committee during World War I, and serving as president of the Woman's Land Army of America, training women to work on farms to help in food production, taking the place of men who went off to war. These are just a few of the many activities, both civic and social, which she was involved with during her years in Peterborough. Because of her close relationship to the church, she is buried in a crypt beneath the sanctuary, along with her husband, William Schofield, and her son, Lt. William Cheney, an aviator who died in a training accident in Italy in 1918. The design of the church is significant, being a perfect representation of the Norman Revival style of architecture, a category of the Romanesque Revival style, which Ralph Adams Cram is said to have been based on St. Mary the Virgin Church at Iffley in England, built in 1170. One historian has stated "in the basic simplicity and strength of the building material" this church "is surprisingly, if not ideally, suited to New Hampshire, both in style and temperament."[74] The church itself is distinguished by its granite construction, cut in ashlar form and quarried in Peterborough, as well as its square central tower and a rose window with tracery above the entrance. However, this is not all; the finest craftsmen of the period were commissioned to craft the stained-glass windows, decorative woodwork, and ornamental iron-work, and other details, making the entire church a true work of art. The landscape around All Saints Church is also masterfully planned, resulting in a fully realized medieval English churchyard in the heart of a New Hampshire town. Not only is the church set far back from busy Concord Street, with a forested setting as a backdrop, but as one approaches the church, a well-planned courtyard featuring a flagstone walkway is encountered, on the sides of which are a vestry to the north and a rectory to the south, each rectangular in form and finished in a gray-painted stucco that blends in well with the church. Standing in the middle of this courtyard and beholding the church that stands before you, one has the feeling of stepping back in time.

Pittsburg

Farnham Memorial United Methodist Church
Built: 1875
Location: 1613 Main Street

This church is interesting not only for being the most northerly located church in New Hampshire, but also for being the only church ever built in this small North Country town. The town of Pittsburg was incorporated in 1840 and has an interesting early

Above: All Saint's Episcopal Church, Peterborough.

Right: Doorway detail, All Saint's Episcopal Church, Peterborough.

history, the area, sharing a border with Canada, being once known as the Indian Stream Republic for a period due to border land disputes. The people inhabiting this region were, and still are, independent minded, but that does not mean they were not religious. The Congregationalists formed a society here in 1822, while later on the Free Will Baptists did the same, but neither group built a house of worship, instead meeting in local homes and schools. The same circumstances held true for the Methodists for many years after having first sent circuit riders here to organize classes in 1826. In 1874, local families donated land for a church and the following year construction on not one, but two Methodist churches would begin. The village church construction was underway by April 1875 and was completed that summer. The other edifice in the southern part of Pittsburg was nearly finished in the spring, but was blown down during a wind storm, rebuilt, and blown down again. As far as is known, neither doomed structure was fully completed or held services within. The church in the village, however, was completed without incident, and from that time forth it has played a vital role in the life of the town. The church is a pleasing and well-executed example of a modest country church, distinguished by its pedimented porch and a projecting two-stage tower. The sides feature tall and narrow 1 × 1 rectangular sash windows which are given their Gothic appearance by the application of an arched wood panel at the top of the frame. All of these features date from a remodel

Farnham Memorial United Methodist Church, Pittsburg.

of the church which occurred in 1925. Prior to this time, the structure was a simple barn-like structure with little adornment and a simple two stage steeple built directly on the roof. The congregation here has always been small and despite a lack of financial means at times, has always maintained regular preaching, for many years sharing a pastor with nearby Canaan, Vermont. The church's most active members, however, have been the women of Pittsburg over the years, usually comprising the majority in numbers. These women, first through the Ladies' Aid Society, then the Women's Society for Christian Service, and later the United Methodist Women groups, have been the backbone of the church, instrumental in raising funds to help pay for ministerial services in lean years, as well as raising funds to help maintain and repair the church and to make interior improvements. Indeed, the church gained its current name in 1929, being renamed in honor of Mrs. Flora Farnham, who was not only an active and enthusiastic church member, but also donated $3,200 to pay off the mortgage on the church building.

Portsmouth

St. John's Episcopal Church
Built: 1807–08
Architect: Alexander Parris
Location: 101 Chapel Street

The site of this, the oldest surviving church structure in Portsmouth, was originally fortified and known as Graffort's Fort, not surprising given its ideal defensive location close to Portsmouth Harbor. In 1732, the small Anglican congregation in town bought the site with the hopes of building their own church. Anglican services had first been held in Portsmouth in 1638, but for only four years before their minister departed. As far as is known, Anglican services would not return until 1732 when a new congregation was formed. The first church on this site, Queen's Chapel (the name changed to St. John's after the American Revolution in 1791), served the congregation for many years until it burned down on Christmas Eve in 1806, the prominent minister Rev. Arthur Browne serving as pastor from 1736 to 1773. Plans to rebuild a new edifice on Church Hill began in short order, with the church hiring a young, up and coming architect, Alexander Parris, who had been making a name for himself in Portland, Maine, over the last several years building homes and commercial structures. The master-builder of this church was James Nutter of Newington, a man highly regarded for his joinery skills and the builder of a number of other local structures. The foundation was laid in June 1807, with the church open for worship in May 1808. Among the other local craftsmen that contributed to the structure, the first brick church built in New Hampshire, was gravestone carver Noah Smith, who executed the marble-trim around the triple entryways, and figurehead carver William Dearing, who carved the Ionic capitals on the interior wood columns. While the construction of this church went off smoothly, pranksters took advantage of a lift left at the site to aid in hoisting materials up to the steeple, and one night, after a horse went missing, it was discovered in the unfinished belfry.[75] The church is a Federal-style building and shows influences from both Asher Benjamin and Charles Bullfinch, men whose work Parris had undoubtedly studied. Notable features include the octagonal lantern above and the keystones and other marble trim work around the windows and doors. The blind arcade on each side, featuring an upper circular window is also an unusual feature, demonstrative of the skills of both the architect who designed St. John's and the masons who did the work. One major change to the church was the alteration of its façade in 1848; while it now has a Greek Revival-style pediment, the original design featured a flat-topped parapet above the three façade windows, with the center parapet slightly taller, while the parapets on either side were decorated with scroll-work and finials at their corners. While the interior of the church has also changed with the times, it nonetheless contains many historic artifacts, including a chair which George Washington used while attending services here in 1789, as well as a copy of the interesting and mistake-filled Vinegar Bible, printed in 1717. The original bell in the belfry was recast by Paul Revere, using the remnant of the bell destroyed in the fire of 1806, which had been captured at the Siege of Louisbourg, at what is now Cape Breton, in Canada, in 1745. The Revere bell subsequently cracked in 1896 and was recast at the Blake Bell foundry in Boston in 1896, and was recast yet again in 1905, vestiges of the original Louisbourg and Revere bells now entirely gone except in lineage only. The site surrounding this downtown church is also of note and quite unusual—one cannot help but notice the tomb doors facing the street, indicative of the large expanse of underground tombs on the church's western-facing side. In fact, the churchyard was in use at least by 1745, with the land formally deeded to the church by Theodore Atkinson (whose tomb door is plainly marked) in 1754. There are hundreds of individuals interred in the underground tombs, some of whom are memorialized on plaques inside St. John's. Interestingly, there was once a tunnel running under the street that connected the church basement with the Portsmouth Brewery, which went out of business with the advent of the Prohibition era in 1920. The brewery rented the space from the church and here conditioned its India pale ale and other brews.

South Church Unitarian Universalist
Built: 1824–26
Location: 292 State Street

This church is significant in northern New England for both its form and the materials used. The congregation the church serves can trace its roots back to 1627, with the town divided into a north and south parish in 1713. The South Parish would, by the 1750s, become the more liberal of Portsmouth's churches, and in

Right: St. John's Episcopal Church, Portsmouth.

Below: South Church Unitarian Universalist, Portsmouth.

the aftermath of the Toleration Act of 1819, became Unitarian in doctrine under the leadership of Rev. Dr. Nathan Parker. Their original meetinghouse was built in 1731, but by this time, it was in need of repair, so a new house of worship was eventually decided upon, being built over the course of nearly two years. The building of this church was a massive undertaking, the granite blocks in ashlar form being quarried in Rockland, Massachusetts. The architect for the church is unknown for certain, though Alexander Parris has been called by many a likely candidate—not only did he design St. John's Church (see above) seventeen years prior, but he had great expertise when it came to stone structures of a monumental nature. This church is significant because of its granite construction, coming at a time when the use of granite in the construction trade, as well as its quarrying on a large scale, was in its beginning stage in New England. The Greek Revival style of South Church, distinguished by its impressive temple-like appearance with a portico supported by four massive Tuscan columns, is also notable as an early example of the use of this style north of Boston. Interestingly, the belfry on the roof of South Church, which houses a 2,540-lb. bell cast by the Boston Copper Company in 1828, was criticized from the very beginning as the only flaw in a building that was otherwise seen as the embodiment of "classic architecture."[76] The Universalists in Portsmouth also have an extensive history, being organized in 1777 as the first church to fully subscribe to liberal doctrines. They built their own church, first on Vaughan Street, then on Pleasant Street in 1808, and it is here where Rev. Hosea Ballou, a native of Richmond, NH, preached from 1808–1815 and wrote the first published Universalist treatise. Another meetinghouse would follow, and was used by the Universalists until it was lost by fire in 1947. Having federated with the South Parish Church in 1945, the two groups immediately merged in the aftermath of the fire and since that time the church has continued under this same organization.

Temple Israel (former Methodist Church)
Built: 1828
Location: 200 Court Street

First built as a Methodist church, this structure became available when they built a new church on Miller Avenue. A sale was negotiated between them and the Temple of Israel in 1911, and by 1912, the building was occupied as the first Jewish house of worship in the state of New Hampshire. The Jewish presence in New Hampshire dates to about 1780, when Abraham and Rachel Isaac came here from Prussia, with Abraham employed as an auctioneer and merchant. After his death in 1803 (his gravestone can be found in North Cemetery), his wife moved away and it appears that there were no practicing Jews in town until the 1880s when many immigrants arrived here to find employment in local manufacturing, including the Portsmouth Naval Shipyard. By 1900, there were about thirty Jewish families in town and soon efforts to organize began. The Temple of Israel (later shortened to Temple Israel) congregation was formed beginning about 1905, with land for a Jewish cemetery purchased on Banfield Road in 1908. Responding to an advertisement placed in Boston and New York newspapers, Rev. Harry Liberson, a native of Latvia, was hired as the first rabbi and would remain a prominent citizen both in the Jewish population and in Portsmouth overall up to his death in 1973. The building purchased by Temple Israel, in its original form, is a simple two-story brick structure built in the Federal style, featuring triple entryways with fanlights above facing State Street. The trim of the compass-headed windows above each entryway features granite sills and keystone molding above. The temple has had several additions over the years, including a Community Center built in 1967 directly behind the original building and a side annex facing Court Street built in 2007, featuring an entryway with a pedimented porch, with circular and semi-circular windows on the façade. Overall, Temple Israel and its associated buildings are a pleasing mix of new and old, the entire complex fitting in well with the historical nature of the city and reflective of its diverse nature. Since the organization of Temple Israel, the Jewish population expanded at a steady pace, many families moving to the historic area, once known as "Puddledock," now known by the historic name of Strawberry Banke, directly around the temple. Many of the men were employed in the shipyard across the river, but there were also many

Temple Israel, Portsmouth.

Jewish businesses established, including bakers, butchers, and markets to serve the specific needs of the Jewish residents. About seventy-five families were members of Temple Israel by 1940, that number currently standing at about 300.

North Church of Portsmouth
Built: 1854–55
Architects: James D. Towle and Francis Foster
Location: 2 Congress Street

Located in the heart of the city in Market Square, this towering church, though not the oldest in town, is easily Portsmouth's most recognizable and beloved landmark, visible from far away. This site is important, as here was located a predecessor meetinghouse that was also an imposing structure, it being a triple-decker built in 1712, with a bell tower and 150-foot spire added later on, and served until it was taken down in 1854 after having become worn out and outdated in style. The Congregational church served by North Church today is the oldest continually operating religious organization in town, being organized in 1671. For much of its history, especially after the establishment of the South Parish Church (see above), this church was the most orthodox in town. Amongst its many ministers was Rev. Jabez Fitch (1672–1746), known as one of New Hampshire's first historians and chronicler of the Great Throat Distemper Epidemic, which devastated the New Hampshire seacoast in 1738. When it was decided to tear down the old meetinghouse and build a "New North" church, the enthusiasm of the congregation and town in general was very high, with $20,000 in pew sales made on the first day they went up for sale. The total cost of the new structure, which has a seating capacity of about 1,000, came in at $30,000, it being built by a Boston firm, Towle & Foster, that were known for the Italianate-style churches they built throughout New England from 1851–1863. Interestingly, the church steeple included a clock stage in which was mounted the clock from the previous meetinghouse, which was crafted in 1803 by the noted clockmaker Simon Willard of Boston. This clock, however, lasted for a just a short time until it was replaced in 1856. The most notable, and noticeable, feature of North Church, of course, is its five-stage steeple; early on, the possibility of omitting the steeple altogether was seriously discussed due to the high cost of the overall building, but the church members ultimately decided in favor of the 180-foot spire, continuing the sky-high traditions of the church. Indeed, the spire is so beloved in town and viewed as an asset all its own, that when a storm severely damaged the steeple during the course of renovations in 2006, a Market Square Steeple Fund was created by members of the community, raising nearly $1 million of a $1.5-million restoration project. While the steeple is the structure's central focus, there are many other elaborate Italianate and high-Victorian details of interest, including the tall and narrow arched windows topped with elaborately scrolled window hoods, as well as the Italianate brackets supporting the projecting eaves on the main block of the building, as well as on the eaves of the tower.

North Church of Portsmouth.

People's Baptist Church (former Free Will Baptist Church)
Built: 1858
Builder: Nathan Tarleton
Location: 48 Pearl Street

Known locally as "The Pearl" or "The Portsmouth Pearl," this historic structure was first built as a Free Will Baptist Church. As the congregation grew here, the building was enlarged by 10 feet with a front bay addition and a steeple above in 1868, this work costing about $2,500. The building is interesting from an architectural standpoint due to its Italianate styling, directly influenced by the recently built North Church (see above) and then quite popular in Portsmouth. This styling is most evident in the tall and narrow rounded-arch windows with hood molding above featuring acorn-style pendants. However, by the end of the nineteenth century, church membership was declining, and in 1915 the Free Will Baptist Church merged with the Middle Street Baptist Church. Just weeks after this, the Free Will Baptist Church on Pearl Street, complete with its furnishings, was sold to the People's Baptist Church for $1,200. This change in ownership resulted in the first African-American owned church in the state of New Hampshire, which is this building's true historical importance and legacy. The People's Baptist Church, first known as the People's Mission, was founded in 1890 by James Slaughter, who arrived in town from Virginia in the previous year and started Bible classes in his home. The People's

Mission first met in the South Ward Hall (see below) and formally organized as the People's Baptist Church in 1892, with Rev. James Randolph as pastor and Slaughter as church deacon, as well as fellow Virginian George Straughn. Both deacons were active and highly respected in the community. At first, the People's Baptist Church was affiliated with the all-white Middle Street Baptist Church, though worship services were conducted separately. In 1908 the People's Baptist Church became an entirely independent church and began raising funds for a church building of their own. Once the old Free Will Baptist Church was purchased in 1915, the first person to be baptized was Cynthia Hall, who though affiliated with the church, had previously stated that she would only officially join once they had their own church.[77] From this point on, and for the next sixty-nine years, The Pearl, as it soon became known, was a vital institution in Portsmouth's black community. One important date in this church, and the town of Portsmouth's, history is October 26, 1952. On this day, a graduate student from Boston College named Martin Luther King was a guest preacher here, while in the visiting choir was a young woman, Coretta Scott, who was a music student and destined to be King's wife within a year. The People's Baptist Church, though strong for many years, experienced divisions during the turbulent era of the 1960's. The "reserved Yankee style" of preaching did not sit well with everyone in the congregation and then "came the ultimate question of whether continuing a Black church was relevant in this time of struggle for equal civil rights and integration."[78] In 1967, the church split into two groups with the formation of the New Hope Baptist Church, while the other members of the church eventually disbanded altogether in 1968. In the following year, the New Hope Baptist Church occupied The Pearl and would later take ownership, continuing to worship there until they sold the building in 1984, and within a few years built a new church all their own on Peverly Hill Road. Since that time, the church has been sold several times and used as a function hall. What the future may hold for the structure is uncertain, though the building is on the National Historic Register, as well as being a stop on Portsmouth's Black Heritage Trail.

South Meetinghouse (South Ward Hall)
Built: 1866
Architect: Isaiah Wilson
Location: 260 Marcy Street

This meetinghouse has been a landmark on in Portsmouth's South End since it was built and, true to the form of original New England meetinghouse structures, has seen a wide variety of uses over the years. The site it occupies was that for its predecessor, the 1731-built South Meetinghouse, and the structure was town-owned and remains so to this day. It cost $9,600 to build and its building involved dozens of contractors and suppliers rather than one single individual or firm. Architecturally, the South Meetinghouse is an eclectic mix of Italianate and Greek Revival styling,

Above: Former People's Baptist Church, Portsmouth.

Right: South Meetinghouse, Portsmouth.

the former seen in its tall and narrow rounded arch windows with hood moldings, as well the paired brackets supporting the broad eaves at the top of the two-stage tower. The Greek Revival influence is primarily seen in the porch supported by four Doric columns. While not as sophisticated as other Italianate-styled buildings constructed in Portsmouth during that time period, the building is nonetheless well proportioned and, sited on a rise of land, has a commanding presence. The original clock in the tower was crafted by local clockmaker H. H. Ham and originally had just two faces until it was replaced in 1901. A true community structure, this meetinghouse has had many functions over the years: it was originally built for the Third Ward of Portsmouth as a meeting and voting place, as well as a school. However, like the meetinghouses of old, it has also hosted religious services over the years. Most significantly, it became the first church for Portsmouth's black residents when a worship group was formed by Edmund Kelly in 1873, albeit only for a short time. Later on, from 1892–1915, the People's Baptist Church (see above) worshipped here regularly until they purchased their own church. It was also here in 1882 that Portsmouth first celebrated the anniversary of President Abraham Lincoln's Emancipation Proclamation, an annual event that was held for many years thereafter. By the 1940s, the building was boarded up and virtually abandoned and was used by a variety of groups over the years before being acquired via lease by Strawberry Banke, the organization holding many cultural events here. In 1980, faced with mounting repair bills, the city put the building up for sale, but it was instead, eventually, leased to the Children's Museum of Portsmouth, they occupying the building from 1983 to 2008. Currently the building is occupied by Portsmouth Public Media TV, a community based public television company.

Rindge

Rindge Meeting House (First Congregational Church)
Built: 1796
Builders: John and David Barker
Location: 6 Payson Hill Road

An impressive wood frame structure with a commanding presence, this meetinghouse is important not only as one of the largest meetinghouses ever built north of Boston, but also as one that has continued to serve the original functions for which it was designed. In the aftermath of the passage of the Toleration Act of 1819, many towns quit the shared tradition of the meetinghouse, either the church building a new structure all their own or the church taking over the old meetinghouse, with town offices moved to a new town hall. This is was not the case for Rindge, as in 1820, an agreement was reached whereby the town owns the land and building and leases space to the church. To this day, the meetinghouse is a shared space, with town offices at the lower level and the church occupying the upper space. The two tiers of windows across the façade of the church are unusual and indicative that this meetinghouse may once have had two tiers of galleries, a rarity in meetinghouse construction. The meetinghouse once had a projecting bell tower on its west gable end, but was altered to its present form in 1839 when that end of the building was enlarged by 10 feet, the window arrangement altered, the bell tower enclosed, and a new steeple built. Interestingly, the steeple height was reduced by 12 feet at this time because the town's fire engine at the time could not spray water high enough to reach the height of the original spire, though its height was increased again in 1895 with the addition of the town clock. This fine example of simple colonial architecture, immaculately maintained, is distinguished by its façade with two rows of windows, the lower being large 20 × 20 sash windows, while the upper row consist of the standard 12 × 12 sash windows. The twin entryways, which feature sidelights and decorative molding, are also very pleasing to the eye. This meetinghouse is also one of the most pleasantly situated in the state, located on a knoll of land, adjacent to it being the original town cemetery that was laid out in about 1764 when the first meetinghouse was built on this site. The cemetery is notable for its finely carved gravestones and is the final resting place for many of the town's founding families. Behind the church is a row of horse sheds (there were once two rows) that have been repaired in recent times and add to the site's historic nature. The first two ministers to preach in this meetinghouse were highly respected men who had long tenures,

Rindge Meetinghouse.

indicative of the harmony within the town. I have already discussed elsewhere in these pages the activities of Rev. Seth Payson, who served from 1782 until his death in 1820, in getting this church built, and it is no surprise that Payson Hill Road was named in his honor. His successor was Rev. Amos Burnham, who was ordained in 1821 and served through 1867, though his pay of $400 a year (which remained unchanged for forty-six years), plus use of the parsonage house and land, was paid by the church members themselves, and religiously so once a year on the same day, not the town as a whole.

Rochester

First Church Congregational (former First Parish Congregational Church)
Built: 1780
Location: 63 South Main Street

Of the many hundreds of people who pass this church on a daily basis, few realize its historical nature. The main block of this much-altered structure was built as the town's second meetinghouse and was located on the Rochester Green a short distance to the south. It was raised during the forty-nine-year tenure of Rev. Joseph Haven, who graduated from Harvard in 1774 and was ordained here in 1776. Its original form was that of a standard Type II meetinghouse, without a bell tower or steeple and porches on three sides, built to replace the first 1731-built meetinghouse, which stood on Haven Hill but had become so rickety it was feared a strong wind might blow it down. The need for a new meetinghouse was agreed upon, but the Revolutionary War made both men and money scarce, so its building was delayed until 1780. Prior to this time, timber had been gotten out for the new meetinghouse and was laid on the green, while some timbers from the old meetinghouse were also used in the new one. The meetinghouse, which had never been painted and still had no steeple or bell, was eventually taken over by the Congregational Church after the Toleration Act of 1819 was passed, and moved to its current location in 1843. The building being somewhat dilapidated and out of fashion, was renovated and raised, with a vestry added below. In 1868, it was enlarged and remodeled to its current form at an expense of $8,500, a hefty sum for the time, with all vestiges of its colonial exterior removed. The result is a pleasing structure built in the prevailing Italianate and high Victorian styles. The former is most evident in its tall and narrow rounded arch windows, those on the façade featuring arched hood moldings, while those on the long sides feature pedimented window hoods. The steeple of the church features Victorian details, including the applied trim on the plain first stage. Most unusual in this church building are the polygonal additions on the façade, located on each side of the base of the pavilion that supports the tower. Today, the First Church, as it has been since its founding in 1743, is a vital part of community life in

First Church Congregational, Rochester.

Rochester, providing meeting space for such diverse programs as scouting activities, adult education programs, and addiction and recovery groups, as well as operating their own food pantry.

Walnut Grove Baptist Church (Second Baptist Church)
Built: 1867
Location: 1022 Salmon Falls Road

This beautiful country church had its beginnings in two events, one that was regional in nature, the other deeply personal and tragic. Itinerant Free Will Baptist preachers were active in Rochester by the early 1800s, with one regular visitor being Rev. Enoch Place, who was preaching sermons here by 1818. The First Free Will Baptist Church was founded in the Gonic area of Rochester in 1829 (building their first church in 1840) and residents in this area of Rochester along the Maine border attended services there, as well as across the river at Lebanon, Maine. A Sabbath School was established in 1861 in the Walnut Grove area, which met in a local schoolhouse. While the area residents were clearly interested in religious meetings, thoughts about their own salvation took a personal turn in July 1863 when two young children of Samuel and Francis Wingate, Clara (age eight) and James (age three) died, followed by the death of Albert Tebbets later that fall. Perhaps serving as a catalyst for local residents, the Walnut Grove Church was formed in June 1864, being the second Baptist church formed in town. The treasurer of the church was the above-mentioned Samuel Wingate, while many other prominent local family names, including Tebbets, Meserve, Hanson, and Mills, are found among its earliest members. Monthly meetings were held at the house of Samuel Meserve, but by 1867, plans to build a church were underway, with land donated by Benjamin and Wesley Mills. It was a small piece of land (the parking lot land was not acquired until 1990), with just enough room for horse sheds in the rear. The hayfields on three sides of the church were owned by the Mills and the lands to this day are still hayfields. The small church was built by members of the church at a cost of $1,500, funded by the sale of church pews. The church had a bell early on, but this was removed and later came up missing. The current form of the steeple likely dates from the early twentieth century, it being subsequently renovated in 2006. The façade of the church is highlighted by twin entryways with transom lights above and corner pilasters. The church is three bays in length featuring 12 × 12 sash windows with paired shutters. The building has been well-maintained over the years and, except for the Gothic-pointed steeple, retains most of its original character. Despite the fact that Walnut Grove did not have a full-time minister until the 1990s, it has always been an active group within the community and averages about fifty attendees for their Sunday services. Though Walnut Grove is part of one of New Hampshire's largest cities, this church and the landscape surrounding it has remained true to its rural origins.

Walnut Grove Baptist Church, Rochester.

Rumney

Rumney Baptist Church
Built: 1838
Location: 375 Main Street

The Baptist faith in this Lakes region town got its start as early as 1777, with services to believers offered by itinerant Baptist ministers. The Baptist church was subsequently organized here in 1780 and was early on affiliated with the Baptist church in Woodstock, but by 1789, it was part of the Baptist Association in Meredith, uniting with the church in that town, as well as those in Holderness and Sandwich. Early services were held in local homes and barns until the first meetinghouse was built about 1795 on the town common. After a great revival in 1810, the Baptist Church numbered nearly 300 members, though by 1813, after Rev. Ezra Wilmarth left Rumney, the church would have no preacher for over a decade, and would languish until the arrival of Rev. Noah Nichols in 1829. Following his revival of the congregation, the current church was built on land donated by Josiah Quincy, costing $3,000. Quincy was a well-known and highly regarded lawyer who served as President of the New Hampshire Senate in 1841–42. In 1866, when the church was extensively repaired and altered, Quincy paid half of the $2,000 cost. The church today is a mix of the Greek Revival and Victorian styles, the former characterized

Rumney Baptist Church.

by its façade, which features corner pilasters and pilasters flanking the central arched window. The arched stained-glass windows, as well as those above the twin entryways are Victorian in styling and were likely part of the 1866 remodel. The church also features a three-stage tower topped off by a simple arrow weathervane. The upper octagonal stage is unusual in that it is capped by a segmented metal dome that is silver in color and is most certainly, based on older views of the church, a modern replacement for the original dome.

Salisbury

Old Baptist Meeting House
Built: 1791–93
Location: 655 Old Turnpike Road (Route 4)

This venerable structure is located in the historic village of Salisbury Heights and may be considered its crown jewel. Its building was the result of the moving of the town's original meetinghouse to a new location, leaving those in the old center of town and to the west very dissatisfied. The idea of moving the old meetinghouse and the resulting controversy arose in 1773, but it was not until 1790 that the move was actually made. In the meantime, a Baptist Society was formed in the Salisbury Heights area in 1789, the meetings held near the house/tavern of Abel Elkins, whose establishment was across the street from where the church would be built and is still in existence today. Meetings were first held in private homes, but within a year, it was decided to build a church and building and pew committees were formed to attend to the required work. The name of the master-builder or carpenter chosen by the building committee is unknown, but it was likely a local man, perhaps Abel Elkins, who built his own tavern across the street. As originally built, the meetinghouse sat closer to the road and had twin steeples, one at each end of the building, that on the north side having a bell. This plan was unusual for the time, as few meetinghouses built in New Hampshire had twin spires. The structure remained unchanged until it was set back from the road in 1839 and totally remodeled into its current form. The work was done by Deacon William Parsons at a cost of $1,100, and consisted of interior changes as well as removing the south spire and enlarging the north steeple, adding new 6 × 6 sash windows, and painting the entire building. The pleasing church we see today is the final result of all these changes. It was also at this time that the clock in the steeple was made by Josiah Green, though he retained ownership and could take it down at any time. The building is an eclectic mix of styles, being largely Federal in nature, but with touches of Gothic and Greek Revival. The Gothic Revival elements are starkly evident in the pinnacles used on the corner of the tower, as well as those atop the columns that flank the twin entryways. The Greek Revival style is evident in the pavilion that supports the forward part of the tower and gives the

Right: Old Baptist Meeting House, Salisbury.

Below: Façade detail, Old Baptist Meeting House, Salisbury.

façade its temple-like appearance. The first minister to preach in this meetinghouse was an interesting and accomplished, albeit somewhat scattered, figure. Rev. Elias Smith, a native of Lyme, Connecticut, became a Baptist in Vermont in 1789 and was ordained a priest in 1791, preaching his first sermon in Salisbury. When he first preached in this church, its interior was unfinished, without a pulpit or any pews, but when he preached here again and was offered a settlement in February 1793, he stated to a friend that "They have a new meeting-house, completely finished, the society is large, rich and liberal, and propose to give me two hundred dollars a year, and to find me a home and wood. There is a prospect of doing good in this and surrounding towns."[79] Smith accepted the call, but within a few years, the official enthusiasm died down and he turned to other pursuits, including teaching and becoming a merchant, partnering with church member Josiah Green. He also became somewhat erratic in his preaching methods, and by 1797, he left town. Smith would subsequently settle in Portsmouth and in 1808 published the "Herald of Gospel Liberty," a religious newspaper said to be the first publication of its kind in America. The Baptists would continue to use this church into the 1920s before its ownership passed to the United Baptist Conference of New Hampshire. In 1956, it was deeded to the town, and subsequently sold to the Salisbury Historical Society for a nominal sum in 1966. Despite periods of neglect, and damage suffered during the Hurricane of 1938, the church since 1966 has been well-maintained.

Sanbornton

Sanbornton Congregational Church
Built: 1834
Location: 21 Meetinghouse Hill Road

Built as a successor to the town's first meetinghouse, this church is notable for its setting as part of the Sanbornton Square Historic District. Permanently settled in 1764, the town built its first meetinghouse by 1775, but it was not completely finished until 1797. By the 1830s, the old meetinghouse was in such disrepair that the town voted to hand the building over to the Congregationalists, and build a new town house. Likewise, the church decided to build a new house of worship a short distance away, right next to the Woodman-Sanborn Academy school building and adjacent to the new town house. Like many New Hampshire towns, the folks in Sanbornton were frugal and materials from the old meetinghouse were hauled to this site from a short distance away where it had once stood for use in the new church, which was dedicated in September 1834. From that time to this, the exterior of the church has remained largely unchanged, with the exception of rear and basement additions, as well as stained-glass replacing the original clear glass. The style of the church is largely Gothic Revival, as is evident in the pinnacles flanking the twin entryway

Sanbornton Congregational Church.

columns and the arched louvers of the tower and belfry, as well as above the side windows on the façade. The pediment, with its semielliptical louver, is a throwback to the Federal style. The church is a pleasing example of rural architecture, built by an unknown but experienced carpenter. The church is made all the more pleasing by its historic setting, being flanked by two town owned historic buildings, the 1825-built Woodman-Sanborn Academy Schoolhouse that now serves as the town library, and the Sanbornton Town Hall, which was also built in 1834. Also included in this historic area are a number of period residences. It is interesting to note that the first minister to preach here, Rev. Abraham Bodwell, was ordained in 1806 and continued here for forty-six years until he requested a dismissal due to his age and poor health in 1852. Several revivals were experienced during his tenure, especially in 1816, when about 100 new members were added to the church, but by the time this new church had been built, times had changed and from then to the end of Bodwell's ministry, there were no revivals and the church gathered but few members in these lean years.

Second Baptist Church (Bay Meetinghouse)
Built: 1838
Builder: Capt. Smith
Location: 322 Upper Bay Road

This meetinghouse, beautifully sited overlooking Lake Winnisquam (once called Sanbornton Bay), was originally built for the Free Will Baptist Society, which was organized in the early 1800s and incorporated in 1816. The first church on this site was built in 1808, but was in poor condition by the 1830s. The society debated in early 1836 whether to repair the structure or to build a new church of either brick or wood. Eventually, the latter option was chosen and the present structure was completed by October 1836. A Captain Smith of Dorchester was chosen as builder, but nothing certain is known of him or his work. It is highly likely that he was a relation to the man in charge of the building project for the church, Zebulon Smith, Jr., perhaps even being his father, the elder Zebulon Smith, who owned a sawmill just northwest of the Bay Meetinghouse. Overall, the structure cost about $2,200 and is largely built in the Federal style, though with Gothic Revival detailing, as seen in the corner pinnacles on the two-stage tower and above the side trim flanking the doors of the twin entryways, as well as the arched louvers above the side windows. The church has changed but little since its building, though an 1886 remodel changed the sash windows on the side. This pleasing church is well-maintained and currently features distinctive black-painted trim in the pediment and the doorway pinnacles. The view from the front doors of this church are exceptional, one being able to see the "bay" (thus inspiring the church's original name) many miles in the distance, and it is no surprise that such an inspiring spot was chosen for a house of worship.

Second Baptist Church (Bay Meetinghouse), Sanbornton.

Sanbornville

The Episcopal Church of Saint John the Baptist
Built: 1876–77
Architect: Charles Haight
Builder: William Lang
Location: 118 High Street

The building of this church was inspired, quite simply, by the deathbed wish of a woman with both local ties, as well as those to some of the most prominent merchants of the day in New England and New York. Rebecca Phippen Dow, just hours before her death on July 7, 1875, told a family member of her desire that an Episcopal church be established in Sanbornton. She was a native of Salem, Massachusetts, and the widow of Josiah Dow (1782–1850), a native of Wakefield who made a fortune in the shipping and mercantile trade in Salem, Boston, and Brooklyn, NY, being involved with such enterprises all over the world. The Dow children married into Brooklyn's famed Low family, who were heavily involved in the China trade, with one son being a notable clipper ship captain. The Dows would return to Wakefield and even established a private school, Dow Academy, on their own property. While Josiah Dow was a Unitarian, his wife was an Episcopalian, but had no local church in which to worship when the Dows returned to Wakefield. Her granddaughter, Harriette Low, with the assistance of an aunt, Harriet Dow, carried out Rebecca Dow's final wishes with determination, and by November 1876, the ground was broken for the church, which was consecrated in September 1877. The architect chosen for the project was New Yorker Charles Haight, a well-known architect of his time but now largely forgotten, who was very much influenced by the work of Richard Upjohn. The church was constructed by local builder William Lang of Brookfield and cost about $7,000. The land was donated by John Sanborn, a railroad superintendent and the man for whom the village is named, while the church building was almost entirely funded by members of the Low and Dow families. Additional land was donated by the Low family in 1887 to increase the site to its present-day size. The Gothic Revival church building is notable for its fine board and batten construction and cruciform plan, the shingling details and prominent buttresses on the tower, as well as fourteen beautiful stained-glass windows and the tall and narrow side windows featuring small diamond-shaped panes of glass. Just as this church had to be built, so too did a church organization itself have to be established. Saint John the Baptist was first a mission church, with services held at other locales beginning in 1876, and would not gain parish status until 1961. The bell in the tower, donated by the Low family, is indicative of the rural nature and nascent status of the church, it having the words "The Voice of One Crying in the Wilderness" engraved on its side. It is interesting to note that close to the church there is one burial, that for an infant daughter of one of the ministers.

The Episcopal Church of St. John the Baptist, Sanbornville.

Sandown

Sandown Meetinghouse
Built: 1774–75
Location: 27 Fremont Road

This structure is notable as one of the best-preserved meetinghouses of its type in all of New England and the finest in New Hampshire, as well as for the excellent quality of workmanship that is demonstrated in its many details both inside and out. Once a part of the town of Kingston, Sandown was incorporated as an independent town in 1756, with a Congregational Church organized in 1759 as the standing order. The first meetinghouse was a small structure, possibly built of logs, but by 1772, the town had grown substantially and it was decided to build a larger structure. As was often the case, siting the meetinghouse took time, and it was eventually decided to choose the geographic center of town. However, since the exact spot was bog-land and not suitable, a new spot was chosen a short distance away, the land purchased from John Colby. There are few details to be had about the meetinghouse's construction: just who built or finished the interior of the meetinghouse is unknown, but one historian suggests Peter Colby as a likely candidate, he being known as a skilled carpenter who lived in the still extant house just across the street.[80] Indeed, Peter and John Colby's names appears on a town list of twenty-seven men who were paid for their work on the meetinghouse, but no master-builder is named. While some have speculated that, based on the craftsmanship, someone outside the community was hired as either master-builder or to complete the interior finish-work, there is no evidence that tells us whether or not this was the case. Some of the anecdotes recorded about this meetinghouse, though unsubstantiated, are quite interesting and not too far-fetched; it is said that the large timbers, beams measuring 10 × 12 inches and rafters 8 × 10 inches among them, required for the building could not be found locally as the area had long been settled and larger trees harvested, and were thus procured in northern New Hampshire, presumably dragged here by teams of oxen. In regards to the building of the meetinghouse, one story that has been told in Sandown through the years is that during its raising, the town ran out of rum to supply the workers, they refusing to work until another barrel of rum was procured, it being brought from nearby Newburyport.[81] The Sandown meetinghouse is a Type II meetinghouse, a standard of its day in rural New Hampshire, but is so unusual because it has not been altered over the years in any significant way. The interior, known for its wine-glass pulpit and finely constructed box pews, has seen several changes, the addition of two stoves (since removed) in 1826 and 1839, as well as the removal of pews in the south gallery to make way for an organ. The exterior is also largely original, except for the panes of glass in the 16 × 12 sash windows. Of these panes, about a third are original, the remainder being replacements due to the ravages of time and weather, including the Hurricane of 1938, which is said to have resulted in much breakage. This meetinghouse's notable features have been well-described and documented over the years, the building itself so notable that in the 1920s famed auto-maker Henry Ford offered $40,000 for the building for his museum in Dearborn, Michigan. While Ford was able to purchase other historic buildings during his New Hampshire trip, the folks in Sandown had the wisdom to not let their meetinghouse be one of them.

I have already described elsewhere some of the fine interior finish work on the pulpit and the box pews, but what fascinates many people during their visit here are the slave pews, located in the gallery in the corners near the pulpit. While most accounts state that there were but few slaves in town to use these pews, and that they were instead used by household servants, the names of some Sandown slaves on the eve of the American Revolution are indeed known. Robin, Scipio, and Archelaus perhaps attended religious services here with their masters, and may have even attempted to enlist for military service within this meetinghouse's walls. These three men, though rejected for service in New Hampshire, did fight for Massachusetts and did so honorably. However, one free black resident of Sandown, Thomas Griffin, likely knew this meetinghouse well; in April 1775, he was married to his wife, Anna, probably in the meetinghouse, by Sandown town minister Rev. Josiah Cotton, and two weeks later enlisted for service in the Revolutionary War as a drummer and a fifer. While he was in the service, his new wife, Anna Griffin, stayed in Sandown with friend Mary Bailey, and it is not hard to imagine her sitting in the slave pew every Sunday, wishing and praying for her husband's safe return, which occurred sometime in 1779.

As to the exterior of the Sandown meetinghouse, there are many details which stand out and no mere drive-by view of this structure will do. In fact, a full walk around is a must to appreciate it to the fullest. On the south side facing the modern town center is the main entryway, distinguished by its fluted pilasters and a finely formed pediment with modillions. On the west side facing the road is another entryway featuring pilasters and transom lights above, as well as another well-done pediment with modillions. The third entryway on the east side was executed in similar fashion, though somewhat more subdued in its styling with no modillions in the pediment. Finally, the north wall is notable as well, featuring a fine central compass-headed pulpit window with rounded molding above. The meetinghouse, which has always been painted white as far as is known, is beautifully maintained and in excellent condition. It hosted annual meetings and voting for every election, both local and presidential, from its building to 1929, when meetings were moved to the new town hall. That same year, the Old Meetinghouse Historical Association was formed to preserve the building for future generations. This it has done with great dedication and success.

Sandown Meetinghouse, west gable-end view.

View from the gallery, Sandown Meetinghouse.

East doorway detail, Sandown Meetinghouse.

Sandwich

Community Church of Sandwich (former Baptist Church and Free Will Baptist Church)
Built: 1792–93
Builder: Ezekiel French
Location: 12 Church Street

This church structure embodies the interesting religious history of this once-remote town, which was established in 1763. The first church established here was that for the Baptists in the early 1770s, Elder Jacob Jewell arriving here from Weare. Though the Baptists were active here and built a crude meetinghouse early on, a more substantial house of worship was needed within less than two decades, so this meetinghouse was built as a replacement. The structure was owned by the town and was shared by the Baptists and Methodists, with annual meetings also held here. As originally constructed, the building was a Type II meetinghouse without a bell tower or steeple. Its builder, Ezekiel French, was a trained carpenter who came here from Epping and would later become prominent in town affairs and serve as selectman. Upon the building of this meetinghouse, the first formal Baptist religious society in Sandwich was organized in 1793, but it would turn out to be short-lived. In 1799, the church withdrew from the Baptist Association and, in 1801, voted to ask for instructors from the Free Will Baptists in New Durham to spread their faith. In 1803, the church was formally accepted as the Free Will Baptist Church of Sandwich and this denomination worshipped here for over 100 years. In 1847, the meetinghouse was turned to face south toward Center Sandwich and was cut down in height by 4 feet and remodeled in the Greek Revival style. The changes were so extensive that some historians have recorded that a new church was built altogether. The church gained much of its present form in 1862 when a bell tower and steeple were added, and became what we see today in 1925 when the tower was given a clock and reconfigured in the Colonial revival style that was then popular, the whole designed by Boston architect J. Randolph Coolidge, Jr. The addition of the tower at the gable end in 1862 was somewhat unusual and old-fashioned for the time and is indeed the most notable feature of this church, distinguished by the Gothic corner pinnacles on the lower stage, while the upper stages feature Federal-style corner finials in the shape of an urn. The Free Will Baptist church in Center Sandwich remained strong for many years but, as with many rural New Hampshire communities, declining numbers occurred as the town itself shrank in population from the late nineteenth and continuing through the early twentieth centuries, with Sandwich's residents reduced from just over 2,200 in number at the start of the Civil War to less than a thousand by 1910. Though the town was a popular destination for summer residents and still is today, the number of year-round worshippers made it difficult for the Free Will Baptists and the Methodists to hire a full-time

Community Church of Sandwich (former Baptist Church), Sandwich.

minister on their own, with the result that the two churches federated. As a result, the Sandwich congregation withdrew from the Quarterly Meetings about 1912. The church today is community oriented with no specific denomination, and is a popular place for worship still among summer residents. This church is also notable as being a highlight of the Center Sandwich Historic District, with many historic period residences in its immediate surroundings, as well as for the burying ground, called the Rural Cemetery today, though often also referred to as the Baptist Cemetery that is adjacent to the church and still in use today. This historic cemetery predates the church itself and is notable for the many finely carved stones found within which date at least as far back as the 1780s, though earlier unmarked burials most likely also occurred here.

Community Church of Sandwich (former Methodist Church)
Built: 1848
Builder: Jonathan Hanson
Location: 2–22 Main Street

The Methodists got their start in Sandwich beginning in 1803, with circuit riders coming from Landaff to the north, a difficult journey on horseback through the heavily forested White Mountain region. The town became a Methodist station in 1810 and conducted worship services in private homes and in the 1792-built meetinghouse (see above), sharing that space with the Baptists. This situation prevailed until their numbers had grown so greatly, becoming the largest denomination in town, that they built their own meetinghouse on Skinner Road (Route 113) in 1825. This structure served the congregation until it was severely damaged by fire in 1847. Under the influence of church member Moulton Marston, a prominent local businessman, banker, and town and state official who twice served on the Governor's Council, it was decided to build a new church on Main Street. Not only was Marston on the church building committee, but he also donated the land for the new church and was one of its most active benefactors. In fact, the church was built adjacent to Marston's own home, a historic Federal-style structure that is still standing today to the right of the Greek Revival structure that he helped to bring into being. A local builder was hired for the job and he and his workmen, along with church volunteers, proceeded to raise and outfit a new church, the total cost being about $2,200, with most of the amount financed by the sale of church pews. The resulting structure is considered by many historians today to be one of the finest Greek Revival churches in the region. The building is distinguished by its gable-end façade, which features a steep and unadorned pediment and towering corner pilasters and matching pilasters flanking the central entryway. The church is topped with a three-stage tower, the lower two stages, including the open belfry, being square in plan, and the upper-stage being octagonal in form with a dome on top. The church is a beautiful example of rural architecture and, with the old Baptist Church just around the corner, is one of the crown jewels in the Center Sandwich Historic District.

North Sandwich Meeting House
Built: 1881
Builder: William Quinby
Location: 354 Quaker Whiteface Road

This structure is important as the best-preserved Quaker meetinghouse in Carroll County, being the home of the Sandwich Society of Friends, established in 1783. The Friends were active from the earliest beginnings of the town, with as many as forty members living here by 1777. The group continued to grow and were recognized as a Monthly Meeting in 1802. The first activity of the Friends took place in Center Sandwich, where a meetinghouse was built early on, but those residing in North Sandwich soon organized, building their first meetinghouse on this spot in 1814. This meetinghouse served the North Sandwich Quakers for many years, but had grown dilapidated as its membership went into a slow decline, matching the downward trend in the town's overall population as residents sought greater economic opportunities in the big cities to the south or through emigration to the farmlands of the Midwest. However, the arrival of the Quaker minister John Cartland, noted for his "great acceptance … honesty and devotion to duty … as

Right: Community Church of Sandwich (former Methodist Church), Sandwich.

Below: North Sandwich Meeting House, Sandwich.

well as by his verbal ministrations," in 1876 sparked a revival amongst the North Sandwich Quakers.[82] Indeed, while the Quakers in Center Sandwich disbanded in 1884, those in the north soon formed plans to either repair the old meetinghouse or build a new one. After some deliberation, it was decided in the spring of 1881 that enough funds could be raised by subscription to build a new meetinghouse and local builder William Quinby, who lived just down the road, was hired to build the structure from the foundation upward at a cost of $700. Though records are lacking, it would seem that the meetinghouse was completed later in 1881, though at a cost of $916 rather than the original amount agreed upon. The resulting meetinghouse has served from that time to the present as the home of the North Sandwich Meeting, one of the oldest active Quaker meetings in the state. The meetinghouse exterior has remained virtually unchanged since its building, with the exception of the sign on the facade and its front steps, the building a nice example of a rural nineteenth-century church. It is distinguished from Quaker meetinghouses from an earlier era (see Dover above) by its single entryway, an indication that by this time the North Sandwich meeting for its male and female members was integrated. The meetinghouse is distinguished by its fine granite foundation and the 6 × 6 sash windows which provide ample light for the two and a half-story structure. The beautiful rural setting of this meetinghouse at the junction of Quaker-Whiteface and Durgin Bridge roads is also notable. Indeed, part of the experience in viewing this meetinghouse is the journey to get there along narrow country roads that appear to have changed but little over the past 100 years or more. One route to reach this meetinghouse involves crossing the Cold River by way of the Durgin Bridge, a historic covered bridge built in 1869. The previous bridge on this spot was a link in the Underground Railroad between Sandwich and North Conway which carried runaway slaves from the south northward to freedom in Canada with the help of those sympathetic to their plight, possibly including the North Sandwich Quakers as members of the sect were amongst the most active groups who opposed slavery.

Seabrook

Old South Meetinghouse
Built: 1764
Location: 651 Lafayette Road

Located along heavily-travelled U.S. Route 1, the old King's Highway, it is easy to miss this historic meetinghouse. The area comprising Seabrook today was once a part of the town of Hampton Falls and was settled by 1638. Established first as a southern parish because of a ministerial dispute in the Hampton Falls Congregational Church, the parish, taking the name of Seabrook, became an independent town in 1768. This meetinghouse was built earlier in 1764, the same year that the parish was established and a Presbyterian church formed, with Rev. Samuel Perley settled as their minister. Though his tenure here only lasted until his dismissal in 1775, it was an active one. In 1775, the Boston Presbytery, through which Rev. Perley was ordained, conducted organizational meetings here. After Perley was dismissed, the town had no settled minister for nearly twenty-five years and preaching even after that time was only sporadic, the house occupied by the Congregationalists, Baptists, and other groups up to the mid-1800s, as well as continuing to serve its civic functions as the seat of town government. As originally built, Old South was a standard Type II meetinghouse with twin porches. It had no bell tower or steeple until one was added in 1820, though there was no bell in the belfry. One account states that the framing timbers came from six different towns, likely due to a lack of old growth timber within the town limits. However, by the 1850s, the meetinghouse was seldom used except for annual town meetings and had fallen into disrepair, "it having become deserted even as a place for the children to play in."[83] However, the meetinghouse got a boost in 1858 with the formation of the Seabrook Baptist Church. In that year the structure was repaired and renovated into its current form and turned so that its main entrance faced the road, being dedicated for services by the Baptists in March 1859. Among the changes at this time were the addition of the current three-stage steeple, as well as the altering of the interior, with the first floor renovated at town expense for use as a town hall, while the gallery was removed and a second story created, which would be used by the newly-formed church. The cost of the entire project was just over $3,500, with the town paying $950 for the renovation of their space. From that time until a new town hall was built in 1954, town business, including meetings, voting, as well as social events, were conducted here, while religious services were also conducted here off and on until finally ceasing about 1967, when the meetinghouse was leased to a funeral home. Interestingly, at this time, a hole was cut in the upper floor to allow the installation of a ramp to facilitate the transfer of caskets to the upper sanctuary. The meetinghouse was taken back by the town in 1974 and is now owned by the Seabrook Historical Society and has undergone extensive repairs from 2016–18. Old South is notable for its large, 15 × 15 sash windows, each sash separated by a wood panel in an atypical fashion, as well its simple yet elegant three-stage steeple, topped off with an attractive banner-style weathervane all of which features date from the 1859 remodel. The bell in the steeple was donated by Charles Sanborn and was first rung in 1861 to mark the inauguration of President Abraham Lincoln. The façade of the church, featuring twin entryways, corner pilasters, and a broken pediment with a semielliptical fan louver, is reflective of the Greek Revival style.

Old South Meetinghouse, Seabrook.

Stark

Stark Union Church
Built: 1853
Location: 1190 NH Route 110

Originally built by pew owners rather than a specific denomination, this beautiful church is still owned by pew owners today, an arrangement that has now continuously lasted for over 160 years, likely a record for any church of its kind in New Hampshire. Originally granted in 1774 under the name Percy, the town was incorporated in 1795 and gained its current name in 1832. Stark's early settlers were nominally Congregationalists, with a society formed by 1810, but the group was neither large nor robust. The Methodist circuit riders also made their appearance here in the early 1800s, as did the Free Will Baptists, they being the most active religious groups in town. Worship services and meetings for both groups were held in local homes, neither large enough to support a settled minister. There was no town-owned meetinghouse in Stark, and no town house for civic functions was built until one was finally voted for in 1847. This church was the first and only church building ever to be built here, a union-type church decided upon as no one religious group could afford to build their own or hire their own full-time minister, there being less than 500 people residing in town. This beautiful church, a combination of the Gothic and Greek Revival styles with a seating capacity of 250, was decided upon in 1854 by a building committee consisting of three men, Solomon Cole, Andrew Cole, and Benjamin Thompson. Its construction was certainly a town-affair, but who served as master-builder is unknown, it costing $1,050 in all and considered early on to be "the finest church for the cost ... ever put up in the county."[84] The church has always been non-denominational and remains so even today, though early on the Methodists and Free Will Baptists were its most frequent users. Likewise, pew owners have always maintained ownership of the church, the Pew Owner's Association doing so since the 1950s, doing a great job in maintaining the structure. The Stark Union Church, whose exterior remains largely unchanged, is distinguished by its façade featuring twin entryways with pediments above, with a 12 × 12 sash window in-between, as well as corner pilasters. The two-stage tower is noted for its Gothic Revival-style pinnacles on the corners, as well as the arched belfry opening framed by pilasters with keystone trim above. As beautiful as this church is, it is made even more attractive by a village setting which features the Stark Covered Bridge. Built *c.* 1857 and crossing the Upper Ammonoosuc River, the bridge is just yards from the church and is distinguished by its portal featuring beautifully turned pendants, the whole complementing quite well the architecture of Stark Union Church. The bridge allowed those living across the river to attend church, while horse sheds once stood on the ground between the church and the river adjacent to the bridge. Finally, directly opposite the church is the Stark Village School, built in 1890 and noted for its distinctive tower, while to the immediate southeast of the

Stark Union Church.

church, across Route 110, is the hillside location of the picturesque and historic Stark Village Cemetery. All of these features, with the church central among them, make this quintessential New England village one of the most heavily photographed locations in the state.

Stoddard

Stoddard Congregational Church
Built: 1836
Location: 1549 Route 123 North

This fine example of a Gothic Revival church was built when the Congregationalists in town were unsatisfied with sharing the 1789-built town meetinghouse with the Universalists. That sect had grown in popularity by the 1830s and seems to have claimed the old meetinghouse for most Sabbath days, on a proportionate basis, leaving the Congregationalists with no convenient house of worship. This situation continued until, in 1835, they decided to build their own church. Interestingly, the framing timbers for the church were hewn on the lawn of the tavern of Capt. Jonathan Sanderson, located across the street from the church. This large public house was built in 1833 and today is known as the historic Loomis-Hadley House. The

Stoddard Congregational Church.

cost of the church was just over $2,000, and while its master-builder or architect is unknown, history tells us that one local carpenter, John Mellen, saved the day when he "noticed that one major cross beam was insufficiently supported below" and secured a supporting timber just in time to prevent the frame from collapsing.[85] The church today has seen no major changes over the years and is noted for its arched twin entryways and windows, as well as a two-stage tower featuring a crenelated parapet and pinnacles. The bell in the tower was purchased at an additional cost of $289, the equivalent of about $7,000 in today's currency. The first minister to preach here was Stoddard's longtime minister, Rev. Isaac Robinson, who was settled here in 1803 and remained here the remainder of his life, preaching his last sermon in July 1854 before his death on the following Sabbath after serving for fifty-one years.

Strafford

Third Baptist Church
Built: 1857–58
Builder: Dennis Foss
Location: 30 Strafford Road

Located in Center Strafford, a part of the town once better known as "The Ridge," this church was one of four Free Will Baptist churches established in Strafford. The Free Will Baptist faith gained a foothold in this town early on at Strafford Corner beginning in 1779, even before Elder Benjamin Randall of New Durham organized the mother church, he being one of its inaugural members. In succeeding years, three other churches were established so as to reduce the hardships in travelling to a house of worship, with churches organized in North Strafford, Bow Lake, and "The Ridge." The Third Baptist Church was organized in 1819 and their first house of worship was built that same year, probably a standard Type II meetinghouse. The first minister of the Third Church, Rev. Enoch Place, preached here twice a month for thirty-six years, alternating his time between two of the Free Will Baptist churches in town. Many members of the Foss family, who came early to Strafford, were members of this church, so it is not surprising that a builder by this name also constructed the church. The church is a beautiful combination of the Greek Revival and Italianate styles, the former seen in the corner pilasters and those flanking the central doorway. The emerging popularity of the Italianate style is distinctly visible in the paired brackets supporting the wide eaves and cornices of the building, the overall combination of styles, topped off with a simple three-stage steeple, making for a pleasing church structure. The church has been well-maintained and cared for over the years and the exterior remains largely original, with exception of the window glass, which was changed from clear to stained-glass in 1922. Just a short distance from this rural church is the historic Austin Hall, the school building for

Third Baptist Church, Strafford.

the Austin Academy, built in 1833 under the encouragement of Rev. Place and an "outgrowth of that church on the Ridge," becoming "the first, high class educational organization of the Free Will Baptist denomination."[86]

Stratham

Stratham Community Church
Built: 1837
Location: 6 Emery Lane

The location of this church has a long history in Stratham, having been the site of the town's previous meetinghouses. The second meetinghouse on this site, built in 1769, was taken down in 1837, with the Congregationalists building this church and dedicating it by November of that same year. However, church and state still remained connected in Stratham, as space in the basement of the new church was reserved for town meetings. This situation remained in effect until 1877, when a new town hall was built. The church is an interesting mix of architectural styles, tastefully blended: the arched louvers above the twin entryways, windows, and the belfry are Gothic Revival stylings, while the corner pilasters; those on the tower are Greek Revival elements; and finally, the octagonal cupola portion of the three-stage tower is in the Federal style. The tower is topped off with a fine heart-shaped banner weathervane, which is one of the finest in the area. It was created by blacksmith and mechanic Joseph Emery (1802–1840), member of a prominent family that was among the town's first settlers. Emery Lane is named for the family and Joseph Emery's farm was very nearby, he being the owner of pew No. 27 in the church. The building of this church came at a time when its membership was in flux, with declining numbers and no hired minister from 1834–36. The first minister to preach in the new church was Rev. William Newman, who served the town from November 1836 to 1849. During his time here, periods of revival were experienced and the church added new members. Later minister George Savory, installed in 1885, was long remembered for the "giving box" that he hung on the wall inside the church, asking that members donate a tenth of their income, though local John Emery recalled that it seldom held that amount. The exterior details of the church remain largely the same, with the significant exception of the side addition, which was built in 1998 to link the structure to two other buildings on the site. One of these is the now steeple-less, 1840-built former Stratham Baptist Church, which was gifted to the church in 1964 and moved to this site in 1981, now housing a preschool. On the east side of the church may be seen the old Congregational Cemetery, which predates the church and is the final resting place of many town notables, including some older stones toward the front for young members of the Boardman family and for prominent townsman and church deacon, Samuel Lane.

Stratham Community Church.

Sugar Hill

St. Matthew's Episcopal Chapel
Built: 1893–94
Architect: Frederick C. Withers
Location: Junction, Route 117 and Birches Road

This beautiful Episcopal chapel was built by a New York architect to serve the many summer tourists who visited Sugar Hill (part of the town of Lisbon until 1962) and the White Mountain area beginning in the 1860s. By the 1880s, the town was famed as a tourist destination and had a number of grand hotels to serve their needs. However, what these folks did not have—many of them wealthy Episcopalians from New York who stayed the entire summer season—was a church in which to worship, they being forced to make the long-distance journey to Littleton. Episcopal services were held for a time in the ballroom of the Sunset Hill House, but a permanent solution was found when the owner of the Miramonte Hotel, located just across the street from St. Matthew's, donated land for a church. The architect for the new church was Frederick Clarke Withers, who donated his services and was likely a summer visitor here. Noted for his Gothic Revival designs, Withers was by this time in the twilight of his career, and St. Matthew's was the only wooden church he ever designed. The cornerstone was laid in 1893, and by August 1894, the new chapel was dedicated for service. In the beginning, the interior was rudimentary, with benches provided for worshippers, while the stained-glass windows of today were not yet procured, instead filled with paper colored to look like stained-glass. Eventually, real stained-glass was obtained, including three windows donated by the Cammann family of Huntington, NY, and coming from an Episcopal church in Cold Spring Harbor, New York, that was being torn down. Today, the church continues to serve many summer residents and tourists and has been beautifully maintained. The historic chapel is notable for its steeply pitched roof and beautifully shingled gable-end tower, while the barrel-vaulted ceiling of the sanctuary inside is beautifully executed. The church has seen several exterior changes over the years, most notably in its paint scheme. In the beginning, the church was painted a dark red color, consistent with late Victorian-era tastes, and remained this color into the 1930s. In addition, the foundation was originally constructed of stone, but due to moisture issues was replaced with one of concrete, this covered by the lattice work that is seen today, while the parking lot and circular drive are modern conveniences added at a much later date, the lot around the entire chapel being originally a mixture of wild grass and trees. In fact, one side of the church remains as grassland and is known for the purple lupine flowers that grow here in abundance every June, a sign that St. Matthew's will soon be open again for the summer season.

St. Matthews's Episcopal Chapel, Sugar Hill.

Sutton

First Free Will Baptist Church of Sutton (former North Sutton Meetinghouse and First Baptist Church)
Built: 1797
Builder: John Harvey
Location: Route 114

This town meetinghouse was built at the same time that the town's south meetinghouse was built, mainly due to the rough terrain that divided both areas of town and made the journey from one end of Sutton to the other quite difficult in the days of horse and buggy travel. First granted in 1749, Sutton was originally called Perrystown, but difficulties delayed settlement and the town was regranted in 1784, eventually gaining its present name after settlers who arrived here from Sutton, Massachusetts. While it is believed that a crude log meetinghouse was first built to serve the town's needs, a true meetinghouse was not debated until 1792, and involved much controversy over the levying of a "penny tax" to raise the funds for building. Eventually, the matter was settled and each section of town chose their own building committee and master-builder, each meetinghouse to be of the same dimension and similar to that in nearby New London. Pews were sold in advance to offset the costs beginning in 1794 and the meetinghouse was raised in 1797 and finished the following year. The timber for the meetinghouse is said to have been cut from the exact spot where it now stands. One interesting aspect of its finishing was the procurement of the original lock for the front door and pulpit hinges of the meetinghouse. The lock became a subject of dispute between its maker, Thomas Stevens of Weare, and Matthew Harvey of the building committee, as to its cost, Harvey deeming the original cost of $5 too high. Eventually, a price of $4 was agreed upon by both parties, and today that same lock is on display inside the old meetinghouse. The interior of this church from the very beginning seems to have been fraught with peril, the floor in the upper gallery said to have been as steeply inclined as the roof itself, so much so that "it was truly an awful operation to take one's place in the singing seats."[87] As originally constructed, the structure was a Type II meetinghouse with side porches, but began to gain its present form when it was remodeled in 1855, with the gallery replaced with a level floor to create a full second-story and the porches removed. This space was occupied by the church, while the lower space was used as the town hall. In 1870, the structure gained its current configuration when the two-stage tower with open belfry and bell was added at a cost of $1,153, $800 raised by the men in town who called themselves the "Bell Company," while the ladies of the town raised $350 through the formation of a knitting society who sold their work and arranged fundraising events. The church is plain, but the massive size of the main block is impressive, while the single entryway on the long side facing south, flanked by tapered pilasters, offers some pleasing detail. The rear porch of the church is a modern addition, but offers some hint of how the structure with its original porches would have once appeared, while inside some of the original beams are visible. The tower also features a Seth Thomas clock dating from 1921, which came from Bradford and whose working mechanism is on display for all to see. The meetinghouse for years was shared by the various denominations in town, even after the Toleration Act of 1819, as well as serving community needs, at one time housing a library, but ceased functioning as a town hall when Sutton built Pillsbury Memorial Hall in 1891. From about that time on and through the 1940s, the structure was the home of the First Baptist Church, though cared for by the Meeting House Society. This congregation merged with the Free Will Baptists from Sutton Mills in 1977, the historic meetinghouse then gaining its current designation.

South Sutton Meeting House
Built: 1839
Location: 17 Meeting House Hill Road

This meetinghouse is the third such structure to stand on this prominent hill in the southern part of town. The first meetinghouse was built under the same circumstances and to the same plan as the North Sutton Meeting House (see above) by Daniel Page in 1797, but it caught fire and burned during cleanup of the site upon

Above: First Free Will Baptist Church of Sutton.

Below: Original front door lock, former North Sutton Meetinghouse. This hardware, along with the key and other hardware are now framed and hanging inside the church.

its completion. The second meetinghouse, too, was built by Page within a short time, and lasted up to 1839, but details of its fate are unclear—it is likely that if fell into disrepair and was simply replaced in 1839 with a new building, which fact is stated in the 1890 town history without any details. While some believe that the original second meetinghouse was simply renovated to its current form, architectural historians dispute this and consider the current structure to date entirely from 1839. Sadly, the name of its builder has gone unrecorded, but he was likely influenced by similar period meetinghouses built in nearby Warner and Webster (see below). The meetinghouse is a fine example of the many Greek Revival churches then being built throughout New Hampshire, and is notable today for its largely original condition. The meetinghouse is notable for its three-stage tower with arched openings, as well as for its temple-like façade featuring a pediment with a semielliptical fan louvered vent, as well as for its twin entryways with sidelights. The central window is unusual in form, featuring a 12 × 8 sash window flanked by 3 × 2 sidelights, the combination allowing a good amount of light inside. The church is also notable for its prominent site on the town green which also features the town's Civil War monument. The church, like its North Sutton counterpart, hosted the worship services for several of the town's denominations, with the Baptists predominating in numbers, but also including the Universalists, Seventh Day Adventists, and possibly the more unusual

South Sutton Meeting House.

First Society of Spiritualists of Sutton beginning in 1858. The meetinghouse would eventually decline in use and is now owned by the Sutton Historical Society, with two annual services held on Old Home Day and the Children's Christmas Pageant. The structure has remained in relatively good condition over the years, but the tower as of this writing is in need of repairs and stabilization. The historical society is currently considering whether to apply for grant money or to turn ownership of the building over the town, subject to voter approval, in order to provide the needed insurance and resources to preserve this important town building.

Tamworth

Chocorua Community Church (former Free Will Baptist Church)
Built: 1885
Location: 40 Deer Hill Road (Route 113)

The roots of this village church can be traced as far back as 1781, when the founder of the Free Will Baptist faith in New England, Rev. Benjamin Randall, visited here to preach and thus planted the seed for future growth. When the Free Will Baptists in Tamworth joined the Sandwich Quarterly Meeting in 1802, it was the oldest of the towns joining to form the meeting. Formerly known as Tamworth Iron Works, the village built the first Free Will Baptist church structure in town here in 1835, and the number of church members fluctuated with the times, it having 100 members in 1812, fifty in 1833, 171 in 1843, and ninety-six in 1889. Though uncertain, this edifice seems to have been built during the pastorate of Rev. John Runnels, who was ordained in 1852 and served until his death in 1887. However, there are those who believe that this church is the original 1835 structure and that it was only remodeled in 1885. Whatever the case may be, the structure, which has not changed significantly since 1885, is a nice example of a rural church with some Gothic Revival details in the arched louver above the doorway and in the belfry of the three-stage tower. This church remained affiliated with the Free Will Baptist Church after Rev. Runnels' death, but by the early twentieth century, membership had declined. The church gave up its Baptist name by 1941 and in that year joined with the Congregational Church, with one hired minister supplying both churches because of their weakened financial state. By 1956, the two churches together could not afford to hire a minister, so in 1957, the Tamworth Associated Churches organization was formed when St. Andrews-in-the-Valley Episcopal Church joined the group. This organization, however, is no longer in effect and the Chocorua Community Church is today an independent entity.

Chocorua Community Church, Tamworth.

Tilton

Fred Andrew Smart Chapel (former Free Will Baptist Church of Canterbury)
Built: 1852, 1963
Location: 43 School Street

This elegant chapel on the campus of the Tilton School has a long history, beginning its life in the nearby town of Canterbury. The original structure served the Free Will Baptist Church in that town, being built at a cost of $1,400 at the junction of Baptist and Baptist Hill roads. This structure served the town for over a century, but as numbers declined in the two remaining churches in Canterbury (the Congregationalists and the Free Will Baptists), it was decided by the early 1960s that the two congregations should merge. This they did, making it official in 1965, choosing to use the smaller Congregational church building at Canterbury Center as their house of worship. The old Free Will Baptist Church no longer being needed, it was subsequently sold to the Tilton School and moved there in 1965. Once in Tilton, the old church was enlarged and modified, being dedicated as the Fred Andrew Smart Chapel in 1966. It is named after the school's long-time English teacher, a graduate of Brown University in 1898 who came here early in his career

Fred Andrew Smart Chapel, Tilton.

to become a dedicated and highly regarded instructor. During its conversion for use by the school, it was lengthened by 40 feet and given a lower basement level, but otherwise the church remains largely true to its original Greek revival form. The original tower of the Baptist church was in three stages, the chapel retaining these elements, including the squat first stage, but adding a tall spire to top it off. The temple-like façade is largely unchanged, featuring corner pilasters and central pilasters flanking the entryway, as well as a pediment with a semielliptical fan louver. The paired brackets in the pediments and supporting the eaves are, however, an interesting Italianate influence. All of these features are well-blended and speak to the prominence of both the original church in Canterbury as well as the school it serves in Tilton today. Though the chapel is named for Fred Smart today, we should not forget those Free Will Baptist elders who first occupied the pulpit of this church in Canterbury, first and foremost among them being Rev. Jeremiah Clough, who served the church from 1840 up to his death in 1879 and was one of the most prominent and respected men in town. After his death, it was recorded in the church record that "his funeral was largely attended at the church.... He has been ... its preacher and pastor for a long time. He came to his grave full of years and good works. We shall greatly miss him."[88]

Troy

Troy Town Hall (former Troy Meetinghouse)
Built: 1814–15
Builder: Thomas Spaulding
Location: 16 Central Square

This meetinghouse turned town hall has a long and varied history that is as old as the town of Troy itself. Discussions were first held about the town's formation from parts of Fitzwilliam and Marlborough in the 1790s, and by 1812, a building committee was formed for the planning of a meetinghouse even before the establishment of Troy as a separate town in 1815 occurred. Members of this committee went so far as to visit Templeton, Massachusetts, to see the new meetinghouse built there by Elias Carter in 1811. The following year, the men involved in organizing Troy even voted to build a meetinghouse based on that in Templeton. After a delay in raising the needed funds, the timber for the church, supplied by citizens of the Troy, was gathered on the town common and the meetinghouse was raised in June 1814. Carpenter and builder Thomas Spaulding of Sullivan was chosen for the job, paid $550 to raise and frame the meetinghouse, while Samuel Morse of Templeton was chosen to finish the interior. Spaulding not only built this meetinghouse and one in his own home-town, but also worked on that in Hancock (see above). The raising of this meetinghouse, however, was interrupted and came close to disaster when news came, just as the frame had been partially raised, that a boy had fallen into the mill-pond and was in danger of drowning. "Quick as thought, a large number rushed to the water, leaving their companions in labor in a most perilous position. For a little time, a few only, thoughtful and brave men, stood at their posts, though they were almost led to tremble lest the weight they had to sustain should prove too much for their strength, and they should be crushed beneath the falling timbers."[89] Luckily, the men were able to hold on and the drowning boy was quickly saved and those men who had left their posts were able to return and continue the job to its successful conclusion. The completed meetinghouse, while not as refined as the Templeton meetinghouse it sought to copy, is nonetheless an impressive Federal-style building and important as an early part of the Templeton Run of meetinghouses in the Monadnock region. It is distinguished by its gable-end facing the town common, which features a portico supported by four towering Doric columns, the portico itself partially supporting the three-stage tower whose upper stages are octagonal in form. The façade is also notable for its paired corner pilasters and triple entryways featuring Federal-style trim. The structure was used for both religious and civic functions until 1859, when it no longer hosted religious services. The first minister to officiate here was Rev. Ezekiel Rich, an evangelist preacher who served the town from 1815–1818, but lived in town and conducted occasional services up to his departure in 1845. A well-liked and learned man, Rich

Troy Town Hall.

was also somewhat eccentric, publishing a proposal in 1844 to reform the English alphabet through the use of numbers and inverted letters. The Congregationalists stopped using the meetinghouse by 1846, with other denominations following suit. After the meetinghouse became solely owned by the town in 1853, it was several years later turned 90 degrees to its current position facing the town common, a basement level was added, and the interior was remodeled to accommodate civic functions and activities. By the early 1860s, the space below the meetinghouse served as the firehouse and housed Troy's steam fire engine, and the town jail was also located here for a time. In 1893, a rear addition was built to accommodate a stage and dressing rooms in order to host community events, and the structure to this day serves as the seat of town government. Though enlarged and somewhat altered, the original form of the building's exterior is largely intact and the old Troy Meetinghouse still serves the town today, just as it did when it was first built over 200 years ago.

Tuftonboro

Tuftonboro Corner United Methodist Church
Built: 1853
Location: 129 Mountain Road (Route 171)

This notable structure is home to one of the oldest Methodist congregations in the Lakes Region. The first Methodist services were held here in 1804, and the following year, the town became a station for circuit riders who spread the faith in the Lakes Region, the circuit called the Tuftonborough Circuit because it was the first town in the area to establish the faith. By 1809, the Methodists counted some 300 members, worshipping in local homes, barns, schools, and even outdoors in the summer months. Though records for this early church are lacking, their first house of worship in this town was built in 1820. This replacement church was built by January 1854 on a piece of land that was acquired by a five-man meetinghouse committee at a cost of $108. Just who the builder of the structure may have been is not known, but Joseph Nutter of nearby Wakefield is a good candidate. He is known to have built the First Free Will Baptist Church in Ossipee (see above) in 1856, which shares similar features, and was likely a relation of Jacob Nutter, one of the members of this church's meetinghouse committee. No matter who built the structure, their efforts resulted in one of the area's finest Greek Revival structures. The façade is notable for its twin pedimented entryways, which feature sidelights and pilasters topped with Ionic capitals, as well as for the row of three 6 × 6 sash windows with matching pediments above. The three-stage tower of this church is also impressive, notable for the finely executed corner pilasters on the two lower stages. The location of this church in the historic Tuftonboro Corner is also notable—an old home that served as a tavern and stage coach stop is located adjacent at the corner of Mountain and Durgin roads, while a short distance away is the Tuftonboro Corner Cemetery where many early congregants of this church, including members of the Drew, Canney, Nutter, and Durgin families, have been buried.

Unity

Unity Town Hall (former First Baptist Church of Unity)
Built: 1831
Builder: Col. William Abbott
Location: 713 2nd New Hampshire Turnpike

Granted in 1764 and first settled in 1769, Unity's religious history is indicative of both its remote location and the independent spirit of its early inhabitants. The town never settled a minister, instead reserving the traditional minister's lot for the

Right: Tuftonboro Corner United Methodist Church.

Below: Entryway detail, Tuftonboro Corner United Methodist church.

use of the local school, and it was the Baptist and Methodist denominations that were most prominent here beginning in the early 1800s and lasting through much of the century. The Baptist faith was at the height of its popularity in town when they decided to build this fine church, and though records are lacking to document its building, the structure was almost certainly designed and built by William Abbott of Boscawen, known for the meetinghouses he built throughout the state, including that in Webster (see below). This structure is a quite pleasing example of the many transitional churches that were being built throughout New Hampshire, William Abbott being recognized for his expertise in the field, in the 1830s and combining the old Federal style of architecture with that of the Greek Revival style that was then in vogue. The structure is noted for its temple-like façade featuring double pediments with modillions, with the pavilion supporting the front of the two-stage tower above. The twin entryways are particularly notable for the Federal-style fan louvers above the door and flanking pilasters with half-round molding featuring a series of diamond shapes with quatrefoil insets, the whole beautifully executed. Likewise, the tower, which contains a later-day Revere Copper Company Bell and was renovated in 2001, is notable for its Federal details, including the urns on pedestals marking the corners of each stage and the rectangular louvers topped off with fan louvers on its first stage. This church served the Baptists until that sect slowly faded away by the 1870s after its membership had declined. Now in disrepair after years of neglect, the town of Unity acquired ownership of the structure in June 1877 when it was purchased at public auction for the measly sum of $25, the only stipulation being that religious services would be allowed within. The structure was subsequently renovated and from that time, and for many years after, the building served as the sole seat of government in Unity until the town offices were eventually relocated. The town hall today is used by the town for many community events, including Cub Scout and school groups, as well as local conservation committee and selectman meetings. Of course, the town hall also hosts such traditional activities as the annual town meeting and as the place where Unity citizens exercise their right to vote. Unity gained the most attention ever in this regard in July 2008, when the town was chosen, due to its name, as the site where Democratic presidential rivals Hillary Clinton and nominee Barack Obama met to unify the party after a spirited primary season. Thousands of people attended this event, which took place just down the road from the Unity Town Hall and put the town in the national spotlight.

Above left: Unity Town Hall.

Above right: Door detail, Unity Town Hall.

Warner

United Church of Warner (Former Congregational Church)
Built: 1819
Location: 43 East Main Street

In 1772, the early inhabitants of Warner chose the Congregationalist faith as the standing order, installing Rev. William Kelley, a Harvard graduate, as the first town minister. The church worshipped in the town's first two meetinghouses, the second built in 1770, but in the aftermath of the passage of the Toleration Act of 1819, the town already having experienced difficulties in taxing its citizens to support Rev. Kelley as far back as 1800, the Congregationalists decided to build their own house of worship. The final straw for them, as was the case in many towns, was the fact that they had to share the meetinghouse with other denominations, especially Universalists who "rushed in and claimed the right to occupy whenever they pleased."[90] Their church, its cornerstone laid in June 1819 and dedicated in October, cost $2,300 and was originally located in Lower Warner, but was moved to its current site in the village in 1845, subsequently modernized in 1856, and enlarged by 15 feet and improved in 1868. Membership in the church fluctuated over the years in the nineteenth century, with periods of decline and periods of great interest and revival, most notably in 1827–28 and 1831–32, it has always remained intact. Many prominent town-folks were members of this church, but one of its more interesting members was Revolutionary War veteran Anthony Clark. A free-black from Massachusetts who previously lived in Dunbarton, he was married to his wife, Lucy Moore, by Rev. Kelley in 1804. Clark over the years grew to be one of Warner's most prominent and respected citizens and was a worshipper at this church—perhaps relegated to a seat in the upper gallery, as was common for African-American communicants. The 1856 military funeral services held for Clark, who lived to the age of 100, in this church were said to be a "splendid affair," indicative of the respect Clark had gained over the years. Though the church has been altered over the years, it is nonetheless a venerable structure with many notable details. First and foremost, among them is the three-stage tower, which is Federal in style and features a Palladian window in the lower stage, and an octagonal lantern upper stage topped off with a swallowtail banner weathervane. The pavilion that supports the front of the tower is notable for its pediment, which features a semielliptical window with tracery. Later additions to

United Church of Warner.

this church include the stained-glass windows, and the prominent porch supported by natural stone pillars that runs the length of the pavilion.

Lower Warner Meetinghouse
Built: 1844–45
Location: 232 East Main Street

This pleasing church structure had a short active life and never had a settled minister. When the Congregational Society in Warner announced plans to move their church from Lower Warner to the village in 1844, a group of twenty-eight families in Lower Warner, led by Stephen and Joshua George, became disaffected, unhappy with the prospect of a having to travel further to attend Sabbath services. As a result, they withdrew from the Congregational Church and formed the Second Orthodox Congregational Society. The land for their meetinghouse was provided by Stephen George, the structure built between the homes of Stephen and Joshua George, but details about its building or builder are unknown. The church was used for no more two years before many of the disaffected families joined again with their old church in the village, and this meetinghouse was effectively abandoned. The deed to the property, not surprisingly, stipulated that the building itself could not be moved, so

Lower Warner Meeting House, Warner.

it has remained all these years in its original location. What functions it may have subsequently hosted over the years is uncertain, but the building was nonetheless faithfully maintained by the George family and their descendants before being presented to the Warner Historical Society by them in 1969. Today, the church is the site of an annual Christmas service, as well as an occasional site for weddings. While earlier historians state that this church was built and used by the Methodists in town, this information is now known to be incorrect based on recently discovered documents. The simple Greek Revival structure is notable not just for its beauty, but also for its virtually unaltered state; the church once had a steeple, this being lost in a storm about 1893, but otherwise both inside and out remains in its original state with no modern conveniences of any kind added. Its most notable features are the 20 x 20 sash windows, the recessed entryway flanked by boxed columns, and the pediment above that contains a triangular fan louver. The two stages of the tower that remain feature simple boxed corner-boards that match the corner trim on the façade. All in all, the church is an excellent example of period rural architecture.

Warren

Warren United Methodist Church (former Warren Meetinghouse)
Built: 1818
Builder: John Whiton (1859)
Location: 2 School Street

This imposing structure was first built by town vote on the town common across the way, being raised on the Fourth of July and dedicated for use later that fall. The "good old oaken" frame used in the meetinghouse's construction was hewed from timber "hauled from many a dark recess of the old woods by the laboring oxen-the inhabitants ready to assist, giving many a long day's work; and by the first of July it was ready for erection."[91] The building committee consisted of Jonathan and Abel Merrill, Nathaniel Clough, and James Williams, but the name of its master-builder is not known. By the fall of 1819, the pews inside the church had been sold and the meetinghouse was finished except for being painted, the meetinghouse used by the Congregationalists, with space inside reserved for town offices. Other religious denominations in town also likely used the building, but by the late 1830s, the Universalists seem to have become predominant, their first hired preacher being Rev. John Palmer in 1838. The Methodists had a society formed in Warren by 1799 and had their own chapel, but when the town decided they wanted to clear the common of buildings and to dispose of the meetinghouse, it was purchased by them in 1859 and moved just off the common to its current location, where it was remodeled into its present form. This work was done by John Whiton. The church as originally constructed was a simple Type II meetinghouse, as reflected in the main block of the building. The remodeled church features a notable double pavilion, which

Warren United Methodist Church.

supports the three-stage tower, while the paired brackets supporting the eaves and the tall and narrow stained-glass windows are all distinct Italianate features, an architectural style then coming into vogue. It was also at this time—when being placed on a new foundation—that a lower level was provided for the church. From 1859 onward, the Methodist Church in Warren has remained an important institution in town. However, while its fine form and commanding size cannot help but draw attention, it may, perhaps, have been a bit upstaged in 1971 when a Redstone rocket was placed on the town green within a stone's throw from the church entrance and dedicated on the Fourth of July, exactly 153 years after the meetinghouse was raised. It is likely the only historic church in America sited next to a Space Age relict of this size and type.

Washington

Washington Town Hall (former Washington Meetinghouse and Townhouse)
Built: 1787–88
Builders: Joseph and Church Tabor and Goodhue Farley
Location: 7 Halfmoon Pond Road

Originally named Camden when the town was first settled in 1768, its name was changed to Washington in December 1776, one of the first towns to so honor the then-future first president—just twelve days before his historic crossing of the Delaware River. Life early on was hard due to the economic effects of the war, and the winters were particularly bitter in the early years, causing much privation. However, with a minister settled by the end of the war, thoughts soon turned to building a meetinghouse, with a committee formed in 1785 to draft plans and subsequent committees formed to procure the building materials, including ten-penny nails, stone and bricks for the underpinning, glazed panes of glass for the windows, and black birch plank to finish the interior. These committees also chose the master-builders and set the wages for both their work, as well as that of the lesser carpenters. Joseph and Church Tabor were experienced builders who were chosen to raise the frame of the structure and fashion the window frames, while Goodhue Farley was chosen to finish the exterior. One specific provision regarding the procurement of materials was "that all the hewing timber should be cut in the old of the moon in September and October" in 1786.[92] Because of a lack of currency at the time, the Continental dollar being worthless, some wages for work on the meetinghouse were paid in goods and commodities, such as flour, rye, flax, and maple sugar. Though the exact time when the structure was raised is not recorded, the frame was likely raised by mid-1787, with meetings about boarding the house held in September 1787, and those for finishing the work in February 1788. Once completed, the large meetinghouse was one of the finest in the area but, unlike in many other towns, this meetinghouse has evolved as time and customs have changed and has remained a vital town asset for over 230 years. While the Congregationalists were the standing order in Washington, the meetinghouse was shared with other denominations in town, including the Universalists beginning about 1802. By 1820, that sect had their own hired minister and used the meetinghouse more frequently, so much so that by the 1840s, the Congregationalists abandoned the meetinghouse after building their own house of worship right next door (see below). With the growth of the Methodist and Seventh Day Adventist faiths in town, both of whom built their own churches, by about 1850, the meetinghouse was no longer the site of religious services in town. It was at this time that the interior was completely remodeled, with the box pews on the main floor and the gallery above removed and a full second story built to accommodate community activities and town offices. Annual town meetings were still held here, however, and this tradition would continue into the 1990s. As to the exterior, it has seen only a few changes since it was originally built as a standard Type II meetinghouse with twin porches. In 1825, the prominent bell tower was added to replace one side porch, with a 9 × 9 transom window also added over the main entryway, but since that time, there has been no change, and as late as 1841, the bell in the bell tower was available to any denomination in town to use to call their meetings. The meetinghouse today is notable for its three-stage tower, the upper two being open and octagonal in shape, a nod to the Federal style. The original main block of the meetinghouse is notable for its large size, pedimented single entryway on the long side, and the large 20 × 20 sash windows. The site of this church is also notable, an excellent example and unique survivor of a mid-nineteenth-century village

Washington Town Hall.

center that, at an elevation of 1,532 feet, is the highest town center and meetinghouse location in the entire state. Just yards away from the meetinghouse is the Washington Congregational Church (see below), whose architecture, compared with that of this meetinghouse, clearly demonstrates the progression of meetinghouse and church architecture in rural New Hampshire over the years. Between the two buildings is the historic 1883-built Center School, which now serves as the town police station. The Washington Meetinghouse has been well-cared for over the years, and in 2017–2018, the structure underwent substantial renovation and restoration work.

Washington Congregational Church
Built: 1839–40
Builder: Peter Cook
Location: 1 Halfmoon Pond Road

This Gothic Revival-style church is notable for both its historic village setting, as well as being a fine example of the many rural churches that were being built in New Hampshire during the 1830–1850 time period. The Congregationalists got their start in Washington in 1780 under the name of The Church of Christ in Washington, with Rev. George Leslie serving as the town's first settled minister, he coming here despite being offered a professorship at Dartmouth College. The church occupied the town meetinghouse (see above) for years, but the ever-present difficulties entailed in having to share that building with other denominations in town would eventually cause the church to seek a house of worship that was all their own. This was, as time would show, an ideal time to build, as both the town population and the membership of the church was at an all-time high, reaching numbers that would not be reached again until 2010. In 1839, the town voted to allow the selectmen to lease a parcel of land on the common to the Congregationalists so they could erect their own building. The church was erected by master-builder Peter Cook at a cost of $1,177, with another $466 for additional supplies, fixtures, and expenses, the building erected by early 1840. The first man to preach a sermon here was Rev. Samuel Mason, but his stay here was short. Over the years, the difficulties of maintaining regular preaching at this church, as elsewhere in rural New Hampshire, had its ups and downs, but through it all, the church here has prevailed and remains a strong community and spiritual presence in Washington. As for the church itself, its exterior has changed little over the years and is notable for its pleasant façade featuring a pediment with Gothic-arch fan louver, twin-entryways with sidelights, and geometric-style molding. The two-stage tower is the highlight of the building's Gothic Revival stylings, featuring corner pinnacles at each stage, the upper stage finished off with a crenellated parapet. The structure is well-maintained and underwent interior renovations in 2017. Two

Washington Congregational Church.

interesting and unanswered questions about this church exist: evidence shows that the back of the church was painted red up to 1890, though the façade has always been painted white. What the reasoning was for this paint scheme is unknown, but likely due to a combination of cost and style—white paint was the preferred color for churches at this time, but white lead was more expensive than the iron oxide used to make red paint. Finally, the pews inside the church appear to be of two types of wood construction: hand-planed and machine-planed. The reasoning for this is unknown, but local historians speculate that the older hand-planed pews may have come from the old meetinghouse when its interior was renovated for secular use.[93]

Webster

Old Webster Meeting House (former Westerly Meeting House)
Built: 1791
Builder: Samuel Jackman
Location: 1220 Battle Street

Long before its incorporation in 1860 as the town of Webster, the area the town encompasses was known as Boscawen West, the so-called "westerly" parish in the town of Boscawen, beginning in 1791. The parish was formed because the local inhabitants found it a hardship to travel the 5 miles required to attend Sabbath Day services at the meetinghouse in the center of town. In that same year, the parish built this structure, their first and only meetinghouse. Its builder, Samuel Jackman, was known in town as "Joiner Jackman" to distinguish him from a blacksmith in town with the same name. Of Jackman, it is stated that "He was a man of marked ability and sterling integrity, and of great strength; and athlete; he could climb trees feet foremost."[94] At first, Boscawen's regular town minister at the time, Rev. Samuel Wood, divided his time between the town's two parishes, but in 1804, the Westerly Religious Society was formed, uniting with the Second Congregational Church in Boscawen and hiring a minister at their own expense. This church group used the meetinghouse until 1823, when a dispute between them and the Christian Union Society prompted the Congregationalists to abandon the meetinghouse and build a church of their own (see below). Formed in 1820, the Christian Union Society demanded that they be allowed to use the meetinghouse, resulting in a dispute that was eventually taken to superior court. Once the Congregationalists were gone, the other group became the majority occupants of this meetinghouse. The structure served both religious and civic functions for many years, with the interior remodeled in 1844, the gallery being floored over and the second floor made into a chapel, while the ground floor was used for town offices. As originally built, this Type II meetinghouse had twin porches, these being removed in 1844, but otherwise the exterior of the meetinghouse remains largely original and is one of only a handful of eighteenth-century meetinghouses

Old Webster Meeting House.

remaining in New Hampshire. The building is notable for its size, seven bays wide on the front featuring 16 × 12 sash windows, and the doorway with transom lights which also dates from the 1844 remodel. Though a historic building, this meetinghouse was nearly lost in the 1940s as the result of a flood control project in the town of Webster planned by the U.S. Army Corps of Engineers. Condemned in 1941, the building was planned for demolition, but the newly-formed Society for the Preservation of the Old Meeting House in Webster came to the rescue and purchased the structure. It was subsequently moved in 1942 about a half-mile south to its present location in a village setting and is well maintained to this day by the society that saved it for future generations. Behind the meetinghouse is a row of horse sheds, these being historic replicas of the original sheds that once stood adjacent to the meetinghouse at its original site, constructed between 1972 and 1979 and used for storage.

First Congregational Church of Webster
Built: 1823
Builders: George Pillsbury and Col. William Abbott
Location: 1011 Long Street

This Federal-style church is one of the most notable in the area, distinguished by its fine workmanship, historical integrity, and continuity of ownership. The building of this church by the Congregationalists in town, then known as Boscawen West, came about in the aftermath of the Toleration Act of 1819, when the Christian Union Society was formed and demanded a share in the parish meetinghouse (see above). Unhappy with this arrangement, the Congregationalists eventually sold their share to the society and built this church. A building committee was formed in May 1823, with one its members being master-builder and future church deacon

George Pillsbury. He would be the man who raised and framed the structure, while the experienced builder and joiner William Abbott was hired to finish the interior, being paid $517 for his work. While the underpinning of the church was supplied by Ezekiel Evans of Warner, most of the rest of the work was supplied by workman who were members of the church and likely to purchase a pew. This arrangement offered a mutually beneficial solution to paying for the cost of building the church, which totaled about $4,800. Among the other costs included in this amount that are interesting include the weathervane with lightning rod made by Joseph Morse for $5.50 and the sash windows, with 959 square lights (individual panes of glass) in all, fashioned by Daniel Pillsbury for $43. The timber for the church was cut in May 1823 and the frame was raised on July 3–4, with dedication services held late that year on Christmas day. Exactly how many men were employed in raising the church is uncertain, but provisions for the traditional event included 209 lemons, 54 pounds of sugar, and nearly 13 gallons of rum to quench their thirst. The site of the church on Corser Hill, which accounts for its sometime designation as the Corser Hill Meetinghouse, was purchased from Rev. Ebenezer Price, who had been settled in 1804, was the first to preach in this church building, and remained until his dismissal in 1837. The finely finished structure is noted for its beautiful façade, featuring triple entryways with rayed fanlights above, the central doorway having sidelights, while above is a Palladian window flanked by arched windows with tracery details. The three-stage tower is also well executed, notable for the balustrades with corner

Above left: First Congregational Church of Webster.

Above right: Main entryway detail, First Congregational Church of Webster.

urns at the top of each, as well as the corner columns on the two upper stages. The interior here is also notable and remains largely original, featuring box pews and a gallery with exquisitely carved cornices and molding supported by turned columns. Climbing the narrow steps to the tower is a unique experience, giving one a glimpse of the massive timbers used in the framing and rafters, as well as the mechanical works of the E. Howard tower clock. As of this writing, the pastor of the church is Rev. David Richardson. He not only lives in the house directly across the street from the church, but grew up in a house next to this church and attended services here in his youth and is thus well-versed in the history of this historic structure.

Wentworth

Wentworth Congregational Church (former Wentworth Meetinghouse)
Built: 1828–29
Builder: Col. William Abbott
Location: 38 Wentworth Village Road

Erected by one of New Hampshire's finest church builders of the early nineteenth century, this pleasing structure occupies a prominent position on the village green. By 1827, Wentworth's original meetinghouse was outdated and in poor condition and the town debated its replacement or repair. The Wentworth Meeting House Association was formed that same year and soon voted to build a new meetinghouse. However, before this could take place, the problem of the old meetinghouse was solved when a fire broke out in a blacksmith shop and spread to neighboring buildings, include the meetinghouse, a tavern, and several outbuildings. The meetinghouse was subsequently destroyed by the fire and efforts to find a new site and build a new meetinghouse were begun straight away. The land acquired for the church, once the site of a tavern, was purchased for $300. William Abbott of Boscawen, the builder of fine churches in Webster and Unity (see above), was awarded the contract and the frame of the structure was raised in September 1828, with the building finished by July 1829 and dedicated for service in August. Pew sales to finance the building costs began that summer, with nearly $2,500 raised through the sale of sixty-two pews—the remaining pews, twenty-two in all, were allocated to the shareholders of the Wentworth Meeting House Association. In all, the meetinghouse cost $3,250, with an additional $418 raised by subscription to purchase the 1,113-lb. bell, which was placed in June 1829. The exterior of this church has remained largely unchanged over the years and is Federal in style. The facade features a central entryway flanked by 16 × 12 sash windows, while above are two 12 × 8 sash windows whose larger panes were installed during an 1867 remodeling of the interior, while the pediment features a large semielliptical fan louver with decorative molding. Most notable is the three-stage tower, a hallmark of an Abbott-built church, each stage of which features a balustrade with a decorative carved

Wentworth Congregational Church.

panel at the center, with Federal-style urns placed at the corners, the whole topped off by a dome and a beautiful scrolled weathervane. Sited prominently on a hill, this tower is a dominant feature on the town landscape. The meetinghouse was shared by several denominations over the years, but in 1856, the First Congregational Society was formed and became the primary occupant. In 1867, the meetinghouse interior was renovated into its current form, the gallery floored over to create a second story, with the church occupying the upper floor, while the main floor was reserved for the town, with the pulpit and box pews removed and more modern pews installed, the whole project costing $2,100. The lower story was reconfigured again in 1876 with the addition of a community stage and kitchen. The structure was used as the town hall until a new town hall was built in 1899, thereafter becoming a Congregational church. The church is notable to this day for its unique function within the community; as one historian states, though the building is not tax supported, "its people protect it as if it was their own. No one owns it but everyone claims it. In an out-of-the-way hamlet, it is an unexpected beauty against the sky."[95]

Westmoreland

Park Hill Meetinghouse (former Westmoreland Meeting House)
Built: 1764
Architect: Simeon Cobb (1826 remodel)
Location: 531 Route 63

This attractive meetinghouse underwent many changes during the first century of its existence and is today considered to be one of the finest meetinghouses in the

Monadnock region. It was originally built further to the south at the corner of what is now North Cemetery because that area was the most heavily settled. The meetinghouse was completed and dedicated by November 1764 and was a Type II meetinghouse, the standard for the day, with no bell tower or steeple. However, the location turned out to be inconvenient and plans were put forth to move the building but problems arose when the Baptist element in town, whose taxes had also helped to build the meetinghouse, opposed the move. Ultimately, the building was turned over to the town, it being put up for auction in the hopes that the Baptists could be bought out. However, the Baptists had the higher bid, after which the auction sale was cancelled by town vote. This muddled affair was ended when a town committee awarded the building to the Congregationalists and ordered them to reimburse the Baptists on a proportional basis. This matter was settled in 1779, whereupon the meetinghouse was moved to the Park Hill location that summer with the help of many men, log rollers, and teams of oxen. The men moving the meetinghouse intended to place the structure at the bottom of Park Hill, not desirous of moving it up the hill, but, bribed with a barrel of rum from the nearby tavern owner, they completed the job. Within several years, side porches were added to the meetinghouse to make for more interior space, and so configured it would stay for over forty years. In 1826, the church was moved another 90 feet to the top of Park Hill, the side porches were removed, and the front was lengthened by 20 feet with the addition of a portico and a

Above left: Park Hill Meetinghouse, Westmoreland.

Above right: Tower detail, Park Hill Meetinghouse, Westmoreland.

three-stage bell tower and steeple, a new bell purchased from the Revere Company at this time. This work was done to plans drawn up by a prominent local man, Simeon Cobb. The portico is supported by four towering columns, each 25–30 feet in length, fashioned from trees that were cut 2 miles north of the meetinghouse and dragged here by oxen. Though this meetinghouse is not considered by most historians to be a part of the Templeton run of churches inspired by the Massachusetts builder Elias Carter, the façade of this meetinghouse was certainly inspired by the churches in that group within the corresponding time period, its façade featuring corner pilasters and columns, as well as a pediment with an ovoid window, a close match to that in Fitzwilliam and elsewhere. The three-stage tower is also beautifully executed, featuring a Palladian window on the lowest stage, while the top two stages feature corner pilasters and well-carved molding details that are distinctly of the Federal style, as is the uppermost octagonal stage. It is on the side of the building where we can see how the building has evolved over the years; five bays in length, the lower windows are original 12 × 12 sash windows, while the five above are larger in size, dating from the 1853 remodel when the gallery of the meetinghouse was floored over to create a second-story enclosed space. The Congregational church in Westmoreland would have its ups and downs over the years until 1873, when two rival congregations united to call themselves the Congregational Church of Westmoreland, thereby settling matters down that had been ongoing for decades between rival factions. Though notable for its architectural details and its high state of preservation and maintenance, the Park Hill Meetinghouse is also notable for its prominent hilltop setting, one of the finest in the entire state, as well as the historic buildings in the immediate area, including the *c.* 1780-built parsonage house (now a private residence) just to the right of the meetinghouse.

Wilmot

North Wilmot Union Meetinghouse
Built: 1829
Builder: Josiah Stearns
Location: Junction of North Wilmot, Tewksbury, and Piper Pond roads

Located in an isolated rural setting at the junction of several backroads, this meetinghouse is a surprising hidden treasure. It is also indicative of an area that was once populous and economically viable, with the ability to support their own house of worship. As with many rural New Hampshire towns, Wilmot suffered a significant population decline by the late 1800s, and what was once a booming part of town eventually reverted back to a quiet wilderness and a school, sawmill, blacksmith shop, and many residences that were once located here are now long gone. This meetinghouse was first located at the top of Tewksbury Hill, about a mile to the north up the unpaved Tewksbury Road, near the site where the historic cemetery can still be seen and was built to serve the five denominations then active in the area, the Congregationalists, Methodists, Universalists, Free Will Baptists, and the Christian Baptists. None of these groups had a large membership nor the financial means to build their own church, so they combined to build this union meetinghouse, the Sunday services divided up proportionately based on pew ownership, the sale of which financed the building costs. The builder of this beautifully designed house of worship was a local man, Josiah Stearns, who was a master-carpenter and stonecutter, said to have built many of the buildings in North Wilmot, as well as the Wilmot Center Meetinghouse (destroyed by fire in 1957). The meetinghouse remained at its original location until 1850 when it was moved downhill to its present site, this accomplished with the use of rollers and thirty-yoke of oxen. Not only was Tewksbury Hill a difficult spot to reach, especially in wintertime, but the population of North Wilmot had also shifted. Despite the move, the exterior of the church remains almost entirely original, a rural builder's combination of Federal and Greek Revival elements. The former styling is visible in the Palladian window with a central fan louver above the entryway and the keystone molding of the open belfry stage of the tower, while the corner Tuscan pilasters of the vestibule are a Greek Revival influence. The two-stage tower is topped off with Gothic Revival-style pinnacles, which were likely added around or after the time the meetinghouse was moved. The bell in the tower was placed in 1915. The meetinghouse for years was used by the town's varying denominations, but with these groups in decline, with only two religious groups using the structure by 1866, it became a Congregational church in 1917, but eventually they too would abandon the meetinghouse. Now maintained by the Union Meeting House Society, no regular services are held here today, though the meetinghouse does host occasional town services and community events, and is also available for weddings and other private events. Behind the meetinghouse are horse sheds that were once used by those attending services.

Windham

Windham Presbyterian Church
Built: 1834
Location: 1 Church Road

Once a part of the town of Londonderry, Windham was set off as an independent town in 1742. Its earliest settlers were largely Scotch-Irish, and the Presbyterian faith here took hold and was established as the town's standing order, services being conducted in the town's first meetinghouse's, including that built at the center of town (which still serves as the Windham Town Hall today) in 1798. The Presbyterians would continue to use the old meetinghouse even after the Toleration

Above left: North Wilmot Union Meetinghouse, Wilmot.

Above right: Windham Presbyterian Church.

Act of 1819, but the dissatisfaction between the town and the Presbyterian Religious Society which arose in 1833 brought on change. With the rise of other religious denominations in town by this time, most notably the Methodists and Unitarians, the issue as to who controlled the meetinghouse, as well as the ministerial funds for the support of the gospel (sometimes referred to as the Wilson Fund after the man who donated it, James Wilson), came to the fore. The Presbyterians claimed the entire meetinghouse and the fund, due to their long history, but when it came to a town vote, they lost out and were forced to share the meetinghouse. Unhappy with this situation, the Presbyterian Society withdrew entirely from the meetinghouse and worshipped in a local hall until they built their own house of worship, just a stone's throw away from the old meetinghouse. The frame of the church was raised on June 27–29, 1834, and the building dedicated for service in January 1835. Ever since this time, it has been the home of the Presbyterian Church in Windham. Interestingly, though religious services were conducted here from its dedication onward, business meetings for the Presbyterian Society were still held in the old meetinghouse as late as 1841. While the interior has undergone many changes over the years, the exterior is largely original. It is notable for its two-stage tower with dome and a fine lyre-style banner weathervane, the upper belfry stage being octagonal in form with columns and rounded-arch opening with louvers, a throwback to the Federal style. The bell in the steeple was not added until 1847 after the necessary repairs and alterations were made, the funds for the project raised by voluntary subscription. The façade of the church features a pediment within which may have been a central window (now boarded over) flanked by rayed fan louvers, while below are twin entryways with transom lights, between which are a pair of narrow arched windows with matching shutters and with keystone molding above. The church has been well-cared for over the years, with the steeple renovated and stabilized in 2016, the bell silenced due to a cracked yoke for the previous two years. Fundraising by a local group, People for the Steeple, raised over $18,000 to aid in the $40,000 repair cost.

Wolfeboro

First Baptist Church of Wolfeboro (former Free Will Baptist Church)
Built: 1840
Location: 116 Center Street

The Free Will Baptist Church was formed in 1792 and was the first church to be organized in Wolfeboro. Among the attendees at the first meeting was a committee from New Durham, which included the founder of the denomination, Elder Benjamin Randall. Isaac Townsend was ordained as the church's first minister and meetings early on were held in private homes. For some years, Townsend, who served the church for fifty-four years, was the only ordained minister in Wolfeboro. In 1801, it was voted by the group to build a meetinghouse that would be shared by the Baptists and the Methodists. It was erected in the eastern part of town near the border between Brookfield and Wolfeboro, that area then a population center. This meetinghouse was subsequently replaced by the current First Baptist Church, which was built in the Wolfeboro Falls area, that part of town growing steadily with milling activities in the area. It cost $1,000 to build and was dedicated for service in the fall of 1840. The building was originally a plain meetinghouse, without a steeple or tower. Horse sheds were eventually built behind the church, but these were destroyed by fire in 1888, which also damaged the back portion of the structure. As a result, then-pastor Rev. Lincoln Given led efforts to repair and upgrade the church. In 1890, about $2,100 was spent, much of it raised by private donations, to reconfigure the church, building a vestry in the rear, enlarging the main auditorium (which had previously been remodeled in 1881), and, most significantly, adding a bell tower to the front with two entryways. In 1929–30, the front of the church was again reconfigured, the twin entryways replaced with a central door. Today, the church is a nice example of a late Victorian-era building, distinguished by its shingled bell tower featuring Tuscan pilasters on the louvered belfry, the bell gifted to the church in the first decade of the twentieth century by a prominent local businessman. The lot on which the church sits was once surrounded with a row of maple trees planted in 1857 by Rev. Levi Brackett and Benjamin Franklin Parker, a member of the church who later published a definitive history of the town. In 1951, the church gained its current name and is now affiliated with the American Baptist Churches USA.

First Baptist Church, Wolfeboro.

Wolfeboro Community Church (former Union Meeting House)
Built: 1841
Location: Governor John Wentworth Highway (Route 109)

This simple church was built at a cost of $800 and was dedicated for service in November 1841. The building costs were financed through the sale of pews, with the Christian Religious Society and the Free Will Baptists having the largest shares. The union aspect of the structure is demonstrated by the fact that Methodist, Free Will Baptist, Christian, and Congregationalist ministers attended its dedication service and offered readings and prayers. This area, known then as Wolfeborough Center, is near the geographic center of town and was conveniently located for many local residents in a time before the economic center of town shifted to its current lakeside location. The clapboard-sided structure is a simple yet attractive rural church, nearly square, with a façade that features twin entryways, standard for the day, and a center 12 × 12 sash window with double-hung shutters. The interior, consisting of a large auditorium, is notable for the placement of the reading desk used by the presiding minister at the front, between the twin entryways. Referred to as a "reversed seating" plan (the pulpit or desk traditionally located on the far wall opposite the entryways), this configuration was once common in rural northern New England churches of the period, but soon fell out of fashion, making this a rare

Wolfeboro Community Church

survivor. As the town's center of activities shifted and the population here decreased, the use of this church declined by the early twentieth century. Though no regular worship services are held here today, special services are conducted from time to time and the historic structure is well-maintained by a private association.

Cotton Mountain Community Church (former Wolfeborough, Brookfield, and Wakefield Meetinghouse)
Built: 1852
Location: Stoneham Road

Located off the beaten path in the scenic Cotton Mountain area, this rural church was essentially a union church, built by members of the Baptist and Methodist societies in the eastern part of Wolfeboro. It was a replacement for an earlier 1801-built meetinghouse located a short distance away. A surviving document shows that this church was originally intended to be built on the site of the original meetinghouse, but these plans subsequently changed, it being built on land sold by Elliot Cotton, later a town selectman and state representative, to the group in 1852 for $50. No details of the church's building are known, except that its building cost was about $1,000, financed by pew sales at the rate of approximately $25 per pew, and that it was slated for final completion by November 1852. In size and general plan, this church

Cotton Mountain Community Church, Wolfeboro.

structure is quite similar to the earlier Wolfeboro Community Church (see above), but it is distinguished by its greater degree of architectural styling. A pleasing example of a Greek Revival building, the church is distinguished by its façade, featuring twin entryways with sidelights covered by louvered shutters, a central 12 × 12 sash window with double hung shutters, simple corner pilasters, and a plain yet well-defined pediment, the elements well-blended to give the church a temple-like appearance. As with other union churches in Wolfeboro and other Lakes Region towns, the use of this church declined as the local population declined, shifting toward the rapidly developing lakeside area of modern Wolfeboro by the end of the nineteenth century. In 1957, the Church was deeded to the local Community Church Association, whose members, including the prominent Maxfield family, have done a nice job in continuing to preserve and maintain the historic church. A visit to this church must include travelling the length of Stoneham Road and adjacent roads in the Cotton Mountain area, where scenic vistas of Lake Winnipesaukee in the distance are to be had.

First Christian Church
Built: 1858
Location: 83 North Main Street

The First Christian Church was organized here in 1812, following visits made by the itinerant preacher, Elder Mark Fernald, of Kittery, Maine. Fernald was pastor of the church for the first twenty-six years of its existence and was active in this and surrounding areas preaching the word of God. He also worked in harmony with Elder Isaac Townsend of the Free Will Baptist Church (see above), the two men the most prominent religious figures of their time in Wolfeboro. Meetings were first held in the town meetinghouse during the summer months, and in schoolhouses that could be more easily heated in the winter. Their first meetinghouse was built in 1838 by James Edmunds towards the geographic center of town, but when the Smith's Bridge Village area by the lake became the town's growing center of economic and civic activity, the society decided to demolish their old meetinghouse and built the current church building at a cost of $1,500. The move was not popular with everyone, with some members, including builder James Edmunds (no doubt incensed that his meetinghouse was no longer to be used), refusing to continue with the church in its new location. However, the location of the church in the growing center of town accounted for its expanded growth in the subsequent years. As originally constructed, the church was a simple affair, without a steeple, but the sustaining membership of the church allowed for continued expansion, with the church gaining its present form in 1892 when it was enlarged, the steeple with weathervane added, and the façade given a makeover. The church today is largely Italianate in style, featuring tall and narrow side windows and paired brackets and

First Christian Church, Wolfeboro.

pointed arch openings on the steeple. The façade, though obscured by trees, is a pleasing one with interesting architectural features, including a central doorway with transom lights flanked by narrow rounded arch windows, with a Palladian window above and a larger Palladian window to the right side. These additions cost $1,000 in 1892, akin to about $142,000 in 2017 dollars, an indicator of the elevated status of the church at the time of this expansion. Today, the First Christian Church continues as one of the town's most venerable spiritual institutions and has a large and active congregation.

Wonalancet

Wonalancet Union Chapel
Built: 1880
Location: 3436 Chinook Trail

This attractive chapel, located in a village in the town of Tamworth, is perhaps one of the most photographed churches in the entire state due to the natural landscape that surrounds it. The chapel was built as a house of worship for summer visitors and has always been non-denominational, the building operated by the Wonalancet Corporation since 1892. Indeed, the area of this village once had a half-dozen or so inns and hotels catering to the tourist trade, including the well-known Ferncroft Inn. Visiting ministers from many faiths, including Roman Catholic, Episcopalian, Methodist, Congregationalist, and Baptist have given sermons here, speaking on whatever subject they desire. The chapel as originally built was quite simple in appearance, having a steep roof and no steeple or tower. The square tower and open belfry were added in 1896, with the steeple above added in 1937 and named after local benefactor Katherine Sleeper Walden. The stylized arrow weathervane topping off the steeple was added in 1963, a gift from Rev. and Mrs. Allen Clark. Overall, this simple chapel is a pleasing example of rural architecture in the Colonial Revival style, as demonstrated by its octagonal belfry with squared-columns as supports and keystone trim, the columns flanking the entryway, and the round window with tracery in the lower stage of the tower. Interestingly, the chapel does have an order of service, using hymns that come from the hymnal used by the U.S. military, readings from the Bible, and prayers from the Book of Common Prayer. Just as important as this chapel is the landscape within which it lies. The vast field that fronts the chapel offers an excellent view of the mountains, which serve as a backdrop to the chapel when viewed from afar, a view that will remain unspoiled as it is protected by a conservation easement. The road on which the chapel is located gained its name from Chinook, a sled dog who was an integral part of the Byrd Antarctic Expedition in 1928. His owner was Arthur Treadwell Walden, a pioneer in the breeding and training of sled dogs who had his kennels here, introduced the sport of dog-sledding to New Hampshire, and was also a part of Byrd's expedition. His wife, Katherine Sleeper Walden, was a native of Boston who came to area in 1890 and decided to open an inn of her own in a historic home, naming it Wonalancet Farm. She became very well known in this area for her many endeavors, including establishing hiking trails for summer visitors and for her efforts in adding 3,000 acres of land to the White Mountain National Forest in 1914. It is no surprise, then, that one of the mountain peaks in this area was named Mt. Katherine in her honor. Having been a previous summer visitor to Tamworth as a young lady, it is said that Katherine Sleeper initiated the first religious services held in this chapel, performed by the rector of the Cathedral Church of St. Paul in Boston, Rev. Treadwell Walden, the father of her future husband. Quite fittingly, both Katherine and Arthur Walden were buried on this chapel's grounds upon their deaths in the 1940s.

Above left: Wonalancet Union Chapel, Tamworth.

Above right: Scenic view, Wonalancet Union Chapel, Tamworth.

Endnotes

Chapter 1

1. Lawrence, R. F., *The New Hampshire Churches* (Claremont, NH: Claremont Power Press, 1856), p. 64.

Chapter 2

1. Batchellor, A. S., Township Grants of Lands in New Hampshire Included in the Masonian Patent, New Hampshire State Papers, Vol. XXVI (Concord, NH: Edward Pearson, 1896), p. 470.

Chapter 3

1. Batchellor, A. S., Township Grants of Lands in New Hampshire Included in the Masonian Patent, New Hampshire State Papers, Vol. XXVI (Concord, NH: Edward Pearson, 1896), p. 117.
2. Cochrane, W. R., and Wood, G. K., *History of Francestown, NH* (Nashua, NH: James Barker, 1895), p. 14.
3. Mitchell, H. E., *The Town Register-Wolfeboro, Ossipee, Effingham, Tuftonboro, Tamworth, Freedom, 1908* (Augusta, ME: Mitchell-Cony, 1908), p. 61.
4. Worthen, M. H. A., *The History of Sutton, New Hampshire, Part I* (Concord, NH: Republican Press, 1890), p. 318.

Chapter 4

1. Wadleigh, G., *Notable Events in the History of Dover, New Hampshire* (Dover, NH: Tufts College Press, 1913), p. 35.
2. Cochrane, W. R., and Wood, G. K., *History of Francestown, NH* (Nashua, NH: James Barker, 1895), p. 81.
3. Benes, P. *Meetinghouses of Early New England* (Amherst, MA: University of Massachusetts Press, 2012), p. 51.

4. Secomb, D. F., *History of the Town of Amherst, Hillsborough County, New Hampshire* (Concord, NH: Evans, Sleeper & Woodbury, 1883), p. 235.
5. Eastman, J. R., *History of the Town of Andover, New Hampshire* (Concord, NH: Rumford Printing, 1910), p. 112.
6. Clark, C. E., *The Meetinghouse Tragedy: An Episode in the Life of a New England Town* (Hanover, NH: University Press of New England, 1998), pp. 44–45.

Chapter 5

1. Lawrence, R. F., *The New Hampshire Churches* (Claremont, NH: Claremont Power Press, 1856), p. 139.
2. Albee, J., *New Castle Historic and Picturesque* (Boston, MA: Rand Avery, 1884), p. 112.
3. Benes, P. *Meetinghouses of Early New England* (Amherst, MA: University of Massachusetts Press, 2012), p. 180.
4. Dibble, A. W., "Major John Dunlap: The Craftsman and His Community," *Old-Time New England*, Vol. 58, No. 3 (Boston, MA: Historic New England, 1978), pp. 50–58.
5. Dow, J., *History of the Town of Hampton, New Hampshire, Vol. 1* (Salem, MA: Salem Press, 1893), p. 374.
6. Thomas, M. F., *History of Fremont, NH* (Manchester, NH: New England Printing, 1998), p. 613.
7. Dow, *op. cit.*, p. 338.
8. Secomb, D. F., *History of the Town of Amherst, Hillsborough County, New Hampshire* (Concord, NH: Evans, Sleeper & Woodbury, 1883), p. 243.
9. Waite, O. F. R., *History of Claremont, New Hampshire* (Manchester, NH: John B. Clarke, 1895), p. 185.
10. Cochrane, W. R., and Wood, G. K., *History of Francestown, NH* (Nashua, NH: James Barker, 1895), p. 81.
11. Hayward, S. *History of the Town of Gilsum, New Hampshire* (Manchester, NH: John B. Clarke, 1881), p. 102.
12. Saunderson, H. H., *History of Charlestown, New Hampshire* (Claremont, NH: Claremont Manufacturing, 1876), p. 271.
13. Smith, C. J., *History of the Town of Mont Vernon, New Hampshire* (Boston, MA: Blanchard Printing, 1907), p. 86.
14. Benes, *op. cit.*, p. 353.
15. Chase, B., *History of Old Chester* (Auburn, NH: Benjamin Chase, 1869), p. 152.

Chapter 7

1. Ferguson, W. A., *History of Coos County, New Hampshire* (Syracuse, NY: W.A. Ferguson, 1888), p. 473.

Chapter 8

1. Lawrence, R. F., *The New Hampshire Churches* (Claremont, NH: Claremont Power Press, 1856), p. 62.
2. *Ibid.*, p. 135.

Chapter 9

1. Tolles, B. F., *New Hampshire Architecture: An Illustrated Guide* (Hanover, NH: University Press of New England, 1979), p. 43.
2. Thomas, M. F., *History of Fremont, NH* (Manchester, NH: New England Printing, 1998), p. 607.
3. Ferguson, W. A., *History of Coos County, New Hampshire* (Syracuse, NY: W.A. Ferguson, 1888), p. 763.
4. Muzzey, F., *History of the Wentworth Congregational Church* (Wentworth, NH: np, 2014), p. 10.
5. Benes, P. *Meetinghouses of Early New England* (Amherst, MA: University of Massachusetts Press, 2012), p. 128.
6. Sinnott, E. W., *Meetinghouse & Church in Early New England* (New York, NY: Bonanza Books, 1963), p. 72.

Chapter 10

1. Tolles, B. F., *New Hampshire Architecture: An Illustrated Guide* (Hanover, NH: University Press of New England, 1979), p. xxi.
2. Schjonberg, M. F., "Summering Episcopalians Love their Seasaonal Chapels," *Episcopal News Monthly*, August 30, 2017 (New York, NY: The Episcopal Church), p. 2.

Chapter 11

1. Woodbury, P., Savage, T., and Patten, W., *History of Bedford, New Hampshire* (Concord, NH: Rumford Printing, 1903), p. 329.
2. Benes, P. *Meetinghouses of Early New England* (Amherst, MA: University of Massachusetts Press, 2012), pp. 124–125.
3. Hazlett, C. A., "The Four Meeting Houses of the North Parish of Portsmouth," *The Granite Monthly*, February 1906, pp. 37–44 (Dover, NH: H.H. Metcalf), p. 39.
4. Hurd, D. H., *History of Merrimac and Belknap Counties, New Hampshire* (Philadelphia, PA: J.W. Lewis, 1885), pp. 199–200.
5. Hazlett, *op. cit.*, p. 39.
6. Dow, J., *History of the Town of Hampton, New Hampshire, Vol. 1* (Salem, MA: Salem Press, 1893), p. 338.
7. Seward, J., *A History of the Town of Sullivan, New Hampshire, Vol. 1* (Keene, NH: np., 1921), p. 395.
8. Hazlett, *op. cit.*, p. 39.
9. Coffin, C. C., *The History of Boscawen and Webster* (Concord, NH: Republican Press, 1878), p. 238.
10. For a more complete listing of church clocks in New Hampshire and beyond, the reader is advised to consult the work of clock expert Donn Haven Lathrop online at homepages.sover.net/~donnl/makers.html.

Chapter 12

1. Brown, J. E., *The Years of the Life of Samuel Lane, 1718–1806* (Hanover, NH: University Press of New England, 2000), p. 76.

2. Wallace, W. A., *The History of Canaan, New Hampshire* (Concord, NH: Rumford Press, 1910), p. 148.
3. *Ibid.*
4. Nelson, W. R., *History of Goshen, New Hampshire* (Concord, NH: Evans Printing, 1957), p. 228.
5. *Ibid.*
6. Benes, P. *Meetinghouses of Early New England* (Amherst, MA: University of Massachusetts Press, 2012), p. 59.
7. Child, W. H., *History of the Town of Cornish, New Hampshire, Vol. 1* (Concord, NH: Rumford Press, 1911), p. 362.
8. Peladeau, M. B., "Brother Moses Johnson, 1752–1842," *A Biographical Dictionary of Architects in Maine*, Vol. V, No. 11 (Augusta, ME: Maine Historic Preservation Commission, 1988), p. 3.
9. Andrews, E. D., *A Shaker Meeting House and its Builder* (New Haven, CT: Yale University Press, 1962), pp. 14–15.
10. Peladeau, *op. cit.*, p. 4.
11. Coffin, C. C., *The History of Boscawen and Webster* (Concord, NH: Republican Press, 1878), p. 596.
12. Kowsky, F. R., *The Architecture of Frederick Clarke Withers* (Middletown, CT: Wesleyan University Press, 1980), p. 98.
13. Beard, C. S., "St. Andre's Parish, Biddeford, Maine', *National Register of Historic Places Registration Form* (Augusta, ME: Maine Historic Preservation Commission, 2015), p. 15.

Chapter 13

1. Knoblock, G. A., *Historic Burial Grounds of the New Hampshire Seacoast* (Charleston, SC: Arcadia Publishing, 1999), p. 77.
2. Cogswell, E. C., *History of New Boston, New Hampshire* (Boston, MA: George C. Rand & Avery, 1864), p. 125.

Chapter 14

1. Alton Monthly Meeting, "The Alton Monthly Meeting or church records," (Alton, NH: manuscript record, 1803-1854), pp. 104–107.
2. Lawrence, R. F., *The New Hampshire Churches* (Claremont, NH: Claremont Power Press, 1856), p. 478.
3. Rowe, R. H., *Amherst Historical Moments, Amherst, New Hampshire* (Portsmouth, NH: Peter Randall, 2004), p. 41.
4. Lawrence, *op. cit.*, p. 155.
5. *Ibid.*, p. 159.
6. McDonald, S. R., "St. Ann Church, Berlin, NH (National Register of Historic Places Inventory-Nomination Form)" (Berlin, NH: Department of Community Development, 1979), p. 3.
7. Fuerstman, H. M., 'Seeking Celia: Our Stained Glass Windows', www.bethlehemsynagogue.org/news/2014/3/3/our-stained-glass-windows-seeking-celia, 2014.
8. Lawrence, *op. cit.*, p. 350.
9. Coffin, C. C., *The History of Boscawen and Webster* (Concord, NH: Republican Press, 1878), p. 157.

10. Campton Historical Society, "Historic Site Series, Site #5, Campton Baptist Church" www.camptonhistorical.org/Campton%20Baptist%20Church.pdf.
11. McLee, M., Thompson, P. J., and White, D., "The Reverend John Newton Mars (1804–1884): New England Cleric and Celebrated Standard Bearer in the Wesleyan Tradition," *Methodist History*, Vol. 54:1, pp. 71–80 (Madison, NJ: The United Methodist Church, October 2015), p. 71.
12. Wallace, W. A., *The History of Canaan, New Hampshire* (Concord, NH: Rumford Press, 1910), p. 241.
13. Saunderson, H. H., *History of Charlestown, New Hampshire* (Claremont, NH: Claremont Manufacturing, 1876), p. 243.
14. Chase, B., *History of Old Chester* (Auburn, NH: Benjamin Chase, 1869), p. 325.
15. Waite, O. F. R., *History of Claremont, New Hampshire* (Manchester, NH: John B. Clarke, 1895), p. 99.
16. Paradis, W. H., *Upon This Granite: Catholicism in New Hampshire* (Portsmouth, NH: Peter Randall, 1998). P. 46.
17. *Ibid.*, p. 50.
18. Gifford, W., *Colebrook: "A Place Up Back of New Hampshire"* (Colebrook, NH: News & Sentinel, 1993), p. 29.
19. Ferguson, W. A., *History of Coos County, New Hampshire* (Syracuse, NY: W.A. Ferguson, 1888), p. 609.
20. Lyford, J. O., *History of Concord, New Hampshire, Vol. 2* (Concord, NH: Rumford Press, 1903), p. 729.
21. Holt, A. W., *The History of the First Baptist Church, Concord, New Hampshire* (Concord, NH: Correctional Industries, 1993), p. 10.
22. Child, W. H., *History of the Town of Cornish, New Hampshire, Vol. 1* (Concord, NH: Rumford Press, 1911), p. 124.
23. *Ibid.*
24. Lawrence, *op. cit.*, p. 35.
25. *Ibid.*, p. 41.
26. Blodgett, I. D., *Asahel Blodgett of Hudson and Dorchester, NH* (Boston, MA: T.R. Marvin and Sons, 1906), p. 44.
27. Paradis, *op. cit.*, p. 57.
28. Leonard, L. W., and Seward, J. L., *The History of Dublin, NH* (Cambridge, MA: University Press, 1920), p. 258.
29. Tolles, B. F., *New Hampshire Architecture: An Illustrated Guide* (Hanover, NH: University Press of New England, 1979), p. 127.
30. Lawrence, *op. cit.*, p. 381.
31. Thomas, M. F., *History of Fremont, NH* (Manchester, NH: New England Printing, 1998), p. 606.
32. Lawrence, *op. cit.*, p. 53.
33. Thomas, *op. cit.*, p. 613.
34. *Ibid.*, p. 616.
35. Mausolf, L., "Mid-20th Century Architecture in NH: 1945–1975" (Concord, NH: New Hampshire Department of Employment Security, December 2012), p. 51.
36. Ruell, D., *The Historic Churches of Belknap County* (Meredith, NH: Meredith Media, 1995), p. 59.
37. Nelson, W. R., *History of Goshen, New Hampshire* (Concord, NH: Evans Printing, 1957), p. 228.
38. *Ibid.*, p. 232.
39. Dion, F., *Upon This Rock: A History of the Community Congregational Church, Greenland, New Hampshire* (Portsmouth, NH: np, 1956), p. 20.

40. Noyes, H. E., *A Memorial of the Town of Hampstead, New Hampshire* (Boston, MA: George Reed, 1899), p. 115.
41. Whitcher, W. F., *History of the Town of Haverhill, New Hampshire* (Concord, NH: Rumford Press, 1919), p. 106.
42. *Ibid.*
43. Lawrence, *op. cit.*, p. 390.
44. Evans, G. C., *History of the Town of Jefferson, NH, 1873–1927* (Manchester, NH: Granite Press, 1927), p. 87.
45. Griffin, S. G., *A History of the Town of Keene* (Keene, NH: Sentinel Printing, 1904), pp. 401–403.
46. Ruell, *op. cit.*, p. 89.
47. Lisbon Area Historical Society, "Lisbon Methodist Episcopal Church" (Lisbon, NH, n.d., np.), p. 2.
48. Jackson, J. R. *History of Littleton, New Hampshire, Vol. 1* (Cambridge, MA: University press, 1905), p. 160.
49. *Ibid.*, p. 260.
50. Madison Public Schools, *A Brief History of Madison* (Madison, NH: np., 1926), p. 18.
51. Mausolf, *op. cit.*, p. 81.
52. Hurd, D. H., *History of Merrimac and Belknap Counties, New Hampshire* (Philadelphia, PA: J.W. Lewis, 1885), p. 847.
53. Lawrence, *op. cit.*, p. 213.
54. Scales, J., *History of Strafford County, New Hampshire* (Chicago, IL: Richmond-Arnold, 1914), p. 518.
55. Parker, E. E., *History of the City of Nashua, NH* (Nashua, NH: Telegraph Publishing, 1897), p. 157.
56. Clark, R. S. *First Presbyterian Church 1763–1988, The Community Church of New Boston* (New Boston, NH: np., 1988), p. 11.
57. Garvin, J., "Newbury Center Meeting House" (Concord, NH: New Hampshire Division of Historical Resources, May 28, 2006), p. 4
58. *Ibid.*, p. 6
59. Albee, J., *New Castle Historic and Picturesque* (Boston, MA: Rand Avery, 1884), p. 114.
60. Kelley, F. H., *Reminiscences of New Hampton, NH* (Worcester, MA: C. Hamilton, 1889), p. 41.
61. Ruell, *op. cit.*, p. 155.
62. Tolles, *op. cit.*, p. 257.
63. Wheeler, E. *The History of Newport, New Hampshire* (Concord, NH: Republican Press, 1879), p. 111.
64. *Ibid.*, p. 115.
65. *Ibid.*, p. 116.
66. Merrill, G. D., *History of Carroll County, New Hampshire* (Boston, MA: W. A. Ferguson, 1889), p. 866.
67. Cogswell, E. C., *History of Nottingham, Deerfield, and Northwood* (Manchester, NH: John B. Clarke, 1878), p. 541.
68. Tolles, *op. cit.*, p. 4.
69. Leighton, M. I., *Early Settler's Meeting House at Leighton's Corner, New Hampshire* (Center Ossipee, NH: Independent Press, 1933), p. 3.
70. *Ibid.*, p. 11.
71. Brown, D. A., *History of Penacook, N.H.* (Concord, NH: Rumford Press, 1902), pp. 102–106.

72. Smith, A., *History of the Town of Peterborough* (Boston, MA: George Ellis, 1876), p. 136.
73. *Ibid.*, p. 87
74. Stone, L., "All Saints Church," National Register of Historic Places Inventory-Nomination Form (Peterborough, NH: All Saints Parish, 1978), p. 4.
75. McLaughlin, R. E., *On Church Hill: A Layman's History of St. John's Parish, Portsmouth, New Hampshire* (Portsmouth, NH: Peter Randall, 1982), p. 33.
76. Thoreson, S. W., "South Parish Church," National Register of Historic Places Inventory-Nomination Form (Portsmouth, NH: The Thoreson Group, 1978), p. 2.
77. Sammons, M. J., and Cunningham, V., *Black Portsmouth: Three Centuries of African American Heritage* (Hanover, NH: University of New Hampshire Press, 2004), p. 148.
78. *Ibid.*, pp. 151–152.
79. Dearborn, J. J., *The History of Salisbury, New Hampshire* (Manchester, NH: William Moore, 1890), p. 176.
80. Speare, E. A., *Colonial Meeting-Houses of New Hampshire* (Littleton, NH: Courier printing, 1938), p. 9.
81. Holmes, R., *A View from Meeting House Hill: A History of Sandown, New Hampshire* (Portsmouth, NH: Peter Randall, 1988), pp. 113–114.
82. Merrill, *op. cit.*, p. 690.
83. Hurd, *op. cit.*, p. 486.
84. Ferguson, *op. cit.*, p. 575.
85. Rumrill, A., "Stoddard Meetinghouse," *Sacred and Secular: Historic Meetinghouses and Churches of the Monadnock Region (*Keene, NH: Historical Society of Cheshire County, 2006), p. 60.
86. Scales, *op. cit.*, p. 411.
87. Worthen, Mrs. A. H., *The History of Sutton, New Hampshire, Part I* (Concord, NH: Republican Press, 1890), p. 334.
88. Lyford, J. O., *History of the Town of Canterbury, New Hampshire, 1727–1912, Volume 1* (Concord, NH: The Rumford Press, 1912), p. 334.
89. Stone, M. T., *Historical Sketch of the Town of Troy, New Hampshire, 1764–1897* (Keene, NH: Sentinel Printing, 1897), p. 134.
90. Lawrence, *op. cit.*, p. 416.
91. Little, W., *History of the Town of Warren, N.H.* (Concord, NH: McFarland & Jenks, 1854), p. 91.
92. Gage, G. N., *History of Washington, New Hampshire* (Claremont, NH: Claremont Manufacturing, 1886), p. 31.
93. Jager, R., and Jager, G., *A Cloud of Witnesses: A History of Washington Congregational Church, 1780–2005* (Concord, NH: Wallace Press, 2005), p. 26.
94. Coffin, *op. cit.*, p. 559.
95. Muzzey, F., *History of the Wentworth Congregational Church* (Wentworth, NH: np, 2014), p. 16.

Bibliography

Albee, J., *New Castle Historic and Picturesque* (Boston, MA: Rand Avery, 1884)

Alton Monthly Meeting, "The Alton Monthly Meeting or church records," (Alton, NH: manuscript, 1803–1854)

Andrews, E. D., *A Shaker Meeting House and its Builder* (New Haven, CT: Yale University Press, 1962)

Barstow, G., *The History of New Hampshire* (Concord, NH: I.S. Boyd, 1842)

Batchellor, A. S., *Township Grants of Lands in New Hampshire Included in the Masonian Patent, New Hampshire State Papers, Vol. XXVII* (Concord, NH: Edward Pearson, 1896)

Beard, C. S., "St. Andre's Parish," National Register of Historic Places Registration Form (Biddeford, ME: Maine Historic Preservation Commission, 2015)

Bell, C. H., *History of the Town of Exeter, New Hampshire* (Boston, MA: J. E. Farwell, 1888)

Benes, P., *Meetinghouses of Early New England* (Amherst, MA: University of Massachusetts Press, 2012)

Benjamin, A., *A Reprint* (New York, NY: The Architectural Book Publishing Co., 1917, a compendium of all five of Benjamin's architectural trade books)

Bennett, J. C., *Sutton Homes & Buildings Volume II* (Concord, NH: Town & Country Reprographics, 1996)

Bittinger, J. Q., *A History of the First Congregational Church, Haverhill, N.H.* (Claremont, NH: Claremont Manufacturing Co., 1876)

Blodgett, I. D., *Asahel Blodgett of Hudson and Dorchester, NH* (Boston, MA: T. R. Marvin and Sons, 1906)

Bouton, N., *The History of Concord* (Concord, NH: Benning Sanborn, 1856)

Brigden, T. H., *History of Water Village Community Church Ossipee, New Hampshire* (Wolfeboro, NH: The Kingswood Press, 1978)

Brown, D. A., *The History of Penacook, N.H* (Concord, NH: Rumford Press, 1902)

Brown, J. E., *The Years of the Life of Samuel Lane, 1718–1806* (Hanover, NH: University Press of New England, 2000)

Brown, W., *History of the Town of Hampton Falls New Hampshire* (Manchester, NH: John B. Clarke, 1900)

Byrne, W., *The Catholic Church in the New England States, Volume I* (Boston, MA: Hurd and Everts Co., 1899)

Campton Historical Society, "Historic Site Series, Site #4, Campton Congregational Church," www.camptonhistorical.org/Campton%20Congregational%20Church%20marker%20flyer.pdf

Campton Historical Society, "Historic Site Series, Site #5, Campton Baptist Church," www.camptonhistorical.org/Campton%20Baptist%20Church.pdf

Chase, B., *History of Old Chester* (Auburn, NH: Benjamin Chase, 1869)

Chester Congregational Church, "The Congregational Church of Chester, New Hampshire 1731–2006" (Chester, NH, np, *c.* 2006)

Chichester History Committee, *A History of Chichester* (Chichester, NH: np, 1977)

Child, H., *Gazetteer of Grafton County, N.H. 1709–1886* (Syracuse, NY: Syracuse Journal, 1886)

Child, W. H., *History of the Town of Cornish, New Hampshire, Vol. 1* (Concord, NH: Rumford Press, 1911)

Clark, C. E., *The Meetinghouse Tragedy: An Episode in the Life of a New England Town* (Hanover, NH: University Press of New England, 1998)

Clark, R. S., *First Presbyterian Church 1763–1988, The Community Church of New Boston* (New Boston, NH: np, 1988)

Cochrane, W. R., *History of the Town of Antrim, New Hampshire* (Manchester, NH: Mirror Steam Printing, 1880)

Cochrane, W. R., and Wood, G. K., *History of Francestown, N.H.* (Nashua, NH: James Barker, 1895)

Coffin, C. C., *The History of Boscawen and Webster* (Concord, NH: Republican Press, 1878)

Cogswell, E. C., *History of New Boston, New Hampshire* (Boston, MA: George C. Rand & Avery, 1864); *History of Nottingham, Deerfield, and Northwood* (Manchester, NH: John Clarke, 1878)

Colby, J., *Littleton: Crossroads of New Hampshire* (Canaan, NH: Phoenix Publishing, 1984)

Cutter, D. B., *History of the Town of Jaffrey, New Hampshire* (Concord, NH: Republican Press, 1881)

Dearborn, J. J., *The History of Salisbury, New Hampshire* (Manchester, NH: William Moore, 1890)

De Goesbriand, L., *Catholic Memoirs of Vermont and New Hampshire* (Burlington, VT: R. S. Styles, 1886)

Dibble, A. W., "Major John Dunlap: The Craftsman and His Community," *Old-Time New England*, Vol. 58, No. 3, pp. 50–58 (Boston, MA: Historic New England, 1978)

Dion, F., *Upon This Rock: A History of the Community Congregational Church, Greenland, New Hampshire* (Portsmouth, NH: np, 1956)

Dow, J., *History of the Town of Hampton, New Hampshire, Vol. 1* (Salem, MA: Salem Press, 1893)

East Alton Meetinghouse Association, "The East Alton Meeting House" (Alton, NH: np: n.d.)

Evans, G. C., *History of the Town of Jefferson, New Hampshire, 1773–1927* (Manchester, NH: Granite Press, 1927)

Ferguson, W. A., *History of Coos County, New Hampshire* (Syracuse, NY: W.A. Ferguson, 1888)

Fitzgerald, A., *The Minot Diaries: Life on a New England Farm, 1830–1888* (Bath, NH: Bath Historical Society, 2015)

Fuerstman, H. M., "Seeking Celia: Our Stained Glass Windows," 2014, www.bethlehemsynagogue.org/news/2014/3/3/our-stained-glass-windows-seeking-celia.

Gage, G. N., *History of Washington, New Hampshire* (Claremont, NH: Claremont Manufacturing, 1886)

Garvin, J. L., "Notes on the Date of Construction of the Danville Meeting House," (Concord, NH; New Hampshire Division of Historical Resources, October 7, 1995); "Newbury Center Meeting House, Newbury, New Hampshire" (Concord, NH: New Hampshire Division of Historical Resources, May 28, 2006)

Gifford, W., *Colebrook: "A Place Up Back of New Hampshire"* (Colebrook, NH: News & Sentinel, 1993)

Gray, R., and Bickford, M., *Headwaters Harvest: A History of Methodism in Pittsburg, New Hampshire* (Pittsburg, NH: Farnham Memorial United Methodist Church, 1997)

Griffin, S. G., *A History of the Town of Keene* (Keene, NH: Sentinel Printing, 1904)

Hadsel, C., *Suspended Worlds: Historic Theater Scenery in Northern New England* (Jaffrey, NH: David R. Godine, 2018)

Hall, M. O., *Rambles About Greenland in Rhyme* (Boston, MA: Alfred Mudge and Son, 1900)

Harkness, M. G., *The Tamworth Narrative* (Freeport, ME: The Bond Wheelwright Co., 1958)

Haverhill, Town of, *Autobiography of a Bell* (Woodsville, NH: News Print, 1902)

Hayward, S., *History of the Town of Gilsum, New Hampshire* (Manchester, NH: John B. Clarke, 1881)

Hayward, W. W., *The History of Hancock, New Hampshire* (Lowell, MA: Vox Populi Press, 1889)

Hazlett, C. A., "The Four Meeting Houses of the North Parish of Portsmouth," *The Granite Monthly*, February 1906, pp. 37–44 (Dover, NH: H. H. Metcalf); *History of Rockingham County, New Hampshire* (Chicago, IL: Richmond-Arnold Publishing, 1915)

Holmes, R., *A View from Meeting House Hill: A History of Sandown, New Hampshire* (Portsmouth, NH: Peter Randall, 1988)

Holt, A. W., *The History of the First Baptist Church, Concord, New Hampshire* (Concord, NH: NH Correctional Industries, 1993)

Hoskins, E. B., *Historical Sketches of Lyman New Hampshire* (Lisbon, NH: Charles P. Hibberd, 1903)

Hurd, D. H., *History of Cheshire and Sullivan Counties, New Hampshire* (Philadelphia, PA: J. W. Lewis, 1886); *History of Merrimac and Belknap Counties, New Hampshire* (Philadelphia, PA: J. W. Lewis, 1885); *History of Rockingham and Strafford Counties, New Hampshire* (Philadelphia, PA: J. W. Lewis, 1882)

Jackson, J. R., *History of Littleton, New Hampshire, Vol. 1*(Cambridge, MA: University Press, 1905)

Jager, R., and Jager, G., *A Cloud of Witnesses: A History of the Washington Congregational Church 1780–2005* (Concord, NH: Wallace Press, 2005)

Kelley, F. H., *Reminiscences of New Hampton, N.H.* (Worcester, MA: C. Hamilton, 1889)

Knoblock, G. A., *Historic Burial Grounds of the New Hampshire Seacoast* (Charleston, SC: Arcadia Publishing, 1999); *Strong and Brave Fellows; New Hampshire's Black Soldiers and Sailors of the American Revolution* (Jefferson, NC: McFarland & Co., 2003)

Knoblock, G. A., and Wemmer, D., *Historic Weathervanes of New England* (Jefferson, NC: McFarland & Co., 2018)

Kowsky, F. R., *The Architecture of Frederick Clarke Withers* (Middletown, CT: Wesleyan University Press, 1980)

Lawrence, R. F., *The New Hampshire Churches: Comprising Histories of the Congregational and Presbyterian Churches in the State* (Claremont, NH: Claremont Power Press, 1856)

Leighton, M. I., *Early Settlers Meeting House at Leighton's Corner New Hampshire* (Center Ossipee: Independent Press, 1933)

Leonard, L. W., and Seward, J. L., *The History of Dublin, N.H.* (Cambridge, MA: University Press, 1920)

Lisbon Area Historical Society, "Lisbon Methodist Episcopal Church" (Lisbon, NH: nd.)

Little, W., *History of the Town of Warren, N.H.* (Concord, NH: McFarland & Jenks, 1854)

Lord, E. M., *Melvin Village Community Church History 1837–1973* (Melvin Village, NH: np, 1973)

Lord, C. C., *Life and Times in Hopkinton, N.H.* (Concord, NH: Republican Press, 1890)

Lyford, J. O., *History of the Town of Canterbury, New Hampshire, 1727–1912, Volume 1* (Concord, NH: The Rumford Press, 1912); *History of Concord, New Hampshire, Vol. 2* (Concord, NH: Rumford Press, 1903)

McDonald, S. R., "St. Anne Church," "National Register of Historic Places Inventory-Nomination Form" (Berlin, NH: Dept. of Community Development, 1979)

McDuffee, F., *History of the Town of Rochester, New Hampshire* (Manchester, NH: John B. Clarke, 1892)

McLaughlin, R. E., *On Church Hill; A Layman's History of St. John's Parish, Portsmouth, NH.* (Portsmouth, NH: Peter Randall, 1982)

McLee, M., Thompson, P. J., and White, D., "The Reverend John Newton Mars (1804–1884): New England Cleric and Celebrated Standard Bearer in the Wesleyan Tradition," *Methodist History*, 54:1, pp. 71–80 (Madison, NJ: The United Methodist Church, October, 2015)

Macomber, D. E., "Epsom Churches-The Free Will Baptist Church," *Epsom Vol. III Historical Documents* (Epsom, NH: Epsom Historical Society, 1995)

Madison Public Schools, *A Brief History of Madison* (Madison, NH: np, 1926)

Mausolf, L., "Mid-20th Century Architecture in NH: 1945–1975" (Concord, NH: New Hampshire Department of Employment Security, December 2012)

Merrill, G. D., *History of Carroll County, New Hampshire* (Boston, MA: W. A. Ferguson, 1889)

Merrill, J. L., *History of Acworth* (Springfield, MA: Samuel Bowles, 1869)

Merrill, P. S., "Origins of New Hampton Community Church" (New Hampton, NH: unpublished manuscript, *c.* 1954)

Mitchell, H. E., *The Town Register-Wolfeboro, Ossipee, Effingham, Tuftonboro, Tamworth, Freedom—1908* (Augusta, ME: Mitchell-Cony, 1908)

Monadnock Historical Societies Forum, *Sacred and Secular: Historic Meetinghouses and Churches of the Monadnock Region* (Jaffrey, NH: Savron Graphics, 2007)

Muzzey, F., *History of the Wentworth Congregational Church* (Wentworth, NH: np, 2014)

Nelson, W. R., *History of Goshen, New Hampshire* (Concord, NH: Evans Printing, 1957)

Noyes, H. E., *A Memorial of the Town of Hampstead, New Hampshire* (Boston, MA: George Reed, 1899)

Orford, Town of, *Centennial Celebration of the Town of Orford, N.H.* (Manchester, NH: Henry Gage, *c.* 1866)

Paradis, W. H., *Upon This Granite: Catholicism in New Hampshire* (Portsmouth, NH: Peter Randall, 1998)

Parker, B. F., *History of the Town of Wolfeborough, New Hampshire* (Los Angeles, CA: American Offset Printers, 1988)

Parker, E. E., *History of the City of Nashua, NH* (Nashua, NH: Telegraph Publishing, 1897)

Parker, E. L., *The History of Londonderry* (Boston, MA: Perkins and Whipple, 1851)

Peladeau, M. B., "Brother Moses Johnson, 1752–1842," *A Biographical Dictionary of Architects in Maine, Volume V, No. 11* (Augusta, ME: Maine Historic Preservation Commission, 1988)

Purton, W., "Emmanuel Church, Dublin, N.H.," *The Churchman*, No. 24, p. 368 (London, UK, September 22, 1885)

Rowe, R. H., *Amherst Historical Moments, Amherst, New Hampshire* (Portsmouth, NH: Peter Randall, 2004)

Ruell, D., *The Historic Churches of Belknap County* (Meredith, NH: Meredith Media, 1995); "First Free Will Baptist Church of Ossipee, Wakefield, and Effingham," National Register of Historic Places Inventory-Nomination Form (Meredith, NH: Lakes Region Planning Commission, 1983); "Episcopal Church of St. John the Baptist," National Register of Historic Places Inventory-Nomination Form (Meredith, NH: Lakes Region Planning Commission, 1984)

Ruell, D., and Fonda, C., "Tuftonboro United Methodist Church," National Register of Historic Places Inventory-Nomination Form (Ashland, NH: Lakes Region Planning Commission, 1997)

Saint Agnes Catholic Church, *St. Agnes Centennial Celebration, 1901–2001* (Lancaster, NH: Bar-Jona Enterprises, 2001)

Sammons, M. J., and Cunningham, V., *Black Portsmouth: Three Centuries of African American Heritage* (Hanover, NH: University of New Hampshire Press, 2004)

Sargent, L., "The History of Walnut Grove Church" (Rochester, NH: unpublished manuscript, 2007)

Saunderson, H. H., *History of Charlestown, New Hampshire* (Claremont, NH: Claremont Manufacturing, 1876)

Scales, J., *History of Strafford County New Hampshire* (Chicago, IL: Richmond-Arnold, 1914)

Schjonberg, M. F., "Summering Episcopalians love their seasonal chapels," *Episcopal News Monthly* (New York, NY: The Episcopal Church, August 30, 2017)

Secomb, D. F., *History of the Town of Amherst, Hillsborough County, New Hampshire* (Concord, NH: Evans, Sleeper & Woodbury, 1883)

Seward, J., *A History of the Town of Sullivan, New Hampshire, Volume 1* (Keene, NH: np, 1921)

Sinnott, E. W., *Meetinghouse & Church in Early New England* (New York: Bonanza Books, 1963)

Small, E., *The Old South Meetinghouse Seabrook, New Hampshire 1764* (Seabrook, NH: np, 1975)

Smith, A., *History of the Town of Peterborough* (Boston, MA: George Ellis, 1876)

Smith, C. J., *History of the Town of Mont Vernon, New Hampshire* (Boston, MA: Blanchard Printing, 1907)

Somers, A. N., *History of Lancaster, New Hampshire* (Concord, NH: Rumford Press, 1899)

Speare, E. A., *Colonial Meeting-Houses of New Hampshire* (Littleton, NH: Courier Printing, 1938); *Historic Bells in New Hampshire* (Littleton, NH: Courier Printing, 1944)

Stearns, E. S., *History of the Town of Rindge, New Hampshire* (Boston, MA: G.H. Ellis, 1875)

Stewart, I. D., *The History of the Freewill Baptists, Volume 1* (Dover, NH: William Burr, 1862)

Stone, L., "All Saints Church," National Register of Historic Places Inventory-Nomination Form (Peterborough, NH: All Saints' Parish, 1978)

Tamworth Civic Association, "Wonolancet Chapel," *The Tamworth Civic News*, Vol. XXI, No. 5 (Tamworth, NH: Civic Association, July 1, 2016)

Thomas, M. F., *History of Fremont, N.H. Olde Poplin* (Manchester, NH: New England Printing, 1998)

Thoreson, S. W., "South Parish Church," National Register of Historic Places Inventory-Nomination Form (Portsmouth, NH: The Thoreson Group, 1978)

Tolles, Jr., B. F., *New Hampshire Architecture: An Illustrated Guide* (Hanover, NH: University Press of New England, 1979)

Wadleigh, G., *Notable Events in the History of Dover, New Hampshire* (Dover, NH: Tufts College Press, 1913)

Waite, O. F. R., *History of Claremont, New Hampshire* (Manchester, NH: John B. Clarke, 1895)

Wallace, W. A., *The History of Canaan, New Hampshire* (Concord, NH: Rumford Press, 1910)

Wheeler, E., *Croydon, N.H., 1866. Proceedings at the Centennial Celebration* (Claremont, NH: Claremont Manufacturing, 1867); *The History of Newport, New Hampshire* (Concord, NH: Republican Press, 1879)

Whitcher, W. F., *History of the Town of Haverhill, New Hampshire* (Concord, NH: Rumford Press, 1919)

Whitney, H. J. E., and Nankervis, A. D. M., *A Brief History of The Church of the Epiphany Lisbon, New Hampshire* (Lisbon, NH: np, 2007)

Woodbury, P., Savage, T., and Patten, W., *History of Bedford, New Hampshire* (Concord, NH: Rumford Printing Co., 1903)

Worthen, Mrs. A. H., *The History of Sutton, New Hampshire, Part I* (Concord, NH: Republican Press, 1890)

About the Author

Glenn A. Knoblock is a historian, author, and lecturer with over a dozen books to his credit that highlight various aspects of New Hampshire and New England history. He has a B.A. in history from Bowling Green State University in Ohio and has been studying and documenting aspects of New Hampshire history for over thirty years. For nearly two decades, he has given lectures on the topics he has written about state-wide as part of the New Hampshire Humanities and their Humanities To Go program. He resides in Wolfeboro, New Hampshire, with his wife, Terry, daughter, Anna, and their goldendoodle Shiloh.